THE POWER OF MARKET FUNDAMENTALISM

T0324652

THE POWER OF MARKET FUNDAMENTALISM

Karl Polanyi's Critique

FRED BLOCK
MARGARET R. SOMERS

Harvard University Press

Cambridge, Massachusetts
London, England

First Harvard University Press paperback edition, 2016
Third Printing

Library of Congress Cataloging-in-Publication Data
Block, Fred L.
The power of market fundamentalism : Karl Polanyi's critique /
Fred Block and Margaret R. Somers.
pages cm
Includes bibliographical references and index.
ISBN 978-0-674-05071-6 (cloth : alk. paper)
ISBN 978-0-674-97088-5 (pbk.)
1. Polanyi, Karl, 1886–1964.   2. Free enterprise—History.
3. Economics—History.   4. Economics—Sociological aspects—History.
I. Somers, Margaret R.   II. Title.
HB102.P64B56 2014
330.15'7—dc23   2013038788

*In memory of Daniel Bell and Albert Hirschman:
two intellectual giants who shared our admiration
for Karl Polanyi and who continue to inspire.*

CONTENTS

Preface   ix

1 Karl Polanyi and the Power of Ideas   1

2 Beyond the Economistic Fallacy   44

3 Karl Polanyi and the Writing of
The Great Transformation   73

4 Turning the Tables: Polanyi's Critique of Free
Market Utopianism   98

5 In the Shadow of Speenhamland: Social Policy
and the Old Poor Law   114

6 From Poverty to Perversity: Ideational Embeddedness
and Market Fundamentalism over Two Centuries
of Welfare Debate   150

7 The Enduring Strength of Free Market Conservatism
in the United States   193

8 The Reality of Society   218

Notes   241

Bibliography   253

Index   287

PREFACE

This book is the culmination of a decades-long joint effort to construct and make available a usable form of Karl Polanyi's social theory. The two of us first met at the end of the 1960s as activists in the student and antiwar movements, when we discovered a mutual enthusiasm for Karl Polanyi. After years of thinking and brainstorming together, we began writing in the late 1970s and early 1980s—with only the carnage of Thatcherism and the early years of the Reagan Administration to portend the future. We published our first Polanyi piece in Theda Skocpol's *Vision and Method in Historical Sociology* (1984), after which we took a bit of a writing hiatus, but hardly a thinking one. We began writing together again in the second half of the 1990s and continue right through the present.

Ours has been a remarkably fruitful collaboration, one stimulated by our deep mutual admiration and our ability to be inspired continuously by the other. It has also been a challenging one. While we write as scholars and engaged intellectuals, we have been at all times deeply attuned to and profoundly roiled by the always worrisome political environment. Our good fortune is that we share the most foundational political and social commitments. At the same time, we have very different political temperaments; one of us has an affinity with Pollyanna while the other tends more towards Cassandra. If either of these perspectives is more or less appropriate for the age, it is impossible to judge. It is never a good idea to prognosticate, as Polanyi himself surely learned the hard way after his premature eulogy for market fundamentalism began to unravel in the years after *The Great Transformation* was published in 1944. There is little doubt, however, that because of the different strengths each of us brings to the table, the end result is better than what either of us could have done alone.

Over such an extended period of time, we have incurred many more debts than can possibly be acknowledged here. Fred first wants to thank his spouse, Carole Joffe, and his two daughters, Miriam and Judith Joffe-Block, who grew into adulthood while this book was underway. All three have tolerated endless conversations about Karl Polanyi. His sister Elizabeth has been a source of support and bibliographic assistance. He is also deeply grateful to a group of close colleagues who have given him support over many years; these include Karl Klare, Matthew R. Keller, Magali Sarfatti Larson, Michael Peter Smith, and Howard Winant. Margaret wants to thank her partner, Michael Steltzer, and her beloved friend, Leslie DePietro, both of whom have been so supportive of her work that they insist they now know Karl Polanyi on a first-name basis. She also is blessed with a circle of colleagues without whom the intensity of scholarly life would be a barren place indeed. Margaret also expresses her deep gratitude to the late Daniel Bell for years of intellectual support and encouragement, always delivered in his own idiosyncratic and delightful fashion.

Together we want to thank those who have played a particularly important role in keeping us on track. Greta Krippner and Peter Evans have intervened at key points to help us focus our arguments and escape from some of the more complex Polanyian tangles. Michael Aronson at Harvard University Press has been infinitely patient during the long gestation of this volume and he has provided critical encouragement at some of our low points. Claire Whitlinger provided tireless support as a research assistant during the early phases of her graduate career. Parul Baxi and John Kincaid assisted at the end of the project. And this whole effort would not have been possible without the ongoing work of Marguerite Mendell, Kari Polanyi-Levitt, and Ana Gomez to create and sustain the Karl Polanyi Institute at Concordia University in Montreal. Their deep friendship as well as the global network of Polanyians that they have assembled has sustained our work over many years. Very early in this project, Margaret was fortunate enough to discuss Polanyi's life with a number of people knowledgeable about his world and Hungarian history. Sadly, these include some who have since passed away, notably Istvan Eorsi, Gyorgy Litvan, Harry Pearson, and Hans and Eva Zeisel. These invaluable conversations, as well as the insights of Gyorgi Markus, Gabor Vermes, Giovanni Arrighi, Daniel Bell, George Dalton, E. J. Hobsbawm, Peter Lange, Anthony Leeds, Larry Miller, and John Myles, all contributed significantly to the material in chapter 2. In 1986, Margaret attended the Centennial Celebration of the life of Karl Polanyi in Budapest, sponsored by the Hungarian Academy of Arts and Sciences. At that occasion Polanyi-Levitt oversaw the burial of the ashes of Karl Polanyi, and his wife, Ilona Duczynska in a Budapest cemetary. It was there that she and Margie Mendell made public their plans for the forthcoming Karl Polanyi Institute in Concordia. It would be impossible to acknowledge adequately just how meaningful was the privilege of sharing in that experience.

For their generous readings and critical feedback on earlier drafts of this volume, we would like to thank Elizabeth Anderson, Phineas Baxandall, Daniel Beland, John Bowman, Howard Brick, Rogers Brubaker, Michael Burawoy, Leonardo Burlamaqui, Ayse Bursa, Craig Calhoun, Michele Cangiani, Ana Celia Castro, Bill Domhoff, Phil Harvey, Donald Herzog, Alex Hicks, Larry Hirschhorn, Albert Hirschman, Dan Hirschman, Arlie Hochschild, Jerry Jacobs, Don Kalb, Michael Katz, Ira Katznelson, Michele Lamont, Bill Lazonick, C. K. Lee, Sandy Levitsky, Kristin Luker, Mick Mann, Jeff Manza, David Matza, Mark Mizruchi, Mary Nolan, Sean O'Riain, Jamie Peck, Frances Fox Piven, Guenther Roth, Bill Roy, Andrew Schrank, Gay Seidman, Eric Sheppard, Beverly Silver, Theda Skocpol, Brian Steensland, Marc Steinberg, Wolfgang Streeck, Richard Swedberg, Ron Suny, Claus Thomasberger, Dan Tompkins, John Walton, Josh Whitford, Karl Widerquist, Erik Wright, Mayer Zald, and Viviana Zelizer. We presented pieces of the book at NYU's NYLON Workshop, UCLA's Comparative History Workshop, York University's Social Theory Workshop, and various sessions of the American Sociological Association. We appreciate the thoughtful readings and commentary provided by so many of the participants of these workshops and presentations. Finally, Greg Clark, Peter Lindert, and Norma Landau at UC Davis and Tom Green at Michigan were extremely helpful when we were immersed in the details of the Old Poor Law in England.

A number of students are also to be thanked for their research assistance, including Jane Rafferty, Claire Whitlinger, Dan Schimmerer, Dan Samson, and Miguel Ruiz. We are also indebted to Leslie Ellen Jones for her superb work in copyediting the manuscript.

Fred's main institutional debt is to the Ford Foundation and specifically to Leonardo Burlamaqui, who supported his research over the last seven years. It would have been difficult to complete this manuscript without Leonardo's ongoing support for the project. Margaret would like to acknowledge support over the years from the American Sociological Association's Fund for the Advancement of the Discipline; the

Agrarian Studies Program, Yale University; George and Eliza Howard Foundation, Brown University; the University of Michigan's Institute for the Humanities, Institute for Research on Women and Gender, the Office of the Vice President for Research, and the College of Arts and Sciences; the Center for the Critical Study of Contemporary Culture, Rutgers University; the National Endowment for the Humanities; NYU's International Center for Advanced Studies; the Center for Advanced Studies in the Social and Behavioral Sciences, Stanford University; and the Eisenberg Institute for Historical Studies, University of Michigan.

Several of these chapters appeared earlier in other locations, although all have been substantially revised for this volume. "Beyond the Economistic Fallacy: The Holistic Social Science of Karl Polanyi" appeared in Theda Skocpol, ed., *Vision and Method in Historical Sociology* (Cambridge: Cambridge University Press, 1984). "Karl Polanyi and the Writing of *The Great Transformation*" was published in *Theory and Society* 32 (2003): 275–306. "In the Shadow of Speenhamland: Social Policy and the Old Poor Law" appeared in *Politics & Society* 31, 2 (2003): 283–323. "From Poverty to Perversity: Ideas, Markets, and Institutions over 200 Years of Welfare Debate," appeared in *American Sociological Review* 70, 2 (2003): 260–287. Chapter 7 draws on "Understanding the Diverging Trajectories of the United States and Western Europe: A Neo-Polanyian Analysis," *Politics & Society* 35, 3 (2007): 1–31.

THE POWER OF MARKET FUNDAMENTALISM

1

KARL POLANYI AND THE
POWER OF IDEAS

It was a little more than twenty years ago that the decades-long Cold War between the United States and the Soviet Union ended. When the Soviet Union collapsed, some analysts optimistically claimed that we had reached the "end of history" because the institutions of Western societies had definitively proven their superiority over all others (Fukuyama 1992). Since then the United States has suffered the trauma of the September 11, 2001 terrorist attacks, fought extended wars in Afghanistan and Iraq, and has experienced the worst economic downturn since the Great Depression. Over this same twenty-year period, politics in the United States has become ever more polarized, stalemated, and dysfunctional. From the attempted impeachment of Bill Clinton, to the deceptions and manifest incompetence of the George W. Bush Administration, to the excesses of the Tea Party during the Obama Administration, the political system continues to career out of control. Suffice it to say, the triumphalism expressed when the Soviet Union collapsed is now only a distant memory.

Nonetheless, however ludicrous "the end of history" may sound to us now, the proclamation cannot be dismissed as simply the hubris of a handful of overly optimistic prognosticators. After all, very little in contemporary social and economic theory prepared us for the multiple traumas of the last two decades. Economists were particularly complacent as they vigorously promoted the doctrine that "deregulation," labor "flexibility," tax cuts for the wealthy, and unfettered free markets would produce unprecedented prosperity. In fact, the U.S. model was held out as an example to others as a preferable alternative to both the "Eurosclerosis"[1] that allegedly plagued Continental Europe and the "crony capitalism" that undermined the major Asian economies.

1

There were, of course, some important exceptions to the celebratory mood. Starting in 2000, the Nobel-winning economist Joseph Stiglitz (2000, 2002, 2003) challenged the wisdom and sustainability of the economic policies that Washington was urging on the rest of the world. The financier and philanthropist George Soros produced a series of books (1998, 2000, 2002) questioning the arguments underlying the spectacular growth of global financial markets. John Gray (2000), the British political theorist who had earlier been a supporter of Margaret Thatcher, questioned whether the bad "Anglo-American" version of capitalism was undermining the stability of the more productive type of capitalism that had flourished on the European Continent. And Mark Blyth (2002), a Scottish born political scientist, questioned the dramatic increase in wealth of the top 1% of households in the U.S. that resulted from Reagan-era policies.

Many of these dissenters and skeptics explicitly drew inspiration from the work of Karl Polanyi (1886–1964), a twentieth-century Hungarian refugee intellectual and economic historian, whose most important book, *The Great Transformation* (hereafter GT), was originally published in 1944.[2] In that work, Polanyi sought to understand the historical forces that had led to the Great War (World War I), the Great Depression of the 1930s, the New Deal, the rise of fascism, and the coming of World War II. He develops what many consider to be the twentieth-century's most powerful and systematic critique of free market ideas and practices, one that has extraordinary relevance for understanding our own historical period.

Our project in this book is to show that Polanyi's thought is as critical as ever for making sense of the surprising political-economic developments of the past few decades and their contemporary social and economic consequences. Our focus is on the rebirth in the 1970s and 1980s of the same free market ideas that were widely assumed to have died in the Great Depression. Driven by this free market ideology, conservative politicians have engaged in a decades-long campaign to reverse the reforms originally introduced in the 1930s by Franklin Roosevelt's New Deal and extended in the 1960s by Lyndon Johnson's Great Society programs. Those regulations and programs had placed severe restrictions on speculative activity by financial institutions, reduced the extreme inequality of income and wealth distribution of the 1920s, provided organized labor with a stable and recognized position in both the workplace and in the polity, and created protections for citizens from the risks involved in becoming unemployed or growing old. Businessmen and right-wing intellectuals had railed against these changes for many decades, but their fortunes changed in the 1970s as conservatism again became a powerful force in United States politics. Once Ronald Reagan gained the presidency in 1980, the conservative movement began to make significant headway in dismantling much of the New Deal framework (Phillips-Fein 2009; Smith 2012).

The fruits of these efforts are now glaringly familiar. Income inequality in the United States has increased dramatically since 1981, the labor movement has suffered a precipitous decline in numbers, and ordinary citizens are substantially less protected from risks that diminish their incomes (Hacker 2006; Wilkinson and Pickett 2009; Hacker and Pierson 2010). Most spectacularly, the share of income going to the top 1%—including capital gains—grew from 10% in 1981 to a peak of 23.5% in 2007 just before the crisis and the level for the most recent year—2012—was just below that peak (Saez and Piketty 2013, Table A3).[3] Jeffrey Winters (2011) has estimated that the top 400 taxpayers in the United States exercise 10,000 times the material power of the average citizen in the bottom 90%. This differs little from the power differential in Ancient Rome between the Senators, and slaves and farm laborers who made up most of the population. This enormous imbalance of power and dominance—itself facilitated by the spectacular rise of finance and the relaxation of its regulatory framework—inexorably set the stage for the catastrophic global financial crisis in the fall of 2008 (Stiglitz 2010).

The extraordinary influence of free market ideas in justifying the project of dismantling the New Deal over the last thirty years is no longer disputed. There is some dispute as to what to call them. Some use the term "neoliberalism," others "laissez-faire," and still others just plain "free market ideology." Following George Soros (1998), we use the label "market fundamentalism" because the term conveys the quasi-religious certainty expressed by contemporary advocates of market self-regulation. Moreover, we want to emphasize the affinity with religious fundamentalisms that rely on revelation or a claim to truth independent of the kind of empirical verification that is expected in the social sciences (see Chapter 6). But whatever the term, these free market theories and policies were successfully revived in the 1970s in response to the perceived failure of New Deal and Great Society policies to address widespread economic and social problems. Pushed by powerful interest groups, they quickly defeated the entrenched Keynesian ideas and policy prescriptions that had been dominant in the United States from the mid-1930s through the 1960s. Over the next four decades, this updated version of laissez-faire moved from the margins of influence to become conventional political wisdom with world-transforming effects that continue today (Cassidy 2009; Burgin 2012; Jones 2012).

To be sure, others have stressed the importance of free market ideas in the recent transformation of politics in the U.S. (Blyth 2002; MacKenzie 2006; Quiggin 2010; Peck 2010). Valuable work also traces out the history of these ideas and the elaborate networks that disseminated these ideas and assured their influence over critical political elites (Krugman 2009b; Phillips-Fein 2009; Crouch 2011; Frank 2011; Burgin 2012). Our focus, however, is somewhat different. We are seeking to explain what it is about these free market ideas that give them such extraordinary command. What, we ask, is the source of this power? How is it that ideas once marginalized and seemingly defeated in the 1930s and 1940s again became this society's conventional wisdom?

We approach these questions using theoretical tools we derive from our engagement with Polanyi's work. We recognize that despite Joseph Stiglitz's observation that " . . . it often seems as if Polanyi is speaking directly to present day issues" (GT, ii), Polanyi's ideas have never achieved the broad public circulation of those of John Maynard Keynes, Milton Friedman, and Friedrich Hayek. Yet in a way that differs from much of what we read today, GT's account of the origins of the crises of the 1930s and 1940s, written seventy years ago, reveals a profound understanding of the very same free market ideas that have loomed so large in transforming our recent world. In fact, the target of Polanyi's critique—the early nineteenth-century classical political economy of T. R. Malthus and David Ricardo—is credited proudly as their theoretical inspiration by the two intellectual figures most closely associated with the revival of free market ideas in the second half of the twentieth century—Friedrich Hayek and Milton Friedman. Indeed, it is the very success of his theoretical opponents in reestablishing the moral and political authority of free market doctrine that has made Polanyi's analysis even more relevant for understanding the present era. It is for this reason that we seek to introduce his ideas to a wider audience.

Introducing Karl Polanyi

As we elaborate in the next chapter, Karl Polanyi was a Jewish-born European refugee intellectual who was repeatedly displaced by war and social conflicts. Born in the Austro-Hungarian Empire in 1886, he was a founder of the Galileo Circle, a club of Hungarian intellectuals that included Karl Mannheim and Georg Lukacs. He fought in World War

I and supported the October 1918 Aster Revolution that overturned the landed aristocratic regime. Just months later, the Communist Béla Kun revolution created a Soviet Republic in Hungary. The revolution was quickly defeated. Polanyi left for Vienna, where he was a witness to its fifteen-year "socialist municipality"—an urban laboratory of working class co-operative life, from housing to health care, from work to education. He later described this period as one of the formative experiences of his intellectual development: "Vienna achieved one of the most spectacular cultural triumphs of Western history . . . an unexampled moral and intellectual rise in the condition of a highly developed industrial working class which, protected by the Vienna system, withstood the degrading effects of grave economic dislocation and achieved a level never reached before by the masses of the people in any industrial society" (GT, 299).

The rising tide of fascism, however, ultimately brought this socialist and democratic experiment to a brutal end in 1934. Warned that he was personally in danger because of his strongly anti-fascist views, Polanyi departed for England in 1933 where he made his living by teaching adult education courses to British workers through the Workers' Educational Association—the extramural outreach arm of the Universities of Oxford and London. His direct encounter with English workers and the English class system had a deep impact on him. Comparing the English working class with Central European workers, he was shocked by the former's political views and ignorance of their own past struggles. His experience with England's working people became central to his analysis in GT, which he wrote with the support of a fellowship from the Rockefeller Foundation after leaving England for what he expected to be a brief visit at Bennington College in Vermont. After World War II, he taught in the Economics Department at Columbia University before retiring to Canada, where he died in 1964. In 1986, both Karl and his wife Ilona Duczynska were welcomed back posthumously by the Hungarian Academy of Arts and Sciences for a full-fledged academic celebration of the centennial of Polanyi's birth.[4]

His multiple homelands and a nontraditional academic career that bridged history, economics, sociology, classics, and anthropology contributed to Polanyi's tenuous place in both scholarly and policy discourse. He was initially invited to teach at Columbia because his work was compatible with the institutional economists then dominant in that department. But by the end of the 1940s, institutionalism had gone into sharp decline in mainstream economics (Yonay 1998), and he was left without a disciplinary home. In the political climate of the Cold War, moreover, Polanyi's complex and unique understanding of different economic systems had little purchase for an intellectual world highly polarized between East and West. His vision of a moral social democracy supported by vigorous democratic participation from civil society did not fit neatly into either of the dominant categories of the 1950s and 1960s. With a few critical exceptions, his work had little impact on mainstream scholarship in the social sciences until the late 1970s.[5]

With the rise of Thatcher and Reagan at the end of the 1970s, however, Polanyi's influence began to grow, as his critique of their free market ideas and policies became ever more relevant.[6] As the crisis of socialism deepened with the 1989 fall of the Berlin Wall, a number of scholars who were searching for a non-Marxist alternative to the triumphalist celebration of the *status quo* discovered Polanyi's work. As the world began to seem more and more like "Everything For Sale" (Kuttner 1996), his powerful analysis of how the unchecked dominance of the market would inevitably devastate social solidarity and the foundational institutions of civil society was increasingly illuminating and convincing. Polanyi's argument that markets are invariably embedded in social relations also challenged the ascendant precept that freedom and individual rights depended exclusively on an economy driven by a system of self-regulating markets and severely diminished government spending on social and economic provisioning and protection. His work also critiqued the ideology that associated prosperity, choice, and efficiency exclusively with the free market, while attributing inefficiency, corruption, and coercive power entirely to government. He insisted that the economic sphere is as much a site of power as the state, and that a robust human freedom depends on a coalition of state and civil society that has the power to protect society against the destructive forces of marketization.[7]

Perhaps most influentially, Polanyi's work challenged the idea that the market and the state are separate and autonomous entities, a premise that was built into the assumptions of classical and neoclassical economic theory alike. He demonstrated that underneath the claim that only a self-regulating autonomous market can produce optimal results was the conviction that the laws of the market are no different from the biological self-regulatory organisms of nature—a claim that throughout this book we call *social naturalism*. By deconstructing these assumptions that had long passed as proven truths, Polanyi undermined the claim that protecting people against some of the market's worst inequalities was tantamount to tampering with nature itself.

Even today, however, Polanyi's writings defy easy classification. He was an expansive social theorist and social democratic thinker who still believed in the indispensable role of markets: " . . . the end of market society means in no way the absence of markets" (GT, 252). He was dedicated to social protection, but from a government held accountable by the democratic participation of an active citizenry (GT, 264–265). He held tenaciously both to individual rights and to an enlarged idea of freedom—which, like that found in FDR's "Second Bill of Rights," included not just civil and political rights but also economic justice and freedom from want.[8] And while there are others equally dedicated to democratic theory and economic justice, Polanyi is unique in his understanding of both the vitality, endurance, and appeal of free market ideas, as well as the profound threat they pose to human civilization.

Most importantly, Polanyi's writings defy the main intellectual traditions of his era and of our own. As we have noted, he was fiercely critical of the tradition of economic liberalism in both its nineteenth- and twentieth-century variants. But while he described himself as a socialist and was deeply influenced by the Marxist tradition, he expressed great disagreement with other strands of socialist and Marxist thought. He was particularly cynical about the "economistic fallacy" that he attributed in part to Marxist theory (GT, 158–159; Polanyi 1977). He was also unique in insisting that the idea of a self-regulating market was nothing short of "utopian"—a term that had previously been reserved by conservatives to use against leftist critics of market societies (see Chapter 4). Moreover, he also saw the world very differently from the twentieth century's most important theorists of political liberalism because he was, above all, a theorist of social discontinuities. His analysis of the three centuries previous to the twentieth emphasized radical breaks and reversals rather than slow and relentless progress.[9]

Precisely because of his distance from these other more familiar traditions, understanding Polanyi's arguments calls for significant interpretive work. It requires the reader to bracket some of the more recognizable assumptions that he or she has about how the world works. In fact, one cannot make sense of Polanyi's arguments without a willingness to at least suspend belief in those very assumptions. To facilitate this kind of work, our book is an exercise in interpretative social science—digging beneath the words on the printed page to uncover the deeper structures of meaning and argument that gives Polanyi's analysis its remarkable ability to make sense of recent events.

We are not, however, claiming to adjudicate definitively what Karl Polanyi "truly" meant when he used a particular concept or developed a specific line of argument. The work of the canonical figures of social thought, whether it be Adam Smith, Marx, Weber, Freud, or Keynes, is full of complexities and ambiguities and open to multiple interpretations. Karl Polanyi is no different, and our interpretation is only one of many possible readings (for other recent readings, see Burawoy 2003; Buğra and Agartan, eds. 2007; Gemici 2008; Dale 2010). Our purpose is instead to elaborate an emergent inventory of concepts that provides leverage for illuminating and explaining the complex socioeconomic and political developments that have brought us to the crisis we find ourselves in today.[10]

Polanyi's Conceptual Armature

To guide the reader through the substantive breadth of the chapters that follow, we have devised a three-pronged conceptual armature to unify our analysis. Polanyi's writings are so multidimensional that different interpreters would certainly emphasize different themes than these. But these are the themes that have captured our attention over our years of engaging with his work, and they serve as a foundation for the arguments of this book.

First, while markets are necessary, they are also fundamentally threatening to human freedom and the collective good. They are necessary, as we learned from the tragic experiment in Communism in the Soviet Union and Eastern Europe, because they are mechanisms through which individuals exercise choice. At the same time, most of what makes life possible is not actually produced to be sold on the market and will be endangered by being treated as such. These are the necessities of social existence that, along with material sustenance, make it possible for us to be full members of the social world we all inhabit interdependently— above all, education, health care, a sustainable environment, personal and social security, and the right to earn a livelihood. It is when these public goods are turned into commodities and subjected to market principles that social life is threatened fundamentally and major crises ensue. According to Polanyi, these necessities of social life have to be protected from the market by social and political institutions and recognized as rights rather than commodities, or human freedom will be endangered.

Our second theme is that the free market celebrated by economists and political libertarians has never—and cannot ever—actually exist. For Polanyi, the human economy is always and everywhere embedded in society (see Chapter 3, this volume). By this he means that even "free" market economies consist of cultural understandings, shared values, legal rules, and a wide range of governmental actions that make market exchange possible. Economists deny this fundamental reality by conceptualizing the economy not as embedded but as an autonomous self-governing entity. They argue against government involvement in everything from innovations to protecting the environment and advocate a self-regulating system of interconnected and unfettered markets. Polanyi surprisingly calls this conservative and libertarian vision "utopian," because it cannot possibly be realized. Like all utopias, it is both doomed to fail and destined to produce dystopian consequences.

Polanyi's argument here is subtle and complex; he argues that free market ideologues claim that they are disembedding the market from all kinds of destructive controls and constraints. They deny that their favored policies—rolling back welfare provisions, dismantling regulations, and shrinking government—will leave people dangerously exposed to market forces. In reality, however, they are not setting the market free from the state but are instead *re-embedding* it in *different* political, legal, and cultural arrangements, ones that mostly disadvantage the poor and the middle class and advantage wealth and corporate interests. Polanyi's paradigmatic example of this process is the 1834 Poor Law Amendment Act ("New Poor Law"), which dismantled the centuries-old system of English poor relief. The political economists who justified this legislation claimed it would free the labor market of an archaic set of rules and practices that only encouraged laziness and economic irresponsibility. In reality, they simply created a new and different set of coercive institutions—a centralized Poor Law Commission and local work houses—designed to make the rural poor "responsive" to the signals of the market (see Chapters 5 and 6).

Similarly, what has frequently been described as the "deregulation" of the financial sector in the United States should actually be understood as "reregulation." In place of an older set of rules that were designed to protect the public from fraud and excessive risk-taking by financial institutions, politicians established a new set of rules that provided government protection for the financial sector to engage in predatory lending and a huge expansion in dangerous speculation. During the real estate boom of the 2000s, for example, a number of state governments sought to pass legislation that would outlaw some of the most dangerous mortgage lending practices. But the financial institutions appealed to their federal regulators, who told the states—in no uncertain terms—that their proposals conflicted with federal rules that had priority in this area (Tabb 2012, 165). As these examples of what we dub the "always-embedded economy" demonstrate, Polanyi is using "embeddedness" as a placeholder term for politics, social relations, and institutions. For Polanyi, an always-embedded market economy means that markets are *always* organized through politics and social practices.

Polanyi's always-embedded economy leads directly to his concept of the double movement. As market fundamentalists and their allies attempt to construct their ideal world of a self-regulating market system, the destabilizing consequences set off countervailing movements by other groups in society who recognize the need to protect themselves and others from exposure to unmediated market forces. These counter-movements are just as likely to be conservative, even populist and fascist, as market destabilizations will mobilize the right no less than the left, as we illustrate in Chapter 7. But in Polanyi's framework, these ongoing and polarizing conflicts are more complex than the Marxist idea of class struggle between the bourgeoisie and the proletariat; rather, particular policy ideas create shifting constituencies of groups that favor or oppose expanding or constraining markets. And since the project of creating a self-regulating market is ultimately impossible, there will be times that even the largest businesses will defect and openly embrace the use of government for protection against market turmoil.

Our third theme is that the seductive persistence of free market ideology is rooted in its promise *to reduce the role of politics in civic and social life*. Since politics inevitably entails conflict over the scope and character of government, as well as morally unsatisfying compromises among competing interest groups, the wish to narrow its scope is understandable. The desire to eliminate the tyranny and ugliness of politics was part of the historical appeal of movements inspired by a Marxism that anticipated the "withering away of the state." And one sees this just as clearly in the libertarian rhetoric of Tea Party activists in the United States as they express their intense distaste for Washington's bail out in 2008–2009 of Wall Street banks (Skocpol and Williamson 2012).

Polanyi argues that in a complex society we cannot escape the necessity of politics and governmental coordination of economic and social life. Utopian calls from either the right or the left to end politics as we know it are likely only to end up expanding the scope of politics. But this insight did not lead Polanyi to despair. While his eyes were open to all of the ugliness of the political realm, he believed that an expansion of political democracy was the only guarantee against both government coercion and market tyranny. In the final pages of GT, he lays out his still-persuasive argument that recognizing the inevitability of politics and political conflicts could be the foundation for a society with a greater degree of freedom than ever before: "Uncomplaining acceptance of the reality of society gives man indomitable courage and strength to remove all removable injustices and unfreedom. As long as he is true to his task of creating more abundant freedom for all, he need not fear that either power or planning will turn against him and destroy the freedom he is building by their instrumentality" (GT, 268).

The Great Transformation and the Hundred Year's Peace

This book is being published in 2014—the centennial of the outbreak of World War I. Polanyi began GT with an analysis of the One Hundred Year's Peace that preceded the outbreak of World War I a century ago. To be sure, Polanyi acknowledges that this peace had been disrupted by smaller wars between European powers such as the Crimean War, the Franco-Prussian War, and an almost continuous series of military encounters between the European powers and local populations in Africa and Asia. Nevertheless, he views it as remarkable that these wars were limited and that Europe successfully avoided a larger conflagration for a full century. For Polanyi, both the durability of the peace and the abrupt outbreak of a general European war were not accidental. He views World War I as marking the end of nineteenth-century civilization; it was the consequence of a terminal crisis of the institutions that had maintained the long peace.

Polanyi identifies four institutions on which nineteenth-century civilization rested: the balance of power system in Europe, the self-regulating market, the liberal state, and the international gold standard. By the balance of power system, he means the system of changing alliances among the European powers, which prevented any single power from gaining a dominant position. Polanyi argues that these shifting alliances helped maintain the peace through deterrence, as the high probability of retaliation by a group of opponents made armed aggression within Europe too costly.

The other three foundational institutions share a common history; they were all interconnected products of England's early industrial success and they all contributed to the dramatic economic growth of Europe's long nineteenth century of peace. The first was the idea of the self-regulating market, elaborated by the newly invented nineteenth-century political economy—especially Malthus and Ricardo--and built on Adam Smith's idea of the "invisible hand."[11] Although there were significant differences between Malthus and Ricardo, they both asserted that only the price mechanism and other incentives built into the market economy could effectively bring supply and demand into balance and assure the optimal use of economic resources. For this to happen, it was essential that government power be used only to legally reinforce these market processes, not to try to override them or alter them in any way. Governments must protect property rights and enforce contracts, but politicians had to resist the temptation to intervene with market outcomes lest perilous results ensue.[12] The self-regulating market gave rise to the liberal state, the third of Polanyi's four pillars. It was the liberal state that enforced the doctrine of "laissez-faire," embraced the orthodoxy of free trade, and consistently campaigned against the protectionist measures of the previous mercantilist regime. Pursuing free trade, the politicians claimed, would expand the market internationally and assure more rapid advances in the division of labor.

The international gold standard was the final piece of Polanyi's puzzle. It required each nation-state to fix its national currency to the value of gold and allow market forces to drive the movement of gold, trade, and capital flows across national borders. In combination with the previous policies of free trade and laissez-faire, an international gold standard regime was supposed to achieve an automatic system of global adjustment.[13] Nations that spent more than they earned in foreign transactions would experience an outflow of gold that would diminish their money supply; this in turn would slow economic activity and bring them back into international balance. Nations that earned more abroad than they spent would have gold inflows that would expand the money supply and accelerate economic activity, which also would help their economies move back to a position of international balance. England had adopted the gold standard in the last part of the eighteenth century and restored it after the Napoleonic Wars. Other European nations gradually followed the English model and by the 1870s, it was the standard for developed nations and widely seen as a critical pillar of global prosperity.[14]

Polanyi argues that the triad of the self-regulating market, the liberal state, and the gold standard were central to the growing prosperity of nineteenth-century Europe. He insists, however, that these arrangements represented a radical and dangerous break with previous institutional patterns and set off countertrends that would ultimately lead to crisis and war. His argument here is complex and multifaceted, but it is possible to trace out a few of the critical causal chains in his argument.

Polanyi argues first and foremost that the goal of creating a self-regulating market and a liberal state is ultimately unachievable—hence "utopian." He states unequivocally on the first page of the book: "Our thesis is that the idea of a self-adjusting market implied a stark Utopia. Such an institution could not exist for any length of time without annihilating the human and natural substance of society; it would have physically destroyed man and transformed his surroundings into a wilderness" (GT, 3). Our entire book could be seen as an extended effort to explicate these two sentences.

Polanyi's thesis can be illustrated through the experience of unemployed urban workers in market economies. Market economies go through economic cycles that alternate periods of prosperity and high demand for labor with periods of crisis and elevated unemployment. What are the unemployed to do during these crisis periods when there is no demand for their services? Free market economists advise that the unemployed must adjust to the situation by accepting reduced wages. But even the unemployed who hold up signs saying "will work for food" usually find little interest in their services during an economic downturn. Absent unemployment insurance or other forms of welfare, these displaced workers and their families are at risk for starvation. If political authorities were bound by laissez-faire principles during periods of mass unemployment or failed harvests, there would be mass starvation.[15] This is what Polanyi means by "such an institution could not exist for any length of time without annihilating the human . . . substance of society." Under pressure from their citizens, even undemocratic governments had little choice but to move away from strict laissez-faire principles during the course of the nineteenth century.

This nineteenth-century resistance was part of Polanyi's "double movement." The movement to impose laissez-faire on society generated a countermovement to protect society from the devastating consequences of markets—not only from the threat of mass starvation, but also from environmental degradation and destructive economic cycles. The newly emergent working class was often the main force of this countermovement for protection, but it often had other powerful allies. In England, for example, parts of the old landed elite fought to constrain market forces and supported a series of Factory Acts designed to constrain the most horrific consequences of rapid industrialization (Somers 1992, 1995, 1997). Polanyi goes on to argue that these protective countermovements successfully organized to win government assistance to the unemployed, regulation of the length of the working day, Bismarck's pioneering welfare policies in Germany, and an enormous expansion of regulatory actions designed to offset the many negative consequences of market competition (GT, ch. 13).

Polanyi then complicates his historical argument with a paradox. Just as governments were under increasing pressure to buffer their citizens from mass unemployment and other market shocks, the spread of the gold standard system magnified the impact of market forces on national economies. In particular, the gold standard's automatic economic adjustments created new and deeper outbreaks of mass unemployment. In the 1870s, governments abandoned the orthodoxy of free trade by embracing protective tariffs to cushion their citizens from the global market. Indeed, in Polanyi's view the rush to empire in the last decades of the nineteenth century was a direct response to the pressures created by the gold standard. The profits and protected markets available in overseas colonies buffered nations from the disastrous consequences of the gold standard. For example, nations could avoid painful domestic deflation by drawing down gold and other foreign exchange earned by their colonies.

Polanyi observes the dramatic irony of these developments. One of the core claims of the economic liberals was that the universal embrace of free trade and the gold standard system would usher in a period of international peace and harmony, since all nations would benefit from expanded global flows of trade and capital. But exactly the opposite happened. Since governments had no choice but to protect their citizens from the disruptions caused by market processes, the protective shell surrounding nations hardened. He writes: "The new crustacean type of nation expressed its identity through national token currencies safeguarded by a type of sovereignty more jealous and absolute than anything known before" (GT, 211). This crustacean nationalism was expressed in the heightened Anglo-German global rivalry in trade and arms that began in the 1890s and which ultimately allowed the assassination of an Austrian archduke to escalate into World War I.

The core impossibility of entrusting society to a self-regulating market meant that from the 1870s onward nations were caught in a vise between the logic of the protective countermovement on the one side and the pressures of the gold standard mechanism on the other. This vise exacerbated internal domestic tensions: citizens found it impossible to win many of the protections that they needed, as the gold standard obstructed governmental concessions at every turn. Mounting internal tensions, in turn, translated into growing global tensions as political leaders blamed the machinations of foreign leaders for their domestic difficulties. For Polanyi the outbreak of World War I and the continuing high levels of global tensions in the 1920s and 1930s was the inexorable result.

The Interwar Years, Bretton Woods, and the Return of the Gold Standard Mechanism

Polanyi wrote GT during World War II as an effort to influence the postwar settlement. He wanted to avoid a replay of the post-World War I Treaty of Versailles, where the great powers agreed to restore the gold standard system of 1870–1914. Polanyi saw this as inevitably placing nations in the same internally contradictory position that they had been in before the war—caught between the legitimate demands of citizens for protection from the market and the economic logic of the gold standard system. In the aftermath of World War I, workers—often inspired by the example of the Russian Revolution—demanded both higher wages and greater protection from income insecurity caused by unemployment, illness, and old age. As Beverly Silver (2003) has documented, the result was one of the greatest strike waves in history. Yet the logic of gold standard restoration in the 1920s made it virtually impossible for employers or government to offer concessions to this mobilized working class. Since wartime expenditures had driven up price levels, stabilizing currencies in relationship to gold required a heavy dose of deflation and government budgetary discipline (Maier 1975). Gold standard orthodoxy required strict austerity for both wages and government expenditures.

This was the structural backdrop to the crises of democratic governance symbolized by Mussolini's seizure of power in Italy in 1922.

Since a compromise between the demands of workers and the pressures of the gold standard was impossible, the strains led to the collapse of democratic institutions in country after country. Moreover, in the 1920s radicalization within countries interacted dangerously with the complex system of reparations, war debts, and external financing from the United States. When the stock market crashed in the United States in 1929, cutting off American capital flows to Europe, the result was a string of European bank failures in 1931. Europe's capacity to manage this crisis was severely compromised by the growing political polarization within nations. The result was an accelerating economic downturn with no agreement as to how to reverse it. Moreover, the logic of the gold standard demanded that nations take actions that only strengthened the deflationary pressures. It was in this context that Hitler came to power in Germany, repudiated the gold standard, and began the rearmament program that put Germans back to work and made World War II inevitable.

Polanyi's indictment of the role that the restoration of the gold standard played in the crisis of the Interwar Years was widely shared in the 1940s. William Adams Brown, Jr., of the Brookings Institution had published his monumental book *The International Gold Standard Reinterpreted, 1914–1934* under the prestigious imprint of the National Bureau of Economic Research in 1940. Brown's analysis dovetailed with Polanyi's. Even more importantly, John Maynard Keynes and Harry Dexter White, the two men given the primary responsibility for reconstructing the global financial system by the United Kingdom and the United States, identified the gold standard as playing a central role in these tragic events. On the one side, the pressure on nations to maintain the currency's gold price trumped democracy and made it impossible for societies to respond to the demands of working people. On the other, the system of free capital movements meant that governments were effectively powerless to pursue national objectives such as higher levels of employment or improvements in real wage levels (Block 1977).

Over the course of World War II, this diagnosis of the dangers of the gold standard produced broad consensus over reconstructing the global financial architecture to increase the capacity of governments to pursue domestic policy objectives. While there were serious disagreements between Keynes and White—the two major architects of the Bretton Woods agreements—they were in accord on the fundamental idea of overcoming the deflationary bias of the previous system. They both wanted an international monetary regime that was consistent with the goal of pursuing full employment for the world's labor force. While the Bretton Woods system was not fully operational until the late 1950s, the new policy environment of fixed exchange rates and strict regulation of global capital flows facilitated full employment policies for almost three decades after the end of World War II. This was the "Golden Age" when both developed and developing nations experienced rapid economic growth (Marglin and Schor, eds. 1990).

From the end of the 1960s through the beginning of the 1970s, the Bretton Woods regime faced mounting strains, primarily because the U.S. was unable to bring its balance of payments deficit under control. Under the weight of mounting problems, there was international agreement in 1973 to move from fixed exchange rates to floating exchange rates. While the proponents of floating rates had argued that market-determined exchange rates would adjust smoothly and gradually, the reality was the opposite. With exchange rates now shaped by the actions of financial traders and speculators, they became much more volatile after 1973 (Krugman 1989). As exchange rate movements became more pronounced, a growing number of governments dismantled controls over international capital movements, producing even greater volatility in both exchange rates and capital movements. During the course of the next three decades, there was a spectacular increase in both foreign exchange trading and in the growth of various derivative instruments that were intended to allow investors to hedge against increasingly disruptive and unpredictable movements in exchange rates, interest rates, and other variables that might impact their portfolios.

The cumulative impact of these post-1973 changes effectively undid what had been attempted in the Bretton Woods agreements. In a world of floating exchange rates and instantaneous movements of global capital, governments in developed countries lost much of the policy autonomy that they had gained in the Bretton Woods system. If a government attempted to pursue expansionary policies to increase employment, it would once again risk crippling outflows of capital. Even Scandinavian social democracies that had aggressively pursued full employment policies through the mid-1970s faced periods in which unemployment was reported at 8%, 9%, or even higher. And from 2010 to 2012, as recovery from the worst economic slowdown since the Great Depression was just getting underway, pressures from the global financial markets were forcing countries such as Greece, Portugal, and Spain to pursue austerity policies that would ratchet up unemployment and leave more people unprotected from the economic impact of the global economic downturn.

The Global Economy Today

Tragically, the world economy today has returned to the kind of dangerous conflict between democracy and the pressures of the global financial system that characterized the 1920s (Streeck 2011). Despite the Greek government having been duly elected in 2010 with strong popular support and with millions of people engaged in ongoing mass demonstrations to protect existing levels of government spending, the Greeks have been under relentless pressure from the more powerful members of the European Union. They were given only two bad choices, and both of them involved imposing austerity on their own people. The government could have defaulted on its debt, withdrawn from the European common currency, and then imposed extreme austerity measures. The less unpleasant alternative has been to rely on an aid package from the European community to meet its debt obligations and remain in the Eurozone, but the price has been to impose ever greater degrees of austerity that continue to be strongly opposed by the Greek electorate.

The problems that have been facing Greece, Ireland, Spain, and Portugal since 2010 replicate those that developing nations have been facing for many years. Starting particularly during the 1980s debt crisis, countries that had been encouraged by international bankers to borrow during the 1970s suddenly faced a reckoning.[16] Unable to keep up with their debt payments and yet unable to borrow new funds in the private market, governments had to turn to the International Monetary Fund and the World Bank. These institutions imposed "structural adjustments" as the price for new assistance. Structural adjustment dictated a large dose of austerity—especially reductions in state spending on social programs—as well as much higher levels of unemployment. Again, the preferences of voters in these countries were suddenly irrelevant; democratic outcomes were trumped by the inexorable demands of the global financial institutions. Remarkably, the world had once again effectively restored an out-of-control financial mechanism quite similar to the nineteenth-century gold standard.

This is what makes Polanyi's arguments so relevant to the current problems of the global economy. The world is, in effect, struggling with the unfinished business of the 1920s and 1930s. The most obvious sign of this was the almost instantaneous diffusion of global deflationary pressures from the fall of 2008 through early 2009. To be sure, government initiatives to prop up financial institutions and add demand to the global economy contained the worst of the crisis and narrowly averted even more catastrophic levels of global unemployment or even a second Great Depression. But even as we write in 2013, five years later, there seems to be no end to widespread unemployment coupled with an ongoing deluge of foreclosures. The depth of the resulting suffering makes it more critical than ever to understand the policy choices that ultimately culminated in the global financial crisis.

Suppressing the Lessons of History

When he wrote GT, Polanyi believed that the experience of the 1930s had finally discredited the ideas of his free market opponents. We know now, of course, that he was wrong; in the 1970s those ideas returned from the dead and once again reshaped the world. But the way in which this happened still vindicates Polanyi's emphasis on the extraordinary role that ideas play in justifying certain policy choices that, in turn, can have catastrophic social and economic consequences.

As both the United States and the global economy experienced growing strains in the 1970s, the free market ideas that had been the target of Polanyi's critique experienced an extraordinary revival. Friedrich Hayek and Milton Friedman, working with a network of well-funded organizations and think tanks, had kept those ideas alive since the 1940s.[17] Yet until the 1970s, free market orthodoxy had little traction in political debates, and economics continued to be dominated by scholars who identified as Keynesians.

This changed in the 1970s, as much of the U.S. business community made a sharp rightward turn (see Chapter 7) and as Keynesian economists proved unable to respond effectively to the double challenges of slow growth with high inflation and mounting criticisms by Milton Friedman and his followers. When Ronald Reagan won the presidential election in 1980 he announced, in effect, that the age of Keynes was over and the age of Friedman had begun. But contrary to popular myth, "big government" did not suddenly disappear; instead, government expenditures continued to rise with Reagan's massive military buildup. Moreover, under the guise of "deregulation" and "small government," the Reagan Administration accelerated the processes of what we are calling *reregulation*, which had begun under Jimmy Carter. By the term reregulation, as we suggested earlier, we aim to push back against the belief that the success of neoliberal ideology since the mid-1970s has been matched by markets being increasingly freed from regulations and government management. On the contrary, regulations did not go away; they simply changed. Those that had previously been written to protect employees or consumers were systematically rewritten to support business interests and reduce previous restrictions on business practices. Similarly, the tax code was rejiggered to shift the burden from high-income households to middle class and working class earners.

Reagan's reregulative policies started a dramatic shift of income in favor of the top 1% of households (Hacker and Pierson 2010). As noted earlier, the share of income going to the top 1% increased from 10% in 1981 to 23.5% in 2007 (Saez and Piketty 2013). Much of this shift can be traced to the bold new opportunities that Reaganite reregulation created for Wall Street. Under the new rules, employment and profits in the financial sector grew spectacularly (Krippner 2011; Polanyi-Levitt 2013). Dozens of new billionaires suddenly appeared, who had built their fortunes simply by making deals or trading pieces of paper including newly authorized derivatives such as credit default swaps and collateralized debt obligations.

Moreover, this shift of income and wealth created a powerful feedback mechanism. Some of the new wealth flowed back to Washington to fund right wing think tanks and to finance the campaigns of market-oriented politicians in both parties. With learned studies coming from these think tanks and the promise of more campaign funds, Congress was eager for new rounds of free market reregulation. By the 1990s, Republicans and Democrats alike were singing the praises of the free market and celebrating the extraordinary energy and dynamism of the financial sector. In fact, it was during the Clinton Administration that free market ideas moved from being a partisan weapon to becoming the new ideational regime (Chapter 6). In the late 1990s, Clinton officials such as Robert Rubin and Larry Summers were among the most enthusiastic celebrants of financial markets that were growing rapidly and allegedly regulating themselves.

To be sure, from the 1980s onward, almost every step of reregulation that eliminated previous restrictions on what financial firms could legally do was challenged by powerful voices who warned that the new measures could well lead to a financial disaster. Their warnings, however, were systematically ridiculed and marginalized as pessimistic "Chicken Little" anxieties of those not sophisticated enough to understand how effectively modern financial markets manage and diffuse risk. Even those who were shouting at the top of their lungs that the rise in prices in the U.S. housing market was dangerous and unsustainable were drowned out and ultimately ignored (Tabb 2012). What happened, of course, was that billions worth of subprime mortgage loans were packaged together and resold to financial institutions around the world. When prices in the U.S. housing market turned down, the default rate on those loans skyrocketed, and the consequence was that financiers woke up to the realization that they were holding hundreds of billions of dollars of toxic assets that nobody wanted. In the resulting rush to safety, long-established financial firms collapsed, credit dried up around the world, and economies went into free-fall (Baker 2008; Johnson and Kwak 2010; Stiglitz 2010). As the crisis was unfolding, Alan Greenspan, who had presided over decades of irresponsible financial reregulation as Chair of the Federal Reserve Board, was called to account.[18]After four decades on the national stage as a philosopher of free markets and the cheerleader for tax cuts, he testified to Congress in October 2008 by saying: "Those of us who have looked to the self-interest of lending institutions to protect shareholders' equity, myself included, are in a state of shocked disbelief." Congressman Henry Waxman probed: "Do you feel that your ideology pushed you to make decisions that you wish you had not made?" Greenspan's humbled reply was: "Yes, I've found a flaw. I don't know how significant or permanent it is. But I've been very distressed by that fact . . . I made a mistake in presuming that the self-interest of organizations, specifically banks and others, were such as that they were best capable of protecting their own shareholders and their equity in the firms . . . [the] flaw in the model that I perceived is the critical functioning structure that defines how the world works" (Andrews 2008). Waxman was clearly prodding Greenspan to acknowledge that the decisions he took at the Fed were not simply dictated by obvious and objective economic science. And Greenspan did not dissemble, but stated unambiguously that it was his ideology that told him how the world worked. What others called a dangerous bubble in the housing market he perceived as merely surface disturbance not worthy of interference. He was simply acting according to his dominant creed that because of the "self-interest of organizations," markets will always self-correct.

Greenspan exemplifies the point that when public officials take actions that in retrospect appear wildly irrational, it usually is the case that they are engaging in sober calculations based on mistaken premises derived from theories of how the world works.[19] The politicians and government officials who so carelessly unwound an entire system of financial regulations did so from their fealty to free market assumptions that unleashing finance would pay off mightily. So foundational was this model in sculpting collective perceptions that financial engineers, banking economists, and politicians justified their actions by its authority. The model limited their vision in such a way that made their choices appear to be rational ones. They were, in short, both constrained and enabled by their ideas.

Keynes and Polanyi

In the aftermath of these catastrophic events, it has become clear that the lessons of the 1930s were suppressed. It is now imperative to return to the insights of Keynes and Polanyi, the thinkers who developed the most cogent analyses of that earlier period of economic crisis. Here we can gain considerable appreciation of Polanyi's unique approach by comparing him to Keynes, his much more famous contemporary. Keynes developed his thinking in opposition to the austerity policies imposed by mainstream economic orthodoxy in the 1920s and 1930s, and he fiercely opposed reduced public spending and draconian wage cuts as solutions to the catastrophic crisis of the global depression. As early as the 1920s, Keynes developed a positive sum solution to the economic problems of modern societies. He envisioned a class compromise between workers and employers so that societies could have significant gains in the standard of living at the same time that business firms flourished with rising productivity. A better educated, better housed, and healthier working class could make enterprises more productive, while also providing the growing demand needed to stimulate new investment and new industries (Skidelsky 1994).

Keynes, like Polanyi several years later, believed economic orthodoxy to be a complex system of illusions; he defined his mission to replace this stifling orthodoxy with a new and expansive economic perspective. Equipped with this superior set of economic understandings, political party competition would be freed of the kind of stalemates that had dominated European politics in the 1920s. Parties would draw on skilled government officials who understood how to use a toolkit of government practices to sustain economic growth. Together, this new positive sum economy and a system of pragmatic policy making that learned from its own mistakes would generate continuous economic advance. In the early 1930s, Keynes confidently anticipated that in about a hundred years economies would be so productive that human beings would be free of the age old struggle for subsistence (1963 [1931]).

The General Theory (1936) was enormously influential, and Keynesian ideas dominated economics and government policy in the first three post-World War II decades. All were characterized by strong growth, nearly full employment, and low inflation. Ironically, it was the apparent success of Keynesian policies in these three postwar decades that led both scholars and the public to forget the intense debates of the interwar period. Across most of the political spectrum, there was agreement that Keynesian policies had demonstrated the path to continuous prosperity. Even Milton Friedman acknowledged in 1965: "We're all Keynesians now"(cited in Krugman 2012, 101).[20]

Skidelsky (2009) has observed that Keynes's critique of economic orthodoxy was informed by a deep moral sensibility. But as Keynes's ideas were transformed into Keynesianism,[21] they gradually became a set of administrative and bureaucratic routines that were framed in a language that was primarily technocratic. John F. Kennedy's Council of Economic Advisors in the early 1960s, for example, insisted that Keynesian ideas were so powerful that, under the guidance of skilled economists, governments could set unemployment and inflation at appropriate levels. They described this as a question of fine-tuning, not unlike adjusting the pitch produced by a piano's keys. But the problem with this technocratic adaptation of Keynes was that it meant jettisoning his critically important focus on uncertainty and instability in market economies (Minsky 1986).[22]

As Keynesian government policies were cut off from their moral underpinnings, the ideas themselves became increasingly vulnerable to conservative assault. To be sure, some of this vulnerability can be traced back to Keynes himself. His pragmatism overwhelmed the moral commitments that he brought to his original enterprise. His biographer, Robert Skidelsky, has confirmed this disjuncture between Keynes's deepest views and the arguments that he made to convince other economists: "Deep down, he was not an economist at all. Of course, he could 'do' economics—and with the best. He put on the mask of an economist to gain authority, just as he put on dark suits and homburgs for life in the

City. But he did not believe in the system of ideas by which economists lived, and still live; he did not worship at the temple; he was a heretic who learned how to play the game" (Skidelsky 2009, 59–60). Skidelsky insists that Keynes's insights " . . . were never—could never be—properly integrated into the core of his discipline, which expelled them as soon as it conveniently could" (Skidelsky 2009, 55–56).

In a view that he shared with Karl Polanyi, John Maynard Keynes's unacceptable heresy was his belief that the economy was a means to an end, not an end in itself. He had an abiding suspicion of crass materialism, of money-making, and especially of the "love of money." Skidelsky drives home this point by quoting a speech Keynes gave in Dublin in 1933, in which he said that the system of economic calculation made " . . . the whole conduct of life . . . into a sort of parody of an accountant's nightmare. We destroy the beauty of the countryside because the unappropriated splendors of nature have no economic value. We are capable of shutting off the sun and the stars because they do not pay a dividend" (146). In fact, by the end of the 1930s, Keynes (1982 [1939]:500) explicitly argued for "liberal socialism," despite his continuing rejection of Marxist ideas. He wrote in *The New Statesman and Nation:* "The question is whether we are prepared to move out of the nineteenth century laissez-faire state into an era of liberal socialism, by which I mean a system where we can act as an organized community for common purposes and to promote social and economic justice, whilst respecting and protecting the individual—his freedom of choice, his faith, his mind, and its expression, his enterprise and his property."[23] But no matter how radical the prescriptions he offered, when Keynes "put on the mask of the economist," he conformed to the discipline's core assumption that the economy is autonomous from other social institutions. In a word, Keynes's pragmatism and desire to influence other economists meant that he could not embrace Polanyi's heretical view that actual market economies are embedded in society. The irony, however, is that granting the claim that the economy is autonomous set the stage for the successful free market counterattack against Keynes's influence.

In their subsequent assault on Keynesianism, Milton Friedman and his followers adopted the strategy of resurrecting the orthodox tenets of Malthus and Ricardo. Because the economy is autonomous, they asserted, it must be allowed to govern itself by its own laws. Since it is autonomous, it must also be shielded from "outside" impositions such as moral views that favor equality, "social agendas," or the particular preferences of elected officials. As we elaborate in our discussion of welfare policies in Chapter 5, the Friedmanites evoke a lost Eden of uninterrupted prosperity that thrived precisely because the economy was allowed to self-regulate. By insisting that only a return to those earlier practices would restore prosperity, they were able to defeat deeply entrenched Keynesian ideas.

There was, moreover, yet another problem that contributed to the eventual delegitimation and defeat of Keynesian economic practices in the 1970s. Even though Keynes had once insisted that "The republic of my imagination lies on the extreme left of celestial space" (cited in Clarke 2009, 68), the reality is that he shared the skepticism of the British upper class towards political democracy. While he was fervent in insisting that laissez-faire be replaced by an active state directing the economy, he wanted that role to be carried out exclusively by economic experts and highly trained civil servants. As Sabeel Rahman writes about Keynes in the 1930s: "Indeed, part of Keynes' unease with the more social democratic vision of the Labour Party was precisely that if political agency is invested in a broader democratic public rather than insulated bureaucracies, 'too much will always be decided by those who do not know what they are talking about'" (Rahman 2011, 269). In the end, this failure to give his economic solutions a democratic grounding proved fatal to Keynes's intellectual legacy and legitimacy. When it was most vulnerable to unyielding conservative assault in the crises of the 1970s, Keynesianism had no popular democratic foundation of support to defend it.

Polanyi's Alternative to Keynes

Like Keynes, Polanyi rejected a zero-sum approach to politics in which working class gains would inevitably come at the expense of business profits. He based this conviction on his experience with "Red Vienna" in the 1920s. There he had witnessed a democratic socialist movement successfully create a prototypical welfare state in which a healthier, more educated, and better housed labor force brought benefits to workers and employers alike (see McRobbie and Levitt, eds. 2006; and GT, 298–299). This experience gave Polanyi confidence that there was a way out of the stalemate between labor and capital. However, as with Keynes, Polanyi recognized that opening up this path required a different set of rules for governing the global economy than those that had prevailed between the two World Wars.

At the same time, there are important differences between Keynes and Polanyi. Keynes, to gain credibility among established economists, was willing to cede his critique of market autonomy. Polanyi devotes an entire book to debunking that stark utopian thinking, as well as showing the catastrophic destruction it inflicted on the world. His insistence that the human economy is embedded in social, political, ideational, cultural, and moral structures is designed to preempt the logic of free market theorists who move from the conceit of an autonomous self-activating economy to the normative claim that human freedom depends upon the market being the governing mechanism for all of society.

Polanyi also understood the risks and dangers of Keynes's more technocratic approach to politics. He recognized that a pragmatic politics shorn of moral purpose would inevitably become frail; policies that are legitimated simply on the instrumental grounds of short-term success will be vulnerable as soon as conditions change, as we show in Chapter 6. This belief motivated him to make democratic politics an essential cornerstone of his political economic vision. Only active participation from below could counteract the tendency of politics to degenerate into a cynical contest for power between rival factions. It is not that he was naïve about the limitations of existing forms of democratic governance; it is rather that he took the long view of democratization as a process developing over many decades to bring government under popular control.

While Polanyi was a strong defender of parliamentary democracy, he believed that the democratization of society had to go beyond citizens choosing their leaders in periodic competitive elections. In the 1920s, Polanyi had been drawn to the ideas of "guild socialism" proposed by G. D. H. Cole (Dale 2010). Cole (1920) sought to avoid the twin dangers of state socialism on the one side and anarcho-syndicalism on the other by envisioning a separation of powers between a system of worker representation that would own and manage the production process and a parliamentary state that would continue to represent the population on a territorial basis.

There are no explicit references to guild socialism in GT, but Polanyi's belief in expanding democracy to include the economy is expressed in his idiosyncratic definition of socialism: "Socialism is, essentially, the tendency inherent in an industrial civilization to transcend the self-regulating market by consciously subordinating it to a democratic society" (GT, 242–243). Implicit in this definition is a critique of the Marxist stipulation that the coercive power of the state would "wither away" once the socialist revolution ended class exploitation. Polanyi sees this claim as a parallel utopian fantasy to that of the self-regulating market. Indeed, he explicitly follows Weber in recognizing that political authority and power would inevitably continue into any future social order, especially as a countervailing source of power to that of the economy (Polanyi, GT, ch. 13).

Two fundamental points follow. First, socialists could not ignore the difficulties entailed in imposing democratic accountability on governmental power. Second, Marxists were guilty of imagining that a shift in property relations would—by itself—usher in a new and better society (see Chapter 2). According to Polanyi, Marx mistakenly had accepted the claims of the classical economists, especially Ricardo, that property relations can and will determine the entire shape of the social order.

Polanyi's view here is based on his unique insight that market society was imposed in the nineteenth century through political means. What we think of as "modern capitalist society" was, for Polanyi, not the result of underlying inevitable economic mechanisms, but rather the consequence of a series of political choices and explicit government policies. The pretense now stripped away of the economy as a "force of nature," it follows logically that these arrangements can be undone and reversed through the same mechanism—the use of political power. While Polanyi is usually not explicit on this point, his argument is consistent with those who have argued that private property represents a bundle of different rights that owners had at one particular moment in time (Berman 2006, 168).[24] It follows that political and legal changes introduced over time can change that bundle of rights until many of the most important structural inequalities in labor markets, capital markets, and product markets are effectively eliminated.

For example, like Keynes and Harry Dexter White (Block 1977), Polanyi argued that limiting the right of property owners to move capital across national boundaries would eliminate one of the most powerful devices by which the wealthy are able to bypass democratic constraints by forcing governments to pursue their own policy preferences. For Polanyi, moreover, that markets and property rights are fundamentally political constructs is an historical claim not just a theoretical one. In GT he explains the history of the previous century as a series of partially successful efforts to transform market relationships through political means. So, for example, Bismarck's social welfare measures in the 1870s not only provided workers with insurance against illness, disability, and old age; they also transformed the labor market by politics. In the same way, trade unions winning rights on the shop floor politically reorganized class and property relationships (GT, 210–217).

In sum, one of Polanyi's most essential arguments concerns political democracy. Only a profound commitment to democratic practices could assure that economic activity was constrained within a framework that meets the shared needs of the citizenry. Because he also recognized the importance of global institutions, Polanyi was convinced that successful democratic governance at the local and the national level required supportive global arrangements that worked in tandem. Subordinating the economy to democratic governance was for Polanyi a global imperative.

Polanyi's Distinctive Ideas

Up to this point, we have provided a general introduction to Polanyi's main arguments and sought to place him in historical context as well as in relation to other important intellectual traditions. Now we turn to some of the more specific arguments that make Polanyi such a distinctive and generative thinker. We have identified seven key ideas that correspond to the remaining seven chapters of this book. Our exposition of these seven ideas are not intended as introductions or summaries of the later chapters, but rather to clarify and bring to attention the fundamental theoretical issues at stake in each chapter. To be sure, each chapter is far more complex in its argument than one single key idea. Still, we think this is the best way to introduce readers to the richness and complexity of Polanyi's intellectual project. Read through the prism of our own interpretations, each of these Polanyian ideas challenges familiar assumptions about how the world works. Together, they add up to a powerful critique of existing social and economic arrangements and a vision of a real alternative.

In this task we face a problem that was identified by Karl Polanyi's brother, the philosopher Michael Polanyi. The relationship between these two extremely gifted brothers is a fascinating story in itself. While the two were very close at times in their adult lives, they found themselves during the Cold War on opposite sides of the era's polarized politics. In fact, Michael Polanyi attended the initial meeting of the Mont Pelerin Society in 1947, the organization through which Friedrich Hayek and Milton Friedman worked tirelessly to move free market ideas from the margins of discourse to global dominance. Yet despite his alliance with his brother's key theoretical opponents, Michael offered effusive praise when his brother sent him GT in manuscript (Fleming 2001).

Michael began his career as a scientist working in England, where he came into direct conflict with a group of scientists influenced by Marxism, who believed that the progress of science, like that of the economy, would be improved through a regime of planning. In order to challenge this idea, Michael developed a theory of scientific development that emphasized the tacit and personal elements of scientific knowledge. He insisted that neither individual scientists nor the scientific community could ever enumerate all of the ideas that were incorporated into a specific scientific theory. Scientific theories were like icebergs; the textbook version of the theory was what appeared above the surface, but it was supported by a huge structure of invisible assumptions and implicit claims that only became visible through the spontaneous and unplanned efforts of individual scientists to make sense of data (M. Polanyi 2009 [1966]).

Michael's insight is particularly relevant for his brother's theoretical corpus. Karl Polanyi's thinking was complex because his concepts are intertwined with the historical experiences that he was seeking to explain, and his framework included various tacit assumptions that are never stated explicitly. It is tempting to try to develop a systematic, step-by-step, exposition of his key ideas. The effort, however, would be easily defeated by the interconnectedness of Karl Polanyi's theoretical framework. Each of Polanyi's key ideas is connected and dependent on other key ideas, so it is impossible to work one's way up from the foundational ideas.

The Economy Is an Instituted Process (Chapter 2)

Karl Polanyi defined himself as an institutionalist—both to distinguish himself from conventional mainstream economics and to make clear that rather than the "laws of the market," social, political, and cultural institutions shape how economies actually work. He made the critical distinction between the formal and the substantive view of the economy; the former focuses on the economizing of scarce resources while the latter centers on how human beings organize and allocate the pursuit of the things needed to sustain human life. This distinction makes clear that the lens used by most economists is not wide enough to capture the complexity of actual substantive economies—both historically and in the present.

This substantivist view of the economy is grounded in Polanyi's understanding that society and its institutions make up the foundation upon which an economy is built. Aristotle insisted that humans are fundamentally political animals; they realize themselves only living in a polis—a political community. Polanyi would modify this and say that humans are social animals; they define and realize themselves in relation to others. It is collectively through social arrangements that human beings work out how they will secure their livelihood. It follows from this argument that market exchange is only one of the institutional arrangements by which humans organize economic activity (Polanyi 1968 [1957]).

Polanyi stressed the continuing role of three other institutional complexes—redistribution, reciprocity, and householding. Redistribution is the pattern in which goods are accumulated at a central point and then distributed out to households. Reciprocity is the pattern associated with gift-giving, through which items are passed along to others with the expectation that the giver will also be a receiver. Householding is the pattern in which families provide for their own needs. The role these institutions play in modern society is invisible to those who focus only on markets and processes of economizing.

These are the foundations for Polanyi's profound rejection of what he terms the "economistic fallacy"—the belief that human society is fundamentally shaped by the needs of the economy. His view is that Western societies are as much shaped by culture as are tribal societies; it is just that the *content* of our cultural beliefs now reflect the core ideas of Western liberalism—belief in the sovereignty of the self-interested, materially-motivated individual, and the sacred status we effectively attribute to a rapidly developing economy (Sahlins 1976; Thomasberger 2013). Just like any tribal individual who finds it difficult to think outside of the framework provided by his or her own culture, we are ourselves prisoners of modernity's culture of the market's natural inviolability. The consequence is that we understand ourselves and our social relationships in ways that are radically incomplete.

Polanyi argues that, in the nineteenth century, Western societies came to be organized in a way that made the pursuit of individual self-interest *appear* to be the innate motivation of human nature. Yet, like Durkheim (1964 [1893], 242), who emphasized the noncontractual bases of contract, Polanyi recognized that this utilitarian notion of self-interest was far too brittle and socially corrosive to ever forge any kinds of deep solidarities (Somers 2008, ch.2). Were it to be an accurate description of the social world, we would be living in a Hobbesian universe of constant war of all against all. And wars and social conflict notwithstanding, it is clear we do not live in that kind of world—in large part thanks to the fundamental role played by the government provisioning, legal power, our social bonds, the normative constraints of our political culture, and our institutions of civil society. All of this, however, is obscured by the economistic fallacy. Our taken-for-granted cultural framework is one that makes us think that we do not actually have a culture and that the state's growth in size and importance is a threat and a coercive antagonist to nature, rather than a constitutive support for the actual functioning economy.

Challenging the Concept of the Autonomous Economy: The Always and Everywhere Embedded Economy (Chapter 3)

Polanyi directly challenges the conventional view that the Industrial Revolution and the rise of the bourgeoisie ushered in an historical epoch in which the economy became an autonomous and self-regulating entity, separated entirely from government and society. He was painfully aware that the classical economists aimed to turn this view into orthodox "common sense," and he also knew that they had been extraordinarily successful in creating broad legitimacy for laissez-faire and free trade policies. England in the nineteenth century did become "the workshop of the world" and its embrace of free market and free trade policies was accepted by conventional wisdom as the explanation for its industrial primacy. But while Polanyi acknowledges the unprecedented influence of T. R. Malthus, David Ricardo, and classical political economy, he also insists that there was a huge discrepancy between their ideas and the actual policies that governments adopted.

The conceptual tool that Polanyi uses to show the incoherence of classical political economy and its later neoclassical intellectual heirs is his theory of fictitious commodities. At the core of the vision of a self-regulating and autonomous economy is the idea that the price mechanism coordinates the supply and demand for both key economic inputs as well as for final products. The economy consists of many decentralized producers who compete with each other and continuously take account of price signals in the market. If, for example, a particular raw material becomes scarce and significantly more expensive, firms that ordinarily rely on that input will search for substitutes and suppliers will increase the supply. The combination of more supply and the substitution of alternatives will soon bring those prices down to a more reasonable level that will readjust supply and demand. Through this constant adjustment process, the price mechanism assures that the decentralized economic actors make the best possible use of available resources.

This vision of a self-equilibrating economy was still just an abstract ideal for the classical political economists. By the mid-twentieth century, however, economists worked out the mathematics of a general equilibrium model which, under restrictive conditions, will demonstrate the optimal outcomes that the classical economists expected. Yet even before this model was fully developed, Polanyi recognized that there was a fundamental flaw in this entire way of thinking. The capacity of the market mechanism to balance supply and demand works for commodities—those things that are actually produced for the purpose of being sold in the market. But Polanyi argues that while land, labor, and money are all critical inputs into the production process, they do not meet the definition of a commodity. Labor is simply organized activity of human beings, land is nature that has been subdivided, and money is a unit of accounting and a way of storing value.

Polanyi insists that land, labor, and money should be understood as fictitious commodities; they cannot behave or be treated in the same way as true commodities because they were not produced to be sold on a market. The opportunities to substitute for these economic inputs are distinctly limited, moreover. The idea of the self-regulating market economy, however, requires that land, labor, and money be treated "as if" they were real commodities.[25] The vision of a self-regulating market economy thus rests on a fiction; it describes something that cannot actually exist.

The only way to bridge the gap between the pretense and the reality of actually existing market economies has been to use the powers of government to manage the markets for these fictitious commodities in ways that produce over time the illusion of their commoditization, and thus some rough balancing of supply and demand. So, for example, governments always need to structure the market for labor in order to produce the particular skills that employers need and to mitigate the extremes of labor scarcity on one side and mass unemployment on the other. Even before the birth of the modern welfare state, governments used such tools as emigration and immigration policies to achieve some balance in the labor market, and public agencies dispensed relief to assist the unemployed. To be sure, the effectiveness of this governmental management of the labor market varies over time and usually leaves some groups with no protection from the deprivations caused by lack of earnings.[26]

The case of land is quite similar. Governments create markets in land in the first place by establishing property rights, conducting land surveys, creating localities with specific boundaries, and enhancing the value of certain plots of land by building appropriate infrastructure such as roads, canals, parks, and other urban amenities. And most importantly, predictability in the market for land requires sets of rules as to what types of economic activity are permitted or prohibited in particular localities. One would not expect the supply and demand for suburban real estate to reach some kind of equilibrium level if residents were each allowed to begin smelting coal in their backyards.

As for money, Polanyi argues that during the course of the nineteenth century, most nations created central banks in order to mitigate the disastrous alternation between rapid expansion and rapid contraction of the supply of money and credit. When management of money and credit is left in the hands of the private sector, the historical experience has been boom-bust cycles—inflationary credit cycles followed by crashes. As we know from recent experience, even with the creation of Central Banks, the danger of such boom-bust cycles does not disappear. It is governmental management of the supplies of money and credit that has facilitated long periods of stable economic expansion.

Polanyi's point is quite simple. According to free market doctrine, market economies make a radical separation between the economic and the political realm. The political realm simply enforces a stable set of background rules, such as laws of contract and property, and it allows the market to proceed autonomously within those rules. Polanyi uses the examples of the fictitious commodities to show that this radical separation is mythical. The government is centrally involved in overseeing the markets for land, labor, and money; its activities help to constitute the very core of the economy.

To be sure, Polanyi recognizes that this governmental involvement in the economy goes well beyond these three fictitious commodities. They are simply illustrative of the deep ways in which the economy and the state are intertwined. He also discusses the case of antitrust policies. The autonomous market model rests on the idea that different firms are competing with each other, but this competition can sometimes leave a small number of firms in a dominant position where they no longer are compelled to respond to price signals. So even some of the more radical proponents of laissez-faire historically endorsed the government's role in assuring that a competitive marketplace is actually present. However, contemporary market fundamentalists have mostly abandoned this support for government antitrust initiatives (Crouch 2011).

The Seductive Appeal of the Autonomous Economy (Chapter 4)

But what accounts for the seductive appeal of these erroneous claims that the economy is both autonomous and self-regulating? How is it that extremely intelligent people have been so convinced by an idea that lacks empirical grounding? After all, an autonomous economy is invisible to the naked eye. Polanyi offers the surprising explanation that the free market idea is so appealing because it is utopian. While many generations of conservative thinkers have derided communism and socialism as utopian ideas that are completely inconsistent with what we know about human societies, Polanyi turns the tables and insists that the theorists of the free market have constructed a utopian vision of the good society that is appealing, impossible, and ultimately destructive, even catastrophic.

To understand the appeal of the free market utopia, we must recognize that it promises to reduce radically the role of politics in social life. Distaste for politics is deeply rooted in the modern Western tradition in several ways. First, those who have political power too often use it to place limits on individual rights. In the absolutist monarchies of both early modern Europe and contemporary dictatorships, people could be thrown in prison or be killed for simply falling out of favor with those with political clout. Even in democratic regimes with separations of power and the recognition of civil rights, abuses are not uncommon. Franklin Roosevelt interred tens of thousands of innocent Japanese citizens during World War II, and since the tragedy of the World Trade Center on September 11, 2001, the United States has routinely denied constitutional protections to people deemed to be threats to our national security.[27]

Second, even when political power is not being used to limit the freedom of the individual, the practice of politics is almost always conflict-ridden and ugly. The political arena is where different groups contend over competing views of how society should be organized, and inevitably the clashes over deep value disagreements produce polarization and hostility between rival camps. At the same time, elected officials must approve budgets and pass laws that bridge some of these fundamental disagreements, and the inevitable compromises that they make frequently appear to be arbitrary and unprincipled. The political arena routinely offends the sensibilities of ordinary citizens because it necessarily includes both actors who are excessively driven by principles and those whose only principle is making whatever deals will advance their own individual political careers. The market, by contrast, has been seen as a rational "haven" from the passion-inflamed world of political combat (Hirschman 1977).

The idea of ending politics has therefore long been deeply appealing. Polanyi argues that free market theorists especially promise a world where politics would largely disappear because the state's functions would be radically restrained as the self-regulating market becomes the central institution governing society. Threats to individual liberty would be eliminated and we would be safe from those ugly conflicts and unprincipled politicians because the scope of governmental action would be effectively limited.

Precisely because there is no such thing as an autonomous economy, Polanyi defines this vision as utopian, and therefore impossible. But he also emphasizes that the policy recommendations that are designed to realize this utopia pose fundamental threats to society. On the one hand, measures based on the unrealistic vision of self-regulating markets often expose social groups to extreme hardship and the most dangerous forms of social exclusion (see Somers 2008, chs. 2, 3). On the other, pursuing the free market utopia requires anti-democratic measures that limit what citizens are able to accomplish in the political sphere. The ideal of limited government means that citizens must not be allowed to expand government spending for pensions and unemployment insurance if those measures are seen as interfering with market self-regulation.

Polanyi recognizes that democracy is itself put at risk by such anti-democratic efforts to derail popular protective measures. He argues that the fantasy of escaping from a world in which political power exists actually paves the way for dictatorship. Vigorous democratic institutions are the only way to protect ourselves from political tyranny. But those who strive for a society organized around a self-regulating market are forced to weaken democracy and limit the public's capacity to make its own decisions. It is precisely those weakened and unresponsive democracies that are most vulnerable to attack by extremist leaders bent on imposing authoritarian solutions.

The Political Embedding of Markets:
The Speenhamland Story (Chapter 5)

Polanyi argues that market fundamentalists naturalize the market economy into something that is autonomous of human artifice and operates according to its own inner logic of nature. Polanyi challenges this way of thinking by showing that the state was by necessity very directly involved in governing the markets for the fictitious commodities of land, labor, and money. He elaborates this position by showing that both the initial construction of a modern labor market and its continual functioning requires a very substantial expansion of the state's capacity for coercion: "The road to the free market was opened and kept open by an enormous increase in continuous, centrally organized and controlled interventionism" (GT, 146).

Polanyi devotes several chapters of GT to the famous Speenhamland Act. Speenhamland is a village in Berkshire County, England, where in 1795, in response to an extended harvest failure and downturn in the world market, the magistrates adopted a policy to support the wage levels of agricultural laborers using a schedule that linked the amount of "poor relief" to the size of the family and the cost of bread. Under the Old Poor Laws dating back to 1563, local parishes were the basic administrative unit. Although they were required to provide assistance to their indigent parishioners, there was considerable local discretion over the precise rules, forms of assistance, and degrees of generosity.

Responding to the acute distress in 1795, the Speenhamland policy represented an attempt to rationalize the system by creating some degree of uniformity in relief practice. In practice, the new policy was actually implemented in a limited number of counties in the south of England. Nevertheless, the Speenhamland Act was blamed by a chorus of Poor Law opponents as being responsible for what was claimed to be a widespread collapse in rural wages and rural productivity that occurred in the 1810s and 1820s. (The argument by which a form of social assistance came to be blamed for creating the very poverty it was meant to alleviate is also the central topic of Chapter 6 on the "perversity thesis"). Critics of the Old Poor Laws insisted that the only solution was to abolish the Speenhamland system and all forms of "outdoor relief"—assistance that allowed the indigent to continue to live in their own houses while receiving assistance. Their solution was to abolish the old system completely and universalize the work house, in which the indigent and "able-bodied" workers, both men and women, would be required to do menial and demeaning labor in exchange for meals and forced lodging.

In 1834, the radical anti-welfare forces were victorious in abolishing the Old Poor Law and substituting the "Poor Law Amendment Act" or "the New Poor Law." This widely unpopular national legislation, among the very first passed by the newly reformed 1832 Parliament (now filled by representatives of newly enfranchised business interests), created a national system of poor houses that were administered centrally by a Poor Law Board based in London. Polanyi analyzed the New Poor Law as ushering in a fully modern labor market, the kind envisioned by the classical economists in which working people had no choice but to obey the signals of the labor market regardless of how degraded the working conditions or how debased the compensation. Polanyi stresses the role of government coercion in making the dreadful and degrading experience of the work house the only alternative to starvation. Only then did the English poor finally accept the working conditions of the "dark Satanic mills" of early industrialism.

Speenhamland and the Poor Laws—Old and New—loom so large in Polanyi's account because their history provides powerful evidence that economic arrangements are neither natural nor autonomous, but they are deeply embedded within the state's exercise of power and authority. In Chapter 5 we support the basic thrust of his argument about the underlying intentions of those who pushed the New Poor Law through Parliament, as well as its enormous significance in shaping the modern industrial order. But we also directly challenge his interpretation of the Speenhamland period overall. Polanyi may simply have put too much stock in the "evidence" supplied by the now thoroughly discredited 1834 Report on the Poor Law.

The Continuing Power of the Perversity Narrative (Chapter 6)

The campaign against the Old Poor Law relied heavily on what we call "the perversity narrative"—the claim that policies meant to assist the rural poor were, in fact, responsible for their poverty. Remarkably, the very same arguments used against the Old Poor Law—that poverty is caused by welfare, rather than vice versa—were revived by conservatives in the United States in the 1980s and played a central role in bringing about the end of "welfare as we know it" in legislation passed in 1996.

Adopting the language of Albert Hirschman (1991), we label these arguments as the "perversity thesis" and explore its astonishing revival after 200 years of history. This presents a compelling puzzle: since we usually assume that dominant ideas are those perceived to best make sense of *current* issues, such continuity across vast swaths of time and space is difficult to reconcile with the ways in which we think about the contextual importance of policy debates and influential ideas.

A central aspect of Polanyi's critique of the economistic fallacy is his argument that the classical economists were mistaken or misleading in both their understanding of human beings (ontology) and their theory of knowledge (epistemology). Polanyi is explicit in arguing that these mistakes were incorporated into the fabric of mainstream economics and continued to have negative consequences well into the twentieth century. GT draws attention to what we call the "naturalistic fallacy" of classical political economy—the belief that society is governed by the same laws that govern nature and the physical world. We term this idea "social naturalism" and show how important a role it plays in the initial formulation of the perversity thesis in Malthus's famous *Essay on the Principle of Population*.

In that essay, Malthus begins by asserting that human population tends to grow geometrically while agricultural output grows only arithmetically, so societies are in constant danger of outgrowing the food supply. This is precisely why, according to Malthus, poor relief is so destructive; it encourages (incentivizes, in today's language) the poor to have children even when they lack the resources to provide for their offspring through their own labor. The central moment in Malthus's argument comes when he proposes a "thought experiment" of what might happen if the system of poor relief were eliminated from one day to the next. He foretells that the poor would quickly see the folly of having children that they are not able to provide for, and society would quickly move back to the lost "state of nature" when those without resources responsibly postponed sex and marriage until they had accumulated a sufficient stake to provide for their children. At that point, population and food supply would again be in balance.

But while Malthus is justly celebrated for placing the ratio of population growth to food supply on the agenda of the social sciences, his reliance on social naturalism and the "biological" essence of human beings makes this part of his argument highly problematic. While it is true that human societies have long struggled with the balance between resources and population growth, Malthus simply invokes an imaginary state of nature and biology to solve the problem. Moreover, he ignores the variety of social mechanisms that societies have used to manage population growth and to augment the supply of food. The reality is that the reproductive practices of both the rich and the poor are also embedded in social arrangements and are not governed directly by nature or by economic incentives.

At the same time, that Malthus had to resort to a thought experiment to clinch his argument against poor relief demonstrates the epistemological shortcomings of classical political economy. We term this approach to knowledge *theoretical realism*—a philosophical precept that rejects empirical evidence as the primary condition for positive knowledge. It instead uses theory to deduce that hidden forces and properties are the causal mechanisms that underlie social processes that are the real foundations for knowledge. Malthus and Ricardo developed their theories in the shadow of Newton's discovery of the unseen underlying laws of motion that explained the movements of the planets. For the economists, the market-induced balancing of supply and demand and the differential growth of population and food supply were equivalent unobservable laws that account for the "natural" movement of self-regulating markets to equilibrium.

The critical difference between physics and economics, of course, is that the stable trajectories of the planets *can* be observed and carefully measured. Physics is indeed a science. By contrast, the assertion that there is an underlying movement of self-regulating economies towards equilibrium is not based on empirical observation; it is simply a methodological axiom. Absent empirical evidence, however, their basic assumptions about how economies work can be neither falsified nor confirmed—thus conveniently insulating them from standard social science scrutiny. No matter; both classical political economy and modern economics are built on top of this nonempirical "as if" axiom. Polanyi's ideas help us to see that particular market arrangements are not just socially and politically embedded; they are also embedded in ideas, a phenomenon we dub *ideational embeddedness*. When free market advocates mount their arguments against welfare spending or for tax cuts that benefit the wealthy, they are seeking to embed economic practices within a worldview that rests on social naturalism and theoretical realism.

The Contradictory Relationship between
Big Business and the State (Chapter 7)

In Polanyi's historical account, big businesses and corporations are frequently caught between their ideological support for the free market and their practical need for ever greater government action to organize and stabilize markets. This can be seen as another face of the tension between regulation and deregulation. Businesses often define as regulation only those government rules that they feel unfairly limit their ability to shift costs onto others. Eliminating such rules is characterized as deregulation or the act of restoring markets to their natural prepolitical condition. As we suggested above, however, these firms actually demand as many—albeit different and more advantageous—rules and regulations that are pro-business. The difference is not the *fact* of regulations; it is what they are called, what their effects are, and who they benefit. Rather than describing these business-friendly laws and policies as regulations, free market dogmatists characterize them as part of the natural, right, and proper workings of the free markets. Classic examples are the rules protecting intellectual property rights, including patent laws, copyright, and protection of trade secrets. These are all very specific historical creations that have been continuously modified and changed over time through administrative actions, judicial rulings, and new laws. Most recently, the digitization of information required major shifts in the legal regime to protect ownership rights in the strings of zeroes and ones that form software programs, as well as music and videos. The Disney Corporation has taken advantage of these recent legislative initiatives to extend the duration of copyright protection so that Mickey Mouse and Donald Duck are still protected more than eighty years after their initial creation.

But when Disney profits from the extension of copyright protection or a pharmaceutical company takes advantage of a government-granted monopoly to sell a particular medication for twenty years, they do not describe this as a government "intervention" or "regulation." On the contrary, government is depicted as simply validating the firm's legitimate right to draw profits from its very substantial research and development effort. Even when the firm has licensed the particular technology for a nominal fee from a government research laboratory that is legally prohibited from commercializing its own discoveries, it still insists that a government-granted monopoly is a legitimate and necessary way to incentivize the firm to oversee the costly clinical trials that are a prerequisite for approval to market the new medication.

This is a great deal more than hypocrisy—although it is that, to be sure. More fundamentally, it is a denial of the fact that in all contemporary market societies, large corporations are always heavily dependent on government in a wide variety of ways. They need government contracts, government help with their research and development efforts, government protection of their intellectual property, government support when they run into problems overseas, and so on. But the business sector also worries that this dependence makes it vulnerable to government pressure to accept policies and limitations on their actions that they find burdensome. In some places, and with varying degrees of intensity, firms deliberately embrace the ideology of the free market as a way to push back and resist those initiatives of government that they do not like. This strategy has been pursued with particular intensity by business firms in the United States.

The Reality of Society: The Need to Subordinate the Economy to Democratic Politics

Even while emphasizing the "stark utopianism" of the self-regulating market, Polanyi's most passionate argument against free market ideology is based on the limits it places on the scope of democratic politics. The hegemony of a self-regulating economy free of government "meddling" is, in the end, an assertion that the preferences of voters in democratic politics must be ignored when they conflict with the logic of a self-correcting market economy. And, in fact, free market theorists such as Milton Friedman and Paul Weyrich have argued explicitly for a legal framework that would prevent voters from taking any actions that "undermine" the autonomous economy. Just as the Supreme Court periodically strikes down a piece of Congressional legislation for violating the system of rights guaranteed in the Constitution, free market ideologues want a set of institutions that will similarly overrule any decisions that interfere with what is not by accident called *free* enterprise.

One of these institutions has been well established in many nations—an independent Central Bank that is autonomous from the Executive Branch and that is supposed to set monetary policy strictly by economic rather than popular democratic criteria. While the United States passed legislation that instructs the Federal Reserve Bank to pursue both price stability and full employment, Federal Reserve Chairs usually focus single-mindedly on price stability and the smooth functioning of financial markets. They occasionally give lip service to the goal of full employment, but they are effectively insulated from the economic preferences of the electorate.

But even this is not enough for free market intellectuals and activists. They also want to erect barriers so that taxes or spending cannot be increased by simple democratic majorities. They advocate requiring supermajorities, such as the two-thirds vote in both houses of the legislature that California required for approval of its state budget from 1933 to 2010 and which it still requires for increases in taxes. In fact, conservatives have been fighting for years for a Balanced Budget Amendment to the U.S. Constitution that would prohibit even large majorities in the Congress from authorizing any deficit spending, unless the deficit results from tax cuts that benefit the very rich. Similarly, free market theorists have sought to erect higher barriers to the legislative enactment of regulations on business activity.

Polanyi saw this institutionalized distrust of democratic politics by advocates of the free market as a profound threat to democracy. If the political system is rigged so that the people cannot win the protections from the market that they need, then they will turn against that system. Indeed, this is precisely the dynamic that destroyed democracy in many countries of Europe in the 1920s and 1930s. In fact, Polanyi's view was that his free market antagonists in Vienna, Von Mises and Hayek, had paved the way for the rise of fascism by preaching that popular preferences on economic matters should be ignored. In Polanyi's view, the way to preserve democratic institutions is to extend their influence over economic decisions. Precisely because he saw the autonomous economy to be a fiction, he had little concern that an expanded government role in providing services and regulating private business would destroy the market. On the contrary, his experience of municipal socialism in Vienna had persuaded him that businesses could prosper in a polity that was responsive to the needs of working people.

To be sure, Polanyi recognized that democratic institutions are inherently imperfect; voters will periodically elect people who promise things that are neither possible nor desirable. But the solution to the problems of democracy is *more* democracy, not less. Leaders who claim they will deliver the unattainable can be voted out of office at the next election or brought down by a parliamentary vote of no confidence. Similarly, government enactments that are economically destructive will later be reversed as voters recognize that taxes have been pushed too high or that certain government programs are overly generous. In Polanyi's view, while democracy is imperfect, along with constitutional rights it remains the core mechanism we have for protecting human freedom.

2

BEYOND THE ECONOMISTIC FALLACY

Karl Polanyi's major contributions to the social sciences can be best understood by tracing the essential touchstones of his life—from his youth and young adulthood in Budapest's hothouse intellectual and political environment, his time as editor of an Austrian financial newspaper, through his difficult but life-transforming years in England, his brief time in Vermont, and then to Columbia University. After acquainting ourselves with his remarkable life, this chapter explores Polanyi's most widely recognized contribution, *The Great Transformation* (hereafter referred to as GT).

We attempt to distill from his complex and sprawling historical writings some of his most important theoretical and methodological innovations. These include Polanyi's foundational critique of the "economistic fallacy"—the tendency in Western thought to analyze all aspects of life through an economic determinism. Polanyi countered this tendency by emphasizing the primacy of the social, by which he meant that even the mechanisms that societies adopt to secure the livelihood of their members are socially constructed and heavily dependent on both political institutions and robust social relationships of community and civil society. Through his criticism of the economistic fallacy, Polanyi also made contributions to our understanding of how to conduct exemplary historical and social analysis. Among the most important of these is his demonstration that sufficiently rich and multifaceted social analysis can only be accomplished by taking into account three distinct levels of analysis, levels that cannot be reduced to each other: 1) the global context in which the society is situated, 2) the actions of states, and 3) the conflicts among social classes and other groups.

Although he wrote his masterpiece some seventy years ago, Polanyi's GT still commands our attention today because its story resonates so powerfully with the current clash between economic globalization and world-wide democratic aspirations. Just as in Polanyi's accounting of the late nineteenth and early twentieth centuries, once again there appears to be an intractable contradiction between the imperatives of the global market system and a genuine democratic politics within nation-states. We have in so many ways, it seems, witnessed a virtual replay of Polanyi's "great transformation," as another historical epoch has been rocked to its foundations by the self-defeating project of creating a world dominated by an allegedly self-regulating global market.

Polanyi's Life

There exists no full biography of Karl Polanyi, but such a project would be worthy of the efforts of the most skillful intellectual historian.[1] Polanyi's life spans five countries, he wrote in three languages, and he was actively engaged in political events from the reform politics of pre-World War I Hungary to the North American peace movement of the 1960s. Together with his wife, Ilona Duczynska, his personal networks included the major figures of the classical period of European communism to dissident Hungarian intellectuals active in the 1950s and 1960s. To sort out the people and events that Polanyi influenced, or was influenced by, would require a broad canvas that encompasses many of the central events and ideas of the twentieth century.

For our purposes, a brief glimpse at Polanyi's life will have to suffice.[2] He was born in Hungary in 1886 to a remarkable family. His brother, Michael Polanyi, was internationally known first as a scientist and then as a philosopher. Their father was a Hungarian Jew who became wealthy as a builder of railroads. Polanyi's Russian mother, a strong intellectual, hosted a salon that became an intellectual center in prewar Budapest. As a young man, Karl was a founder of the Galileo Circle, a group of intellectuals committed to the liberating potential of social science and planning in vigorous opposition to "clericalism, corruption, against the privileged, against bureaucracy-against the morass that is ever-present and pervasive in this semi-feudal country" (Duczynska 1977, xi).

Polanyi's ideas can be traced to the formative period of Hungarian history from 1908 to 1918, when a generation of middle-class intellectuals was radicalized by the stagnation of the Austro-Hungarian Empire and ultimately by the barbarity of World War I. Polanyi was typical of this generation in his dissatisfaction with the Socialist Party, despite an intense sympathy for the working class that led him and other members of the Galileo Circle to participate in worker education projects. The Socialists were unattractive because their adherence to a deterministic version of Marxism made them cautious and conservative. The Socialists, moreover, were unwilling to espouse the cause of the Hungarian peasantry, which Polanyi supported vigorously. Despite the size of the rural population, the Socialists dismissed the problems of the peasantry with problematic Marxist phrases about the "idiocy of rural life."

Polanyi passionately rejected the Second International's belief that predetermined stages of historical development inevitably resulted in social progress. Central to him and others of his generation was the idea that progress could only come through conscious human action based on moral principles. The contrast between his view and that of the Socialists is encapsulated in Polanyi's memorial address for the poet Endre Ady—a personal symbol of the younger generation's hopes for a renewal of the Hungarian nation: "The truth is 'that the bird soars despite rather than because of the law of gravity' and 'that society soars to stages embodying ever loftier ideals despite rather than because of material interests'" (quoted in Congdon 1976, 179).

Only months after these words were spoken, the hopes for Hungarian renewal were dashed. With the end of World War I, power passed from the Empire to the Karolyi regime, a coalition government dominated by the Socialists. Polanyi was associated with the Radical Party of Oskár Jászi, a part of the coalition, but their reformist hopes came to nothing as external pressures and internal disagreements blocked effective action. Dissatisfaction with political stalemate led many to turn to the newly formed Hungarian Communist Party, which recruited many radicalized middle-class intellectuals. Many Socialists joined with the Communists in creating the Hungarian Soviet Republic under the leadership of Béla Kun. But in the absence of support from the Soviet Union, the Béla Kun regime collapsed in 1919 from both internal and external pressures, and the right wing seized power.

It seems likely that Polanyi considered the creation of a Hungarian Soviet Republic to be dangerously ill-advised. He would never return to Hungary, except for a brief visit toward the end of his life. In Vienna, he worked as a journalist for *Oesterreschische Volkswirt*, a position that allowed him to study closely the turbulent political and economic events of the 1920s. There he met his wife, Ilona Duczynska, once an active participant in the Béla Kun regime, who had been forced to flee from the White Terror that followed the revolutionary regime's collapse.

As the political situation in Vienna turned to the right in the early 1930s, Polanyi emigrated to England, where he eventually found a job in worker education. In England he became associated with a group of Christian Socialists and Quakers and collaborated with them on a book, *Christianity and the Social Revolution* (1935). His own essay in that book, "The Essence of Fascism," prefigured some of the arguments in GT in pointing to how the corporatist fascist state reduced human beings to mere products. In 1940, Polanyi was able to get an appointment at Bennington College in Vermont, where he crystallized his thoughts and wrote GT, published in 1944. After the war, Polanyi was invited to Columbia to teach economic history, a position that he retained until 1953, when he retired to Toronto, Canada, to join Ilona, who had settled there because anti-communist immigration statutes blocked her from settling in the U.S.

During the Columbia years and in Canada, Polanyi's research shifted from the history of market society to the analysis of archaic and primitive economies. A collaborative research project at Columbia led to the publication of *Trade and Markets in the Early Empires* (1957). With the exception of a number of essays, the rest of Polanyi's work was published after his death in 1964. A research monograph, *Dahomey and the Slave Trade,* was published in 1966, and in 1968, George Dalton collected a number of the published essays, chapters from the three books, and some unpublished material in a volume called *Primitive, Archaic, and Modern Economies.* Finally, in 1977, Harry Pearson published an unfinished manuscript, *The Livelihood of Man,* containing both general material on Polanyi's theory of society and economy and an extensive analysis of ancient Greece.[3]

Polanyi's interest in primitive and archaic economies grew directly out of his analysis of nineteenth-century market society. In GT he demonstrates that the market played a subordinate role before the rise of capitalism and argues that previous scholarship, particularly of the ancient world, had wrongly interpreted the role of markets in those societies using anachronistic theoretical categories derived from modern capitalism. Despite his devastating criticism of a market-dominated society, however, Polanyi was never interested in generating visions of a return to a preindustrial past; his concern was to conceptualize and realize social arrangements that would reconcile technology and human needs, freedom and social justice, markets and democracy. This commitment was reaffirmed in a little-known collection of writings of Hungarian poets, *The Plough and the Pen*, which he edited with his wife shortly after the Hungarian revolution of 1956. He revisited these beliefs as well in his final project, the launching of the journal *Co-Existence,* which absorbed much of his energy in the final years of his life. The page proofs of the first issue arrived the day Polanyi died.

The Great Transformation

While Polanyi's work in anthropology and classical studies originally had more immediate influence on subsequent scholarship in those fields, GT remains his major achievement; today it is by far the work by which he is most known and has been most influential across a broad spectrum of intellectual perspectives. It is his only complete book-length, sole-authored manuscript, and it develops many of the themes he pursued in his later work. Befitting a scholar with such an irregular career, Polanyi wrote the book that brought together all of the themes of a lifetime at the beginning of his formal academic career, not the end. Hence, it is appropriate to focus our analysis on GT, considered today by many as one of the most important books of the twentieth century.

Polanyi wrote GT as a conscious political intervention in the hope he could influence the shape of the post–World War II world. Fascism and the war had brought about the collapse of "civilization as we have known it," but this catastrophe had occurred behind the backs—without the comprehension—of the historical actors. Polanyi believed that only a deep understanding of the terrible events of the previous decades could prevent a recurrence of barbarism and war in the future. While it was on the European continent that the weaknesses of the market caused the most tragic damage, Polanyi was persuaded that the long-term factors that had caused the wreck of civilization must be analyzed in the birthplace of the Industrial Revolution—early nineteenth-century England.[4] Polanyi sought to point the way toward a more humane and rational structure for the postwar world by illuminating the origins of fascism and World War II in the rise of the self-regulating market. This developmental project structured his entire approach.

The driving forces of GT are Polanyi's passionate hatred, not of markets, but rather of a society dominated almost entirely by a market system. But he was not willing simply to extend and elaborate the arguments characteristic of the socialist tradition; he sought instead to rebuild the socialist analysis of market society from its very foundations. This led him to reanalyze precapitalist societies and to reappropriate such pre-Marxist theorists as Aristotle, Hegel, and Robert Owen. The audacity and originality of Polanyi's effort to reconstruct the socialist critique of market society gives his work its lasting power.

GT is the account of the rise and fall of market society. There are two critical transformations: the emergence of nineteenth-century market society out of eighteenth-century mercantilism and the collapse of market society in the twentieth century into fascism and world war. Polanyi's political purpose led him to analyze the second transformation more fully than the first, but there are lacunae in both analyses. Nevertheless, both transformations were central to his understanding of large-scale historical change.

The book begins by demonstrating that England's transition from a commercialized mercantilist society to market society was neither inevitable nor the result of an evolutionary process. He challenges the prevailing wisdom that deemed nineteenth-century market society to have emerged "naturally" from the preindustrial era with the steady expansion of market activity. Instead, Polanyi points out that while markets became increasingly important in the sixteenth century, there was no sign until the early nineteenth century of markets becoming the controlling forces of societies. Rather, the state's determined regulation of these markets, as well as of long-distance and local trade, consistently limited their impact and prevented the creation of potentially threatening national markets (GT, 280–285; see also Katznelson 1979; Somers 1993; 1994a).

In opposition to the familiar evolutionary view, Polanyi argues that the emergence of national markets did not result from the gradual or natural extension of local or long-distance trading. Instead, it was only when mercantilist states began to see economic development as a foundation for building national strength that they deliberately turned to creating national markets as central to their state-building strategy.[5] Even the creation of national markets, however, fell short of the full development of market society. This required a still more monumental societal disjuncture—nature, money, and human beings had to be transformed into the unnatural commodities of "land, capital, and labor" (GT, 71–80).

In his discussion of England's 1795 Speenhamland Act, Polanyi takes up the most important of these transformations: for the purpose of buying and selling their labor in the market, human beings had to be turned into commodities.[6] Speenhamland is the story of how, in the last quarter of the eighteenth century, rural England was suddenly beset by a disturbing and acute increase in poverty. Looking across the channel to the French Revolution, fear of pauper rebelliousness was intense among the landed classes. This fear coexisted with a concern for the potential depopulation of the countryside as higher wages in the emerging rural-industrial villages attracted impoverished country people.

Although it was not understood at the time, pauperism was a product of a marked increase in both the extent and volatility of England's world trade. The volatility was most intensely experienced in the countryside, as rural unemployment went hand in hand with severe dislocations of both village and town occupations. When economic downturns reduced commercial and manufacturing employment, the laboring poor were left only to drift back to their country parishes for survival. The eradication of the family plot by enclosures had done away with any vestiges of informal unemployment insurance for the unemployed, so that even those employed in rural industry had no means of security other than state-provided poor relief. For Polanyi, pauperism was only the overt sign of the dislocations soon to explode with the onset of the Industrial Revolution and the market economy. Yet the outcome was not inevitable; expanding trade and markets would not have by themselves been able to make a qualitative leap into a market society. Only conscious political intervention could bring about this historically unique event. This analytic perspective underlies Polanyi's focus on Speenhamland.

In 1795, the Speenhamland Act was introduced in the south of England as a new practice of poor relief. As an institution it reflected the principle of the "right to live" through a system of family allowances and "grants-in-aid of wages" based on the going price of bread. It was an act in response to the structural problems of economic hardship intended to protect the labor force in the countryside while simultaneously preventing itinerant pauperism. As relief was only available to residents in their local villages, Speenhamland helped maintain the local political power of the landed classes and slowed the release of cheap labor from the countryside. According to Polanyi, however, the Act had devastating consequences for the people it was intended to help.[7] Knowing full well the public coffers were obligated to keep workers alive, albeit at bare subsistence levels, employers allegedly had no incentives to pay decent wages, preferring to let tax-payers pick up the slack. Actual wages thus crashed beneath subsistence while parish relief payments to working people skyrocketed. While squires took on the role of the benevolent almsgivers in their positions as political rulers, as employers they benefited from virtual gang labor, while the taxes to support labor came only from the pockets of the rural middle class.

Speenhamland, a system supposedly organized to support the poor, was in fact benefiting the employers by using public funds to subsidize their labor costs. In some areas only those who were on relief had a chance of employment, and those who tried to keep off it and earn a living on their own were hard pressed to find a job. According to Polanyi, the consequence was a vast demoralization of the poor, as the able-bodied laboring poor became indistinguishable from paupers—being forced onto welfare (see our critique, chapter 5). Polanyi recounts how incentives to work were undermined and the dignity of the English worker was stripped away by this method of welfare, which crystallized in one system the mutual incompatibility and unworkability of the protectionist "right to live" with the wage system of the labor market—two contradictory impulses that prefigured the entire development of the nineteenth century.

The crux of Polanyi's discussion of Speenhamland is thus the tension between an early kind of social insurance system and the emergence of an unalloyed market for labor. Polanyi points to the importance of the passage in 1799 and 1801 of the anti-Combination Laws that criminalized union activity, making unionization a form of treason against the state. These laws prevented workers from being able to resist collectively and bargain for power through the mechanism of unionism. On the one hand, the wage system compelled working people to gain a living by selling their labor. On the other, Speenhamland's system of aid-in-wages attempted to protect workers from the dangers of being fully exposed to the market. The combination of the two, in tandem with union illegality, prevented workers qua "labor" from establishing their own value in negotiations with employers. A new class of employers had been created but, in Polanyi's words, rural workers could not constitute themselves as a class (GT, 81–89).

Speenhamland was repealed in 1834. According to Polanyi, repeal followed the political victory in 1832 of the new industrial middle class, now armed not only with new legislative power but also with "scientific" laws of Malthusian population theory. The 1834 Poor Law Reform Act (usually called "the New Poor Law") eliminated "outdoor" relief to the unemployed (provided in their own homes) and forced those displaced from the countryside into the hated workhouses as the only alternative to the despised factories. In this single institutional change, English workers were transformed into virtual commodities. Now, they had only themselves to sell in order to survive. They either had to lose their citizenship through workhouse imprisonment or accept the terms of an unfair wage system. The "social safety net" disappeared in favor of the market, not the state, setting wage levels. In Polanyi's view, industrialization achieved its true inaugural moment.[8]

Polanyi was no romantic; he was not contrasting the "golden age" virtues of Speenhamland to the vices of market capitalism. Indeed, despite the subsequent catastrophic impact of its repeal, the forced urban migration that followed, and the unprecedented "scientific cruelty" of the New Poor Law, his assessment of Speenhamland's impact on social life is unequivocally negative. A plague on both houses, he charges: " . . . if Speenhamland meant the rot of immobility, now the peril [of the market] was that of death through exposure" (GT, 87).

Polanyi places great emphasis on the Speenhamland interlude for several reasons. First, Speenhamland illustrates that the market's development was neither evolutionary nor continuous. It was the political and violent intervention by the Poor Law Reform in 1834 that institutionalized the first true labor market. This emphasis on the role of the state in unleashing market forces is essential to Polanyi's argument that the nineteenth-century market economy and its accompanying ideological distortions were complete historical novelties. The road to the free market was paved with continuous political manipulation, whether the state was actively involved in removing old restrictive regulations, as in the case of Speenhamland, or in building new political administrative bodies to bolster the factors of production of the new market economy, as in the administrative mechanisms of the New Poor Law (GT, 147). The political mechanisms surrounding the Speenhamland interlude—its institutionalization, its dynamics, and its final repeal—all serve to demonstrate the degree to which the "natural" self-regulating market was politically constructed in its origins.

Second, Polanyi argues that the experience of and the debates around Speenhamland established the fundamental assumptions of liberal economic ideology. The reform of the Poor Law occurred when "economic liberalism burst forth as a crusading passion, and *laissez-faire* became a militant creed" (GT, 143). Polanyi returned to Speenhamland and the birth of the "liberal creed" to show how the fundamental assumptions that continued to shape economic thought in the 1930s and 1940s were mistaken from the start and dated from that century-old passion for a "self-regulating market." There was nothing more central for Polanyi than these three points: that the ideology of economic liberalism was pervasive and politically established, that it was fundamentally mistaken, and that it had become "one of the main obstacles to the solution of the problems of our civilization" (1977, xvii).

To make this point persuasively, he also used Speenhamland to argue that the effort to create a free market for labor was ultimately doomed to failure because of the contradiction between arrangements that sought to protect human communities and the wage system that made no adjustment for social needs. For Polanyi, labor's commodification is the paradigm of market society; the attempt to transform human beings into commodities is the core, and the core weakness, of market society. It is the core weakness because no sooner was market society institutionalized than it catalyzed a powerful countermovement, which Polanyi defines as collective efforts to protect society from the market. Precisely because turning people into commodities represented such a fundamental threat to the fabric of early nineteenth-century society, it set in motion an inevitable counterpressure for the protection of society. In contrast to the calculated efforts of industrialists and state builders to create a market society, Polanyi argues that like all countermovements, these early nineteenth-century ones were spontaneous, unplanned, and came from all sectors of society in response to the devastating impact of the market.

Polanyi uses comparative historical analysis to show that, despite the varying ideological configurations of the different European governments, all of them, including England, passed through a period of laissez-faire, followed immediately by a period of legislative intervention designed to address the dominant social problems of the time. New laws regulating public health, factory conditions, social insurance, trade associations, public utilities, and so on all reflected the essential contradictions of industrial development within a free-market system. Polanyi describes the opposing principles of market society and the protectionist countermovement in the following terms: "The one was the principle of economic liberalism, aiming at the establishment of a self-regulating market, relying on the support of the trading classes, and using largely *laissez-faire* and free trade as its methods; the other was the principle of social protection aiming at the conservation of man and nature as well as productive organization, relying on the varying support of those most immediately affected by the deleterious action of the market-primarily, but not exclusively, the working and the landed classes-and using protective legislation, restrictive associations, and other instruments of intervention as its methods" (GT, 138–139).

Ironically, because the successive victories of these countermovements effectively impaired the self-regulating markets and the unimpeded supremacy of markets over people, even deeper economic disorders and even stronger movements for protection inexorably followed. Behind the backs of all concerned, these clashing processes—all similar to the contradictions of Speenhamland—gradually undermined the basis of nineteenth-century stability, leading to World War I and the seemingly sudden collapse of civilization. Sadly, the 1920s and 1930s only ushered in another period of stalemate, during which a new order struggled to be born.

While he does not mention it directly, Polanyi's argument draws on Keynes's critique of classical economics. Because the classical economic tradition is founded on the theory of the self-regulating market, it obviates any problem of insufficient demand; shifts in factor prices, including the price of labor, will always restore equilibrium and high levels of investment. But as Keynes (1925) insisted, working class organization significantly diminished the flexibility of wages, so that the equilibrating mechanism no longer worked. Without that mechanism, investments were likely to be withheld, and the problem of inadequate demand became chronic. As a result, the progressive strengthening of the working class from the 1830s to the 1920s served to diminish the curative powers of periodic economic crises, leading to progressively more serious economic downturns. In the end, these culminated in the Great Depression of the 1930s. Polanyi, like Keynes, criticizes those who deny that social legislation and trade unions have interfered with the mobility of labor and the flexibility of wages, insisting that such a position implies "that those institutions have entirely failed in their purpose, which was exactly that of interfering with the laws of supply and demand in respect to human labor, and removing it from the orbit of the market" (GT, 186).

Polanyi's discussions of the protection of land and money are parallel to his discussion of labor. Drawing on the historical experience of Germany, he argues that the major mechanisms for protecting the land were agricultural tariffs that aided the peasantry by slowing competitive food imports. This, too, hampered the equilibrating mechanisms of the self-regulating market, while also enhancing the political position of those traditional social groups—the old landed classes, the church, and the army—that supported agricultural protection. Precisely because the protection of the land was a general social interest, these groups were given a mission that allowed them to preserve their influence, enabling them later to be available to provide reactionary solutions when the collapse of liberal society occurred.

Whereas the protection of labor and land were associated primarily with social groups critical of unfettered markets, the movement for the protection of money was a concern among all social groups and classes. Monetary protection took the form of the growing importance of national central banking as a mechanism to protect nations from the vagaries of the world market. The gold standard was the lynchpin of the self-regulating market because it was intended to ensure equilibrium in international payments. When a nation was spending more than it was earning, gold would flow out and the money supply and the level of economic activity would diminish. This, in turn, would lead through price and demand effects to higher exports and lower imports, and a restoration of balance.

The problem was that, as the nineteenth century wore on, there was a decline in the willingness of all groups in society to accept the periodic economic downturns and resulting crises of the credit system that were imposed by this mechanism. Workers agitated against unemployment, capitalists against a fragile banking system, and farmers against falling prices. The result was a series of gradual measures to insulate the national economy from the world market. The growing resort to trade protectionism from the 1870s on also falls into this category, but Polanyi's emphasis is on those measures that tended to decrease the impact of gold movements on the domestic supply of money. The growth and elaboration of central banking created a variety of means by which the impact of international forces was lessened. Polanyi insisted: "Central banking reduced the automatism of the gold standard to a mere pretense. It meant a centrally managed currency; manipulation was substituted for the self-regulating mechanism of supplying credit, even though the device was not always deliberate and conscious" (GT, 204).

This protection of money had two important consequences. First, dampening the automatism of the gold standard reduced the gold standard's capacity to operate as an equilibrating mechanism. Another key link in the theory and practice of market self-regulation was impaired, so the fragility of the market system increased. Second, the creation of central banking tended to solidify the nation as a cohesive unit whose economic interests were in conflict with those of other nations. The effort to protect the national market from the world market led directly to efforts to manipulate the global market in one nation's favor. "The import tariffs of one country hampered the exports of another and forced it to seek for markets in politically unprotected regions" (GT, 226). The result was economic imperialism as the European nations rushed in the last part of the nineteenth century to secure control over Africa and Asia as a means of exporting domestic economic strains. The more serious the economic pressures on each nation, the more intense the inter-imperialist rivalries. Hence, in Polanyi's view, imperialism is the international protectionist institution par excellence, in both its attempt to combat market strains and in its destructive impact.

World War I was the result of these intensifying international conflicts. Throughout the second half of the nineteenth century, high finance—the international banking community—had served successfully as a peace interest. Whenever the European powers moved close to a general war, the bankers mobilized to mediate the conflict, since such a war would endanger their position and profits. However, as the inter-imperialist conflicts grew more intense, the effectiveness of this peace interest diminished. Furthermore, the freezing of Europe into two hostile alliances meant that it was no longer possible to avoid war through a system of shifting alliances. Polanyi suggests that the actual timing of World War I was contingent on a variety of factors, but its ultimate occurrence was an expression of the contradictions of nineteenth-century civilization.

Because the war was not understood as the final crisis of the self-regulating market, every effort was made to reestablish the key institutions of nineteenth-century civilization in the post-World War I world. In particular, a doomed effort was made to restore the gold standard despite the reality that the war had swept away its main bulwark—Britain's international hegemony. Polanyi notes, however, that this restoration was not simply the work of the political right, but that leftists from the Bolsheviks to the German Social Democrats were also unable to imagine a world without the gold standard.

This restoration in a context where the gold standard could not possibly work resulted in a fundamental conflict between parliamentary democracy and markets. The working class, through electoral politics, sought to further protect itself from the market through the passage of various forms of social legislation. But this social spending came into conflict with the needs of each economy to maintain its international competitiveness and its capacity to respond to international market pressures. The result was a period of intense stalemate. The working class lacked the strength and perhaps the imagination to push for a genuine alternative; all it could do was weaken the system by pressing for an extension of protection. The employers were unable to effectively resist these pressures within parliamentary rule, but this meant that they were also unable to make the market system work.

This period of paralysis gave way to the stock market crash and the world depression. In the midst of the depression, fascist movements provided a real although barbaric solution to the contradictions of market society. The solution "can be described as a reform of market economy achieved at the price of the extirpation of all democratic institutions, both in the industrial and in the political realm" (GT, 245). Fascism also broke with the gold standard system by substituting political controls for the market in managing international economic transactions. For Polanyi, the power and dynamism of fascist movements was not a function of their capacity to recruit supporters but rather a result of their ability to provide a solution to the impasse of liberal capitalism. Writing of Hitler's accession to power, Polanyi argued that "to imagine that it was the strength of the movement which created situations such as these, and not to see that it was the situation that gave birth in this case to the movement, is to miss the outstanding lesson of the last decades" (GT, 247). While Polanyi recognizes that fascism took different forms in different societies, he insists that it was ultimately an international movement that was rooted in the structure of the world economy.

Those nations that did not become Fascist responded to the pressures of the 1930s in one of two other ways. Polanyi saw the New Deal as representing one paradigmatic solution to the impasse of market society, one that retained democracy but instituted a number of measures to insulate the national economy from the world market, such as Roosevelt's decision to abandon the gold standard. While Polanyi is not explicit on this point, his view of the New Deal rests on the assumption that the reform measures of the 1930s represented the beginning of a transition to social arrangements under which the market would again be subordinated to social relations (see also Berman 2006). Rather than seeing the New Deal leading to a reinvigorated market society, he views it as the beginning of a transition to socialism.

The other paradigmatic response to the crisis of the 1930s was that of the Soviet Union, with Stalin's decision to build "socialism in one country"—a decision that Polanyi links to the crisis of the world economy. For Polanyi, it was self-evident that these diverse responses to the crisis of market society could not coexist for long without war. Hence, World War II was a direct outcome of the breakdown of market society. Unless this lesson was fully understood, Polanyi believed that the post-World War II period would be as disastrous as the interwar period.

Polanyi's Underlying Concepts

To fully understand Polanyi's contribution, it is necessary to go beyond this brief summary of the major arguments of GT to grasp the conceptual framework upon which Polanyi constructs his specific historical analyses. The foundation on which all his concepts rests is the idea of holism, an analytic commitment to societal interdependence as the necessary context for grasping particular social dynamics.[9] As with Marc Bloch's notion of "totalizing history" (Bloch 1961; Febvre 1973), Polanyi seeks to demonstrate the structural and cultural relationships among all parts of the social whole, while rejecting the genetic determinacy of any one aspect. In this orientation, Polanyi saw himself continuing the tradition of Aristotle: "In terms, then, of our modern speech Aristotle's approach to human affairs was sociological. In mapping out a field of study he would relate all questions of institutional origins and function to the totality of society" (Polanyi 1968 [1957], 96).

Polanyi's intellectual commitment to holism is evident in his specific views of the relationship between the social and the economic, the nature of market society, the role of social classes, and the position of the state in society. Indeed, his entire critique of market society rests on his belief in the dominance of the social. He considers the process of analyzing people's interests in terms of a distinction between material and ideal concerns to be fundamentally misguided. For Polanyi, all human behavior is socially shaped and defined; whether a person is trying to make money or achieve inner peace, the source of the action is a set of socially created definitions that make one or the other goal appear either dangerous or desirable. Religion, for example, is considered an ideal interest, whereas hunger a material one. But Polanyi recounts anthropological findings that in a culture where fish are sacred objects rather than food, more than one tribe has been found to have starved to death on the banks of a river overflowing with fish (GT, 165–166).

The proper distinction is not between different types of interests, but among different social arrangements that generate different belief systems and different institutional opportunities. In striking contrast to those theorists who begin from the individual actor in developing theories of "economic man" or "rational man," Polanyi's starting point is society, and for him any analysis of individuals in isolation from *society* is merely fanciful.

This focus on social arrangements and the way in which they generate different types of human behavior leads directly to Polanyi's critique of what he saw as the economic determinism of both liberalism and orthodox Marxism. For Polanyi, nineteenth-century society was unique in the way that economic imperatives had become dominant in shaping human life. In earlier societies, the economy—the arrangement for ensuring humanity's livelihoods—was embedded in social relations, subordinated to religion, politics, and other social arrangements.[10] In opposition to Adam Smith, Polanyi stressed that the orientation toward individual economic gains played only a minor role in these earlier societies. Only in the nineteenth-century self-regulating market did economic self-interest become the dominant principle of social life, and both liberalism and Marxism made the ahistorical error of assuming that what was dominant in that historical moment had been dominant throughout human history.

Polanyi called this mistake "the economistic fallacy"—a distortion in thought that paralleled the distortion of a society dominated by the market. His attack on this fallacy led him to his extensive study of non-market societies to substantiate his argument for the historical specificity of market society. Even to embark on such a project, however, Polanyi was forced to make a critical distinction between two different meanings of the word *economic*. The formal definition refers solely to the process of economizing scarce means to make the most efficient use of what is available for particular ends. The substantive definition is "an instituted process of interaction between man and his environment" through which material needs are met. The point is that as long as analysts use the first definition, they will find in pre-capitalist societies the same basic dynamics that exist in market societies. Only with the second definition is it possible to escape the tendency to project what presently exists back into the past. The substantive definition of the economy necessarily serves to place the economic back in the context of the social whole: "The human economy, then, is embedded and enmeshed in institutions, economic and noneconomic. The inclusion of the noneconomic is vital. For religion or government may be as important for the structure and functioning of the economy as monetary institutions or the availability of tools and machines themselves that lighten the toil of labor" (Polanyi, Arensberg, and Pearson 1957, 250). As for the "natural economic" motivations ascribed to people by liberalism, Polanyi decries hunger and gain as no more economic than love or hate:

> Single out whatever motive you please, and organize production in such a manner as to make that motive that individual's incentive to produce, and you will have induced a picture of man as altogether absorbed by that partic-ular motive. Let that motive be religious, political or aesthetic; let it be pride, prejudice, love, or envy, and man will appear as essentially religious, politi-cal, aesthetic, proud, prejudiced in love or envy. Other motives, in contrast, will appear distant and shadowy since they cannot be relied upon to operate in the vital business of production. The particular motive selected will repre-sent "real" man. As a matter of fact, human beings will labor for a large vari-ety of reasons as long as things are arranged accordingly (Polanyi 1968, 68).

Only in a market society could this economistic view of people prevail precisely because total marketization establishes a set of institutional mechanisms of production that make human survival depend on eco-nomic drives. If so-called economic motives were natural to humanity, Polanyi suggests, we would have to judge all early and primitive society as thoroughly unnatural.

Polanyi's belief in the dominance of the social also led him to the conclusion that a society that elevated economic motivation to abso-lute priority could not survive. For this reason, he insists that the nine-teenth-century self-regulating market was a utopian experiment that was destined to fail.[11] This is one of Polanyi's most important insights, and it provides the basis for his argument concerning the protectionist countermovement. Pure human greed, left to its own devices, would place no limit on competition, Polanyi argues, and the result would be a destruction of both society and environment. Workers would be exploited beyond the point where they could even reproduce themselves, food would be systematically adulterated to expand profit margins, and the environment would be devastated by pollution and the unrestricted use of resources. Moreover, even before these catastrophes, a society in which each individual pursued only his or her economic self-interest would be unable to maintain the shared meanings and understandings that are necessary for human group life. As with Durkheim's emphasis on the noncontractual basis of contract, Polanyi saw that market transactions depended on collective goods such as trust and regulation that could not possibly be provided by market processes. For this reason, the protectionist countermovement was a necessary response to the threatened destruction of society caused by the unregulated market.

The second concept that is shaped by Polanyi's holism is the notion of market society itself. For Polanyi, the distinction between the existence of markets in society and a market society is fundamental. The followers of the economistic fallacy consistently jump from the fact that markets existed in a particular society to the conclusion that the laws of supply and demand operated as they do in contemporary society. But Polanyi devoted much effort to showing that markets could operate on very different principles. In many precapitalist societies, prices were administratively set, so that supply and demand played a marginal role at best. Moreover, even when price-making markets existed, as during mercantilism, the systematic regulation of those markets meant that markets played a subordinate role in social life. Hence, market society was created only in the nineteenth century when these restrictions were eliminated and land, labor, and money were treated as commodities. The issue is not the *existence* of markets, but the *relationship* of markets to the social whole. The category of market society is used only to describe that social whole in which the market principle extends to and organizes land, labor, and money and structures society around the fiction that these are true, not fictitious, commodities.

The concept of market society also has a spatial dimension for Polanyi. Analysis of particular societies has to take place within the broadest relevant context—in this case, the global economy. Indeed, Polanyi was among the first to recognize that the international sphere was of critical importance for understanding developments within particular nations. But he approaches the international dimension as more than simply a world market in which nations compete. He recognizes that on the international level, just as on the national level, market society requires an institutional order to function. Unregulated and unstructured international economic competition would lead to a continuing state of war. Thus, analysis of globalization requires a focus on the international economic regime that sets the rules within which competition takes place. The gold standard system that plays a central role in the unfolding of his story was such an international regime.

The third important aspect of Polanyi's holism is his unique view of the role of social classes in history. Polanyi uses the standard sociological and Marxist class categories such as bourgeoisie and working class, but he does not accept the practice of treating conflict between these classes as the central engine of history. Instead, the development of society as a whole provides social classes with opportunities, and their capacity to respond to these opportunities depends on proposing solutions that are in the interests of society as a whole. Thus he organizes his argument not around the story of classes themselves, but around the three social substances—land, labor, and money—that classes sought to protect as part of the countermovement against the market. Moreover, because he rejects the view that individuals are motivated solely by self-interest, Polanyi considers no mistake to be greater than to define classes as aggregates of economic interests. On the contrary, classes are social constructions; they represent collective responses to changes in the organization of society. In particular, Polanyi insists that reducing the working class to its economic situation and interests distorts the entire history of its political development.

Polanyi's critique of the economistic fallacy originates from his argument that cultural disaster is even more significant than economic exploitation. Addressing the liberal defenders of the Industrial Revolution who use economic statistics indicating improvement in the standard of living to dispel charges of exploitation, Polanyi characterizes their position: "For how could there be social catastrophe where there was undoubtedly economic improvement?" (GT, 164). Here, setting the stage for an entire generation of social historians yet to come—E. P. Thompson (1963) was the most important[12]— Polanyi uses anthropological evidence to demonstrate that social calamities are primarily cultural, not economic, phenomena, and as such cannot be measured by income figures or population statistics. Cultural catastrophes involving broad strata of common people are infrequent occurrences, and the cataclysm of the Industrial Revolution was an exceptional landslide in history, one that within less than half a century transformed vast masses of the inhabitants of the English countryside from settled folk into something resembling unprotected market commodities bought and sold on the market. If the infrequency of so dramatic an event makes it difficult to grasp, Polanyi makes it easier by drawing an analogy between the imposition of market society and the impact of colonialism on peoples of the Third World. He argues that, in both situations, "not economic exploitation, as often assumed, but the disintegration of the cultural environment of the victim is then the cause of the degradation" (GT, 164 and appendix 12, 300–303).

For this reason, Polanyi sees classes as social and cultural, not economic institutions, constituted primarily to redress the cultural devastation created by market society. Polanyi viewed the goals for which individuals will strive as culturally determined over and above crude economic necessity, and the entire countermovement for protection is primarily a cultural and social phenomenon, and only secondarily an economic one. For this reason, it represented not just a different class interest from that of the market, but a fundamentally different *principle* from the economic one. In this struggle for greater protection from the market, working people found unlikely allies and were effective precisely because they represented the general needs of society against the market. This lengthy quotation conveys Polanyi's views on this issue:

Once we are rid of the obsession that only sectional, never general, interest can become effective, as well as of the twin prejudice of restricting the interests of human groups to their monetary income, the breadth and comprehensiveness of the protectionist movement lose their mystery. While monetary interests are necessarily voiced solely by the persons to whom they pertain, other interests have a wider constituency. They affect individuals in innumerable ways as neighbors, professional persons, consumers, pedestrians, commuters, sportsmen, hikers, gardeners, patients, mothers, or lovers—and are accordingly capable of representation by almost any type of territorial or functional association such as churches, townships, fraternal lodges, clubs, trade unions, or most commonly, political parties based on broad principles of adherence. An all too narrow conception of interests must in effect lead to a warped vision of social and political history, and no purely monetary definition of interests can leave room for that vital need for social protection, the representation of which commonly falls to the persons in charge of the general interests of the community-under modern conditions, the government of the day. Precisely because not the economic but the social interests of different cross sections of the population were threatened by the market, persons belonging to various economic strata unconsciously joined forces to meet the danger (GT 154–155).

In sum, social classes play a key historical role, but it is not a role that can be understood in terms of economic self-interest (see Somers 1992, 1996, 1997). Finally, Polanyi's theory of the state also reflects his commitment to holism. As one would expect from his view of social classes, he rejects the Marxist tendency to explain state policies in terms of economic interests. Instead, he inclines toward a view of a "universal" state that acts to preserve society by transcending particular conflicts in favor of the needs of society. However, there is more to Polanyi's view than this; paradoxically, the very success of the protectionist counter-movement led directly to disaster. State action was not able to produce the idealized outcome that one expects from such a universal conception of the state.

This added complexity rests on the insight that the self-regulating market created a peculiar situation in which development was caught in the contradictory conflict of two sets of "general" interests. On the one hand, the working classes, landed classes, and others who pushed for social protection were acting on behalf of social organization and natural resources, and the state was responsive to their pressures. On the other hand, the very market they were opposing, as oppressive as it may have been, was now the material foundation of the society; survival of the new civilization—shaped and organized by market principles—depended on the survival of the market. Market interests had also become general interests and the state had little choice but to respond to these interests as well.

Thereby, politicians acted in the interests of society as a whole when they passed protective legislation, and yet the same was true when they passed pro-market laws; the state clearly did not "belong" to either market or society. It was, rather, necessarily both universal, representing society against the market, while also serving as a market-driven government. The state, in short, crystallized the nineteenth century's fundamental struggle between market and society.

Polanyi analyzes political and governmental actions in terms of society as a whole, rather than of some particular interests. He is not theorizing here about government efforts to secure legitimacy from the subjective perceptions of the citizenry. Polanyi is instead explaining how an ever-expanding market so endangers basic social relationships and institutions that the state is impelled to do whatever it takes to stabilize economy and society.

Polanyi's view of the state fundamentally conflicts with market fundamentalism's appropriation of classical liberal political theory. While political liberalism developed in opposition to a tyrannical English government and retained a fundamental suspicion toward political power,

Polanyi viewed politics and the exercise of power as constitutive of all human societies that strive for both freedom and social justice. The distinctiveness of Polanyi's approach is clearest in his treatment of the ancient irrigation empires of Babylonia and Assyria. While historiography assimilated these societies to the category of "tyrannical administrative bureaucracy," Polanyi's view is very different. He argues that these empires prospered because the state sanctioned gainless transactions regulated by the king and the rule of law. The spread of such transactions "multiplie[d] manyfold the productivity of labor in a flood-controlled agriculture." Polanyi continues: "The absence, or at least the very subordinate role, of markets did not imply ponderous administrative methods tightly held in the hands of a central bureaucracy. On the contrary, gainless transactions and regulated dispositions, as legitimized by law, opened up, as we have seen, a sphere of personal freedom formerly unknown in the economic life of man" (Polanyi 1977, 74). It is difficult to imagine a view of politics, the state, and social justice that is further at odds with market fundamentalist approaches.

Polanyi's Methodological Contributions

Polanyi's holistic approach to historical analysis represents his most significant contribution to historical and comparative analysis. The formulations we discussed in the previous section comprise a significant legacy to contemporary scholarship. Yet there are also other methodological principles that can be extracted from Polanyi's writings that bear on the vexed questions of historical and comparative analysis. The discussion that follows will touch on three of these: the centrality of institutional analysis, the role of metaphor, and the management of multiple levels of analysis. In addition, the discussion will touch upon one key weakness in Polanyi's approach: the limitations of his analyses of nonmarket societies.

Polanyi's primary task was to develop a method that avoided the assumption that all societies operated on the same economic principles. He thus focused his analysis at the level of societal and political institutions. He saw this as the best way to avoid the conscious or unconscious introduction of theories of motivation that could lead the analyst to findings that simply confirmed his or her initial biases. For example, many theorists had approached primitive societies with the question of how these people economized scarce resources, but for Polanyi this question assumed a motivation that might not be there. Polanyi's contrasting approach would be to ask what the institutional arrangements are by which this *particular* society ensures its own livelihood. His focus on institutions also allows Polanyi to distinguish among different subtypes of institutions. Hence, just because markets existed in a particular society does not imply a full-blown market society, making markets-in-society altogether unlike market society. Instead he carefully differentiates among the different kinds of markets, showing how some were price making while others operated within a system of administered prices. Similarly, Polanyi shows that money fulfills different functions in diverse societies.

It must also be acknowledged that, despite Polanyi's commitment to holism, an exclusive concentration on concrete institutions has its limits. Polanyi also needed to develop concepts that embraced societies as a whole without reintroducing the biases of motivational analysis. For this reason, he developed his classification of the different societal arrangements by which human economies organize themselves—reciprocity, redistribution, and exchange (GT, ch.4, and Polanyi 1977, 35–43). Each of these is an institutionalized pattern of relationships by which individual social units are linked together to form a social whole. Different patterns always coexist within the same society, but there is usually a dominant one. Furthermore, Polanyi remarks: "It would be a mistake rigidly to identify the dominance of exchange with the nineteenth-century economy of the West. More than once in the course of human history have markets played a significant part in integrating the economy, although never on a territorial scale, nor with a comprehensiveness even faintly comparable to that of the nineteenth-century West" (Polanyi 1977, 43).

Although this schema is on a different level of analysis than specific economic institutions, its referent is still an institutional issue—how different societies integrate their economic subunits. While it appears to have certain affinities with what some call functionalism (analysis of how different societies all satisfy certain universal needs [see, e.g., Parsons 1966]), there are more differences than similarities. Polanyi does not produce a catalog of "functional requisites" for human societies; rather he limits his list to those institutional arrangements necessary for the "livelihood of man" and those necessary for some degree of coordination among subunits. In both cases, the answers that Polanyi found could be expressed in terms of specific institutional arrangements rather than abstract functions.

Polanyi's method is to compare the different means by which different societies manage similar problems. This allows him to demonstrate the hidden links between seemingly diverse phenomena. Redistribution, reciprocity, and exchange are all comparable responses to the problem of how societies configure their different institutions. From this point of view, even fascism, the New Deal, and socialism are but different national responses to the same problems brought on by the collapse of the world market. In a sense, Polanyi's procedure anticipates such later classics as that of Barrington Moore (1966) and Alexander Gerschenkron (1962), both of which compare by asking how different societies manage a particular problem, such as how to generate the savings necessary for industrialization. Polanyi's institutional focus allows him to distinguish arrangements that appear to be the same while comparing those that do not at first glance seem to be comparable.

A second important aspect of Polanyi's method is his use of metaphor. The most spectacular aspect of GT is its effort to explain the rise of fascism in terms of how classical political economy and industrialism emerged more than one hundred years earlier. This connection is expressed in terms of a metaphor of organic misdevelopment: the ultimate collapse of market society followed from fundamental strains that were inherent in market society from the beginning. The acorn was flawed, and that is why the seemingly mighty oak of nineteenth-century society crashed so dramatically and so suddenly. To be sure, when Polanyi expresses this idea in his own language—the collapse occurred because society had to save itself from the market—there is more than a hint of reification. The abstract entity, society, appears to have a life of its own, which acts against another abstract entity, the market. Measured against the standards of contemporary scholarship, in which hypostasizing entities and resorting to theories of organic development or misdevelopment are often seen as cardinal sins, Polanyi's argument appears at first glance to be seriously flawed.

Yet such a view misses what is most powerful and useful in Polanyi's argument: the way he moves back and forth between metaphor and metatheory, and a series of concrete causal arguments. In analyzing large-scale historical change, using metaphors such as those of organic development or misdevelopment is indispensable. The indispensability does not rest on the fact that development is immanent in history, but that the effort to make sense of large-scale historical change requires frameworks that are able to link together a variety of concrete processes.

For such frameworks to be intelligible, they must rest on analogies with familiar organic or mechanical processes.[13]

While the effort to rid historical analysis of metaphors is shortsighted, there is an important truth in the debunking of metaphor. Quite simply, the metaphor can only operate as a heuristic; it cannot be used to carry the argument. Absent specific causal explanations, analysts cannot rely on assertions such as that evolution or system maintenance requires certain outcomes. Specific causal mechanisms must be invoked to explain each step in the process. In short, analysis must operate on two levels. The first is the level of metaphor and hypostasization, providing a summary of the major historical dynamics that are being analyzed. The second is a set of causal arguments based on institutional mechanisms and class forces, explaining the various processes of institutional transformation. One measure of a piece of historical analysis is the skill with which the analyst moves between these levels, and in this respect Polanyi is exemplary. The metaphoric structure gives the book its power, but Polanyi does not rest on the metaphor for explanation. As the following passage indicates, Polanyi was acutely aware of the need to fill in the metaphor with a set of concrete historical arguments: "A civilization was being disrupted by the blind action of soulless institutions the only purpose of which was the automatic increase of material welfare. But how did the inevitable actually happen? How was it translated into the political events which are the core of history? Into this final phase of the fall of market economy the conflict of class forces entered decisively" (GT, 219).

Polanyi fills out his analysis of the protectionist countermovement with a discussion of historical actors and the specific dynamics that their actions set in motion. He can be faulted, of course, on the accuracy of some of his historical arguments, as well as for an occasional lack of clarity when he fails to emphasize which are the most important processes. He does not, however, allow the metaphor to substitute for history.

The third important dimension of Polanyi's method is his approach to managing multiple levels of analysis. Because he recognizes the centrality of the world economy, he brings to bear the global level while simultaneously incorporating both the political level of state activities, as well as the conflicts among classes and other social groups. These three levels of analysis—global, national, and local societal groups—became the subject of much discussion after the publication of Immanuel Wallerstein's *The Modern World-System* (1974).[14] This was not purely coincidental, as Wallerstein acknowledges Polanyi to be one of the major inspirations for his world-system theory.

There are nonetheless many important differences between Polanyi's formulations and those of Wallerstein, two of which are particularly relevant here. First, Wallerstein tends to define the global level of analysis primarily in terms of a world market in which nations compete. He pays far less attention than does Polanyi to the institutional arrangements, such as the gold standard system, by which the world market is organized. This omission makes it harder for Wallerstein to integrate international politics into his analysis of the world market, since the strength or weakness of international economic regimes is closely linked to the balance of political and military power among states. Second, as a number of his critics have noted, Wallerstein tends to collapse the three different levels of analysis into one; at times both class relations and state action are seen as determined by the dynamics of the world system (for such criticisms, see Skocpol 1977; Gourevitch 1978). On the other hand, some of Wallerstein's critics make the opposite error—they tend to collapse both world economy and state action into economic class relations, which are seen as determining (Brenner 1977). Polanyi, in contrast, makes a significant effort to grasp the interrelations among the three levels without collapsing any one in another.

He does this by using an implicit concept of opportunity structures. His historical argument suggests that particular moments in the organization of the international economic regime provide unique opportunities for states to act. At these times, it is the degree of latitude open to the state that in turn shapes the spectrum of possible actions for societal struggles. One example is found in his analysis of the 1920s. The restoration of the gold standard after World War I closed off opportunities for creative response by national governments. They had little choice but to obey the rules of the game, but this obedience ensured the frustration of working class goals, resulting in political stalemate. The situation changed dramatically with the coming of the world depression in the 1930s. The failure of the gold standard mechanism created a more open international opportunity structure, which Hitler was quick to use to his advantage. Polanyi writes: "Germany at first reaped the advantages of those who kill that which is doomed to die. Her start lasted as long as the liquidation of the outworn system of the nineteenth century permitted her to keep in the lead" (GT, 246).

Germany, as well as Japan and Italy, gained advantage from breaking with the nineteenth-century rules of the game before the rest of the world had come to understand their obsolescence. Precisely this opportunity to experiment with economic autarchy and an aggressive foreign policy gave fascist movements their power. While Polanyi insists that the fascist impulse was international, it is logical that it should have fully achieved state power in those dissatisfied powers that had the most reason to oppose the existing international rules of the game.

Hence, the three levels of analysis are linked by two different opportunity structures. First, there is a global opportunity structure that shapes what is possible for particular governments. This set of constraints, in turn, creates a national opportunity structure that influences how social groups or class forces can be most effective in influencing state policy. This implicit framework leaves unresolved the critical question of whether the opportunity structures are completely determining or if it were possible, for example, in a period such as the 1920s for a more imaginative working-class movement to have created new opportunities. Still, this framework suggests a method by which the three levels of analysis can be managed without losing a sense of the analytic autonomy of each level.

In fact, the opportunity structure argument is also helpful for understanding what motivated Polanyi to write GT, as well as in accounting for the failure of his aspirations. GT was intended to be a primer for the British workers whom Polanyi taught when he was a worker educator in the 1930s. He believed that the end of the war would once again create an open international opportunity structure and that Britain could be particularly influential in responding to that new structure. This in turn would give the working class the opportunity to push Britain toward democratic socialism and to break with the gold standard. Polanyi correctly perceived that such a move by Britain would have a major impact on the European continent and through much of Africa and Asia. At the same time, Polanyi assumed that the U.S. would continue on its New Deal course.

This was where Polanyi was wrong. With the end of World War II came an almost immediate intensification of the Cold War and the abandonment of the domestic reform project that Franklin Roosevelt had launched. The U.S.'s superior military and economic strength in turn constrained the international opportunity structure and served to block any impulses toward socialism or alternative international economic arrangements in Britain and other European countries (Block 1977). Polanyi quickly recognized the changing reality, and in his essay "Our Obsolete Market Mentality," published in 1947, he pleaded for a shift in American policy away from the restoration of a self-regulating world economy.

While there is much to Polanyi's method that is still of great use, it is also important to note one central weakness. Although Polanyi is able to understand important aspects of nonmarket societies by contrasting them with market societies, his concepts have little analytic power for understanding the dynamic processes within nonmarket societies. The contrast is particularly striking because the conflict between self-regulating markets and social protection makes his analysis of market society especially attuned to processes of change. One is struck, by contrast, that his study of premodern Dahomey provides little analysis of internal change processes beyond descriptive references to the centralization of political-military power by particular families (Polanyi 1966). To be sure, his intellectual project lay elsewhere; he was more concerned to show that a society like Dahomey was able to contain and control the destructive impact of international trade than to explain its own internal dynamics.

Conclusion

Polanyi is unequivocal about his central concern in GT—to explain the destruction of nineteenth-century civilization and its giving way to fascism in the twentieth century. Against all alternatives, he insists that the disintegration was a result of the protective measures that "society adopted in order not to be, in its turn, annihilated by the action of the self-regulating market" (GT, 249). Polanyi thus looks to the conflictual dynamics of social and economic institutions to explain both the construction and subsequent destruction of market society.

Polanyi's institutional focus also leads directly to his conviction that power and political governance are part of the elementary requirements of any organized social life. He does not avoid the implications of this position; for him, it is hopelessly wrongheaded to imagine that even an idealized socialism would solve the problems of politics and bureaucracy. Politics and the state cannot just wither away. The achievement of human freedom will require conscious action to restrain the necessary but dangerous exercise of political power: "The true answer to the threat of bureaucracy as a source of abuse of power is to create spheres of arbitrary freedom protected by unbreakable rules. For, however generously devolution of power is practiced, there will be strengthening of power at the center, and, therefore, danger to individual freedom" (GT, 255).

What was most important for Polanyi was that society must overcome the illusion that the difficult problems of human governance could be solved either through the end of scarcity or the self-regulating market. On the contrary, as he states in the final passage of GT: "As long as man is true to his task of creating more abundant freedom for all, he need not fear that either power or planning will turn against him and destroy the freedom he is building by their instrumentality. This is the meaning of freedom in a complex society; it gives us all the certainty we need" (GT, 268).

In a letter written "to the love of his early youth" in 1958, Polanyi, after mentioning his "martyrdom of isolation," suggests that "one more decade—and I would stand vindicated in my lifetime" (1977, xx). In a way, the remark was prophetic in that 1968 was the year of the May events in France, of the Tet offensive in Vietnam, and of the most dramatic indications of crisis in the post-World War II international economic regime. Once again market society was under serious attack and its central institutions were in crisis. Although these events confirmed Polanyi's diagnosis of the fragility of market society, it took several more decades before Polanyi's intellectual contribution began to receive the recognition that it deserves.

3

KARL POLANYI AND THE WRITING OF
THE GREAT TRANSFORMATION

Now that Polanyi's masterpiece, *The Great Transformation* (referred to as GT hereafter) has begun to gain the attention it deserves, it is vitally important that Polanyi's text be subjected to the kind of close, critical scrutiny that scholars normally direct at classical works. This is particularly important because Polanyi advances complex and sometimes contradictory arguments from which readers can easily derive sharply divergent interpretations. Although there have been a number of important secondary writings on GT (Sievers 1949; Somers 1990; Polanyi-Levitt 1990, 1994; Block 2001), there have been few efforts to place the arguments of the book in the context of Polanyi's development as a theorist.

The focus of this chapter is on a reading of GT that centers on Karl Polanyi's shifting relation to the Marxist tradition. He developed the outline for the book while he was still in England in the latter part of the 1930s. In his English years, Polanyi developed his own Hegelianized Marxist position that had distinct commonalities to arguments developed by Lukacs in *History and Class Consciousness* (1971 [1923]). However, as Polanyi began writing the book in the United States in 1941, his theoretical framework shifted. But since Polanyi composed the manuscript across a period of time when his thinking was changing, the resulting manuscript was left with a number of contradictions and conflicts. Since circumstances did not allow for a major rewrite of the text, he did not have the opportunity to resolve some of these tensions, which can therefore be explained by Polanyi's shifting relationship to certain Marxist formulations.

It is this shifting relationship that explains one of the core paradoxes of Polanyi's contribution. Polanyi glimpsed the idea of *the always-embedded market economy*, but he was not able to give that idea a name or develop it theoretically because it represented too great a divergence from his initial theoretical starting point. And yet, we argue, it is the idea of the always-embedded market economy that provides the most powerful and enduring way to make sense of Polanyi's core arguments in GT. This is not simply an exercise in the history of theory. Polanyi's ideas, particularly the concept of embeddedness, loom large in contemporary scholarship and are the subject of increasingly intense debate (see Krippner 2001, Burawoy 2003, Krippner and Alvarez 2007, Gemici 2008, Dale 2010). For scholars to build on these ideas in a durable way, it is important to develop a theoretically coherent interpretation of his text. This means, above all, understanding the ways in which his analysis of capitalism is similar to and different from other formulations.

Polanyi's Second Encounter with Marxism

As a young man in pre-World War I Budapest, Polanyi rejected the Marxism of the Second International. As we say in Chapter 2:

> In particular, Polanyi passionately rejected the Second International's belief in the inevitability of progress as a consequence of predetermined stages of human development. Central to him and others of his generation was the idea that progress could only come through conscious human action based on moral principles.

Moreover, Polanyi also kept his distance from the Marxism of the Third International with its emphasis on revolutionary action. But the story does not end there, as Polanyi had another encounter with Marxism.[1] The precise timing is unclear, but there are clear traces of it in both his published writings and in materials that are available in the Polanyi archive at Concordia University in Montreal. A formative moment of this encounter for Polanyi was his reading of Marx's *Economic and Philosophical Manuscripts*, first published in German in 1932.[2] These were the "early" or "Paris" manuscripts that the young Marx had written in 1844 elaborating his theory of species being and alienation. When these texts were finally translated into English and French in the 1950s, they generated an intense debate about the relationship between the "young Marx" of the *Manuscripts* and the "mature Marx" of *Capital*. The French philosopher Louis Althusser famously claimed that there was not continuity in Marx's thought, but rather that Marx made an "epistemological break" between his earlier humanism and his mature anti-humanism.

Ironically, Polanyi's reading of Marx was almost the opposite of Althusser's; for Polanyi the humanism of the young Marx was the missing key to the *mature* Marx. In an essay published in 1938, Polanyi wrote: "The early works of Marx were often regarded as a mere preparation for *Capital*, and these writings on philosophy were therefore discounted. The idea was current that Marx had a philosophical period before he branched off into economics, an interest which he put behind him as soon as he came to years of discretion. This notion is entirely erroneous. The philosophical presuppositions, without which *Capital* could not have been written, are the actual content of the early writings of Marx. His works up to 1847 were not "wild oats" of which he afterwards repented. During the forties, he laid the general human basis for all his work" (Polanyi 1938, 5).[3]

Polanyi read Marx's early writings against the backdrop of the Great Depression and the rise of fascism. The collapse of global capitalism and the fascist threat had a radicalizing impact on him as he struggled to find a way to defend democratic and humanistic values. As with other radicalized intellectuals, Polanyi came to see a proletarian revolution as the only viable alternative to fascism. Not ready to join any of the existing Leninist parties, however, during his stay in England in the 1930s he worked instead with a succession of radical Christian groups that allowed him to elaborate his own interpretation of Marx.

Polanyi's position can best be understood in relation to the tradition of Western Marxism. In the 1970s and after, scholars in Europe and North America assembled the thinking and writing of heterodox left-wing intellectuals of the 1920s, 1930s, and 1940s who rescued Marxism from the mechanical thinking of the Second and Third Internationals (Howard and Klare, eds. 1972; Anderson 1976; Jones et al., eds. 1977; Gouldner 1980). The key figures of what was to become a new tradition were Continental European thinkers including Georg Lukacs, Karl Korsch, Antonio Gramsci, Walter Benjamin, and the writers of the Frankfurt School. More recently, Michael Denning has argued that there were important figures in the 1930s in the U.S. who also belong to this tradition, including Kenneth Burke, Sidney Hook, and the Caribbean theorist C. L. R. James (Denning 1997). Polanyi's work in England in the 1930s fits squarely into this expanded tradition of Western Marxism.[4]

Writing in 1934, Polanyi stated his viewpoint starkly: "Mankind has come to an impasse. Fascism resolves it at the cost of a moral and material retrogression. Socialism is the way out by an advance towards a Functional Democracy. A great initiative is needed. Failure or success depends upon the recognition of the central truth that it is *not by following their own immediate material interests* that the working class can prove their capacity for leadership, but by adapting their own interests to the interests of the indifferent masses in order to be able to lead society as a whole. The fullest understanding of the nature of the present crisis is of paramount importance. If a revision of Marxism is necessary for this purpose, the task should neither be shirked nor delayed" [emphasis added] (Polanyi 1934, 188).

Polanyi shared with many others the idea that democracy and capitalism had reached a deadlock in the crisis of the 1930s, but he was equally insistent that it was not enough for the working class to make a revolution in its own name. In a manner quite similar to Gramsci, Polanyi insisted that the working class had to win leadership of society by representing the interests of society as a whole.[5] "Indeed, the secret of success lies rather in the measure in which the groups are able to represent—by including in their own—the interests of others than themselves. To achieve this inclusion they will, in effect, often have to adapt their own interests to those of the wider groups which they aspire to lead"(Polanyi 1934, 188).

The working class must therefore forge an "historical bloc" of diverse social groups around a counterhegemonic vision of how socialism can make full use of society's productive forces. Implicit in this line of argument is the belief that, if the English working class were to focus only on the militant pursuit of its own class interest, the backlash would strengthen the political right and lead to some form of English fascism.

Polanyi linked this broad theoretical framework to the realities of English history in a number of the Workers Educational Association lecture courses that he delivered in the second half of the 1930s.[6] For example, in the 1937–1938 academic year, Polanyi gave a course at the Heathfield site on "English Economic, Social, and Industrial History from the 16th Century." Polanyi's surviving lecture notes for the course allow us to trace the Marxist influences on his formulations. When he arrives at the Industrial Revolution in lecture nineteen, for example, he writes: "Industrial capitalism is the latest and most important form of capitalism. When we loosely talk of capitalism, we usually mean industrial capitalism. It means the use of capital in industrial production and the creation of capital by means of industrial production; therefore also the existence of a class of capitalists whose interests are identified with those of industrial development" (Polanyi 1937–1938, 94).

A few pages later, he poses a critical question: "The Industrial Revolution presents us with a problem: The productive forces of the country increased enormously, yet the state and condition of the people was miserable. How to account for this?" The answer is that: "The Industrial Revolution was a Social Revolution creating a new civilisation with problems and a character of its own" (Polanyi 1937–1938, 99). The next few lectures trace out the horrors of this period—the Satanic Mills, child labor, the dismantling of the earlier legal regime regulating labor, and the Poor Laws. We find here much of the analysis of the Speenhamland period that appears in the GT. From 1795 to 1834 in England, poor relief was thought to have been provided to able-bodied workers through a system of aid-in-wages that came to be called Speenhamland after the town in which the new policy had been enunciated. Speenhamland policies allegedly produced disastrous consequences for the morale and living standards of rural workers (for more on the Speenhamland story, see Chapter 5). Polanyi's analysis of the Old Poor Law in the lectures culminates as follows: "The worst effects were on the rural population. It [Speenhamland] completed the work done by the enclosures and the engrossing of farms. Destitution and idleness broke the last link that bound the countryman to the land. It drove him, demoralized, and indifferent to the total loss of his independence to the labor market of the city . . . But unemployment meant parish relief with its worst consequences. A considerable part of the nation was thus enslaved and humiliated. This was the price paid for the peace of mind of the ruling classes" (Polanyi 1937–1938, 110).

Examining the Turn

The Marxism of Polanyi's writings of the 1930s revolve around the clash between productive forces and social relations. It can be read as an extended elaboration on the famous passage in Marx's 1859 "Preface to the Contribution to the Critique of Political Economy," where Marx explicitly links some of his youthful writings to his mature version of historical materialism. Marx wrote: "At a certain stage of their development, the material productive forces of society come in conflict with the existing relations of production, or—what is but a legal expression for the same thing—with the property relations within which they have been at work hitherto. From forms of development of the productive forces these relations turn into fetters. Then begins an epoch of social revolution" (1978 [1859]:3–6).

But in the writing of the GT, there are few explicit references to this perspective. Terms such as "productive forces" and "ruling classes" are completely absent, and even "capitalism" is used very sparingly in the GT. Most of Polanyi's references to capitalism in the book occur when he is discussing other sources that use that term. In constructing his own argument, he carefully employs the term *market society* instead of capitalism. Some analysts have suggested that this shift in language was simply tactical because of the political complexities of using a Marxist vocabulary (Halperin 1994, ch.2; Stroshane 1997). Our argument, on the contrary, is that the shift of language is symptomatic of a theoretical shift that distanced Polanyi from the Marxist "forces versus relations" framework.

To be sure, there are continuities as well as discontinuities between Polanyi's thinking in the 1930s and what he writes in GT. This is not an issue of Polanyi's political intentions or his loyalty or disloyalty to particular values.[7] It is a given that Polanyi was continuing to think and write in this period in conscious dialogue with both Marxism and the broader socialist tradition. However, some of the specific concepts that he develops while writing GT are in tension with his own earlier Marxist formulations, and as he elaborates their implications, the text develops internal tensions between more deterministic formulations and more open-ended formulations.

The first of these disruptive formulations is Polanyi's idea of fictitious commodities—the concept that he uses to describe the role of land, labor, and money in economic theory.[8] Polanyi's term sounds like Marx, who spoke of "the fetishism of commodities" and the existence of "fictive capital," but Polanyi actually takes pains in a footnote to say that Marx's analysis of commodity fetishism "has nothing in common with the fictitious commodities mentioned in the text" (GT, 76). Polanyi's argument is that land, labor, and money are not true commodities because true commodities are things that are produced for sale on a market. Yet the theory of market self-regulation rests on the pretense that the supply and demand for these fictitious commodities will be effectively equilibrated by the price mechanism just as if they were true commodities. But as Polanyi insists: "Now, in regard to labor, land, and money such a postulate cannot be upheld. To allow the market mechanism to be sole director of the fate of human beings and their natural environment, indeed, even of the amount and use of purchasing power, would result in the demolition of society" (GT, 76).

Polanyi goes on to insist that to avoid the demolition of society, the supply and demand for these fictitious commodities in actual market societies must be managed through the political process. His formulation is quite distinct from Marx's analysis of the contradictions of capitalism. Marx sets up an analytic model of a fully functioning capitalist economy and then argues that the resulting system is subject to intense contradictions that can be expected to manifest themselves in periodic crises. Marx analyzes an ideal version of capitalism and finds it prone to crises, while Polanyi insists that there can be no pure version of market society because land, labor, and money are not true commodities. In Marx, the contradictions come at the end of the analysis; for Polanyi, the system is built on top of a lie that means that it can never work in the way that its proponents claim that it works.

In making his argument, Polanyi was reflecting on decades of historical development that had unfolded since Marx had written. Polanyi had the distinct advantage of observing the dramatic increases in the state's role in managing market economies and he was working out a theoretical framework that placed the state's role close to the center of analysis. The idea of fictitious commodities can be seen as a way of deepening Marx's critique of capitalism. But the theoretical tension increases as Polanyi goes on to use the idea of fictitious commodities to develop his second disruptive concept—the idea of the embedded economy, a concept that has often been misunderstood. Some interpret Polanyi as making the argument that before the rise of market society economies were always embedded in social relations, but with the rise of market societies the situation is reversed and the market becomes dominant. A similar argument had been made explicitly by Lukacs (1971 [1923]), who argued that historical materialism as a method of analysis is specific to capitalist societies because in those societies the economy has become the determinant factor. In earlier societies the economy was not autonomous, so analysts must employ a method that is sensitive to the power of culture and other practices.

But what Polanyi actually said is somewhat different. He argues that market liberals wanted to embed society in the autonomous economy, but their project *could not* succeed. As he writes at the beginning of his first chapter: "Our thesis is that the idea of a self-adjusting market implied a stark Utopia. Such an institution could not exist for any length of time without annihilating the human and natural substance of society; it would have physically destroyed man and transformed his surroundings into a wilderness" (GT, 3).

Moreover, in the first sentence, Polanyi is using "utopia" to mean not a good society but an impossible society. The logic is that precisely because land, labor, and money are fictitious commodities, completely subordinating them to the market mechanism would destroy society. Even in market societies, ways have to be found to embed labor, land, and money in social relations.

With this concept of embeddedness, Polanyi is challenging a core presumption of both economic liberalism and Marxism. Both of these traditions are built on the idea that there is an autonomous economy that is subject to its own internal logic. Polanyi's point is that, since actually existing market economies are dependent upon the state to manage the supply and demand for the fictitious commodities, there can be no analytically autonomous economy. Furthermore, it makes no sense to speak of the logic of the market or the logic of the economy, because pretending that land, labor, and money are true commodities is both irrational and socially dangerous.

Some writing in the Marxist tradition have welcomed Polanyi's powerful critique of the irrationality and ideological nature of market liberalism,[9] but his arguments also pose a serious challenge to some Marxist formulations such as classic accounts of the difference between feudalism and capitalism. Marxists emphasize that feudalism is characterized by the use of extra-economic coercion to extract surplus labor from agricultural producers (Anderson 1974; Burawoy 1985). In capitalism, by contrast, surplus is extracted from the laboring classes through the purely economic mechanism of the wage contract. To be sure, this economic extraction is understood to depend upon the coercive power of the state in enforcing contracts and in "disorganizing" political challenges from the working class. Yet, the state's role does not constitute extra-economic coercion; it is simply a means to police the purely economic exploitation of the capitalist market. The state is in the background; the most important relationship is the exploitation of worker by capitalist at the point of production.

This formulation was central to Marx's and Engels's belief that state power in capitalist society was ultimately an expression of the class power of the bourgeoisie. Once that class power was effectively broken by a revolution that "expropriated the Expropriators," they could confidently predict "the withering away of the state" since there would no longer be any need for institutionalized political coercion. Over the last three or four decades, particularly in response to the failures of state socialism, some working within the Marxist tradition have incorporated the Weberian view that the core of state power—the monopoly over the legitimate use of force and the power to tax—is autonomous from class power.[10] But this revisionist analysis is in conflict with the way that Marx and Engels defined the dividing line between the economic and the political.

Significantly, Polanyi in GT explicitly embraces the Weberian view; he argues that power and compulsion are inevitable in a complex society: "No society is possible in which power and compulsion are absent, nor a world in which force has no function. It was an illusion to assume a society shaped by man's will and wish alone" (GT, 266). Polanyi also insists that justice requires that mechanisms exist to subject the power of the state to democratic control (GT, 262–265). But Polanyi's analysis of state power and of the relationship between politics and the economy form a coherent whole. He is arguing that market society—not just at its moment of formation, but continuously—depends upon extra-economic political coercion. Or even more fundamentally, he is suggesting that classical Marxism tends to exaggerate the contrast between feudalism and capitalism. In both types of society, the processes of extracting surplus from the direct producers involve a complex mix of political, cultural, and economic practices. In neither of these types of society is there a separate economic realm.[11]

Ambiguities in the Text

The argument to this point is that as Polanyi wrote GT, he developed concepts and the embedded economy that distanced him from the Marxist conceptual framework that had been the initial organizing framework for his book. It is common for authors to revisit and revise their conceptual premises in the actual act of writing, but Polanyi's immediate circumstances limited his ability to reconcile the conflicts created by his own intellectual development. As Polanyi states in the author's acknowledgments, the "book was written in America during the Second World War. But it was begun and finished in England" (GT, xl). Polanyi had been granted a two-year fellowship from the Rockefeller

Foundation to write the book while in residence at Bennington College from the fall of 1941 through the spring of 1943.[12] Without this time released from his demanding duties as a Lecturer with the Workers' Educational Association—the extramural outreach arm of the Universities of Oxford and London—it is highly unlikely that the book would have been written at all.

But in addition to the deadline posed by the end of the fellowship period, Polanyi imposed upon himself a second and even more stringent deadline. One of Polanyi's central goals with the book was to influence the debates over the nature of the post-World War II settlement, so he was acutely aware of the need to get the book to press before the end of hostilities. In a letter to Robert MacIver written in October, 1946, Polanyi wrote: "In spite of deficiencies of presentation—*war conditions forced me to rush it to conclusion*—the book has not been overlooked . . ." [Emphasis added]. [13] Polanyi sent the text of the book to the American publisher before sailing to England in June 1943 so that the book could be published in New York in 1944.[14] He simply did not have the time to carry out a major revision of the text to make it more theoretically consistent. The published book contains traces both of Polanyi's initial position and the theoretical innovations that changed his thinking. Once we recognize that the book was written across this theoretical shift, it becomes easier to make sense of its deepest theoretical puzzles.

The Problem of Determinism

In GT, there are two great historical turning points. The first is the passage of the New Poor Law in 1834 that represents the triumph of market society by effectively transforming labor into a commodity. The second turning point is the crisis of the self-regulating market system, which begins in the last decades of the nineteenth century and is completed with the collapse of the world economy in the 1930s. Polanyi describes both of these turning points as occurring with the force of inevitability; they are points at which history *had to* turn. And yet, in both cases, the necessity of the historical change is in conflict with Polanyi's argument about the nature of economic organization. In terms of the theoretical argument, critical changes in the economy should be the contingent results of a convergence of specific factors.

In terms of the New Poor Law there is a further contradiction. On the one side, Polanyi argues that labor had to be turned into a commodity.

He writes: "The mechanism of the market was asserting itself and clamoring for its completion: human labor had to be made a commodity" (GT, 107). And yet, only a few pages before, we were told distinctly that labor could never really be commodified; it is only a fictitious commodity. The first argument is that Speenhamland blocked the full commodification of labor had caused a social disaster and simply had to be repealed. But the second argument is that the full commodification of labor would mean the destruction of society, and so steps had to be taken immediately to protect people from exposure to market forces. In short, how can the adoption of a mistaken and disastrous policy take on the quality of inevitability?

The same tension between determinism and contingency appears in Polanyi's account of how the system of market self-regulation comes into crisis in the last years of the nineteenth century. Polanyi is quite explicit in challenging the views of von Mises and Lippman, who both argued that a "collectivist conspiracy" crippled market society (GT, 148). They argued that starting in the 1870s and 1880s, various forms of quasi-socialist legislation interfered with the mechanisms of market self-regulation. Without the gradual and piecemeal adjustments required by self-regulating markets, the system became prone to much deeper crises, including ultimately the depression of the 1930s. In one of his most eloquent passages, Polanyi thrashes their "collectivist conspiracy" accusations. He shows there was instead a completely *spontaneous* effort in a wide variety of different societies to protect farmers, workers, and businesses from the corrosive impact of the market (GT, ch.12). The difficulty was not with these protective measures, he demonstrates, but with the intolerable costs that market self-regulation imposed on vast numbers of people.

Yet in seeking to refute von Mises and Lippman, Polanyi seems to embrace a key aspect of their argument—that the various protective measures did impair the ability of the market system to work effectively. His Chapter 17 is entitled "Self-Regulation Impaired" and it begins: "In the half century 1879–1929, Western societies developed into closely-knit units, in which powerful disruptive strains were latent. The more immediate source of this development was the impaired self-regulation of market economy. Since society was made to conform to the needs of the market mechanism, imperfections in the functioning of that mechanism created cumulative strains in the body social" (GT, 210).

The next chapter includes this passage that could have been written by one of his ideological opponents: "Protectionism helped to transform competitive markets into monopolistic ones. Less and less could markets be described as autonomous and automatic mechanisms of competing atoms. More and more were individuals replaced by associations, men and capital united to noncompeting groups. Economic adjustment became slow and difficult. The self-regulation of markets was gravely hampered. Eventually, unadjusted price and cost structures prolonged depressions, unadjusted equipment retarded the liquidation of unprofitable investments, unadjusted price and income levels caused social tension" (GT, 210).

These problems of adjustment set the stage for the inevitable collapse of market society in the 1930s. Polanyi writes of the period after World War I, "By inherent necessity the root problems of market society reappeared: interventionism and currency. They became the center of politics in the twenties" (GT, 239). The roots of the final crisis were laid by what Polanyi saw as a heroic but deeply misguided effort to restore the system's capacity for self-regulation. He comments: "Economic liberalism made a supreme bid to restore the self-regulation of the system by eliminating all interventionist policies which interfered with the freedom of markets for land, labor, and money. It undertook no less than to solve, in an emergency, the secular problem involved in three fundamental principles of free trade, a free labor market, and a freely functioning gold standard. It became, in effect the spearhead of a heroic attempt to restore world trade, remove all avoidable hindrances to the mobility of labor, and reconstruct stable exchanges" (GT, 239). But as in earlier moments, this utopian project could not be realized; the result was the collapse of the global economy and its direct political consequence—the rise of fascism. "If ever there was a political movement that responded to the needs of an objective situation and was not a result of fortuitous causes it was fascism" (GT, 245).

This argument about an inevitable crisis of market society has deep Marxist echoes. The attempt to universalize the commodity form sets in motion a powerful countertendency, just as Marx argued that capitalism produced its own gravediggers in the form of the proletariat. The conflict between tendency and countertendency creates deepening tensions and conflicts until a final crisis leads to a radical break with the logic of market society. But here again, this argument is in tension with Polanyi's insistence on the necessity of embeddedness and the inevitability of hybrid forms. If a purely self-regulating market system is an impossibility, how could it be that the lack of purity inevitably produces a crisis?

It is not logical for Polanyi to claim both that a system of self-regulating markets was impossible and that any effort to constrain or limit market self-regulation was doomed to produce a systemic crisis. Fortunately, he suggests a way out of this set of contradictions; it is that the crisis that unfolds in the period from 1879–1929 occurs at a more specific institutional level than suggested either by Marxism or by von Mises and Lippman. The problem lies not with the broad effort to combine market self-regulation with various forms of protectionism, but rather with the misguided effort to establish and maintain the international gold standard. The gold standard is the institutionalization of the abstract logic of market self-regulation. It is the gold standard mechanism that is in contradiction with the various measures taken within nations to buffer their people from market forces. When it is combined with multiple practices that interfere with market logic, the result is deeply contradictory and will inevitably produce a crisis. The implicit counterfactual that he suggests is that if international statesmen after World War I had decided to discard the gold standard, they could have escaped the crisis of the 1930s. The problem, however, was that "Belief in the gold standard was the faith of the age" (GT, 26). He goes on to argue that proponents of all political ideologies shared the belief in the necessity of basing currencies on gold: "It would be hard to find any divergence between utterances of Hoover and Lenin, Churchill and Mussolini, on this point. Indeed, the essentiality of the gold standard to the functioning of the international economic system of the time was the one and only tenet common to men of all nations and all classes, religious dominations, and social philosophies" (GT, 26). But it is clear from the context that Polanyi considers this shared tenet to be tragically mistaken.

In analyzing Polanyi's argument here, we have the advantage of another half century of historical development. The Bretton Woods period, in particular, has taught us that the gold standard was only one of a variety of international monetary regimes that are consistent with a global market system (Eichengreen 1996). When Polanyi was writing, however, it was far more difficult to disentangle the gold standard from the global market. Even so, he was able to identify the gold standard as one of the specific institutional pillars of nineteenth-century civilization (GT, 3). This description of the gold standard as a distinct institutional pillar means that Polanyi had assembled all the elements of the more specific and contingent analysis of the crisis of the 1930s. The core of his argument is that the crisis was rooted not in the fact that self-regulation was impaired; the impairing of market self-regulation was inevitable. The problem was that the various forms of protection practiced by nations coexisted with an international gold standard that rested on the principle of market self-regulation. It was this incompatibility between what was occurring *within* nations and what was occurring *between* nations that created disaster.

This argument has particular relevance in the aftermath of the 2007–2008 global financial crisis. The expansion of international capital mobility over the last twenty years has recreated some of the same constraints that were characteristic of the nineteenth-century gold standard (Greider 1997; Friedman 1999; Skidelsky 2009; Quiggin 2012). Nations that offend the sensibilities of traders in the financial markets can today find themselves subject to huge capital outflows and intense speculative pressures against their currencies. Once again, these arrangements are justified by the principle of market self-regulation. Within societies, however, national governments—even those in the most market-oriented polities—continue to play a central role in economic life by managing the key fictitious commodities (land, labor, and money) and by engaging in a wide variety of measures that protect people from market forces. Hence, the same deep tensions between an international monetary system based on principles of market self-regulation and national policies based on quite different practices characterize our own historical period.

The Speenhamland Problem

The last section suggests an alternative reading that addresses the appearance of determinism in Polanyi's account of the final crisis of market society. But the difficulties explicating Polanyi's analysis of the initial emergence of market society are even more daunting. When Polanyi asserts the inevitability of the New Poor Law, he echoes the Marxist account of the bourgeois revolution. The nascent capitalist forms have emerged within the womb of the old society, but because the existing property relations are holding them back, there is a period of stalemate and crisis. It seems as if he is suggesting that sooner or later the productive forces will inevitably break out and transform the existing political system. In this sense, the coming of the New Poor Law is for Polanyi playing a role similar to successful bourgeois revolution:

"In 1834 industrial capitalism was ready to be started, and Poor Law Reform was ushered in" (GT, 106). And yet the theoretical argument about fictitious commodities and embeddedness has a different logic; the commodity form can never truly complete itself—labor has to remain embedded in social relations because it is a fictitious commodity. Hence, even at its peak, market society is a hybrid; the attempted commodification of labor is combined with policies that embed and protect the working population. Yet if hybridity is the norm, the echoes of the Marxist argument that the market system had to complete itself are misplaced.

This raises two more intertwined questions. Why did Polanyi, a supporter of governmental action to shape economic activity, produce such an eloquent condemnation of the unintended consequences of the Speenhamland intervention on the living situation of the poor? Why did Polanyi devote so much space in the early part of the book to the relatively obscure Speenhamland story that seems only indirectly linked to his broader argument? Even though Polanyi's analysis of the impact of Speenhamland was initially written as part of an attack on market liberalism, his analysis was appropriated in the 1970s by an influential American conservative to make a case against the U.S. system of welfare provision (see Chapter 5). Martin Anderson in his 1978 book, *Welfare*, literally reprints Polanyi's entire Chapter 7 on Speenhamland as part of his demonstration that overly generous welfare programs produce perverse consequences (Anderson 1978). To be sure, scholars have no control over the purposes to which their analyses will be used, but this kind of dramatic appropriation makes it more urgent to understand Polanyi's argument.

In assessing Polanyi's discussion of Speenhamland, our focus in this chapter is not on the historical accuracy of his account (which we do challenge in Chapter 5 below), which requires a much longer review of the vast literature on the Old Poor Law. But it can be said that although there is much that is useful and accurate in Polanyi's analysis of the transition from the Old Poor Law to the New, one of his central arguments does not stand up well against historical evidence. This is the assertion that a widely diffused system of aid in support of wages, the famous bread scale, played a powerful role in depressing rural wages and productivity. A large body of scholarship shows that the use of the bread scale was not widespread enough in rural England to have had the dramatic consequences that Polanyi attributes to it (see Chapter 5).

But what about the theoretical role that Speenhamland plays in Polanyi's larger argument? We saw earlier that his discussion of Speenhamland appears in his lectures from the 1930s as part of an analysis of "the Industrial Revolution as a Social Revolution." Speenhamland was a desperate effort by the rural gentry to hold back the clock, to stop the advance of capitalism. But because the inevitable cannot really be averted, the gentry's initiative had catastrophic consequences for the rural poor. Hence, the significance of the 1834 turning point is that it represents the real birth of both industrial capitalism and of the modern working class. In lecture notes from Bennington in 1941, Polanyi includes among the long-term effects of the New Poor Law that the English working class was constituted as a social class deriving its independent existence from its earnings (Polanyi 1941).

But there is also a second story that helps to explain Polanyi's Speenhamland argument that was deeply rooted in his own biography. Coming to England from Vienna and Budapest, Polanyi was deeply puzzled by the lack of political consciousness of the English working class. In GT, he sketches out a brief comparative sociology of working-class formation in which he notes that the Continental working classes had helped the bourgeoisie fight the battle against feudalism: "But whether the working class won or lost, its experience was enhanced, and its aims raised to a political level. This was what was meant by becoming class conscious. Marxian ideologies crystallized the outlook of the urban worker, who had been taught by circumstances to use his industrial and political strength as a weapon of high policy" (GT, 183).

In contrast, in England "the middle classes . . . were strong enough to vindicate their rights alone" and the British worker was forced to leave "national politics to his 'betters'" (GT, 182–183). This passage continues an analysis of English working class consciousness that Polanyi had first elaborated in 1938: "The worker himself, a safeguarded member of a community which promised to protect him economically, morally, and politically, was prepared to accept a hierarchic class society in which he had a recognized status. Thus the Trade Union came to mean everything to him, and he would make great sacrifices for it. This largely accounts for the outlook and aims of the British worker, and for approval of a class society. It may lead to catastrophe for the British working class is not prepared to take charge, and build, if necessary, a new society" (Polanyi 1938, 24).

Polanyi went on to attribute the inability of British workers to move beyond trade union consciousness to the impact of the Industrial Revolution: "The Industrial Revolution in England was incomparably more harmful than in other countries. Only here were the horrors of licensed child-labour and systemic pauperisation part of working-class history. With the memory of such unspeakable conditions, the British working-class justly feel that they have progressed a long way. . . . *The horrors of that time still haunt the workers;* and this has a distinct bearing on the gradualism which is characteristic of the British working class" [emphasis added] (Polanyi 1938, 25). And again, in GT Polanyi echoes this argument in explaining the political consciousness of Continental workers: "The Continental laborer had not passed through the degrading pauperization of Speenhamland nor was there any parallel in his experience to the scorching fires of the New Poor Law. From the status of a villein he changed—or rather rose—to that of factory worker, and very soon to that of an enfranchised and unionized worker. Thus he escaped the cultural catastrophe which followed in the wake of the Industrial Revolution in England" (GT, 184).

Polanyi's point seems very clear; the trauma of Speenhamland had a long-term impact on the consciousness of the English working class. Because state policies played a central role in destroying the established way of life of the rural working class, it was logical that as the memory of these events was passed along from generation to generation so also was a profound distrust of the state. In fact, in Chapter 8, Polanyi says explicitly: "The hatred of public relief, the distrust of state action, the insistence on respectability and self-reliance, remained for generations characteristic of the British worker" (GT, 105). In short, historical experience had inoculated the English working class against political socialism because that doctrine required viewing the state as a potentially benign force.[15]

The concept of *trauma* may help to understand why Polanyi devotes so much of the early part of the book to retelling the story of Speenhamland and the New Poor Law. His hopes for the post-World War II world required that the English working class would enthusiastically participate in building a new society.[16] He correctly anticipated that a Labor Government would come to power after the war and its prospects depended on a willingness on the part of working people to abandon their historic distrust of state action. Hence, it does not seem farfetched that Polanyi was writing in something approaching a psychoanalytic mode. Perhaps he sought to describe the historical trauma in emotional and graphic detail precisely to facilitate its transcendence. After all, if the memories of a partially repressed trauma can be brought to the surface and validated, then finally the patient might be able to escape the trauma's hold on his or her actions. This psychoanalytically informed political agenda might well have overwhelmed some of Polanyi's other motivations for developing the Speenhamland argument. One of these is clearly stated in the book's endnote on "Speenhamland and Vienna" (GT, 298–299). Here Polanyi says explicitly that he was first drawn to the study of Speenhamland by developments in Austria after World War I. Free-market economists had denounced Vienna's system of unemployment insurance and subsidized rents as another "maladministration of the Poor Law," another "allowance system," which needed the iron broom of the classical economists. Polanyi writes: "What we wish to stress here is the enormous difference in the cultural and moral effects of the two types of intervention: the attempt of Speenhamland to prevent the coming of market economy and the experiment of Vienna trying to transcend such an economy altogether" (GT, 298).

Here Polanyi was trying to combat the generalized use of the Speenhamland story as a cautionary tale against any interference in the market. For this reason, he elaborates the story with a great deal of institutional detail. He stresses, for example, that the depressing effect of the bread scale on wage levels would have been avoided if not for the 1795 Combination Acts, which subjected trade union activity to the laws of treason and so prevented any collective working-class opposition. For the purpose of challenging the market liberals, Polanyi was showing that the negative impact of Speenhamland depended on a range of specific surrounding circumstances; it was illegitimate to see perverse consequences flowing inherently from any interference with the market. Nonetheless, it must be acknowledged that while this aspect of Polanyi's purpose emphasizes contingency, some of his other historical contentions (including the more Marxist analysis of the transition to market society and the narrative that emphasizes the magnitude of the trauma suffered by the English working class) invoke the language of inevitability.

A discussion of Polanyi on Speenhamland would not be complete without addressing what is perhaps his most fundamental reason for analyzing the period from 1795–1834, namely, its outsized impact on the development of classical economic thought (GT, ch.10). We know that Malthus and Ricardo developed the foundational ideas of classical economics by generalizing from the rather peculiar historically specific conditions of the Speenhamland period. It was those conditions that led Ricardo to formulate the "iron law of wages," the claim that, over the long term, wage levels could never rise above subsistence. Ricardo's formulation was based, in turn, on Malthus's alleged discovery that while food supply grows only arithmetically, human population grows geometrically. What they both built into their theories was a model of beastlike individuals who responded instinctively to increasing income with increased procreation and who could only reliably be expected to work by the threat of starvation.

Polanyi calls this way of analyzing human motivations "naturalism," and he sees it as corrupting the tradition of economics from the beginning. Although he recognizes that economists abandoned Ricardo's pessimistic formulations relatively quickly, they did not abandon his Malthusian assumptions about biologically-driven individual behavior. These became the ongoing foundation for imagining that labor could be treated as simply another commodity whose price will be effectively equilibrated by the price mechanism. The whole elaborate vision of market self-regulation is therefore based on a failure to recognize humans as social beings who respond to a range of different motivations. For Polanyi, the roots of this error lie in the Speenhamland period.

This strand of Polanyi's argument represents an important and fruitful contribution to the sociology of knowledge (see Hirschman 1991 and Chapter 6 below). Furthermore, it holds up even if Polanyi's specific claims about the impact of Speenhamland policies on wages do not (see Chapter 5). Malthus and Ricardo were writing in a transitional period, but they wrongheadedly theorized in universal and abstract terms many of the core theorems of the emergent discipline of economics (Redman 1997).

The Ambiguities of Embeddedness and Disembeddedness

We argued earlier that Polanyi is very clear that efforts by market liberals to disembed the economy from society must fail. There are, nonetheless, still ambiguities in his discussion of embeddedness in GT. That he is often read as arguing that the economy is effectively disembedded in market societies indicates that there are contradictory arguments loose in the text.[17] We can make sense of these ambiguities by untangling Polanyi's shifting theoretical formulations as he was writing the book.

Polanyi begins GT with a statement of the impossibility of creating a self-regulating market system: "Our thesis is that the idea of a self-adjusting market implied a stark utopia. Such an institution could not exist for any length of time without annihilating the human and natural substance of society; it would have physically destroyed man and transformed his surroundings into a wilderness"(GT, 3). The passage continues: "Inevitably, society took measures to protect itself, but whatever measures it took impaired the self-regulation of the market, disorganized industrial life, and thus endangered society in yet another way. It was this dilemma which forced the development of the market system into a definite groove and finally disrupted the social organization based upon it" (GT, 3–4).

The initial architecture of Polanyi's argument follows a logic that is parallel to Marx's analysis of the contradictions of capitalism. An initial tendency—the effort to create a self-regulating economy—produces a countertendency—an effort to protect society from the market. But impairing the market's ability to regulate itself produces growing crises and ultimately the collapse of nineteenth-century civilization. In this initial formulation, Polanyi does not introduce the concept of embeddedness. It only appears later, when he contrasts the project of market liberalism with the history of previous social orders in which economic activity had been embedded in social relations. He argues specifically that: " . . . all economic systems known to us up to the end of feudalism in Western Europe were organized either on the principles of reciprocity or redistribution, or householding, or some combination of the three" (GT, 57). He goes on to say: "In this framework, the orderly production and distribution of goods was secured through a great variety of individual motives disciplined by general principles of behavior. Among these motives gain was not prominent. Custom and law, magic and religion co-operated in inducing the individual to comply with rules of behavior which, eventually, ensured his functioning in the economic system" (GT, 57).

With this initial formulation, the task of constructing a market society appears to be one of disembedding the economy because the pursuit of individual gain is suddenly elevated to be the fundamental organizing principle of economic life. But as Polanyi starts to elaborate his argument, he gives the concept of embeddedness a new and unanticipated meaning. Because land, labor, and money are not true commodities, a protective countermovement spontaneously arises to "protect society from the market." And the result of these initiatives is a series of measures that shape and reshape how markets operate.

In Part II of GT, titled "Self-Protection of Society," Polanyi elaborates a thick description of the diversity of means by which "protection" restructures economic life in ways that limit and constrain the pursuit of gain. His intent here is to introduce the idea that protection impairs market self-regulation, so as to put in motion the contradictions that produce both World War I and the Great Depression. But what actually happens in these chapters is that Polanyi demonstrates persuasively that, throughout the whole history of market society, the strength of protection effectively embeds the economy. He suggests that functioning market societies *must* maintain some threshold level of embeddedness or else risk social and economic disaster. Polanyi shows that those advocating protection were not only the opponents of market society; they included its strongest adherents. In tracing out English history he states: "Thus even those who wished most ardently to free the state from all unnecessary duties, and whose whole philosophy demand the restriction of state activities, could not but entrust the self-same state with the new powers, organs, and instruments required for the establishment of laissez-faire" (GT, 147). A few pages later, he writes: "It is highly significant that . . . consistent liberals from Lloyd George and Theodore Roosevelt to Thurman Arnold and Walter Lippman subordinated laissez-faire to the demand for a free competitive market; they pressed for regulation and restrictions, for penal laws and compulsion, arguing as any 'collectivist' would that the freedom of contract was being 'abused' by trade unions, or corporations, whichever it was"(GT, 155).

In short, competitive markets require ongoing state action. Part of what Polanyi is describing here elicits Durkheim's noncontractual bases of contract, the set of legal rules and institutions required to formalize property rights and contractual obligations (Durkheim 1964 [1893], 242). But Polanyi's argument goes well beyond this because he also shows how establishing labor, land, and money as fictitious commodities required new institutional structures. For labor, state initiatives to embed the economy included the administrative apparatus of the New Poor Law; Factory Acts that limited the exploitation of labor; an infrastructure of public health designed to protect the population from disease; and the development of an educational system to provide needed skills. For land, the minimum conditions that Polanyi emphasizes includes assuring a stable food supply at reasonable prices that, in turn, involved protecting the farming population from dramatic income fluctuations that might drive them off the land. With money, much of the infrastructure of embeddedness did not emerge until the last quarter of the nineteenth century with the rise of central banks that stabilized the banking system and smoothed the growth of the money supply. These ongoing efforts to embed the market were often met with resistance and by the opposing pressures of the movement for laissez-faire. Polanyi sees market society as being shaped continuously by this double movement. And although he emphasizes the irrationality and danger of the initiatives by market liberals, he also understands the extraordinary intensity with which they are capable of pursuing their agenda in certain historical periods. In fact, one of his important political arguments is that the resurgent market liberalism of the 1920s bears ultimate responsibility for the rise of fascism. Writing of the 1920s, he argues: "The stubbornness with which economic liberals, for a critical decade, had, in the service of deflationary policies, supported authoritarian interventionism, merely resulted in a decisive weakening of the democratic forces which might otherwise have averted the fascist catastrophe" (GT, 242).

With respect to the inconsistencies in Polanyi's concept of embeddedness, we believe that it is in the chapters on the multiple forms of protection that Polanyi first discovers the concept of the always-embedded economy—that market societies must construct elaborate rules and institutional structures to limit the individual pursuit of gain or risk degenerating into a Hobbesian war of all against all. In order to have the benefits of increased efficiency that are supposed to flow from market competition, these societies must first limit the pursuit of gain by assuring that not everything is for sale to the highest bidder. They must also act to channel the energies of those economic actors motivated largely by gain into a narrow range of legitimate activities. In sum, the economy has to be embedded in law, politics, and morality.[18]

And yet, Polanyi is not able explicitly to give a name to his critical discovery; he returns instead to the original architecture of his argument in which this embedding of the market economy impairs the process of market self-regulation. But even by the logic of his own argument, there can never be a self-regulating market system, so the idea of impairing its functioning is illogical. It is similar to saying that one's efforts to capture a unicorn were impaired by the noisiness of those who came along on the expedition. Here one can clearly see the tension between the two arguments in Polanyi's text. On the one side, the embedding of the market economy is normal and necessary for it to achieve any degree of functionality. On the other side is the argument that the protective countermovement critically weakens the ability of market self-regulation to function so as to produce crises of growing intensity. As we suggested earlier, Polanyi does reconcile the normality of embeddedness with the breakdown of the world economy when he emphasizes the incompatibility of the gold standard with the inevitable and necessary national initiatives to embed economies within protective frameworks. Within the architecture of the book, however, this argument is subordinated to the idea that the protective countermovement impairs the functioning of market self-regulation.

In summary, we are suggesting that although in the course of writing GT, Polanyi discovers the idea of the always-embedded market economy, he does not yet name his discovery. He provides us with some extremely important suggestions about how to carry out an analysis of the always-embedded market economy, but he does not give us that systematic account. However, Polanyi lived for another two decades after sending GT to the publisher; the obvious question is why he did not give his new discovery a more systematic formulation in his later work.

Part of the answer has to do with the intensification of the Cold War in the immediate years after World War II. Many of Polanyi's hopes for the postwar world were dashed by the intensifying conflict between the Soviet Union and the U.S. His 1947 essay, "Our Obsolete Market Mentality," was one of his last public efforts in this period to influence the flow of events as he realized that his views were increasingly marginal and irrelevant.[19] Polanyi responded to the intolerant turn in American politics and academic life by shifting his intellectual energies toward the analysis of primitive and archaic economies rather than deepening his arguments about market economies. Another possible answer is that Polanyi's briefly glimpsed vision of the always-embedded market economy was linked to the specific historical moment formed by both the real political and social achievements of Roosevelt's New Deal, as well as the anticipated social legislation of England's Labour Government. During that brief moment, it appeared that market societies could be fundamentally reshaped by deeply democratic reforms. The historical possibilities were not obviously limited by the existing property arrangements. But with the intensification of the Cold War, that historical moment passed. In that highly polarized context, the idea of the always-embedded market economy appeared superfluous.

Conclusion

In his theory of the always-embedded market economy Polanyi has made one of social science's most significant contributions.[20] Indeed, that he left it underdeveloped also makes it one of the most promising, as economic sociologists and other scholars continue to elaborate and develop the critical concept. We have stressed here in particular the degree to which the idea should make it hard to gloss over or hide the state's fundamental role in shaping actually existing economies. Because the state establishes the noncontractual bases of contract and is centrally involved in constructing the markets for the fictitious commodities of land, labor, and money, it becomes impossible to imagine how the economy would run without its "unnecessary meddling." Moreover, Polanyi also lays the basis for understanding that tax policies, technology policies, competition policies, and trade policies are not incidentals, but fundamental to structuring how different market societies operate.

We also emphasize that the always-embedded concept has a critical cultural or ideational element, which in Chapter 6 we dub *ideational embeddedness*. As Polanyi makes clear, human beings are not born with Adam Smith's propensity to barter and trade. On the contrary, economic actors have to be constructed; people have to learn how to behave in particular market situations (Callon 1998).

Part of what Polanyi was trying to explain in GT was how the ideas of market liberalism had sunk such deep roots into England, and by extension, the U.S. At the same time, he stressed that the ideas of the classical economists had played a far less central role in the construction of market societies on the European continent. The same can also be said for the building of market societies in East Asia (Wade 1990; Gao 1997). Although there have been intense efforts in recent years to export the Anglo-American ways of thinking about the economy to every corner of the world, it would be a mistake to imagine that these missionaries of economic orthodoxy will be uniformly successful in their efforts. It is far more likely that we will see complex forms of syncretism that combine older and newer beliefs.

Finally, the concept of the always-embedded economy suggests that there are no inherent obstacles to restructuring market societies along more democratic and egalitarian lines. After all, if it is not "nature" but political discourses and institutions that drive our markets, then it is those very same political dynamics that are ultimately vulnerable to the power of democratic and egalitarian forces. The multiple ways that business depends on state action provides a critical resource or lever for seeking political change. Even those business interests that profess to believe in the most extreme forms of laissez-faire doctrine need the cooperation of the state, and this often disguised dependence can be employed to renegotiate the legal underpinnings of market society.

It would, nonetheless, go against the spirit of Polanyi to think that gaining significant democratic or egalitarian reforms is ever easy; business interests and their conservative allies have formidable resources with which to resist such changes. Polanyi reminds us, however, just how contingent these resources are; they are not built into the essence of the social system. Hence, although the rules of the international monetary regime, as with the nineteenth-century gold standard, often serve to reinforce the power of business interests, these rules can also be changed (as they were during the Bretton Woods era) to make resistance, at least within developed countries, to egalitarian reforms more difficult.

Similarly, prevailing common sense about the economy tends to reinforce the power of business, but public ideas can be changed as they were during the 1930s and, in some countries, during the 1960s. It is thus possible to make systematic use of Polanyi's insights in GT once we have "unpacked" the text and shown the tensions between Polanyi's original architecture for the book and the new ideas that he developed as he was writing. Most importantly, we can see that Polanyi glimpsed, but was not able to name or elaborate, the idea of the always-embedded market economy. It is this concept that promises new and deeper understandings of market societies, their crises, and their human consequences in the early twenty-first century.

4

TURNING THE TABLES

Polanyi's Critique of Free Market Utopianism

In *The Rhetoric of Reaction,* Albert Hirschman (1991), identifies three distinct "rhetorics" that conservatives have used to discredit reform movements since the French Revolution. Chapter 6 of this volume is devoted to the "rhetoric of perversity"—the claim that a reform will have exactly the opposite of its intended effects and will hurt the intended beneficiaries. The second, "the rhetoric of jeopardy" is exemplified by Friedrich Hayek's *The Road to Serfdom* (2007 [1944]). It is the claim that a reform will erode the freedoms we depend on. Hirschman's third is the "rhetoric of futility"—the insistence that a reform is literally impossible because it goes against everything that we know is natural about human beings and social arrangements. This is the ploy that Malthus used in his *Essay on the Principle of Population* (1985 [1798]) to challenge the egalitarian ideas of William Godwin. Malthus professed to admire the beauty of Godwin's vision, but he ultimately dismissed the vision as impossible. It was futile because Malthus declared it to be against the laws of nature—in other words, utopian.

The rhetoric of futility is the main weapon that conservative intellectuals have wielded against socialists and communists for more than two centuries. They contend that an egalitarian social order would destroy any incentives for effort and creativity, which makes it utterly inconsistent with human nature. But while these arguments are open to debate, there is one aspect of the right's critique that has proven compelling. This is the claim put forward by Marx and Engels and other theorists of the left that ending the class power of the bourgeoisie would also bring an end to political conflicts and the exercise of political power. As Sheldon Wolin (1960) and others have noted, a deep hostility to politics led socialist thinkers to imagine mistakenly that it was possible to escape the necessity of governmental and political power.

One neglected aspect of Karl Polanyi's thought is his showing the parallels between market liberalism and Marxism with respect to their utopian views of state power. They both disdain it and imagine that it is possible to escape from governance and political constraint, and they both prioritize the economy as the central organizing force in society. To be sure, they differ in their normative evaluation of the economy. Economic liberalism celebrates the absolute freedom of unfettered markets as the means to transform politics into a purely technical exercise of maintaining optimal market conditions. Marxism, of course, associates the capitalist economy not with freedom for all but with unfreedom for most, even while it upholds the redemptive powers of a stateless socialist economy.

There is certainly nothing novel about arguments that Marxism is utopian. Where Polanyi is utterly original is in his startling claim that the self-regulating market—the central precept of free-market doctrine—is a utopian idea. A self-regulating market, according to Polanyi, has never and will never exist, making its prescriptive demands for market governance wholly futile. Years before Hirschman's typology of conservative rhetorics, Polanyi mobilized the rhetoric of futility against free-market thinking.

A strong indication of the prescience of Polanyi's rhetorical move was that Friedrich Hayek—arguably the thinker most central to the revival of free-market ideas in the twentieth century—openly embraced utopianism just a few years after the publication of *The Great Transformation* (hereafter GT). In a 1949 University of Chicago Law Review essay entitled "The Intellectuals and Socialism," Hayek proposed his own sociology of knowledge to explain why so many intellectuals had come to embrace socialism. His argument is that, notwithstanding the impracticality of socialism: " . . . theirs has become the only explicit general philosophy of social policy held by a large group, the only system or theory which raises new problems and opens new horizons, that they have succeeded in inspiring the imagination of the intellectuals." Moreover, according to Hayek, the socialists have been able to drive political debate continually to the left by contrasting the status quo to the ideal world of the socialist utopia.

Hayek asserts of his fellow market liberals, "What we lack is a liberal Utopia, a program which seems neither a mere defense of things as they are nor a diluted kind of socialism, but a truly liberal radicalism which does not spare the susceptibilities of the mighty (including the trade unions), which is not too severely practical, and which does not confine itself to what appears today as politically possible." He goes on to say: "The main lesson which the true [market] liberal must learn from the success of the socialists is that it was their courage to be Utopian which gained them the support of the intellectuals and therefore an influence on public opinion which is daily making possible what only recently seemed utterly remote" (Hayek 1949, 432–433.) So, in fact, Hayek and his colleagues proceeded through the 1950s, 1960s, and 1970s to follow this counsel and repackage market liberalism as a utopia. Rather than proposing mild and incremental reforms, they called for radical new measures to overturn what they saw as the drift towards socialism. And just as the socialist utopia had been grounded in a deep moral commitment to equality, the market liberals rooted their utopia in constant appeals to expanding personal liberty. And lo and behold, Hayek was vindicated; free-market ideas made deep inroads among Western intellectuals.[1]

The Elements of Utopia

Ever since Thomas More first coined the term, utopian thinking has been linked with the unrealistic starry-eyed idealism of radical and socialist philosophers who, against all evidence, insist on the achievability of what the Oxford English Dictionary (OED) defines as "an impossibly ideal scheme . . . a place, state, or condition ideally perfect in respect of politics, laws, customs, and conditions." In light of the association between utopia and anti-capitalist movements, how does Polanyi justify attributing an unattainable perfectionism to classical and neoclassical economics? Economics is the discipline, after all, that consistently played a major role in defeating even the tamest of progressive reforms, using its self-confident claims to scientific foundations to accuse movements for social justice of utopianism.

To make his intellectual turnabout even more paradoxical, Polanyi makes Robert Owen the hero of GT. Robert Owen was the early nineteenth-century English industrialist turned philanthropist, socialist philosopher, and architect of the first cooperative industrial village (New Lanark, Scotland). He has long been held up as the poster child for nineteenth-century utopianism. Yet Polanyi insists that it is Owen who is the realist, for it is he who recognized that it is both necessary and right for government to intervene in the economy. By contrast, Malthus and Ricardo, Polanyi insists, are the true utopians, notwithstanding the fact that Thomas Carlyle labeled their political economy as the "dismal science" because of its gloomy predictions about future wage levels and the disasters that would inevitably be wrought by overpopulation. A century of political economy's disciplinary development changed little, in Polanyi's estimation. He applied the same label of utopianism to von Mises and Hayek as he had to Malthus and Ricardo rather than the communists and socialists that they vilified in Vienna.

To get a deeper understanding of Polanyi's meaning and motivation here, we turn to the passage that follows right after he first labels the self-regulating market as a "stark Utopia": " . . . such an institution [a self-regulating market] could not exist for any length of time without annihilating the human and natural substance of society; it would have physically destroyed man and transformed his surroundings into a wilderness" (GT, 3). Polanyi is insistent that the free market utopia is not a harmless fantasy; he is blunt and graphic in characterizing its consequences as producing a *dystopia*—"a society characterized by human misery, as squalor, oppression, disease, and overcrowding."[2]

To understand why and how Polanyi predicts this inevitable slide from utopia to dystopia, it is useful to return to and deconstruct the OED's characterization of utopianism as an "impossibly ideal scheme for the amelioration or perfection of social conditions." Parsing this carefully, we can divide its conception of utopia into three distinct parts—it is an "ideal" of social "perfection," it is a "scheme" to achieve amelioration or perfection, and it is a tragic "impossibility."

The Utopian Ideal

Free-market doctrine is an ideology founded on three assumptions—that power resides exclusively in the state, that political power is a chronic threat to freedom and commerce, and that the economic sphere does not entail the exercise of power. It is the dream of eliminating the need for political power or government that makes these assumptions utopian. It is a dream in which governance and social order are left exclusively to the putatively noncoercive workings of the self-regulating market (Hirschman 1977). Indeed, it is the absence of political power that they see as the precondition for individual liberties, societal prosperity, and the freest of all possible worlds.

Polanyi rejects these assumptions and the normative ideal of a world without power. For him, no society is possible without political power and constraint (GT, 266). He shows historically how government policies and the explicit use of compulsion are necessary to construct and maintain markets. But he pushes this analysis to a more profound philosophical level by asking why anybody would think it desirable in the first place to minimize the role of the state while maximizing reliance on market self-regulation. His explanation centers on "social naturalism," a foundational tenet of classical political economy and modern market fundamentalism (see Chapter 6). Social naturalism is a way of viewing the world built on the assumption that the laws governing natural phenomena also govern human society. Social naturalism can be distinguished from naturalism—the methodological postulate that, because nature and society exhibit the same kinds of regularities, there should be a unified method applicable to both. *Social* naturalism, by contrast, insists that society is governed by those natural laws rather than by institutional rules and social rationalities. For social naturalism, society is not "like" the natural world; the social and natural worlds are one and the same and are subject to the same laws and exigencies. Social naturalism conceptually subordinates society to nature, and society is seen as regulated by natural laws in the same way as falling objects and the evolution of species.

Social naturalism realigns the traditional Enlightenment view of human rationality. It blurs the line between humans and animals by first and foremost defining people first and foremost as animals motivated by the biological instincts to eat and reproduce. Against the rationalist belief that political intervention can alleviate social problems, social naturalism makes scarcity, poverty, distress, and famine inexorable. For Malthus, nature necessitates an endless struggle for scarce resources, but when nature is left to its own devices, it creates a perfect balance of supply and demand. When humans finally abandon the folly and futility of trying to impose their own will over nature, they will find that while not always benign, nature is always a wise governor. "Man" cannot reason with nature because it is nature's utter indifference to reason that distinguishes it from humanity.

The roots of social naturalism can be traced to Joseph Townsend's apocryphal fable about the struggle for survival between goats and dogs on a Pacific island—two originally sparring species that eventually learned to live in harmony only because there was no political interference with the natural condition of scarcity. Polanyi captures the link between social naturalism and government policy in memorable prose: "Hobbes had argued the need for a despot because men were *like* beasts; Townsend insisted that they were *actually* beasts and that, precisely for that reason . . . [n]o government was needed to maintain this balance; it was restored by the pangs of hunger on the one hand, the scarcity of food on the other" (GT, 119).

Since the human poor are biologically indistinguishable from the goats and the dogs, and thus subject to the same laws of nature, their survival should likewise be left to the wisdom of nature without the Poor Law's artificial removal of natural scarcity. Society, as fundamentally biological, is a self-regulating system that when untouched by political intervention will tend toward equilibrium and order: "Essentially, economic society was founded on the grim realities of Nature; if man disobeyed the laws which ruled that society, the fell executioner would strangle the offspring of the improvident. The laws of a competitive society were put under the sanction of the jungle" (GT, 131).

While talk of social naturalism may sound alien to our contemporary political discourse, it is an essential part of free market utopianism. Without social naturalism, there could be no rhetoric about a self-adjusting market regulated by its own natural laws, and about market societies capable of self-governing without a meddlesome government. Social naturalism is also the foundation for the utopian belief in the self-regulating market's benign system of incentives that operate freely without the exercise of power. Social naturalism underlies the market-state binary with its privileging of the market and its precept rather than insistence that these must be separate and autonomous realms.

While Mirowski and Plehwe (2009) advance a different view than ours about the relation between the classical economists and twentieth-century market fundamentalists, they acknowledge that Hayek, Friedman, and their allies " . . . did agree that for purposes of public understanding and sloganeering, *market society must be treated as a 'natural' and inexorable state of humankind*" (435, emphasis in original). Hayek and Friedman evoke social naturalism because it is the source of one of the most powerful political weapons of market fundamentalism—the perversity thesis (Hirschman 1991). Founded on social naturalism, the perversity thesis holds that the "normal" or "natural" state of the market is an equilibrium of self-adjustment. The perversity thesis—or the "perverse-effects doctrine"—holds that any public policy aiming to change market outcomes, such as prices, wages, or inequality, automatically becomes a noxious interference with nature's equilibrating processes. Much stronger than talk of random "unintended effects," the perversity thesis makes perverse outcomes inescapable; the very measures intended for good inevitably will leave the world in a worse shape than prevailed before any "reform" had been instituted (Hirschman 1991). We revisit in Chapters 5 and 6 the battle over the English Poor Laws which were a precursor to struggles over modern welfare benefits waged through the rhetoric of perversity.

Malthus was only the first of a long line to successfully turn the perversity doctrine into a full-scale political campaign to remove or prohibit government-initiated regulations, reforms, and interventions. In the 1880s, Herbert Spencer amplified his attacks on an enlarged franchise with the claim that "uninstructed legislators have in past times continually increased human suffering in their endeavors to mitigate it" (Spencer 1940 [1881]). Von Mises reprised the doctrine by articulating the free-market opposition to unemployment benefits. He argued that if benefits provide livelihoods to the jobless, they will have an incentive not to seek employment but rather to comfortably adjust to a new found leisure (Dale 2008, 512). Finally, Milton Friedman perfected one of the most popular uses of the perversity thesis in his claim that setting a minimum wage induces unemployment and drives down all wages: "Minimum wage laws are about as clear a case as one can find of a measure the effects of which are precisely the opposite of those intended by the men of good will who support it" (Friedman 1962, 180). Friedman's more popular writings show that behind all of the modern bells and whistles of the Chicago School, their policy arguments rely on the same social naturalist-inspired perversity thesis that Malthus elaborated at the end of the eighteenth century.

At the level of ideology, free-market utopianism's promise of a society organized exclusively by the laws of nature eliminates altogether the need for political power to structure or govern human society. In reality, however, the elites who embraced political economy in Malthus's era had no intention of abandoning control over the populace. Their motivation was to eliminate only the protective social policies that interfered with the poor's full exposure to the labor market. With the exception of the socially protective role of the state, they freely used political power to reinforce the logic of markets. To obfuscate this selective anti-statism, free-market utopianism tells a story about how the market's natural mechanisms will not only make for economic prosperity, they will also take over the work too important to trust to government such as providing social order and protecting individual liberty, all without exerting power. After all, if the natural and the social world are organized by the same laws of nature, and these laws are always preferable to the potential tyranny of arbitrary political will, then not just the economic but also the governing functions of society would be better served by the market.

For Polanyi, the idea of a society free of power is an impossible deceit; it is based on the false claim that, in contrast to government, markets and economic relationships are free of the exercise of power. It is utopian not merely because of the idea that society did not need political power; rather it was in the conceit that the market, by contrast, is a site free of power. To characterize it as such plainly reveals free-market utopianism's bias in favor of a definite kind of power.

Utopianism as a Planned Project

Classical political economy staked its appeal not only on the fanciful utopianism of social naturalism's world without power. It also justified its defense of a laissez-faire economy by telling a story about how the historical development of the market economy in the nineteenth century was an entirely natural, spontaneous, and unplanned phenomenon: "Their [economic liberals] whole social philosophy hinges on the idea that laissez-faire was a natural development" (GT, 148). Whereas markets as places of barter and exchange had long existed as elements of all societies, Polanyi's well-known argument is that these were historically always embedded within and regulated by the larger system of social relations. Nineteenth-century political economy claimed that the transformation of these isolated local markets into one big, national market economy was the natural result of their innate tendencies to expand. This was seen as the inevitable result of the even more basic instinctive traits of human nature to barter and exchange.

Classical political economy insists that ever-expanding unregulated markets are the natural condition of society, and—were they left to flourish without interference—the prosperity brought on by self-regulating market economies would be a constant of history. However, a series of corruptions in the form of perverse political and legal interventions blocked this happy outcome. Examples include the efforts of the Tudor monarchy to slow down the enclosure movement and the milder but equally damaging laws restricting the movement of labor. History,

according to this view, entails an epic battle on the part of social natural-
ists to undo the "collectivist" perversions of political power that interfere with the otherwise spontaneous and natural working of markets.
The eventual arrival of laissez-faire and a market economy in the early
nineteenth century was not an act of politics or law; it was rather the
belated restoration of the natural.

The reality is that political economy was a grand and calculated
scheme for the state to actively remake contained and regulated markets into a coordinated self-regulating market society. The irony of
this particular utopian scheme is that it violates the very essence of the
social naturalist ideal. Not only were laissez-faire and the free market not natural but planned; they were, as we discussed earlier, implemented through political interventions: " . . . laissez-faire economy was
the product of deliberate State action" (GT, 147). Revealing the historical planning at the heart of the free-market utopia undermines both
its social naturalist self-representation and its mantle of spontaneity. It
also lays bare once again the hypocritical conceit at its core. The zealotry against the use of state power is selectively conceived and applied.
The self-regulating market abhorred and challenged state intervention
when it came to aiding the poor. For the government to alleviate poverty artificially is to use power in the abuse of nature. But there is no
hesitation whatsoever to use powerful instruments of government coercion to create a new legal regime that enforces the logic of markets.
Polanyi thus disposes of the fiction that market economies are natural.
The market fundamentalist world without power lives exclusively in
the utopian ideology of social naturalism.

Nor, moreover, was political power a onetime exercise in jump-starting
a market economy, only to give way to the natural workings of the
market once it is nicely humming away. The market was never and can
never actually be disembedded. Political power is a constitutive element
at the heart of any functioning market; it can no more be removed than
can the price mechanism. The question is never *whether* the economy
is politically embedded, rather it is what *kinds* of political interventions are used and to whose benefit do they operate. Polany argues that
despite the utopian ideal's anti-statist zealotry, the irony is that political
power is the necessary mechanism to maintain and creatively adjust the
institutional conditions that maintain the appearance of a free-market: "The introduction of free markets, far from doing away with the

need for control, regulation, and intervention, enormously increased their range. Thus even those who wished most ardently to free the state from all unnecessary duties, and whose whole philosophy demanded the restriction of state activities, could not but entrust the self-same state with the new powers, organs, and instruments required for the establishment of laissez-faire" (GT, 146–147).

While it is political power and legislative coercion that exercises the actual heft in this planning process, the ideational scheme is the force that drives that power. The market is not only politically always embedded; it is always *ideationally embedded* (as we argue in Chapter 6 below). Ideational embeddedness, helps us understand how major transformations are ideationally-driven. Put slightly differently, ideas have causal powers. Polanyi was far ahead of his time in recognizing, for example, the central role that the new ideas of social science played in the Industrial Revolution. "Social not technical invention was the intellectual mainspring of the Industrial Revolution. The decisive contribution of the natural sciences to engineering was not made until a full century later, when the Industrial Revolution was long over. . . . The triumphs of natural science had been theoretical in the true sense, and could not compare in practical importance with those of the social sciences of the day" (GT, 124).

Then, almost as if anticipating how today's academics would react, he remarks wryly: " . . . unbelievable though it may seem to our generation, the standing of natural science greatly gained by its connection with the humane sciences. The discovery of economics was an astounding revelation which hastened greatly the transformation of society and the establishment of a market system. . . . It was thus both just and appropriate than not the natural but the social sciences should rank as the intellectual parents of the mechanical revolution which subjected the powers of nature to man" (GT, 124–125.) Polanyi here is insisting that economic theories and social science models do not represent and generalize already existing economic entities but rather *makes* markets, economic practices, and indeed entire market societies. Today, there are new theoretical paradigms that follow Polanyi's path-breaking understanding of the causal powers of economic theories, especially the theory of "performativity" associated with the sociologists Michel Callon and Donald Mackenzie (Callon 1998; MacKenzie 2006; MacKenzie, Muniesa, and Su, eds. 2007).

Utopianism as Tragedy

Even if utopian dreams are ultimately unrealizable (if a society is to survive), Polanyi warns us that attempting to achieve the unachievable nonetheless produces dystopian consequences. The horrors of early industrialization included dark Satanic mills, children maimed and disfigured from sixteen- to eighteen-hour workdays, and the squalor and filth of early industrial cities. For instance, the misguided dream of economic liberals to restore the gold standard after World War I produced a global depression that generated fascism and a second world war. And the last thirty years of market fundamentalism has now produced another dystopian global calamity—a nearly catastrophic financial collapse and a global recession that has thrown millions out of work, and increased hunger and misery in every corner of the globe. But how does Polanyi connect these social tragedies to the utopian project? His answer is not simply that the "best laid plans" will always have unexpected and unintended consequences. It is a more specific argument that the particular utopian ideal of a self-regulating market society creates a dystopian nightmare. The key link is his conception of "fictitious commodities."

Polanyi argues that to create a self-regulating market economy, labor, land, and money must all be subjected to market mechanisms. He calls these the nucleus of a culture "formed by human beings, their natural surroundings, and productive organizations" (GT, 170). Labor and land are "no other than the human beings themselves of which every society consists and the natural surroundings in which it exists." Since commodities are things that are produced to be bought and sold on the market, none of these three vital social entities are true commodities. To include these fictitious commodities in the market mechanism means to subordinate the substance of society itself to the laws of the market. Polanyi argues that this theoretical sleight of hand places human society at risk as it threatens to annihilate the human relationships on which society rests.

Polanyi identifies the noncontractual foundations of contract as necessary for both markets and for human communities to thrive. This is because the humans who are expected to participate in markets are incapable of performing any labor without a life-enhancing social environment and access to social and public goods such as clean air and water, safe working conditions, education, and medical care. In its rush to transform labor into a true commodity, however, market fundamentalism systematically undermines these noncontractual foundations on which human society depends. The tragedy of this is most obvious in the case of turning human beings into labor, which Polanyi says is "only another name for a human activity which goes with life itself" (GT, 75).

In the early years of England's Industrial Revolution, men, women, and children were for the first time treated as commodities subject only to buying and selling on markets. To become commodities, they had to be subjected to the "free labor contract," which required they be ripped away from their prior attachments to families, cultures, and communities. In discussing the process of early marketization in England, Polanyi writes: "[Marketization] was best served by the application of the principle of freedom of contract. In practice this meant that the noncontractual organizations of kinship, neighborhood, profession, and creed were to be liquidated since they claimed the allegiance of the individual and thus restricted his freedom. To represent this principle as one of noninterference, as economic liberals are wont to do, was merely the expression of an ingrained prejudice in favor of a *definite kind* of interference, namely, such as would destroy noncontractual relations between individuals and prevent their spontaneous reformation" (GT, 171).

When rural industry in southern England collapsed in the eighteenth century, thousands of displaced workers were expected to simply relocate to another village, another city, another region, or even another continent to find work. Some economists argue that mass displacement brought with it higher wages, thus making it uniformly advantageous for the working class. Polanyi responds to this dubious claim by illustrating in grim detail that social livelihoods cannot be reduced to material quantification. The Industrial Revolution was a cultural catastrophe that stripped people of the social and cultural supports on which they relied: "The human degradation of the laboring classes under early capitalism was the result of a social catastrophe not measurable in economic terms" (GT, 302). Indeed, he frequently makes the analogy between this early English cultural catastrophe and the devastating consequences on indigenous communities during the European colonization of Africa and Asia: "The catastrophe of the native community is a direct result of the rapid and violent disruption of the basic institutions of the victim (whether force is used in the process or not does not seem altogether relevant). These institutions are disrupted by the very fact that a market economy is forced upon an entirely differently organized community;

labor and land are made into commodities, which, again, is only a short formula for the liquidation of every and any cultural institution in an organic society" (GT, 167).

But even under less extreme circumstances, treating labor as a pure commodity has tragic consequences. It strips people of protection from the periodic bouts of unemployment that are an inevitable consequence of the down phase of the business cycle. It leaves people hungry and unable to feed their families while they wait for employers to once again be interested in their services. And workers who are disabled or ill are simply discarded like any other defective commodity.

Over the last thirty years of market fundamentalism in the United States, the same undermining of noncontractualized social life has occurred. Under the influence of Milton Friedman, a conscious policy of tax cutting has been a principle method of attack (Block 2009). This strategy has been given a name—"starving the beast." It is so dubbed because, as tax cuts inexorably increase government deficits, campaigns are suddenly mobilized to balance budgets by waging ideological combat against "excess spending." But once again, note the selectivity of the anti-statism: the label of excess spending is applied only to social expenditures that support working and middle class people. In the U.S., where the individual states provide many of the critically important protections and public goods, this strategy has proved devastatingly effective. Even after the election of Barack Obama indicated a shift in national mood, state governments—constitutionally required to balance budgets—have engaged in round after round of intense budgetary austerity (Somers 2008, 93–95).

From a Polanyian perspective, the tragic consequences of financial commodification were also predictable. Although it was the financial elite and their political accomplices that pushed the economy over the cliff, the Great Recession took its worst toll on the poor, the middle, and the working classes as unemployment soared. Among the rich Western countries, U.S. residents bear especially painful consequences, as state governments one after the other have eliminated or drastically reduced what little is left of the nation's social safety net. Europeans, we are reminded, do not lose their health care when they lose their jobs: "[Americans] find themselves with essentially no support once their trivial unemployment check has fallen off. We [Americans] have nothing underneath. When Americans lose their jobs, they fall into the abyss. That does not happen in other advanced countries, it does not happen, I want to say, in civilized countries" (Krugman 2009a).

This is free-market utopianism's tragic denouement. When social institutions and public goods are defunded by governments, health, education, and personal safety become accessible only to those who can pay. The result is the "liquidation" of a community's noncontractual foundations. The poor and minorities have long been subject to this kind of strategic defunding of social support. Somers (2008, ch.2) recounts the example of New Orleans in the aftermath of Hurricane Katrina, a recent tragic demonstration of this process. She conceptualizes this development as the *contractualization of citizenship*. Citizenship represents a bundle of rights and obligations, especially the rights to those noncontractual supports necessary for full and equal social inclusion in civil society (Marshall 1964 [1950]). These rights are the legal glue that binds civil society's noncontractual foundations to its people. They are the necessary elements for the essential freedoms and "capabilities" (Sen 1999) that people require to live as equal members of society. For all but the wealthy, government-provided rights to protection against illness, for access to education and literacy, for freedom from hunger and want are the only hope for any semblance of true equality. When these rights are contractualized, they become subject to the rules of *quid pro quo* market exchange, rules that demand something of equivalent value to be exchanged for full citizenship rights. They are thus no longer rights but conditional privileges only available to those who have something to exchange that the market deems of equivalent value, usually money or labor (Somers 2008, ch.2).

Hurricane Katrina shows us what happens to those who have nothing of sufficient market value to exchange for what are no longer rights but now privileges. The indifferent response to the social catastrophe of government at all levels shows what happens to those communities that lack the kind of resources that qualify as worthy of contractual exchange. Quite simply, when rights to public goods dissolve, so too do the rights to inclusion. People are literally cut loose from membership in the broader civil society. Once excluded, they no longer are granted the recognition by others as moral equals; they become superfluous and disposable. As we watched the tragedy of Hurricane Katrina unfold over the course of days, weeks, now years, the status of the largely African-American impoverished population of New Orleans as a superfluous and disposable people was painfully and shamefully exhibited (Adams 2013). No social tableau has better publicized the tragic consequences of commodifying human beings and contractualizing their noncontractual relationship—especially that between government and the people.

Hurricane Katrina shows us *in extremis* what thirty years of free-market utopianism looks like; once having been witnessed, no one can claim ignorance of its inexorably tragic endings (Somers 2008, ch.2).

Polanyi was equally visionary with respect to the second of his fictitious commodities, as he anticipated the dangers that exist with the full commodification of land and nature. For nature to be commodified into property, human habitats must be carved up into parcels; if there are profits to be earned, some of these parcels will be subjected to suffering the most extreme environmental degradation. When agriculture ceases to be a way of life and becomes simply a profit-making activity, entire populations will find themselves at risk of starvation because market signals mean that land will be exploited for raising industrial raw materials rather than food. Today, the scale at which nature is being commodified has expanded to such a degree that planetary annihilation through radical climate change seems almost inevitable.

Finally, Polanyi's designation of money as the third fictitious commodity helps us to make sense of the financial market meltdown of 2007–2008. When the production of money and credit is left entirely to the banking system, it is practically guaranteed that banks and other financial institutions will recklessly multiply the supply of credit in search of higher and higher profits, putting the economy at risk of a devastating crash when investors suddenly lose confidence. This is what drove the severe boom and bust cycles of nineteenth-century market societies and ultimately led to strong central banks and regulations designed to place limits on the ability of financial intermediaries to carry out unsustainable expansions of the supply of credit.

During the current reign of market fundamentalism in the United States, most of these restraints on the ability of financial intermediaries to expand the supply of credit have been systematically dismantled. Seeing the possibility of previously unimaginable profits, financial actors used the efficient markets hypothesis to create a finance-knows-best regulatory climate. This included the dramatic expansion of new financial intermediaries, including hedge funds and private equity funds, largely exempted from any regulatory oversight. Under the eighteen-year reign of Alan Greenspan at the Federal Reserve, the government systematically relaxed the rules that allowed the largest financial institutions to hold substantial liabilities in "off balance sheet entities" and to expand exponentially their ratio of debts to assets. The predictable consequence was that when the inevitable rush to safety by investors finally came, virtually the entire financial system faced insolvency. Only government lending at a previously unimagined level averted a complete financial collapse (Skidelsky 2009; Wessel 2009).

In sum, free-market utopianism's effort to govern society by the laws of supply and demand inevitably subverts necessary forms of social protection and embeddedness. Precisely for this reason, in the course of the nineteenth century, institutions emerged to protect society from the dangers of treating nature, labor, and money as if they were actually true commodities. Critics of free-market utopianism understood that government is the only institution capable of regulating the supply and demand of these fictitious commodities. Policies were set in place that allowed governments to manage shifting demands for employees by providing relief in periods of unemployment, by educating and training future workers, and by influencing migration flows.[3] With respect to land and our natural environment, governments maintained continuity of food production by insulating farmers from the pressures of fluctuating harvests and volatile prices, and they regulated land use to avert environmental destruction. And the rise of central banking was a deliberate effort to manage the supply of money and credit to moderate the cycles of boom and bust.

In the late twentieth century, free-market utopianism undermined the government's ability to manage and protect labor, land, and money. By playing off the deep fears of government-induced unfreedom, it has once again blinded us to the freedoms and human capabilities that only government can ensure. As we discuss in Chapter 8, recognizing what Polanyi calls *the reality of society* is our hope for societal repair.

5

IN THE SHADOW OF SPEENHAMLAND

Social Policy and the Old Poor Law

Karl Polanyi devoted two chapters (6 and 7) of *The Great Transformation* (hereafter GT) to an analysis of the Speenhamland Act—a reference to late eighteenth-century English history that is often puzzling for readers. Yet for two full centuries the Speenhamland story has had a very real impact on social policy debates in England and the United States. Moreover, over the last half century, even Polanyi's interpretation of Speenhamland has had a surprising impact on policy debates. One striking incidence of this influence occurred during the Nixon Administration, when Daniel Patrick Moynihan developed his Family Assistance Plan. As Moynihan recalled:

> In mid-April Martin Anderson, of [Arthur] Burns's staff, prepared "A Short History of a 'Family Security System'" in the form of excerpts on the history of the Speenhamland system, the late eighteenth-century British scheme of poor relief taken from Karl Polanyi's *The Great Transformation* (Moynihan 1973, 179).

The gist of Anderson's memo was that in that earlier historical case, the intended floor under the income of poor families actually operated as a ceiling on earned income, with the consequence that the poor were further impoverished and even discouraged from seeking further work. Anderson worried that Moynihan's income floor might inadvertently produce the same unintended consequence. Anderson's memo was sufficiently powerful that Nixon asked Moynihan to investigate the accuracy of Polanyi's historical analysis. Moynihan's staffers were sent scurrying off to investigate the views of contemporary historians on this question. The Family Assistance Plan was ultimately defeated in the U.S. Senate but only after Richard Nixon had a conversation about the work of Karl Polanyi (Moynihan 1973, 179–180.)

Canada had a similar episode more recently. In December 2000, newly reelected Prime Minister Jean Chretien floated as a trial balloon the idea of a comprehensive anti-poverty program based on a guaranteed annual income for all Canadians. A flurry of press reports followed, including an article in the *National Post* that explicitly referred to the Speenhamland enactment of a guaranteed income scheme in 1795. The article insisted that in this earlier episode, employers had paid below-subsistence wages, and some workers chose the collection of benefits over work: "The first enactment of a guaranteed annual income may have been in 1795 in England, where the Speenhamland system extended subsidies for the infirm to include able-bodied workers. . . . The system revealed the challenge inherent in designing such a policy; the supplement served as a subsidy that allowed employers to hire workers at below-subsistence wages, and allowed landlords to raise rents. Meanwhile, some workers found themselves better off collecting benefits than working" (Chwial-kowska 2000). In both of these cases, the Speenhamland story in which an income floor was inadvertently transformed into an income ceiling served as a chilling cautionary tale against governmental initiatives to establish a guaranteed annual income.

The same argument has been repeated by progressive thinkers in recent debates over the desirability of establishing a universal basic income for all citizens (Van Parijs 1992; Cohen and Rogers, eds. 2001). Analysts who favor using state action to improve the situation of the poor question whether a well-intentioned minimum income would follow the Speenhamland precedent and become a maximum income (Bluestone and Ghilarducci 1996; Howell 1997; Clement 1997). They fear that employers would use the increased income received by the poor as an excuse to lower the wages that they pay these employees. The appearance of this argument would be reason enough to revisit the actual history of Speenhamland. But there is a second and more powerful justification for focusing on this historical episode.

Conservative critics of welfare in the United States in the period from 1978 to 1996 formulated their criticisms of the main federal welfare program—Aid to Families with Dependent Children (AFDC)—in precisely the same terms that English critics of Speenhamland had used in the first decades of the nineteenth century. The parallels in these arguments have been recognized by Albert Hirschman (1991) in his analysis of perversity as one of the three "rhetorics of reaction." The core of the perversity thesis is that well-intentioned policies that provide assistance to the poor by means of state intervention will inevitably harm the recipients by substituting perverse incentives in place of market mechanisms that teach the poor to work hard and exercise sexual restraint (Persky 1997; Reekie 1998; see also Chapter 6).

A number of these conservative critics of AFDC were completely self-conscious about the parallels between Speenhamland and AFDC. The same Martin Anderson who wrote the memo in the Nixon White House published *Welfare* (1978), which was one of the first conservative scholarly attacks on AFDC. Anderson quoted Polanyi's account of Speenhamland at length to argue against both income guarantees and programs like AFDC. In 1984, the neoconservative historian Gertrude Himmelfarb published her influential study *The Idea of Poverty*, in which she carefully recounted the criticisms of the Speenhamland system advanced by Malthus, Burke, de Tocqueville, and others. Later on, she published a series of articles and books (Himmelfarb 1994, 1995) that explicitly drew the parallels between the dire consequences of the English welfare system in the Speenhamland period and the negative consequences of AFDC. Marvin Olasky, a policy intellectual who George W. Bush credited as the theorist of "compassionate conservatism," published an influential book called *The Tragedy of American Compassion* (1992), whose title encapsulated his restatement of early nineteenth-century critiques of Poor Law assistance. As we show in Chapter 6, these self-conscious efforts to mobilize the perversity rhetoric against AFDC had an appreciable effect on both elite and public opinion and contributed to the passage in 1996 of the *Personal Responsibility and Work Opportunities Reconciliation Act* (PRWORA) that ended the long-standing entitlement of poor families to assistance—so much so that it is fair to say that our recent welfare legislation was passed in the shadow of Speenhamland (Weaver 2000).

It is common for social scientists to complain that public policy is made with insufficient attention to history and social theory. In this chapter, however, our argument is that for both discussions of guaranteed incomes and welfare policy, a particular and tendentious reading of social history has been given far too much weight by policy makers and policy intellectuals. This is particularly true in the case of the Speen-hamland story because, over the past fifty years, economic and social historians have produced a large and impressive literature that has rean-alyzed the English Poor Law in general and the Speenhamland period in particular (Blaug 1963, 1964; Baugh 1975; Marshall 1985; Snell 1985; Huzel 1989; Boyer 1990; Sokoll 1993; Lees 1998; King 2000). Yet most of this literature is unknown to social scientists, and its findings about the Poor Law have had little impact on social policy debates.

In this chapter, we propose to rethink and retell the story of Speen-hamland. This means, fundamentally, showing how the findings of recent studies in social and economic history undermine the Speenham-land narratives that have been deployed in social policy debates. But this involves more than simply reporting other scholars' results; we are offering our own analyses of some of the important remaining puzzles in this literature. Our findings and analysis should also have bearing on the history of social theory. While we are critical of Karl Polanyi's history of the Speenhamland episode, we are in fundamental agreement with his insistence that classical political economy was deeply shaped by the effort to explain the persistence of poverty in the Speenhamland epoch (GT, ch.10; Procacci 1991). Specifically, Malthus and Ricardo relied on arguments about biological drives to explain human behavior, and the resulting "social naturalism" became an important assumption behind mainstream economics. We hope to build on that insight by unraveling the naturalizing logic that critics of public assistance continue to invoke. Moreover, we will offer our own alternative narrative that both makes sense of recent historical findings and helps to explain the centrality of the Speenhamland story to classical political economy.

The Speenhamland Stories

Speenhamland refers to a town in Berkshire County, England, where the county squires decreed in May 1795 that the poor should be entitled to a specific quantity of assistance depending upon the price of bread and the size of the family. This form of provision is often called aid-in-wages because when the gap between wages and the price of bread widened, the parish used poor relief funds to supplement the wages of workers and their families (GT, ch.7; Webb and Webb 1927, 168–189). As the program spread (although it is a subject of debate as to how widely it was practiced) among England's parishes, it generated controversy. It was perceived by critics that all precedent had been violated by providing relief not just to the infirm, the aged, or the dependent, but also to the "able-bodied." These criticisms were further fueled by the dramatic increase in local poor rates (taxes) and by the findings of a series of Parliamentary reports that played a considerable role in shaping public opinion.[1] The most important of these was the Royal Commission Report of 1834 that issued a devastating indictment of Speenhamland and created irresistible pressure for the New Poor Law passed later in the same year. Based on what we now know to be a nonsystematic and ideologically driven method of collecting answers to a survey questionnaire, the published report confirmed what the commission had set out to document in the first place (Blaug 1963, 1964; Finer 1972; Cowherd 1977; Henriques 1979, ch.2; Marshall 1985). The main evidence mobilized in the report was hundreds of stories from local parish officials—mostly clergy—confirming the immorality and degradation of the rural poor. The report concluded that Speenhamland and the Old Poor Law more generally were wrongheaded intrusions of state power into self-regulating labor markets. Poor relief created new and perverse incentives that led to increasing pauperization. Exponential increases in childbirth and illegitimacy, declining wages and productivity, assaults on public morality and personal responsibility, and the development of a culture of indolence were only some of the effects attributed to Speenhamland.

The Royal Commission Report was widely distributed, and it influenced a broad range of scholars through the middle of the next century. In fact, until quite recently, the report was treated as one of the important moments in the rise of the social sciences—one of the first times that a government body relied on systematic collection and analysis of data to analyze an important social problem. But a number of scholars have persuasively shown that the Commissioners did very little data analysis and simply used an elaborate structure of appendixes to give more weight to their "findings" (Brundage 1978; Boyer 1990). Moreover, there was little in the commission's analysis that was original; their narrative drew heavily on arguments that had been elaborated by Joseph Townsend and T. R. Malthus in the last part of the eighteenth century.

Joseph Townsend's *Dissertation on the Poor Law* (1971 [1786]) used the "fable of the dogs and goats" on an island in the Pacific to make its case against poor relief. Townsend argued that just as the populations of goats and dogs reached equilibrium as they each adjusted to the changing food supply, so would the population of the human poor naturally reach equilibrium were it not for the artificial intervention of poor relief: "Hunger will tame the fiercest animals, it will teach decency and civility, obedience and subjection, to the most perverse. In general it is only hunger which can spur and goad them [the poor] on to labour; yet our laws have said they shall never hunger" (GT, 118). We have already quoted Polanyi's devastatingly incisive if pithy analysis: "Hobbes had argued the need for a despot because men were *like* beasts; Townsend insisted that they were *actually* beasts and that, precisely for that reason, only a minimum of government was required" (GT, 119).

When the first edition of Malthus's *Essay on the Principle of Population* was published in 1798, there was no mention of Townsend's pamphlet even though Malthus's argument followed along identical lines. (Malthus did, however, cite Townsend in subsequent editions, after being stung by accusations of plagiarism.) Malthus's argument began from two postulates: "First, That food is necessary to the existence of man. Secondly, that the passion between the sexes is necessary and will remain nearly in its present state" (Malthus 1985 [1798], 70).

The identification of these two biological drives—hunger and sex—was the basis for Malthus's central claim that growth of human population will inevitably outstrip the available food supply. Following Townsend, Malthus argued that poor relief interferes with the self-regulating mechanisms that serve as the incentives necessary to drive the poor toward self-disciplined behavior and reproductive prudence. These mechanisms exist in the economy only in its untouched and natural state—the condition of scarcity. So, for example, when poor relief promises child allowances for those parents too poor to make ends meet, young people need no longer delay marriage until they have adequate resources to support a family. Since Malthus strenuously opposed birth control, his goal was for the poor to postpone marriage. Precisely because every additional child promises to produce additional income for the family, the existence of poor relief encourages calculated childbearing as a more expedient means of survival than disciplined productive labor. The consequence is a rise of the birth rate that places an unwanted burden on the rest of society that has to pay the bills.

Malthus also stressed a second line of criticism—that poor relief undermined frugality, personal responsibility, and, above all, work discipline. Once again, the working premise is that the labor market depends on a delicate self-regulating system in which a perfect equilibrium of supply and demand occurs only when it functions in its natural state of scarcity. Remove the scarcity and gone is the spur to labor that only the fear of hunger can provide; no longer will workers be interested in pleasing their employers or in saving for the future. Measures designed to diminish poverty end up making it worse: "Hope and fear are the springs of industry. . . . It is the part of a good politician to strengthen these: but our laws weaken the one and destroy the other" (Townsend 1971 [1786], 17).

For Malthus and those who followed his logic—including the Royal Commissioners—the specific rules for allocating poor relief were not very important; as long as some of the able-bodied poor were eligible for assistance, the negative dynamics were set in motion because people were being protected from the consequences of their own decisions. Hence, supporters of this story tended to assimilate all forms of outdoor relief to the able bodied under the single heading of the allowance system, and as long as per capita poor law outlays were high, they were able to make their case that poor relief was making poverty worse.

The Other Story

Leftist critics of unfettered market allocation have had their own version of the Speenhamland story, although their narrative has had a more limited impact on social policy. Marx and Engels drew from the Royal Commission Report, just as they mined other Parliamentary documents to piece together the story of early industrialization in England. However, their specific references to Speenhamland are brief. Engels wrote in *The Condition of the English Working Class*: "As long as the old Poor Law survived it was possible to supplement the low wages of the farm laborers from the rates. This, however, inevitably led to further wage reductions since the farmers naturally wanted as much as possible of the cost of maintaining their workers to be borne by the Poor Law. The burden of the poor rates would, in any case, have increased with the rise in population. The policy of supplementing agricultural wages, of course, greatly aggravated the position" (1958 [1845], 278). In *Capital*, Marx wrote, "At the end of the eighteenth century and during the first decade of the nineteenth, the English farmers and landlords enforced the absolute minimum of wages by paying the agricultural laborers less than the minimum as actual wages and making up the balance in the form of parish relief" (1930 [1890], 662).

Marx and Engels agreed with the conclusions of the Royal Commission Report, but they rejected its explanatory logic. They agreed that the Poor Law had contributed to the immiseration of the rural poor, but the crucial mechanism was that farmers had pushed wage levels down by shifting costs on to the parish. Since a strapped employer might realistically only be able to pay eight shillings per week to an employee, the parish would add four additional shillings to ensure that the workers' families would have enough bread. But now the employer, having caught on to the dynamic, had a clear incentive to lower his own expenses by paying just seven shillings the next week so that the parish would increase its supplement to five shillings.

It is not difficult to explain why Marx and Engels took this position on the core dynamic of Speenhamland; widespread degradation of the rural poor fit the logic of their broad theory of capitalist development. Both enclosures and the Poor Law were part of the process by which wealth was extracted from the rural poor in order to help finance industrial investment. Moreover, Marx and Engels saw the system of poor relief as nothing more than a feudal remnant. However, Marx and Engels were able to take this position because they were writing a decade or longer after the militant working-class protests that had been engendered by the 1834 New Poor Law. Had they recognized the centrality of the mobilization against the New Poor Law to the development of the working-class movement in England, they might have seen things differently (Edsall, 1970; Rose 1970, 78–94; Knott 1986; Driver 1993, ch.7).

They should have considered why industrial workers in the industrial North of England cared so deeply about a mere "feudal remnant." Their failure to address this issue had unfortunate consequences. Given their political and intellectual authority, the view that the Poor Law between 1795 and 1834 played a critical role in immiserating the rural working class gained credibility that lasted for more than a century. Subsequent historians writing from a perspective critical of capitalism followed their lead. W. Hasbach, a scholar of the German Historical School, published his important study in German in 1894 and in English translation in 1908 (1920). He was followed by J. L. and Barbara Hammond (1970 [1911]), Sidney and Beatrice Webb (1927), Polanyi (2001 [1944]), and E. J. Hobsbawm and George Rude (1968), all of whom concurred in seeing the Poor Law as a factor in rural impoverishment.[2]

But it is not as though the Royal Commission's narrative completely escaped criticism. It was denounced by the rural and urban poor who mobilized extensively against the 1834 New Poor Law, and "Tory radical" opinion allied with the poor in resisting both the dismal implications of Malthus's doctrine and the harshness of the 1834 bill (Hill 1929; Driver 1956; Ward 1962). Even J. R. McCulloch (1938 [1845], 290) an important classical economist, called into question the objectivity of the investigation. Criticism continued in the twentieth century in R. H. Tawney's reference to "that brilliant, influential, and wildly unhistorical report" (cited in Webb and Webb 1927, 84).

Ironically, the most elaborate criticism was offered by the Webbs in Part II of their *Poor Law History*. The Webbs note that the Royal Commission "was not an inquiry into the prevalence and cause of destitution: for the 'poverty of the poor' was at that time deemed to be both explained and justified by the current assumptions underlying the Malthusian 'Law of Population' and the economists' 'Theory of the Wage Fund'" (Webb and Webb 1927, 83). In other words, the Commissioners neglected all structural sources of poverty because they had already embraced theories that explained poverty by Malthusian and Ricardian causes—and prejudices: "The active members of the Commission . . . started with an overwhelming intellectual prepossession, and they made only the very smallest effort to free their investigations and reports from bias—a defect in their work which is not to be excused merely because we are to-day inclined to believe, as they were themselves complacently assured, that their prepossessions against the Rate in Aid of Wages was substantially right" (Webb and Webb 1927, 86–88).

Thus, despite their apparent criticism of the Commissioners' hidden biases, their censure was overshadowed by their endorsement of the report's foundational assumption—that the allowance system set up perverse disincentives to work that were profoundly destructive to society and workers alike. In their admiration of the pseudo-scientism of the report's presentation, moreover, the Webbs helped to perpetuate the image of the investigation as a genuine and exemplary work of social science when they wrote of the commission's investigation: "Their voluminous reports, together with the equally voluminous other statements, were printed in full, comprising altogether no fewer than twenty-six folio volumes, containing in the aggregate over thirteen thousand printed pages, all published during 1834–1835, being by far the most extensive sociological survey that had at that date ever been undertaken" (Webb and Webb 1927, 54). All told, the Webb's ambiguous verdict helped the authority of the Royal Commission Report to survive until the revisionist assault began with Mark Blaug's articles in the 1960s (1963, 1964).

Polanyi's Contribution

When Karl Polanyi began to explore the Speenhamland episode in the 1930s, virtually all of the historical sources available to him affirmed that the Speenhamland episode had degraded the rural poor. Nevertheless, Polanyi was determined to challenge the economic liberals—especially the Austrians von Mises and Hayek—who had demonized Speenhamland as prefiguring the state interventionism of the late nineteenth and early twentieth centuries that they so condemned. They claimed that all efforts to use government to improve the life chances of the poor would end up undermining the economy's vitality and would ultimately hurt the people that the policies had been intended to help. As a supporter of the achievements of municipal socialism in Vienna, Polanyi (GT, 298–299) was determined to demonstrate the flaws in the historical parallels that these free market theorists had developed between Speenhamland and Vienna's extraordinary socialist experiment (see also Polanyi-Levitt and Mendell 1987; Congdon 1990, 78–84).

Polanyi's strategy was to bring a greater degree of institutional specificity to the historical comparison. Instead of just discussing markets and state action in the abstract, he sought to unpack the Speenhamland episode by looking more closely at the actual workings of institutions. His central argument was that the Speenhamland incident could not be generalized to later cases of state action because it occurred before the working class was capable of mobilizing to defend its own interests. This was exemplified by the existence of the Anti-Combination Laws that prohibited all trade union activity. Polanyi (GT, 85) is explicit that had it not been for these laws, Speenhamland's aid-in-wages might well have "had the effect of raising wages instead of depressing them as it actually did." But even more fundamental than the legal obstacles to trade union activity was the fact that the complicated payment system that Speenhamland initiated prevented rural workers from understanding their actual social position: Speenhamland "prevented laborers from developing into an economic class and thus deprived them of the only means of staving off the fate to which they were doomed in the economic mill" (GT, 103). For Polanyi, then, the difference between Speenhamland and Vienna was that in the former case the workers had not been able to organize themselves as a class, so there was no mechanism to block state action from producing perverse consequences.

However, while Polanyi's analysis was clearly an advance over earlier versions of the Speenhamland story, he also was seriously misled by the historical sources. Ironically, Polanyi was warned of the problems in his argument by G. D. H. Cole, the great English labor historian and social theorist. Polanyi had sent Cole the first half of the manuscript of GT in 1943, and Cole wrote back with extensive criticisms: "I think that all through this chapter [7] you treat Speenhamland as much more universal than it was, and also make much too light of county differences in wage policy" (Cole 1943). However, the criticisms arrived too late, since Polanyi had already sent the manuscript to its U.S. publisher.[3]

Divergent Narrative

As Table 5.1 shows, these various efforts to make sense of Speenhamland shares similar conclusions about its ultimate impact on the rural poor. Critics of capitalism saw a very different dynamic at work than that identified by free market advocates, and Polanyi, in particular, added another layer of institutional causality. The body of historical scholarship that has developed over the past fifty years, however, should make it difficult for any of these narratives to continue to be used to justify social and political policy.

Complexities and Causal Gaps

Speenhamland begins to look very different when viewed in the context of England's long and unique Poor Law history (Solar 1995; Lindert 1998). Although initial practices date to the late thirteenth century, the famous 1597 and 1601 Elizabethan Tudor statutes were the most important pieces of English Poor Law legislation. The law established an obligation at the local level to assist those who were impoverished as a consequence of illness, infirmity, family breakdown, or temporary unemployment. There was much variation in actual Poor Law practices as parishes experimented with a variety of different policies designed to protect the poor while maintaining work incentives (Marshall 1926; Webb and Webb 1927). There was also considerable variation over time within parishes; efforts to find the right policy mix at the local level sometimes produced alternating periods of generosity and stinginess (Thomson 1991).

Table 5.1 Divergent Speenhamland Narratives

Proponents	Cause	Key Mechanism	Outcome
Joseph Townsend T. R. Malthus Royal Commissioners Ludwig von Mises Marvin Olasky	Wide use of bread scale undermines scarcity necessary for market self-regulation, discipline, and efficiency.	Poor relief works as perverse incentive to early marriage, increased birth rate, and voluntary unemployment.	Reduced productivity, lower wages, excessive population growth, and increased poverty.
Marx and Engels Hammonds Webbs E. P. Thompson	Wide use of bread scale facilitates unilateral wage reductions by employers.	Farmers shift costs on to the parish to save on their wage bills.	Reduced productivity and lower wages.
Karl Polanyi	Wide use of bread scale and Anti-Combination Acts facilitate unilateral wage reductions by employers.	Farmers shift costs onto the parish at a time when rural workers cannot act collectively.	Reduced productivity and lower wages.
Our synthesis of recent historical scholarship: Mark Blaug, J. P. Huzel, K. D. M. Snell	Bread scale not widely used. Rural impoverishment caused by massive shift of industries to North and deindustrialization in the South, unemployment, enclosures, and decline of crafts.	Economic contraction after 1815, intensified by England's return to gold at the prewar parity, increases agricultural unemployment and rural poverty.	Poor relief significantly buffers rural poor against unemployment and loss of other income sources; provides food and clothing.

Source: Fred Block and Margaret R. Somers

Some degree of controversy over the Poor Laws existed from their inception, but it was in the last years of the eighteenth century that debate intensified with calls for the complete abolition of all "outdoor"—outside the workhouse—relief. Much of the blame for this shift in attitudes is generally placed on the rapidly rising cost of maintaining parish relief in this period. Per capita poor relief outlays are estimated to have more than doubled between 1749 and 1801 (Lindert 1998). Considerable uncertainty about these rising expenditures remains to this day because of the sheer empirical difficulty of understanding a highly decentralized system of social welfare in which critical decisions were made by local parish officials. While we have data on the total Poor Law outlays of fifteen thousand parishes in England for selected years from 1802 to 1834, we do not know precisely how the expenditures were divided among assistance to the vulnerable populations—the elderly, the sick, orphans, and unwed mothers; support for local poorhouses; and various forms of outdoor relief, including assistance to the able-bodied poor. In some parishes, detailed registries of all outlays have survived, but it is often difficult for historians to reconstruct the particular rules under which a specific individual was given six shillings each week. Even after two centuries, historians have closely analyzed the surviving records of a relatively small number of parishes (Huzel 1989; Sokoll 1993). There were some periodic parliamentary surveys that sought to determine the specifics of local relief policies, but generally responses were received from only a small fraction of all parishes, and it is difficult to know if the responses are representative (Williams 1981).

It is clear, however, that the sharp rise in Poor Law expenditures was largely a regional phenomenon—concentrated in southeastern England, both the wheat-growing areas and the pastoral areas where both rural and cottage industries were in decline.[4] In the older cities, it is believed that poor relief for the able bodied was rare, except for periods of acute unemployment or abrupt increases in the price of bread.[5] In the North, the combination of sheep and cattle pasturage, a tradition of small-owner cottage industry, and rapidly growing urban industry meant that per capita poor relief outlays were far lower than in the South (Somers 1993; King 2000). These regional differences were magnified by the greater season variability in demand for labor that was characteristic of the wheat-producing areas, especially as alternative income sources began to dry up (Berg 1994; Valenze 1995).

But if we focus on the southeastern parts of England, there is a second dimension of empirical complexity. During the Speenhamland

Table 5.2 Forms of Relief by Modern Names

1. *Minimum guaranteed income.* This is the Speenhamland bread scale that provides specific amounts of aid in support of wages depending on the price of bread and the size of the family.

2. *Seasonal unemployment insurance.* During the winter months when agricultural work was scarce, some parishes provided unemployed farm workers and their families with a weekly stipend that varied depending upon family size.

3. *Public works.* Some parishes put the unemployed to work building roads or performing other types of work. Sometimes the supervision was done by public authorities and sometimes by private contractors.

4. *Employer subsidies.* Some parishes used poor relief funds to reimburse farmers and other employers who hired the unemployed. This was often called the roundsman system because the unemployed workers would make the rounds of local employers.

5. *Workfare.* Some parishes allocated a certain proportion of the unemployed to each local employer with the idea that they would provide employment instead of paying taxes for poor relief. This is often referred to as the labour rate system.

6. *Child allowances.* Many agricultural parishes provided a supplement to the income of male agricultural workers who had more than two or three children who were not yet of working age.

7. *Workhouse.* Well before 1834, a minority of parishes required that the unemployed seeking relief enter a residential facility that imposed work requirements. Some of these facilities were publicly administered and some were run by private contractors.

8. *Out of parish relief.* Individuals were entitled to assistance in the parish in which they had been born or gained settlement. Sometimes, however, individuals would experience hardship while away from the home parish and request assistance. The implied threat was that if they did not receive help, they would return home and the parish would be obliged to assist them.

Source: Fred Block and Margaret R. Somers

period—1795 to 1834—parishes experimented with a broad array of different ways of distributing relief that would have quite varying consequences. In fact, the range of measures closely resembles the repertoire of relief policies that are still debated two hundred years later. And because of the decentralization of administration, we lack definitive information on how widely each of these particular practices was employed. These policies are listed by their modern names when available (see Table 5.2).

One of the recurrent problems in the literature is that analysts group a number of these distinct policies under one heading and proceed as though all the methods can be expected to have the same consequences. For example, "the allowance system" and "aid-in-wages" are often used to cover the first six different policies. As we will see, these disaggregation problems contribute to the difficulties in developing a clear understanding of Speenhamland.

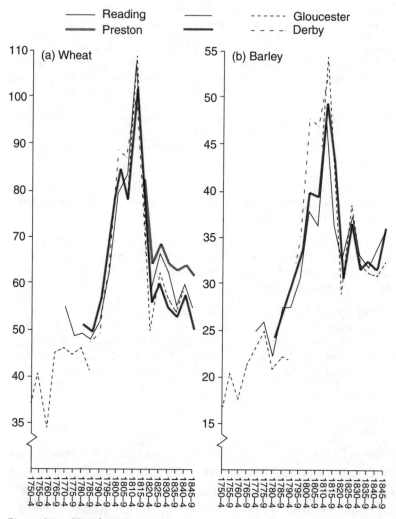

Figure 5.1. Trends in Grain Prices

Source: Richard Perren, "Markets and Marketing," in *Agrarian History,* vol. 6, edited by G. E. Mingay (Cambridge: Cambridge University Press, 1989), 190–274, 231. Reprinted with permission from Cambridge University Press.

A third empirical complexity results from the rapid change in prices that occurs across the Speenhamland period (see Figure 5.1). The first half of the period coincides with the Napoleonic Wars that produced an extremely sharp increase in price levels, particularly for wheat—the dietary staple of both the rural and urban working classes. From 1813 on, as the war winds down, there is a sharp fall in price levels that continues beyond 1834. These dramatic shifts in price levels generated enormous debates among contemporaries and, to this day, economic historians are still debating the appropriate measures of price changes in this period (Snell 1985; Feinstein 1998 Clark 2001).

A final empirical complexity may well be the most serious and the most telling. As only parish officers could be counted on to give the kinds of answers that commissioners or parliamentary investigators were seeking, it is extremely rare that an actual recipient of poor relief would ever be questioned. Hence, the testimony of recipients is not available to counter or compare against the extensive reports from local elites, most of who readily complied with the commissioners in making broad generalizations about the behavior, motivation, and mental states of the recipient population. Only now are we beginning to break these long silences as historians mine letters, wills, and petitions from the rural poor to create a more holistic view of the system of poor relief (Snell 1985; Valenze 1995; Hitchcock et al. 1997).

Causal Gaps

Both the narrative constructed by Malthus and the Royal Commissioners and the alternative narrative constructed by critics of the market have gaps in their causal logics. In the market liberal story, the work disincentive effects of Poor Law assistance are simply assumed and treated as invariant. But let us imagine a parish in which Poor Law assistance primarily took the form of seasonal unemployment insurance. This was often the case in the 1820s, when seasonal unemployment had become the dominant cause of poverty (Boyer 1990, 86–93). When jobs were available on local farms, able-bodied workers would not be eligible for assistance, but as demand for labor diminished in the winter months, those who had been employed would become eligible for unemployment benefits. As long as the administration of the Poor Law blocked those with real work opportunities from receiving these unemployment benefits, it is difficult to see any work disincentive effects. Moreover, it would have been rational for local farmers to provide this seasonal unemployment insurance or much of their labor force would be tempted to move elsewhere.

Indeed, there is reason to believe that many parishes were administered in exactly this way. Given the small size of most rural parishes, parish officials knew well the condition of the local labor market, including whether or where vacancies or layoffs were occurring. Moreover, parish officials were not shy about denying assistance when they suspected that an individual was simply shirking (Sharpe 1997, 99–103). This makes it implausible that large numbers of people were able to cheat routinely and work only when they felt like it. If large increases in Poor Law outlays were primarily caused by the growth of seasonal unemployment insurance, there is no reason to believe there were significant work disincentive effects.

A second causal gap is shared by both stories—a failure to focus specifically on the type of relief that sought to create employment for the unemployed. Public works projects, the employer subsidies, and workfare jobs were all efforts to deal with a growing problem of rural unemployment, and they all faced the classical dilemma involved in "make work" projects. When public agencies create employment specifically with the goal of making recipients work in exchange for relief, supervisors usually find it difficult to elicit high levels of work effort because recipients know that they are not working in a real job.[6] On the one side, the threat of being fired does not have the same credibility as in an ordinary employment relation. On the other, there is no particular reward for hard work since there are no prospects for promotion or greater employment security. These difficulties can be somewhat mitigated if recipients can be persuaded that success in this activity will lead to some form of real employment. But when the unemployment problem is structural and intractable, "make work" efforts are likely to be accompanied by declining morale among recipients.

Many of the specific complaints in the historical record about the corrosive effects of the Poor Law actually center on "roundsmen" or others who were engaged in these kinds of "make work" activities. The Royal Commission Report quotes Mr. Hennant of Thorney Abbey, Cambridge, who describes his experience with employees hired under the labor rate system: "If I complain of the little work done, or its being ill done, the reply is, (interlarded with the grossest blackguardism,) "Oh, we don't care a _____; if you don't like it as it is, you may do your work yourself; for, if you discharge us, you must keep us, or have others of the same sort in our stead" (Royal Commission 1834, 223). A similar sentiment toward such workers follows from Mr. Stephen Cadby of Westbury, Wiltshire: "The greatest evil, in my opinion, is the spirit of laziness and insubordination that it creates; if you remonstrate with these men, they abuse or injure, certain, however their conduct, they shall receive their money" (Royal Commission 1834, 223).

There may be truth to these complaints, but the obvious problem is with structural unemployment that deprived so many of both meaningful work and social dignity. Moreover, there is little reason to credit fears that the attitudes of the unemployed subverted the work discipline of those who were regularly employed. It is much more logical to assume that the sight of the roundsmen would serve to reinforce the regular employees' fear of unemployment. While they might very well sympathize with the plight of the roundsmen, they would not be eager to share that fate. There is little reason to believe that poor productivity on the part of "make work" laborers would subvert the productivity of those who were still gainfully employed.[7]

A third gap in causal logic can be found in the assumption that employers would deliberately lower wages to take advantage of the parish's guaranteed wage supplement. There are several serious problems with this argument. First, we know that farmers competed with each other to attract the most skilled and energetic employees, and there was considerable employment turnover in this period (Kussmaul 1981; Snell 1985). Hence, even though trade unions were outlawed in this period, there were still limits on what employers could do (Rule 1979; Dobson 1980; Rule and Wells 1988). Unilateral reductions in wage levels—even if they were balanced by poor relief supplements—seem like a perfect way to signal that a particular employer was seeking only lower quality workers. Moreover, even if all the farmers in a given parish managed to agree on a collective strategy to lower wages, they would still have to worry that the better workers would defect to higher paying farms in nearby parishes. This was a real threat because agricultural workers were often in walking distance of employment opportunities in neighboring parishes so that they could change employers.

To be sure, employers were able to impose unilateral wage cuts in periods of sharp economic downturn, but this was because employers experienced a general and simultaneous reduction in their need for workers, and rising unemployment deprived workers of any bargaining power. But in the absence of this kind of generalized downturn, there were significant obstacles to unilateral wage reductions. Arguments that assume unilateral wage reductions mistakenly assume that the characteristics of one particular type of parish were general across the countryside. The conventional image of eighteenth-century southern England pictures a homogeneous arable countryside dominated by manorial landholdings of a wealthy semi-aristocratic commercial gentry. Their farming parishes were termed "close" (today, the more easily accommodated "closed" is acceptable) because residential in-migration was restricted and controlled by a very small number of wealthy landholders who governed simultaneously as local magistrates, supervisors of the Poor Law officials, and employers of agricultural laborers. This local property-owning elite sometimes made a practice of demolishing cottages that had earlier housed agricultural workers as a means to reduce the present and future population that would be entitled to Poor Law relief. This had the added benefit of allowing landholders to shift the burden of poor relief onto those living in neighboring parishes (Holderness 1972; Mills 1980; Somers 1993, 601). For their workforce, they relied instead on nonresident workers who commuted from neighboring "open" parishes—so called because, in the absence of dominating landlords, they were open to anyone who could gain settlement there.

The combination of economic and legal power exercised by these parish oligarchs caused great hardship for those subjected to this regime. But the existence of closed parishes hardly sustains the Speenhamland story. For one thing, even though employers in closed parishes were able to shift their Poor Law costs unto others, they also had to worry that lowering of wage levels might mean that vacancies went unfilled. More important, we know now that closed parishes represented a relatively small percentage of all rural parishes and an even smaller percentage of rural population. Among recent analysts, Banks (1988) is highly skeptical of the open/closed distinction, while Song (1998), who considers the distinction important, finds that in Oxford in 1831, 25% of parishes conform to the full definition of closed, with low population density, minimal poor relief outlays, and domination by a few large landholders.

Furthermore, most open parishes had a substantial number of "middling sorts"—small farmers, craftsmen, shopkeepers, and rural artisans—some of whom rotated from being recipients to being those who paid some of the taxes out of which poor relief was financed (Boyer 1990). In their capacity both as ratepayers and as potential recipients of poor relief in bad years, it is unlikely that these middling sorts would see any reason to join with larger agricultural employers in a strategy to keep wage levels low by shifting costs on to the parish.

The final gap in causal logic has been the focus in much of this literature on adult male agricultural wages when the reality of rural life was that family income had been for generations pieced together from multiple different sources, including the earnings of wives and children and money made by men outside of their primary work (Kumar 1988; Berg 1994; Horrell and Humphries 1995; Reay 1996). In fact, when we look at the data on trends of male agricultural wages, the most striking thing is that they move far less dramatically than shifts in the price index. It was possible for farmers to resist more rapid adjustment of wages to price levels precisely because neither employers nor laborers assumed that working-class families could survive on the male workers' wages alone.

This problem of focusing on male wages suggests that when the famous debate between "optimists" and "pessimists" over the impact of the Industrial Revolution on working-class standards of living shifted to the countryside, it often became a dialogue of the deaf (Taylor, ed. 1975). At the beginning of our period—around 1790—most rural laboring families pieced together their household incomes from agricultural wage labor, including that of women and children; from periodic work in rural industries; from their own production on small plots or the parish commons; and from multiple miscellaneous sources of income such as gleaning, fishing, hunting, and casual jobs. By the end of our period, structural changes in the economy including enclosures and the decline of rural industries in southeastern England had undermined some of these important streams of rural working-class income (Snell 1985). Hence, as we shall see, even if wages did not follow the trajectory outlined in the standard Speenhamland stories, the standard of living of many rural people suffered significantly in this period.

Reconstructing the Reality of Speenhamland

The empirical complexities and causal gaps are enough to make us suspicious about both of the Speenhamland stories, but a close examination of the historical evidence is even more devastating. First, the very Speenhamland system that allegedly produced significant work disincentive effects turns out to have been far less common than earlier believed. When properly defined as strictly limited to a bread scale that provided different levels of support depending on family size, it becomes apparent that Speenhamland could not have produced the effects that have been attributed to it. Second, there is strong evidence against the decline in rural productivity that both stories have claimed to have been one of the effects of Speenhamland. Finally, when we look more closely at what happened to the rural standard of living across the period from 1790 to 1834, it is very difficult to resist the conclusion that rising Poor Law outlays were a response to the loss of established forms of family income rather than a cause.

The Limited Pervasiveness and Episodic Nature of the Bread Scale

Speenhamland is itself a contested term. Some have used it to cover the full range of relief policies in which able-bodied individuals and their families received assistance, while others have used it more narrowly to refer to the specific use of a bread scale in allocating assistance. Precisely because of the need to differentiate items numbered 1 and 2 from our list in Table 5.2 from the various forms of employment creation, we will define *Speenhamland* strictly as the use of a bread scale to determine assistance by the size of the family and the cost of wheat.[8] While the Royal Commission Report takes pains to condemn all forms of assistance to the able-bodied, its initial focus is on the allowance system, and it differentiates between parishes that occasionally provide allowances and others where such assistance has been routinized: "In others it is considered that a certain weekly sum, or more frequently the value of a certain quantity of flour or bread, is to be received by each member of a family. The latter practice has sometimes been matured into a system, forming the law of a whole district, sanctioned and enforced by the magistrates, and promulgated in the form of local statutes, under the name of *Scales*" (Royal Commission 1834, 21). This is immediately followed by the printing of a number of representative examples of such scales, including one particularly impressive table from a parish in Essex that provides precise allowances for more than twenty different wheat prices ranging from one to seven shillings per peck. Much of the Report's subsequent fury is then directed against this "allowance system."

Yet few of the indictments of Speenhamland hold up against the evidence. The claim that the use of the bread scale starting in 1795 was unprecedented is simply wrong. Wage-price indexing for the able bodied goes back to the 1349–1351 Ordinance and Statute of Labourers and was most elaborately spelled out in the famous 1563 Tudor Statute of Artificers (Tawney and Power, eds. 1924; Lipson 1943, 253; Tawney 1972 [1938]; Somers 1993, 1994a, 1995). Moreover, bread scales had been used in years of high wheat prices at other times in the second half of the eighteenth century (Henriques 1979; Neuman 1982).

Another misperception is the belief in Speenhamland as a continuous forty-year policy with territorial and temporal uniformity. Mark Blaug (1963, 1964) first called this into question with pathbreaking research that challenged the geographical uniformity of its application. Blaug showed that the use of the bread scale was not geographically universal even in wheat-growing areas. Neuman (1982, 160), in a sample of sixteen parishes in Berkshire County itself, found none that used the Speenhamland scale in the whole period up to 1834. Poynter (1969), Baugh (1975), Huzel (1989), Lees (1998), and King (2000) also stress the limited use of the bread scale. Baugh suggests that it was much more common for parishes to respond to years of very high grain prices by using poor relief funds to purchase grain that was then redistributed to households. In other parishes, the farmers sold wheat to their employees at below-market prices or, as had happened in earlier famine years, extra charitable efforts by the rich provided some of the poor with food (Baugh 1975).

Even so, it is useful to think of the bread scales in certain parishes in 1795 and subsequent famine years as the first Speenhamland episode. In 1795, in 1802–1803, and still again in 1812, a confluence of several factors created the kind of calamity that forced many parishes to take action. In each case, two bad harvests in a row coincided with wartime limitations on agricultural imports from the Continent. The dramatic and severe upward spike in the price of wheat that followed placed this dietary staple well beyond the reach of most agricultural, rural-industrial, and even urban working people. Moreover, as the poor shifted their demand to coarser but cheaper grains, their prices spiraled upwards as well. The consequence was severe distress and the outbreak of food riots in which protesters seized grain from middlemen and bakers (Wells 1988 see also Tilly 1995, 228–232). In 1795, these riots occurred against the backdrop of revolutionary events on the other side of the English Channel, so that local elites had strong incentives to respond to the threat of famine and revolutionary disorder. Despite the arguments of Speenhamland's critics, the use of the bread scale was a very logical method to respond to the threat of famine without permanently altering wage rates or long-term relief patterns. (This is consistent with Sen's [1982] argument that famines are rooted not in an absolute shortage but in political decisions to restrict distribution and entitlement to food.) As soon as the price spike passed, most households would no longer be eligible for assistance because the standard wage would purchase a sufficient amount of bread.

There are two striking features of this initial Speenhamland episode. First, the trend of Poor Law outlays is similar between those parishes that adopted the bread scale and those that used other means to distribute food to the hungry. Baugh (1975) analyzed data from more than seven hundred parishes in Essex, Kent, and Sussex and showed that poor relief outlays very closely tracked the fluctuations in the price of wheat (see Figure 5.1). Sokoll (1993, 138) extensively analyzed Ardleigh, a parish in Essex that did not adopt the bread scale in this early period, and he shows that its outlays also rose and fell in parallel with the other agricultural parishes in Essex that Baugh examined. Second, as Sokoll (1993, 142) emphasizes, these patterns undermine one of the core claims of the Royal Commission Report—that allowances have a kind of addictive and self-expanding effect. The Commissioners claimed, "Profuse allowances excite the most extravagant expectations on the parts of the claimants, who conceive that an inexhaustible fund is devoted to their use, and that they are wronged to the extent of whatever falls short of their claims" (Royal Commission 1834, 49). But in this episode, whether parishes used the formal mechanism of the bread scale or other methods of distributing relief, what is so striking is that outlays fell virtually immediately when the price of wheat fell.

The second discrete Speenhamland episode occurred in the years after the end of the Napoleonic Wars and was not related to famine conditions.[9] With the end of the war, there was a period of severe economic contraction marked by a dramatic decline in wheat prices (see Figures 5.1 and 5.2). There was some downward adjustment of wage rates in this period, but this adjustment was much smaller than the sharp fall in prices. As a consequence, some farms simply went out of business and other agricultural employers sharply reduced their employment levels during the growing season and to a great extent during the winter months. These cutbacks were driven by the introduction of threshing machines—the proximate trigger of the famous 1830 Captain Swing riots—that sharply reduced the demand for labor in the critical months after the harvest. All these processes significantly increased rural unemployment and distress and accounted for the sharp rise in poor relief outlays after 1813.[10]

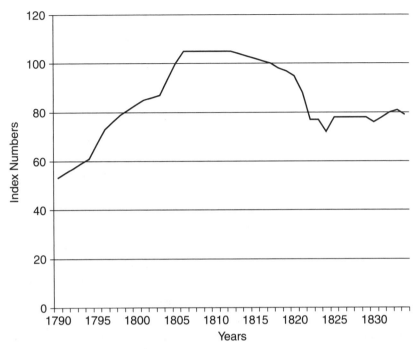

Figure 5.2. Agricultural Wages 1790–1834

Source: Graph drawn from Bowley's series reprinted in B. R. Mitchell and Phyllis Deane, *Abstract of British Historical Statistics* (Cambridge: Cambridge University Press, 1962). The series is for all of England, but his reported data for counties in the Southeast follows the same general pattern.

There is strong consensus in the recent literature that the post-1813 renewal of Speenhamland measures was catalyzed by a shift from inflation in grain prices to structural transformation in employment opportunities, leading primarily to radically new patterns of seasonal unemployment (Snell 1985, Boyer 1990). The period was also marked by the decline of women's farm labor income and an accelerated decline of rural crafts that had provided employment for women (Snell 1985; Berg 1994; Valenze 1995).

But while the bread scale returned, its meaning shifted in an important way. In the earlier period, employed farm workers would receive an income supplement, contingent on family size and the wheat price, to help them get through the period of high food prices. In the later period, the bread scale was used primarily to determine the amount of relief that seasonally unemployed farm workers were entitled to, given the size of their families.[11] The importance of this seasonal dimension of poor relief is amply supported by data showing that poor relief outlays were often two or three times higher in the winter months than in the spring or summer (Emmison 1933; Snell 1985; Boyer 1990; Reay 1996). As Boyer has argued extensively, there were strong reasons for parish authorities to provide relief in the winter for unemployed farm workers. Employers were constantly worried by the threat of out-migration, which would mean labor shortages during the summer months and severe shortages at harvest time (Boyer 1990, 31–43). Without such relief, levels of out-migration, whether to the north or to urban areas, would have been much higher.

This second phase of Speenhamland is exemplified by events in Ardleigh—the Essex parish that has been closely studied by Sokoll. The parish had no earlier history of the use of the bread scale, but a formal bread scale was instituted in September of 1823, followed in 1831 by another Speenhamland statute (Sokoll 1993, 140). This late adoption of the bread scale by parish officials is especially notable because it occurs after decades in which Speenhamland had been denounced for its horrible consequences. This suggests that there was widespread skepticism at the time with the anti-Speenhamland rhetoric and that local officials were undeterred because they were simply trying to find the best practical way to deal with the crisis presented by high levels of unemployment.

Trends in Productivity and Wages

The standard Speenhamland stories insist that rural productivity collapsed in the face of the corrosive impact of the Poor Law. The available data provide no support for this claim. Total wheat production increased substantially between 1790 and 1834; Fairlie's estimate shows that wheat production fluctuated sharply between 1791 and 1811 and then more than doubled by 1834 (John 1989, 1054–1055). This increase was facilitated by an expansion in acreage. Holderness (1972) estimates that acreage increased from about 2.45 million acres in 1801 to 3.4 million in 1836—an increase of almost 39%. But it was not only increased acreage. Holderness suggests that yields per acre might have risen by 33% between 1790 and 1830 (Holderness 1972, 140); Overton (1989) suggests that the increase was 15% between 1801 and 1831.[12]

The official decennial census of population did not begin until 1801. Even then, the early censuses did not ask about employment, so estimates of the size of the agricultural labor force between 1801 and 1831 in the southeastern counties are little more than guesswork. Nonetheless, the labor force seems to have grown substantially more slowly than either wheat output or acreage. Wrigley (1986) estimates that for the whole country, the number of adult males employed in agriculture increased from 910,000 in 1811 to 981,000 in 1831—growth of only about 8%. Since the wheat-growing counties were home to a large portion of English farm workers, it is unlikely that labor force growth in these counties was substantially faster than national growth. Given the doubling of wheat output between 1811 and 1834, there can be little doubt that output per worker rose in this period. Overton (1996) suggests quite substantial increases in labor productivity in agriculture across the whole period from 1800 to 1850. Moreover, even Clark, who has been most outspoken in criticizing the idea of a productivity-increasing "agricultural revolution" in the first three decades of the nineteenth century, acknowledges that labor productivity was either constant or increasing slightly in this period (Clark 1991, 1999).

Since the available data on productivity in the wheat-growing regions are sketchy at best, a number of analysts have supported the Speenhamland thesis by arguing that agricultural wages fell sharply in this period and that it is reasonable to see wages as a reliable proxy for productivity. Influential historians writing in the first half of the century, such as Hammond and Hammond (1970 [1911], ch.7) Webb and Webb (1927, 422–423), and Mantoux (1962 [1928], 431–439) have insisted that wage levels fell dramatically during the Speenhamland period. However, most of the available data series that we have that trace rural wages in this period reveal the same basic pattern. Rural weekly wages for men rise from 1790 through to the end of the Napoleonic Wars. There is then a sharp decline during the agricultural depression, followed by a recovery and a slightly rising trend from the early 1820s through to 1834. The first systematic series on agricultural wages was developed by Bowley at the end of the nineteenth century, and it rises from 53 in 1790 to 105 in 1812, then falls to 72 in 1824 before rising to 79 in 1834 (see Figure 5.2) (Mitchell and Deane 1962, 348). Eccleston found a similar pattern in five Midland counties, and Richardson reports a parallel pattern in wages on a large farm in Essex (Eccleston 1986; Richardson 1991). Clark (2001) has developed a series for weekly winter wages in the southeastern counties based on various surviving estate records, including those used by Richardson, and he finds the same pattern of decline from the peak reached in 1810–1814. The respected historian K. D. M. Snell calculated trends in annual wages for farm servants in a number of southern counties from a unique data set drawn from settlement examinations. For most counties or groups of counties, Snell's (1985) findings move in the same pattern as weekly wages cited elsewhere in the literature, but in some counties he did find that wages fall steadily from the 1820s onward.

Interpreting these patterns of nominal wages has been extremely difficult because of the dramatic price changes that occur across this period. There is no question that in the famine years, such as 1795, 1802–1803, and 1812, the price spike in grains lead to dramatic, albeit temporary, declines in the real wage. Nevertheless, the view advanced by Prothero (1912, 313–315) that wage levels during the Napoleon War doubled while prices actually tripled is no longer accepted. When one brackets the famine years, real agricultural wages clearly rose between 1790 and 1815. Second, since the post-Napoleonic period was one of steadily falling price levels, the small recovery in nominal wages between 1824 and 1834 reported by Bowley understates the gain in real wages in this period.

> In the end, we come to the conclusion that the question that has preoccupied so many analysts—were agricultural real wages higher or lower in 1834 than they were in 1795—is the wrong question for three different reasons. First, the reality was that real wages—with the critical exceptions of the famine years—first rose, then fell, and then rose. Second, when rural workers are compared to the inhabitants of urban England, who had greatly expanded access to a wide variety of manufactured goods between 1790 and 1834, there can be no doubt that their relative standard of living declined sharply during this period of industrial transformation. Finally, translating weekly wages into a standard of living depends critically on the number of weeks of employment available per year, and we know that seasonal unemployment rose dramatically in the countryside after the Napoleonic Wars (Snell 1985).

Instead of focusing on the wrong question, then, it is the Royal Commissioners' claim that Speenhamland policies damaged rural productivity that must be scrutinized. The argument is already undermined by evidence that the bread scale was neither pervasive nor continuous. It is further weakened by both the data on agricultural output and the trends in weekly wages that provide no support for a claimed collapse of rural productivity.

Household Income and the Poor Law

It is precisely because of the variety and variability of the income sources on which families relied that it is extremely difficult to identify any clear trends in average family income across this period. The best estimates that we have come from surviving family budget data that have been compiled by Horrell and Humphries (1995). They indicate that for the low-wage agricultural sector—that tends to overlap with the southeastern counties—there was a small upward trend in real household income between 1790 and 1834. But this average figure conceals much variation, and poor relief outlays represented a rising component of family income, rising from a negligible level in the early period to 8% of family income for the 1821–1840 period. In this context, poor relief can best be understood as a mechanism to sustain family income in a context in which it had become increasingly difficult for the rural poor—through no fault of their own—to piece together an adequate income.

The increasing importance of poor relief can be seen as compensating for three broad trends. First, rural craft industries suffered a dramatic decline in the southeastern counties in the period after 1790 (Snell 1985; Boyer 1990; Allen 1992). Some of this decline had been going on for centuries, but the pace of decline was clearly accelerated by the rapid rise of industrial production in the northern part of the country (Hudson 1986, 1989, 1992; Kriedte, Medick, and Schlumbohm1991). This meant that opportunities for family members, especially women, to supplement income with labor on rural craft production simply disappeared in many places. Second, enclosures and consolidations of holdings meant that many rural laboring families lost the capacity to earn additional income by keeping farm animals or maintaining a vegetable garden. In fact, during the Speenhamland period, a major alternative to the Poor Law that was widely debated was to provide laboring families with allotments—small pieces of land—that would make self-provisioning a real alternative to poor relief in hard times (Barnett 1967). But while the idea was widely discussed, it was implemented only in a few localities. Third, particularly after 1813, the demand for farm labor diminishes, so that there are reduced earning opportunities for wives and children while men experienced longer periods of unemployment in the winter and early spring months.[13] Reay, for example, finds that in one Kent parish, 60% of farm laborers and small farmers required poor relief during the winter months in the 1830s (Emmison, 1933; Reay 1996, 129).

In short, the family budget data provide a different angle of vision that further undermines the conventional Speenhamland stories. Instead of bread scales undermining work effort, we get a picture of a rural population facing broad structural forces that undermined their capacities for self-support. In this context it is difficult to see increasing poor relief as anything but a partial remedy to problems outside the control of the rural poor.

A Revisionist Narrative

The strength of the evidence against the standard Speenhamland stories raises the obvious question of why the past fifty years of historical scholarship have not yet had any significant impact on social policy discussions. There are undoubtedly multiple reasons, but two are especially compelling. The first is that the Malthusian foundation on which the perversity thesis rests followed the logic of Newtonian physics. Just as Newton explained the causal logic behind the fall of an apple not by the simple appearance of things but by explicating the real, albeit hidden, law of gravity, so Malthus explained the perverse consequences of poor relief not by citing data but by invoking a hidden and constant causal logic. By insisting that there was a deeper truth than that of empirical "appearances," Malthus effectively insulated his argument from empirical disconfirmation.[14] This is the reason the perversity thesis has been so effortlessly recycled to analyze poverty populations who live under radically different conditions than those of the Speenhamland epoch. The second is that, since the revisionist work has been produced by a theoretically diverse group of scholars, the findings have not been organized into a coherent alternative account. As of yet, opponents of the perversity thesis lack a compelling narrative structure.

It seems useful, therefore, to suggest an alternative narrative that would place these new historical findings into a framework that social policy analysts might find compelling. This alternative narrative centers on the problems of legitimating the new science of political economy that emerged out of the fundamental contributions of Malthus and Ricardo. Malthus and Ricardo famously disagreed on some key theoretical and policy issues, and later thinkers, such as Marx and Keynes, explicitly embraced one while denigrating the other.[15] But there was also much agreement between the two figures, and ultimately it was Malthus's critique of the Poor Law that helped divert attention from the negative consequences of Ricardo's first great policy success—the decision at the end of the Napoleonic Wars to restore the pound's parity to its prewar level. In short, the construction of the Speenhamland story was intimately connected to Britain's embrace of the gold standard.

The Return to Gold

As described earlier, the second Speenhamland episode resulted from the severe agricultural downturn at the end of the Napoleonic Wars that led to significant increases in Poor Law outlays. But the most important fact is that the agricultural downturn was not just a brief postwar interlude; rather, it became a long-term reality continuing through and beyond the passage of the New Poor Law in 1834 (Gash 1935; Fussell and Compton 1939; Snell 1985, ch.1). In line with Sen's (1982) contemporary analysis, rural distress was itself closely linked to policy decisions, especially England's decision to restore the prewar value of the pound in relation to gold. What happened in this period is remarkably similar to the decision by England to restore the prewar relationship between the pound and gold after World War I. Keynes (1925) had famously denounced this policy as deeply misguided and insisted that it would produce a period of intense deflationary pressure. Less recognized is that Keynes's prescience derived from his knowledge of economic history and the history of economic theory. He realized that English statesmen in the post-World War I era were simply repeating the mistake that had been made—at the urging of David Ricardo—a century earlier.[16]

Ricardo argued forcefully for restoring the pound to its prewar parity from his first publication in 1810 of a pamphlet called "The High Price of Bullion" (Redman 1997, 276). He insisted that the wartime inflation was a direct consequence of the suspension of gold convertibility and that the only way to return prices to their proper level was to restore the prewar parity. His views and those of other bullionists were endorsed by the parliamentary Bullion Committee in its 1810 Report. By 1816, Ricardo had retired from business, and he reasserted his advocacy of a return to gold with a pamphlet titled "A Proposal for an Economical and Secure Currency." With the publication of Ricardo's *Principles* in 1817 and his entrance to Parliament in 1819, his influence on public policy became greater and was central to the government's decision to restore gold to its prewar parity in 1819 (Fetter 1965; Viner 1965 [1937]; Gordon 1976; Hilton 1977).

This restoration, however, occurred against the backdrop of a severe rural crisis that had begun right at the end of the Napoleonic Wars. The fall in wheat prices in 1813 and 1814 produced a massive collapse of rural banks that had failed to hold on to any reserves. Between 1814 and 1816, 240 rural banks stopped payments leading to a destruction of wealth and a disappearance of credit (McCulloch 1938 [1845]; Fussell and Compton 1939). The result was a dramatic increase in unemployment as farmers and other employers were forced to cut back both investment and the size of their labor force. But as the deflation took hold, there was an ironic consequence—the value of the pound started to rise so that the goal of restoring the prewar parity appeared substantially closer. The response of the authorities in 1816 and 1817, therefore, was to prepare for the resumption of gold payments at the old parity, and in May of 1819, Parliament passed legislation to restore gold payments within two years (Viner 1965 [1937], 172). While there is intense controversy over the specific policies that the government and Bank followed in restoring gold, there is widespread consensus that the sustained effort to return to the prewar parity had a profoundly deflationary impact. On the one side, the government was precluded from pursuing the kind of countercyclical policies that could have revived the rural economy. On the other, the sustained tight money policies greatly restricted the availability of the credit that farmers desperately needed.

Moreover, the deflationary pressures did not end with the success of restoration; the gold standard simply made the pressures on the rural economy permanent. Wheat prices continued to fall until 1829, and after that, prices were stabilized at a very low level. The failure of rural banks was also continuous across the whole period from 1815 to 1830 (Fussell and Compton 1939, 186–189). This context of falling prices and limited credit forced farmers to reduce labor costs and that, in turn, produced chronic rural unemployment and increased use of poor relief. The ongoing pressure of low wheat prices forced the more successful farmers to put increasing resources into labor-saving technology such as the threshing machine. Since hand threshing of wheat could represent as much as one-quarter of the whole year's quantity of farm work, mechanization had a huge impact on the rural demand for labor in the winter months (Gash 1935). Triggered by these high rates of unemployment, the machine smashing in the Captain Swing riots of 1830 exploded (Hobsbawm and Rude 1968; Tilly 1995). Another irony was that this outbreak of rural disorder played a key role in undermining elite support for the Old Poor Law (Dunkley 1982; Mandler 1987).

Absent Ricardo's eloquent pleas for a restoration of the prewar parity, policy makers might well have chosen a less deflationary set of policies. Had the rural economy not suffered the additional shock of the deflationary pressures of gold, the wheat-growing areas might have experienced a recovery and an earlier rebound of wheat prices. Without the ideological commitment to laissez-faire, moreover, the government might have embraced policies that helped to cushion the economy in periods of contracting demand, including provisions for a steady flow of credit to farmers (Hilton (1977, 69–97); Gordon (1976, 71–79). Under any set of policies, there would ultimately have been a problem of a rural labor surplus that could only be solved by more rapid rates of out-migration. But the Ricardian policies dramatically intensified the problem—so that this massive readjustment had to be handled over twenty years rather than forty. As Polanyi (GT, 39) eloquently argues, government policies can help protect ordinary people simply by slowing the rate of change, but the Ricardian policies did exactly the opposite; they vastly accelerated the problem of rural surplus population.

Malthus, Parliament, and the Road to the New Poor Law

The New Poor Law of 1834 officially placed the blame for rural distress not on macroeconomic policies but on the Speenhamland system that had allegedly demoralized and degraded the rural poor. But the Royal Commissioner's "solution" did not emerge automatically out of the reality of rural distress. The solution had to be politically and rhetorically constructed, and this construction depended, in turn, on two prior conditions—dramatic changes both in elite opinion and in the political system. In short, the path from Malthus's *Essay* to the Royal Commission Report was hardly simple.

Ironically, the influence of Malthus's call for abolition of the Poor Law probably reached its high point in the period between 1815 and 1818—even before the return to gold. Repeated editions of the *Essay*, along with reprints of Townsend's pamphlet, were extraordinarily influential in shaping elite views. Poynter (1969, 224) suggests that " . . . it was in these years that fundamental disapproval of a legal provision for the poor (and especially for the able-bodied) became sufficiently widespread to be regarded as orthodox, while defence of the Poor Law became, if not quite heretical, at least old-fashioned." This influence was reflected in a series of Parliamentary Reports, culminating with reports in 1817 and 1819 that endorsed the call for abolition of the Poor Laws (see Mandler 1990; Waterman 1991; Poynter 1969; Hilton 1977).

Yet this intellectual influence did not translate into legislation in this period because there was no consensus within the Parliament on the right course of action. In addition to the usual conflicts among factions, some in Parliament were reluctant to abolish the Poor Laws out of the same fear of revolution that had produced the original Speenhamland policy in 1795. Rural unrest was acute in this period, and the unreformed Parliament had good reason to fear that abolition might generate broad protests that would bring together rural laborers, urban workers, and middle-class radicals (Poynter 1969, ch.6).

After 1820, the political strength of the abolitionist position seems to have weakened, but the parliamentary impasse continued. While there were initiatives at the local level to "reform" poor relief to limit outlays, there were still wide disagreements about what to do about rural distress (Poynter 1969, ch.8; Hilton 1977, 98–169). The situation was complicated by further economic downturns between 1819 and 1822 and again in 1825 to 1826. The continuing economic strains generated intense criticisms of the return to gold and calls for aggressive government action to revive the economy. An explicitly anti-Ricardian political economy emerged in this period that drew some of its key inspiration from Malthus's rejection of the view that supply creates its own demand (Link 1959; Hilton 1977, 77–79; Hollander 1997). These underconsumptionist thinkers directly challenged the government's laissez-faire policies and argued for cheaper money, an expansion of rural credit, and programs of public works to increase employment and demand. But these arguments had little impact on government policies.

The Captain Swing riots in 1830 gave new urgency to Poor Law debates. Yet the Parliamentary stalemate was not broken until the Whigs came to power and passed the Reform Act of 1832 that expanded the suffrage and gave the middle class effective representation (Poynter 1969, ch.9; Brundage 1978; Dunkley 1982). While the Reform Act was still pending, the Whig government appointed the Royal Commission to investigate the Poor Laws. While all of the Commissioners had been deeply influenced by Malthus's arguments, they rejected his abolitionist policy solution. Their critical rhetorical move was to adopt the language of reform and to argue that "reformed parishes"—those that replaced outdoor relief with workhouses for the poor—had effectively eliminated all of the negative consequences of Speenhamland. In short, by narrowing Malthus's critique of the Poor Law to focus on the "allowance system" and by proposing concrete reforms rather than abolition, the Royal Commission was able to generate a strong Parliamentary consensus that led to passage of the New Poor Law.[17]

What the Royal Commissioners succeeded in doing was to mobilize and modify Malthus's arguments to rescue political economy from its responsibility for the plight of the rural poor. By effectively blaming the victims for the macroeconomic policy mistakes that had intensified rural poverty, they turned a potential disaster into a policy triumph. In doing this, they made an enormous contribution to the legitimation of political economy. The severity of the agricultural downturn might well have undermined the whole belief in laissez-faire and self-regulating markets. Classical political economy was in its infancy in this period, and its ultimate maturation and worldwide influence were hardly a foregone conclusion.[18] While it is difficult to think through such a radical counterfactual, an alternative and more pragmatic strand of economic thinking might have become institutionalized in the place of the Ricardo tradition. Instead, the ultimate policy triumph of the New Poor Law diverted attention from the new science's first major policy failure and solidified the electorate's faith in market self-regulation.

In sum, the Speenhamland myth was created in the years of agricultural downturn to divert blame for a deep agricultural crisis away from government policy and toward the rural poor who were the major victims of the economic downturn. Since the decision taken by the government on Ricardo's advice to restore the prewar parity of the pound intensified the rural depression, the mythology worked to cover up the first catastrophic policy failure of the new science of political economy. The importance of this myth becomes apparent in thinking about the diffusion of economic liberalism during the course of the nineteenth century. England's ability to persuade other countries to adopt free trade, the gold standard, and the belief in market self-regulation depended on its ability to present itself as a great economic success story (Semmel 1970; Kindleberger 1975). Were other societies aware that the price that England had paid for economic liberalism was severe economic hardship in the countryside in the 1820s, 1830s, and 1840s, both the English model and its policy ideas would have been considerably tarnished. By shifting the blame for the problems on to Speenhamland and all its pernicious evils, economic liberals successfully reframed the agricultural downturn into a problem of individual morality and an enduring parable of the dangers of government "interference" with the market.

Conclusion

The major lesson that we learn from this study is a renewed appreciation for the persuasive power of the metaphors of nature, natural laws, and the "science" of political economy to influence how history is experienced and why certain explanations for distress triumph over others. The Malthusian morality tale about the "perverse" and disastrous consequences of Poor Relief was produced long before any evidence had been gathered and too early for the Speenhamland decision to have produced its alleged consequences. In Malthus's 1798 *Essay on Population,* all the elements of the story line are already in place. Poor relief, by ending the scarcity that is endemic to nature in its untouched state, destroys the incentives both to work (in order to eat) and to control fertility, and thus leads to a precipitous decline in productivity and a rapid growth of the pauper populations. The only way to return the poor to their natural state of self-discipline in both work and procreation is to abolish the system of poor relief and return to the natural state of scarcity and the human discipline it teaches.

In subsequent years, as political economy gained the privileged status of a recognized science, this story was repeated so frequently by political economists, the clergy, and various Parliamentary commissions that it gained the quality of truth. By the time the Royal Commission was created in 1834, the newly reformed Parliament included a significant number of factory owners determined to create an available, cheap, and "free" labor force. The thesis was elevated to an absolute Scientific Truth based entirely on the laws of nature. Despite volumes of literature devoted to the subject, it took the next 130 years before there was a serious scholarly effort to show the shallowness and distortions of that document. But even after years of detailed scholarly work had effectively debunked the Speenhamland legend, as we show in the next chapter, the very same arguments were used to create support for the passage of the Personal Responsibility and Work Opportunities Reconciliation Act in the U.S. in 1996.

Our review of the historical evidence suggests two conclusions. First, the perversity story lacks empirical support. The experience of the

Speenhamland period is that poor relief did not hurt the poor; it helped to protect them from structural changes in the economy that had made it far more difficult for people to earn a living. Second, the doubts that have hung over guaranteed income proposals since Speenhamland lack historical foundations. While it is theoretically possible that a floor under incomes would be transformed into a ceiling, this certainly did not happen during the Speenhamland period, and there is little evidence that it has ever happened. In fact, there are good reasons this theoretical possibility is rarely likely to occur in practice. In contrast to Speenhamland, most contemporary income guarantee proposals, including variants on the negative income tax, do not require that recipients work. Hence, when employees are faced with an employer who is progressively lowering wages to take advantage of the income guarantee program, they are likely to quit and look for alternative employment, since they know that they will be protected by the income guarantee from economic hardship during their period of unemployment. Moreover, under most circumstances, employers avoid unilateral reductions in wages precisely out of the fear that they would drive away existing employees and make it harder to fill vacancies. It seems only logical that if an income guarantee were in place, employers would become even more cautious about imposing wage cuts.

Welfare and income maintenance policies need to be debated free of the mythologies that were created two hundred years ago. Above all, we need to move beyond the naturalized Malthusian accounts that see the behavior of the poor as always determined by their biological drives. Discarding naturalizing blinders and examining the actual situation of the rural poor during the Speenhamland period, we are forced to recognize the central role of larger economic processes such as the severe agricultural deflation and the shift of industry to the North in explaining mounting rural poverty. Relief payments actually provided some protection against these structural pressures. The contemporary lesson is obvious; it is time to reject the ideological claim that the best way to fight poverty is by imposing increasingly stringent conditions on ever-shrinking transfer payments to poor households.

6

FROM POVERTY TO PERVERSITY

Ideational Embeddedness and Market Fundamentalism
over Two Centuries of Welfare Debate

Over the past thirty years market fundamentalism has moved from the margins of debate to become the dominant policy perspective across the global economy (Bourdieu 1998; Campbell and Pedersen, eds. 2001; Fourcade-Gourinchas and Babb 2002; Stiglitz 2002). As we discussed in Chapter 1, the term was popularized by George Soros (1998; 2000) to capture the religious-like certitude of those who believe in a sacred imperative to organize all dimensions of social life according to market principles. Market fundamentalism is the contemporary form of what Polanyi (GT, 3) identified six decades ago as economic liberalism's "stark Utopia" and what we call free-market utopianism—the idea that a "market society" should be created by subordinating all aspects of social life to a system of self-regulating markets.

Social scientists have been surprised by the extraordinary revival of market fundamentalism, which was widely assumed to have died off in the Great Depression of the 1930s. They have had difficulty in explaining its phoenix-like revival. The normal tools of comparative analysis have provided relatively little leverage. Since market fundamentalism's influence depends on global networks, one cannot proceed with comparisons as though each national case is fully independent of the others. Moreover, since no nation could risk following market fundamentalist precepts to the letter, it is difficult even to produce a persuasive indicator of the relative influence of the doctrine in different societies.

150

Even among those who have chosen to engage this difficult terrain, the situation has been further complicated by explanatory disagreements. Some analysts attribute the return of market fundamentalism entirely to structural changes such as the growing integration of global markets (Callinicos 2001; Friedman 1999). Polity-centered institutionalists have been skeptical about the doctrine's actual implementation, especially in societies that are characterized by "varieties of capitalism" that differ from the Anglo-American model (Pierson 1994; Hall and Soskice, eds. 2001; Huber and Stephens 2001; Yamamura and Streeck, eds. 2003). Others have traced market fundamentalism's influence to the enormous investments its supporters have made in propagating their ideas through think tanks, journals, and policy networks (George 1997; Himmelstein 1990; O'Connor 2001; Piven and Cloward 1997; Williams 1996).

As readers of this volume know well by now, we are sympathetic to this emphasis on ideas. Our focus, however, is on that which has been little addressed, namely the *causal mechanisms* that allow certain ideas to exert extraordinary political influence. Haunted by the specter of idealism, social scientists have been wary of attributing causal power to ideas. But if we are to be relevant in today's world, we must both recognize and explain how market fundamentalist ideas have so radically transformed our dominant knowledge culture.[1]

We bring a new analytic strategy to this challenge. Using comparative historical methodology we compare two welfare revolutions. Our first case is the 1996 American "Personal Responsibility and Work Opportunities Reconciliation Act" (PRWORA). The PRWORA is an especially compelling case because a comparable overturning of an existing welfare regime by a market-driven one has occurred only one other time in Anglo-American history.[2] This was in 1834 when England's infamous Poor Law Amendment Act, or "The New Poor Law" (NPL) demolished the centuries-old welfare system of the Old Poor Law (OPL) and replaced it with a radically different system, as we discussed in Chapter 5. In comparing these two cases, our goal is not to explain the nuts and bolts of the Congressional legislative process. Rather, we aim to explain the change in the dominant policy ideas made possible by market fundamentalism's triumph over the previously established ones.

The two cases have several striking similarities. Each episode began at a moment of extraordinary national crisis and social turmoil that led to increased welfare benefits. There followed prolonged periods of political attacks against the existing welfare systems, culminating in sudden

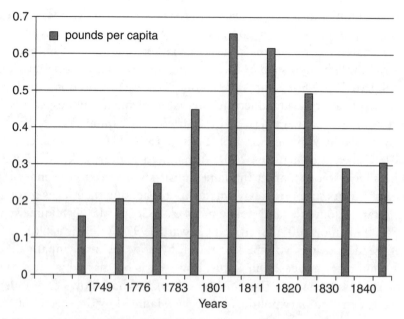

Figure 6.1. United Kingdom Relief Outlays per Capita
Source: Data are from Peter Lindert, "Poor Relief before the Welfare State: Britain versus the Continent, 1780–1880." *European Review of Economic History* 2 (1998): 101–140.

legislative breaks with each nation's long-established legacies of public social provision. Relief expenditures as a percentage of English GDP fell by almost 50% in the decade following reform; in the United States, the decline in the next decade was even sharper and more persistent despite two serious recessions that drove up unemployment levels. (Figures 6.1 and 6.2 trace changes in relief spending per capita.)

What makes these cases so theoretically and methodologically compelling, however, is not simply the fact of their similarities. It is that they exhibit these similarities *despite* overwhelming differences along every *other* significant sociological parameter: England was a small, newly industrializing but still largely agrarian island, while the United States was a postindustrial colossus. England's political system was years away from any semblance of democratic rule while the United States was a liberal democratic polity with an ethos of equality. The eighteenth and early nineteenth-century English "poor" were those who had to work to survive while the rich bore the moral sanction of being idle; in the United the roles were reversed. (See Tables 6.1 and 6.2 for a summary of the similarities and differences across the two cases).[3]

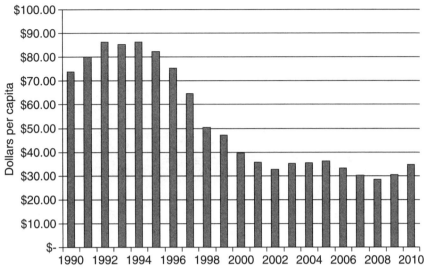

Figure 6.2: United States Benefits per Capita

Source: Population data are from the *Statistical Abstract of the United States;* cash assistance figures are reported in House Ways and Means Committee, *Green Book,* 2012, Additional Tables and Figures, Table 7–3. Available at http://greenbook.waysandmeans.house.gov/sites/greenbook.waysandmeans. house.gov/files/2012/documents/Table%207–3%20TANF_0.pdf. Under the 1996 legislation, states are allowed to use their block grant funds for a variety of different forms of assistance; the figures used here are the state and federal funds that were used to provide actual cash assistance to families.

Table 6.1 Comparing the Two Welfare Revolutions

	England	United States
Similarities		
Timing	Reform in 1834, but crisis dated to 1795 when entitlement was expanded	Reform in 1996, but crisis dated to 1968–1969 when entitlement was expanded
Ideas	Market fundamentalism; perverse consequences of providing welfare	Market fundamentalism; perverse consequences of providing welfare
Differences		
Political System	Up to 1832, franchise excluded the middle class; after 1832, the working class and the poor continued to be excluded	Universal adult suffrage, although participation levels of the poor are low
Beneficiaries	Primarily rural male farm workers and their families	Primarily urban mothers outside of the formal economy
Administration	Legislation shifted power from local parishes to centralized Poor Law Board	Legislation shifted authority to state and local governments

Table 6.2 Perversity Rhetoric in Two Eras

	Laziness	Illegitimacy	Degradation
England	"Ultimately, without doubt, the farmer finds that pauper labour is dear, whatever be its price; but that is not until relief as aid-in-wages] has destroyed the industry and morals of the labourers who were bred under a happier system, and has educated a new generation in idleness, ignorance, and dishonesty" (Royal Commission 1834, 71).	"We have many illegitimate children; and we think that the numbers have increased of late years. If a young woman has two or three bastard children, and receives 2s. 6d. a week for each, it is a little fortune to them" (Royal Commission 1834, 172).	"Whether in work or out of work, when they once become paupers, it can only be by a sort of miracle that they can be broken off; they have no care, no thought, no solicitude, on account of the future . . ." (Royal Commission 1834, 94).
United States	"The welfare system discourages work and self-reliance. The value of welfare's tax-free benefits often exceeds usable income from taxable work. While most Americans expect and want to work, welfare can seduce people into a life of dependency. Worse, the pattern and values of dependency can be transmitted from parent to child, who may come to see welfare as the social norm" (U.S. Domestic Policy Council Low Income Opportunity Working Group 1986, 36).	"There was the single woman who had been having a baby every two years, on purpose—'She told me she thinks two years is about the right spacing.' There was the man who got furious at his girlfriend for losing a baby because 'there went the chance of getting benefits for at least another ten months,' and the women who triumphantly showed up at the Human Services office with a new baby when their eligibility for Aid to Families with Dependent Children had been about to expire" (Murray 1986a, 34).	"Dreams especially died among many poor individuals themselves. They saw that mass pauperism was accepted and pressure to leave welfare was very slight. Sometimes, those (formerly known as the 'worthy poor') who were willing to put off immediate gratification and sacrifice leisure time in order to remain independent, were called chumps rather than champs" (Olasky 1992, 190).

Our Theoretical Approach

Our theoretical approach brings together economic sociology and the sociology of ideas. We decided to couple these fields after finding that both welfare revolutions were preceded by the triumph of market fundamentalism as a new ideational authority. Both cases represent instances of theory-driven legislation—examples of what Bourdieu (1998, 95) referred to as theories "making themselves true" by changing the social world to reflect their abstract theoretical models. It was the ideas of market fundamentalism, we believe, that were the causal mechanisms of revolutionary policy change.

We advance this approach by elaborating several key concepts that will have wider use. The most significant of these is *ideational embeddedness*—a concept derived from Polanyi's insight that markets, even free markets, are always embedded in rules, theoretical assumptions, and institutional arrangements. It follows that even the most aggressive "free market" reforms do not disembed markets but simply re-embed them in different institutional arrangements (see Chapters 1, 2, and 3, and Somers 2008). To date, however, economic sociologists have too often confined their institutionalist imaginations to the standard legal, political, and organizational structures of embeddedness. Zukin and DiMaggio (1990) have enhanced the scope of vision to include "cognitive embeddedness." We go a step further, expanding market embeddedness to include the ideas, public narratives, and explanatory systems by which states, societies, and political cultures construct, transform, explain, and normalize market processes. Like all the familiar mechanisms by which markets are shaped, regulated, and organized, they are always *ideationally embedded* by one or another competing knowledge regime.

Following this principle, we find that in the case of the PRWORA, low-wage labor markets were not disembedded (as is often thought); instead, the new legislation institutionalized a regime in which a new set of ideationally-driven rules and regulations forced the poor to become more directly responsive to market signals (Peck 2001). The role of market fundamentalism in this dramatic policy change demonstrates that ideas have an independent influence on political outcomes. The relative strength of that influence is an empirical question. But once we acknowledge that ideas do exercise this independent role, it becomes clear that many battles over social and economic policy should be redefined as conflicts not over *whether* markets should be embedded but rather *which* ideational regimes will do the embedding.

To theorize about these ideational conflicts in markets and welfare policy, we also call upon the services of Camic and Gross's (2001) proposal for a "new sociology of ideas"—a term they use for an innovative synthesis of recent work in the sociology of knowledge. Focusing on how intellectuals generate and diffuse ideas into the social environment, Camic and Gross reject the sociology of knowledge's traditional explanations of ideas as reflections of social conditions (Mannheim 1968 [1936]). Instead, they see the work of intellectuals as potentially world-changing activity. A similar and compatible attention to ideas has emerged in political science, which builds on historical institutionalism to elaborate a new "ideational institutionalism" (Berman 1998; Blyth 2002; Campbell 1998; Hall 1989; Lieberman 2002; McNamara 1998; Rueschemeyer and Skocpol, eds. 1996).

We concur with the spirit of this new work: Ideas *matter*. But equally important is that *all ideas are not created equal*. Only some ideas can exercise the causal power to undermine, dislodge, and replace a previously dominant ideational regime. We propose the concept of "epistemic privilege" to describe ideas with this kind of comparative advantage. It is sometimes assumed that following the methods of modern science produces this kind of privilege, but this poses obvious difficulties. For example, when Keynes published his *General Theory* (1964 [1936]), both he and his orthodox opponents insisted that their differing theoretical standpoints represented the most advanced fruits of economic science. Likewise, there are also cases where ideas rooted in religious revelation have triumphed over those rooted in the scientific method. Yet another explanation is offered by Camic and Gross (2001); they suggest that epistemic privilege derives from a "fit" between an idea and its local circumstances.[4]

Our explanation is that epistemically privileged ideas come equipped with their own internal claims to veracity. A theory that has "the means of making itself true" (Bourdieu 1998:95) has an obvious advantage over a theory that lacks its own epistemological bootstraps. This has been evident not only for religious revelation, but for Marxism, Freudian theory, and market fundamentalism itself. They have all displayed astonishing immunity to the kinds of empirical challenges that should be evidentially disconfirming. To be sure, "fit" still matters; real people must decide to accept these truth claims. But even in the face of repeated empirical challenges, certain theories have been remarkably persuasive in very diverse localities and across very different historical periods, and we need to understand how they establish their veracity. What makes market fundamentalism stand out even in this rarefied crowd is that it is the only one that lays claims to being an empirical science. That makes its epistemological status even more privileged and its invincibility even more puzzling.

The Perversity Thesis: The Wedge of a Regime Change

To explain such durability, we turn to the "perversity thesis." We adopt this term from Albert Hirschman's path-breaking finding that welfare critics since the French Revolution have used the same "rhetoric of perversity"—the assertion that policies intended to alleviate poverty create perverse incentives toward welfare dependency, and thus inexorably exacerbate the very social ills that they were meant to cure (Hirschman 1991).⁵ The logic behind the rhetoric is impeccable—if assistance is actually hurting the poor by creating dependence, then denying it is not cruel but compassionate, as it restores their morally necessary autonomy. In our two historical episodes, the deployment of the perversity rhetoric worked brilliantly to delegitimate longstanding welfare policies while empowering market fundamentalism to proclaim itself the solution to the crisis of welfare dependency.

By itself, however, the perversity rhetoric is insufficient to ensure success; it requires three external conditions. First, there has to be a severe crisis under the watch of the reigning welfare regime, which creates opportunities for an ideational coup. Second, there has to ensue a battle of clashing ideas fought out in the public arena. Third, the once "extremist" market fundamentalist competitor has to gain a new mainstream legitimacy by establishing itself as the only possible solution to the now teetering old regime. This is when the internal capacities of the perversity thesis come into play. To move into the mainstream, the ideational contender has to reframe the crisis by changing the very definition of reality. It does this by explaining this crisis as a product of the wrong-headed principles and practices of the existing regime, asserting that they violate the inviolable laws of nature. Moreover, the contender has to argue counterfactually that had *it* been the dominant ideational regime, the crisis could have been avoided. The challenging theory then has to be able to explain how and why intelligent and well-intended people could be so deceived into believing the bad ideas of the old regime (Lakatos 1970, 91–196; MacIntyre 1980). Finally, the challenging upstart idea has to take the form of a more powerful public narrative that retells the story of the nation's meaning, morality, and place in the flow of history (Glasman 1996; Lakoff 1996).

This is a high bar, one that only a set of ideas with enormous epistemic privilege could successfully scale. To understand how the perversity thesis exercises such power requires deepening Hirschman's analysis of the rhetoric of perversity, which turns out to be only the tip of the proverbial iceberg. Below the surface, there is a three-dimensional epistemological infrastructure made up of *social naturalism, theoretical realism,* and a *conversion narrative.*

In the analysis that follows, we show how these three factors equipped the perversity thesis with the epistemological bootstraps needed to meet all of the above conditions and to be a causal mechanism in both cases of ideational regime change from poverty to perversity. To change the public understanding of poverty from the fault of the economy to the fault of the poor required the authority of new "poverty knowledge" (O'Connor 2001).

The Two Welfare Revolutions

England: The Crisis of the Old Regime

England was unique in Europe in that it had a highly developed nation-wide preindustrial welfare system (Harvey 1999; Solar 1995; Somers 1993, 1994). The 1597 and 1601 Poor Laws obligated each parish to provide relief to those in need due to sickness, old age, absence of parental support, or unemployment as long as they had legal "settlement" in the locality. The decentralized administrative apparatus left to local parishes the precise form of support, but the great bulk of outlays took the form of outdoor relief—cash or in-kind benefits to people in their own homes, as well as parish-provided employment called "setting the poor to work."[6] By the last decades of the eighteenth century, poor relief had become a standard necessity in the family budgets of "the greater part of the lower working class" (Lees 1998; Marshall 1926; Snell 1985; Wrightson 1980, 2000).

As discussed in Chapter 5, the year 1795 marked a major turning point in Poor Law history. War with revolutionary France, a disastrous harvest, and limitations on food imports caused a dramatic spike in the price of wheat, putting a subsistence diet out of reach for many ordinary working people. Scarcity "so acute and prolonged caused astonishment and dismay" (Poynter 1969, 45), and the poor responded with a wave of food riots (Thompson 1971; Brewer and Styles, eds. 1980; Tilly 1995). Panicked by the specter of revolutionary France, elites searched for policies of containment. The most famous of these was the Speenhamland "Act"[7]—an allowance system assuring subsistence to families of varying sizes (Blaug 1963; GT, ch. 7). As additional assistance reduced discontent, the Poor Laws were again pushed to the background of political debate during the first decade of the new century.

But by the end of the Napoleonic Wars in 1815, rural counties suffered severe economic downturns and high unemployment, parish rates soared, and Speenhamland came under renewed attack. Critics indicted it for having normalized the provision of assistance to able-bodied men and their families, for subjecting public assistance to a "recent unwise benevolence," and for turning relief into an entitlement (Poynter 1969, 45). Even with such elite cricitism and a series of Select Committees in 1817, 1818, and 1824, there was still no consensus for a shift in policy.

Not until the 1832 Reform Bill radically expanded the franchise did the middle class electorate become large enough to oppose the OPL's "interferences" in the labor market. Initially, the new government appointed a Royal Commission to investigate problems with the Poor Law. The commissioners, determined to exploit the opportunity for reform, worked feverishly to produce a report that would legitimate a radical overhaul of the whole system. In a stinging assault on Speenhamland, the influential 1834 Royal Commission Report called for total abolition of outdoor relief for all the able bodied (Brundage 1978, 2002; Driver 1993; Poynter 1969). In the wake of the Report, Parliament passed the infamous 1834 Poor Law Amendment Act in a matter of months. Designed less to rehabilitate than to punish and shame, the mechanism of reform was the principle of "less eligibility"—the practice of making welfare so odious that it was less eligible (attractive) than even the most poverty-stricken life without it. Receiving poor relief became conditional on being incarcerated in a poorhouse, and with it came formal deprivation of political and legal rights under regimes of strict discipline and sexual celibacy— husbands and wives were separated, as were children and their parents (Digby 1978; Henriques 1979; Driver 1993).

As part of the movement in England toward administrative reform and centralization (Brewer 1989; Fischer and Lundgreen 1975; Fraser, ed.

1976), the OPL's porous organizational apparatus was also overhauled. The locus of control shifted from local parishes to a London-based Poor Law Commission that consolidated parishes into large unified districts controlled by state-appointed bureaucrats (Driver 1993; Henriques 1979). The new law encountered stiff resistance from both "monster" popular protests and parish authorities determined to maintain local control (Dunkley 1982; Rose 1970; Steinberg 1999). Within ten years, however, poor relief fell sharply (Figure 6.1); by 1845 only 21,700 able-bodied men still received outdoor relief (Williams 1981, 181).

The United States: The Crisis of the Great Society

The history of Federal welfare assistance in the United States begins with the 1935 Social Security Act's Aid to Dependent Children, later renamed Aid to Families with Dependent Children (AFDC). Previously, assistance to poor families had been based entirely on local discretion, but under the new law, state officials were supposed to provide assistance to poor children (O'Connor 2001; Piven and Cloward 1993 [1971]; Teles 1996). State and local officials, however, maintained considerable discretion even under the federal legislation, especially in the South, where assistance varied by race (Reese 2005).

The War on Poverty and the large-scale migration of African Americans from the rural South doubled the number of AFDC families in the 1960s (Piven and Cloward 1993 [1917], source Table 1). As Supreme Court decisions between 1968 and 1970 made AFDC a legal entitlement (Davis 1993; Teles 1996, 107–16) and media coverage consistently put a dark face on images of poverty, welfare quickly became racialized and criticism increased from all sides. The percentage of AFDC recipients who were African American rose from about 14% in 1936 to a peak of 46% in 1973, before falling to 36% in 1995 (Gilens 1999, 106; Quadagno 1994). Conservatives became more vocal in attacking the misguided "entitlement" policies of the Kennedy-Johnson administrations. Political liberals said AFDC was ineffective in reducing poverty, preferring large-scale jobs programs or a guaranteed annual income. But when the protest movements of the 1960s receded, the impulse to replace AFDC lost steam, and reform efforts under both Nixon and Carter were defeated. Although Reaganites in the 1980s orchestrated a chorus of attacks on AFDC in terms very similar to those of the Speenhamland critics, they were not yet strong enough to overhaul the program. Instead,

Reagan's major initiative was to initiate "waivers" that allowed states to experiment with welfare reform (Teles 1996; Rogers-Dillon 2004). By the early 1990s, thanks to an expansive network of conservative think tanks (George 1997; Rich 2004), conservatives had so radically shifted the political and ideational culture to the right that Clinton campaigned on the promise to "end welfare as we know it." When the Republicans catapulted to power in the 1994 mid-term elections, they held him to his promise. After two years of political pressure, Clinton finally signed the "Personal Responsibility and Work Opportunities Reconciliation Act"—a title that perfectly expressed the newly triumphant narrative of self-inflicted and character-driven poverty.

Restructuring administrative control was as important to conservatives as was the content of the bill. In contrast to the NPL, however, the PRWORA replaced the federally governed AFDC with a program that was funded through block grants to the states, named Temporary Aid to Needy Families or TANF (Weaver 2000).[8] Inspired by a broader bipartisan movement toward "devolution" of government programs (Osborne and Gaebler 1993; Teles 1996), TANF block grants ended the legal recognition of public assistance as an entitlement, while still providing a complex system of rules on how states should allocate assistance.

In parallel form, both the PRWORA and the NPL dramatically ruptured entrenched welfare legacies in a matter of just a few decades. How could such dominant institutional environments have been so vulnerable? Our answer is that in both cases, the real battle was ideational. Before any major institutional change was possible the hard work of ideational regime change was necessary. Once the battle of ideas was won, policy transformation occurred almost effortlessly. It was the ideational transformations from poverty to perversity that did the real work of defeating both old regimes.

England's Old Regime: Pragmatic Institutionalism and the Rational Control of Nature

Nineteenth-century Poor Law critics scapegoated Speenhamland for its unconscionable "break from the past" primarily because it offered aid to the indigent and "able bodied" alike. In fact, its principles were continuous with the two centuries of mercantilism that preceded it, just as its wage-price indexing and relief of poverty for both the sick and able bodied dated to the 1351 Statute of Labourers and the 1597 and

1601 Poor Laws (Minchinton 1972; Palmer 1993; Somers 1993, 1994, 1995). Indeed most of Speenhamland was continuous with the past. In contrast to modern social policy, Speenhamland and the old Poor Law alike did not make moral or practical distinctions among those in need, whether they were employed, unemployed, underemployed, or unemployable (Furniss 1920). Rather than representing a separate poverty policy, the Old Poor Laws made work, poverty, and economic displacement all matters for a broad "Code of Labor" (Marshall 1985; Somers 1993, 1994).

The source of these principles was the centuries-old definition of the "poor" as everyone other than the "idle" rich. They were poor precisely because they had no choice but to work. This conception of the poor was coupled with the first foundational precept of mercantilism—that "People are the Wealth of a Nation." Hence, the purpose of poor relief was to maintain the nation's source of national wealth (Appleby 1978; Furniss 1920; Wilson 1969). With economic growth contingent upon "the miraculous Power of Industry," mercantilist writings overflowed with admonitions to protect by any means the working capacity of the laboring poor. The second mercantilist tenet was the "populationist" belief that national wealth depended on an ever-increasing population of working people. Policies thus encouraged finding steady work for those without employment, attracting more foreign workers, and providing incentives to the poor to marry and have children without the nineteenth-century indictment of childbirth among the poor as an irresponsible tax burden (Appleby 1978).

Even with these strong tenets, mercantilist policy was surprisingly *problem-driven*—its policies were conceived as rational solutions to urgent public crises (Coleman 1969, 1980; Schmoller 1989 [1897]; Wilson 1969). We describe this empirically driven ideational regime as *"institutional pragmatism"*—institutional because it understood labor markets and society as a whole to be rule-driven rather than "natural"; pragmatic because it was problem-driven rather than ideologically teleological. Mercantilism's pragmatism was expressed through its decentralized structures of implementation (Wrightson 2000). National markets were still underdeveloped and prices regionally varied, making it simply practical for local authorities to have maximum discretion and flexibility in determining levels of assistance and necessary rates of taxation (Heckscher 1955 [1935]; Webb and Webb 1927). Decentralized and discretionary policies made it possible for local authorities to assess the current state of need by relying on "signals" (from petitions to food riots) from the local population (Somers 1993; Thompson 1971; Walter and Wrightson 1976; Wrightson 2000:215).

Coupled with mercantilism's pragmatism was its institutionalism— the belief that legal rules and political rationality are the foundation of society's wellbeing. Thus scarcity was not a natural condition of society, but a product of deceptive social practices such as "hoarding" or trafficking in unregulated goods or wages, of failure to enforce existing rules, or refusal to enact effective new rules (Schmoller 1897; Walter and Wrightson 1976).[9] With poverty defined as an inflicted product of rule-breaking or political intention, defending the poor "from the blame of their own poverty" was an "insistent theme" of political elites (Appleby 1978, 140–41, 150; Snell 1985). Institutionalism made poverty not the fault of inevitable market gluts, scarcity, or natural disasters, but of the political failure to prevent their occurrences or to regulate their consequences. Institutional pragmatism reflected an imperturbable faith that ever-greater prosperity was possible with the exercise of political reason in the interest of the well-being, productivity, and increasing numbers of the laboring poor. Nature was a thing apart, driven by natural forces utterly incommensurable with political action and human reason.

Amartya Sen (1981) has argued that famines come not from shortages but from political maldistribution and designed restrictions of entitlement to food. From Sen's perspective, Speenhamland, mercantilism, and Old Poor Law measures taken to avoid famine by redistributing food to the poor and treating it as an entitlement reflected great foresight. By embedding labor markets within a thicket of public laws and institutional pragmatism, the nation's productive capacity became a matter of political rationality and rule making. Both employment and unemployment were too important to be left to their own "natural" state (Somers 1993, 1994).

Population and Perversity: Nature vs. Reason

To change policy, ideas require an opportunity. In the last years of the eighteenth century, a crisis of seemingly intractable poverty and spiraling poor rates (taxes) brought to an end the once-uncontested legitimacy of mercantilist social policies. This presented an extraordinary opportunity to Thomas Robert Malthus. Malthus's *Essay on the Principle of*

Population has justly been celebrated as one of the founding documents of demography. But it was the book's theoretical innovations in the political economy of labor markets, social naturalism, and the perversity thesis that arguably changed the course of history. For sociologists it may be difficult to ascribe so much importance to a single individual. In the case of Malthus, however, it would be difficult to *over*state the extraordinary influence of his ideas. Widely circulated and rewritten in serial editions (1798, 1803, 1806, 1807, 1817, 1826), the *Essay* attacks mercantilism's faith in the use of political reason to overcome nature's ills. It also ridicules the idea that politics is the practice of human rationality applied through positive law (see, e.g., Winch 1992, viii).

Rejecting such political rationalism, Malthus claimed to have found the true cause of the current crisis in the laws of nature, as well as in his novel law of population. In an unprecedented attack on the old regime, he blamed the perversity of the Poor Laws themselves for the escalation in taxation. By inducing the poor to propagate and multiply, Malthus claimed, the laws *caused the very poverty they were designed to cure* (1992 [1803], 100). He attributes much of the blame to mercantilism's populationist fallacy; the Poor Laws were simply the legislative enactment of a wrongheaded idea about the benefits of population growth. That Malthus treated as *fact* what was but a mercantilist *idea* may be one of the great ironies of history. Without his unquestioning belief in the effectiveness of the very mercantilist policies he so loathed, the Mathusian law of population might never have been born. And absent this law, the perversity thesis's case for abolishing the Poor Laws might never have become the ideological engine for market fundamentalism's ultimate success.

Malthus begins his assault by turning the world upside down. "Man" cannot reason with nature because it is nature's utter indifference to reason that distinguishes it from humanity. The first law of nature thus seals the fate of those who would put their hopes in the mind's powers. Regardless of moral capacities, people are first and foremost biological beings motivated by the instinctive drives to eat and have sex. Reflecting the brutal struggle for survival endemic to nature and society alike, however, the two drives are at war with each other. Whereas the need to eat must be satisfied by what will always be a scarce food supply that increases only "arithmetically," the "resources" available to satisfy the sexual drive are limitless. Population thus increases "geometrically."

In this paradigm-changing move, Malthus "proved" that the laws of nature make scarcity a permanent condition of life. Against the rationalist belief that political intervention could alleviate social problems, he declared that scarcity combined with population growth make poverty, distress, and famine inexorable. To explain why the law of population did not wipe out humanity eons ago, Malthus introduces "positive population checks."[10] War, famine, pestilence, infant mortality, are just a few of the ways nature successfully cuts the population to fit scarcity's Procrustean bed. Ironically, this argument reveals Malthus's own utopianism. Despite nature's terrors and its endless struggles for scarce resources, when *left to its own devices,* it creates a perfect balance of supply and demand. When humans finally abandon the folly and futility of trying to impose their own will over nature, they will find that while not always benign, nature is always a wise governor.

From the law of population, Malthus turns to the Poor Laws: "To remedy the frequent distresses of the poor, laws to enforce their relief have been instituted . . . But it is to be feared that . . . [they have] spread the general evil over a much larger surface (1992 [1803], 89). The Poor Laws of England tend to depress the general condition of the poor in these . . . ways. Their first obvious tendency is to increase population without increasing the food for its support. A poor man may marry with little or no prospect of being able to support a family. *They may be said, therefore, to create the poor which they maintain;* and as the provisions of the country must, in consequence of the increased population, be distributed to every man in smaller proportions, it is evident that the labour of those who are not supported by parish assistance will purchase a smaller quantity of provisions than before, and consequently more of them must be driven to apply for assistance." (1992 [1803], 100, italics added).

In this famous formulation, Malthus argues that the very measures intended to help the poor inevitably make them poorer. Scarcity alone creates a balance between available resources and the number of people competing to consume them. Try to cure poverty by alleviating scarcity and nature's disciplinary power over population growth will dissolve. With the Poor Laws' perverse incentives to depend on the parish for family allowances, the self-interested poor marry younger and have more children. Most destructive of all, what should be a scarcity-driven incentive to self-sufficiency through labor instead turns into a culture of entitlement. Morality is corrupted as the poor are robbed of their own independence. Dependence sets in as a permanent feature of life, and with it ever-expanding levels of irresponsible sexuality, sloth, and moral degradation. Ultimately, there is no choice but to recognize that individual behavior is to blame for its own distress.[11]

The result was a clash of warring principles—pragmatic institutionalism versus Malthus's perversity thesis. One was the prevailing ideational regime, the other aspired for the position. It is today hard to comprehend the infamy, notoriety, and contempt that Malthus inspired not only in the first decades of the nineteenth century but for generations to come (Himmelfarb 1984; Winch 1996). The fierceness, rancor, and breadth of the controversy initiated by Malthus's *Essay* are equally remarkable. Looking back from the 1880s, Arnold Toynbee called it a "bitter argument between economists and human beings" (Winch 1996, 6). The depth and breadth of the controversy underlines just how much ideas matter. What it does not do is explain why all ideas are not created equal; only some have the capacity to drive ideational regime change.

Fundamental ideational regime changes are rare. To convert one ideational regime to another, the challenger must meet three difficult requirements. The new theory must, by means of its own logic, be able to demonstrate why the currently dominant ideas cannot possibly solve society's problems. It must be able to explain how intelligent people could have been so misled. And it must be able to provide an alternative view of social reality by means of a more compelling public narrative. Understanding how Malthus's perversity thesis made it possible for market fundamentalism to meet these criteria requires turning to the three components of its epistemological infrastructure—social naturalism, theoretical realism, and the conversion narrative.

Social Naturalism

In using biology to explain society, Malthus was engaged in the project of *social naturalism*. Social naturalism is the claim that the laws of nature govern human society. As we stressed in Chapter 1, it is not just an epistemological stance. It is also an ontology—a theory of being—in which the characteristics of the natural order are mapped onto those of the social order (Somers 1999, 2008). It is an ontology that should not be confused with the more familiar methodology of naturalism. Common to Marx and modern positivism, naturalism is the methodological postulate that because nature and society exhibit the same kinds of regularities, there should be a unified method applicable to both. Social naturalism, by contrast, conflates nature and society. Society is not *like*, but *is* a biological entity, and it is thus subject to biological laws of nature rather than to institutional rules and social rationality.

Society, like nature, is defined as a self-regulating system that, when untouched by political intervention, will tend toward equilibrium and order. Society, like nature, is fundamentally constrained by the scarcity postulate—the constitutive and inevitable reality of material scarcity. Social naturalism in turn makes human nature the same as animal nature and thus constitutively defines it by the immutable biological instincts for food and sex: "These two laws, ever since we have had any knowledge of mankind, appear to have *been fixed laws of our nature*, and, as we have not hitherto seen any alteration in them, we have no right to conclude that they will ever cease to be what they now are, without an immediate act of power in that Being who first arranged the system of the universe, and for the advantage of his creatures, still executes, according to fixed laws, all its various operations" (Malthus 1985 [1798], 70–71, italics added).

The line between humans and animals is thus blurred since human nature is defined as biologically-driven by the instinctual need for food and reproduction. From this axiom of social naturalism, Malthus calls into question the entire Enlightenment distinction between mind and body, between reason and instinct. Much of this he lifts directly from Joseph Townsend, author of one of the most influential political tracts against the Poor Laws (1971 [1786]).[12] Townsend, as we have recounted already, explained the situation of the English poor by telling an apocryphal story of goats and dogs said to have been introduced onto a previously deserted island in the South Pacific by the Spanish in the seventeenth century. The relentless struggle for survival between the two species brought on by the island's scarcity eventually became a harmonious equilibrium: "The weakest of both species were among the first to pay the debt of nature; the most active and vigorous preserved their lives" (cited in GT, 118).

In Townsend's 1786 biological fantasy, Malthus found ample foundations for his social naturalism. The island's harmony was possible only because there was no human interference with the natural state of scarcity. Because the human poor are ontologically indistinguishable from the goats and the dogs, and thus subject to the same biological dynamics, their population should likewise be left to self-regulation by the scarcity of the food supply without the perversity of the Poor Law. "Hobbes had argued the need for a despot because men were *like* beasts; Townsend insisted that they were *actually* beasts and that, precisely for that reason . . . [n]o government was needed to maintain this balance;

it was restored by the pangs of hunger on the one hand, the scarcity of food on the other" (GT, 119, italics in original).

Townsend's social naturalism divides the world by a binary logic between the natural—which was morally and epistemologically privileged—and the much demeaned unnatural. It then maps this hierarchical divide onto the Lockean dichotomy between state and (market) society to create a new social and political ontology, one with a parallel dichotomy of epistemological privilege and moral judgment. On the one side, civil society and the private sphere of market exchange are natural phenomena subject to the certainty, immutability, uncoerced, spontaneous, and scientifically predictable laws of nature. On the other, society's political institutions and rule-driven state policies are perverse: Based on unnatural powers, they are arbitrary, coercive, hierarchical, and a continuing threat to the "system of natural liberty" (Smith 1976 [1776]). By this logic, state intervention into civil society poses a clear and unending danger. It was this Lockean-inspired political gloss on social naturalism that Malthus most appreciated in Townsend and that today still distinguishes Anglo-American political culture from Continental versions of political theory (Somers 1999, 2008).

Malthus's perversity thesis also had to explain the failures of the old regime using his own social naturalist principles. By pointing to the counterintuitive paradox that the greater the poor relief, the greater the poverty, Malthus undermined institutionalism's foundational precept that reason and political judgment were solutions to poverty. Appealing to the laws of nature, Malthus invoked the prestige of the scientific revolution to support his claim that poverty was caused by the conflict between the natural laws of scarcity and the immutable drive for sex and food. He also gained great leverage by attributing much of his scientific learning to the esteemed *Wealth of Nations* (1976 [1776]). It was there that Malthus first read that society was a *"natural system"* and absorbed Smith's self-proclaimed "very violent attack" upon the entire mercantile system of political and economic regulations (Winch 1996:3).[13]

But it was Newton who was the real power behind Malthus's skillful use of social naturalism (Redman 1997). Just as the abstract laws of physics allowed Newton to explain the harmonious motion of the planets, so did Malthus explain the follies of institutionalism using the same natural laws of society (see especially Malthus 1992 [1803], 51). The *Essay* is full of mathematical allusions allegedly provided by Newton's scientific discoveries, and it abounds with images of ballistics, weight springs, and countervailing forces. With this intellectual ammunition, Malthus succeeded in making self-evident that the crisis was beyond the reach of political artifice. The laws of nature could explain what mercantilism could no longer. The stability and order promised by obedience to nature was an irresistible alternative to the failures of human artifice, political will, social institutions, and positive law.

Theoretical Realism

It has been observed by Hume that, of all sciences, there is none where *first appearances* are more deceitful than in politics. The remark is undoubtedly very just, and is most peculiarly applicable to that department of the science which relates to the modes of improving the conditions of the lower classes of society.
—Malthus 1992 [1803], 312, (italics added)

With this observation, Malthus makes clear his intention to uncover the real truth of the politics of poverty and to explain how intelligent and well-meaning people could have been so deceived by pragmatic institutionalism. For these tasks he turned to the Enlightenment project of piercing the "deceit" of "first appearances" and using the light of reason to find the truth of an underlying rational order. This is "theoretical realism" (also called Cartesian rationalism)—a militantly anti-positivist theory of causality for which unobservable or "theoretical entities," such as laws of human nature and the regulative principles governing the relationship between population and food supply are the *real* (hidden) causal forces behind the appearances of experience. It is termed theoretical realism because even though the underlying causal mechanisms cannot be observed, they are more *causally* real than the misleading illusions of empirical observations (Somers 1998). Theoretical realism shares some elements of the epistemic privilege of religious belief. While it does not depend literally on revelation, like religion, it posits the divide between appearance and reality.

The broken clock is the classic metaphor of this Enlightenment project. If we have a clock that does not run, it is futile to try to fix it by fiddling with the face of the clock. Shattering the illusion that the clock's causal mechanisms are empirically observable is a precondition for making the clock's inner workings accessible to science. Malthus knew that the secrets of the social world are not as easily accessible as the gears inside of a clock. To discover these social secrets he found inspiration in the "thought experiment" that Newton had used to discover gravity.[14] Newton had theorized that the only way to access causal powers that we cannot observe is to use logic to "think" our way from empirical effects—the apple falling from the tree—to the hidden causal forces. The thought experiment made the law of gravity the only logical cause for the empirically observable effects—the falling apple (Somers 1998).

From Newton's methodology, Malthus took the lesson that the greatest errors in social knowledge derive from the confusion of cause and effect. Those who imagined that people turned to poor relief only when driven by severe poverty manifested this confusion. The truth was that *poor relief causes poverty,* and not vice versa. Poverty was the *effect* not the cause; it was not the "real" problem, but only the "apparent" one. Malthus reasoned through the logic of the thought experiment that the real causal mechanisms behind poverty are the perverse incentives set up by the Poor Law's violation of nature's law of permanent scarcity. This is the perversity thesis at its best: Instead of ending poverty, child allowances perversely exacerbated it by encouraging childbearing among the poor and thus inducing overpopulation.

But how can this theoretical realist be the same Malthus who so deplored mercantilism's Enlightenment faith in human rationality? His answer would be that using reason in the effort to control nature and mitigate its harsh laws is perversity of the worst kind. By contrast, his use of reason to reveal nature's secrets does not challenge but pays homage to nature's sovereign role in human destiny. Precisely because they are hidden, it is all the more important to bring nature's true causal laws to light for all to see and obey. Malthus saw himself as the spokesman for nature, and in that effort reason ruled.

Nonetheless, the abstractions of theoretical entities and thought experiments still seem at odds with Malthus's reputation as a hard-hitting inductivist and empiricist critic of abstract theory, a reputation he earned from his famous debates with Ricardo (Hollander 1997; Redman 1997). Indeed, there are parts of The *Essay* that present a veritable encyclopedia of facts on bestial life, sickness, weakness, poor food, lack of ability to care for young, scant resources, famine, infanticide, war, massacre, plunder, slavery—to name just a few of nature's checks on population. But these should not deceive: Malthus's theoretical realism prohibited proving causal propositions with empirical evidence. Instead, following the Newtonian strategy of moving from empirical effects to imputed causes, Malthus's list of natural horrors were really just effects, or demonstrative illustrations, designed to "prove" the cause that he by necessity used logic to identify. By reasoning from (observable) effects to causal (imputed) theoretical entities, theoretical realism gives the misleading impression that his causal claims were based on massive empirical substantiation, rather than what they were—entirely theory-driven. Lest we appear to be over-interpreting Malthus's method, in the first edition of the *Essay* Malthus makes explicit his low regard for "facts" in favor of self-evident visionary "plain statement." "The *Essay* might, undoubtedly, have been rendered much more complete by a collection of a greater number of facts in elucidation of the general argument. The Author presumes, however, that the facts which he has *adduced* will be found *to form no inconsiderable evidence for the truth* of his *opinion* respecting the future improvement of mankind. As the Author contemplates this opinion at present, *little more appears to him to be necessary than a plain statement,* in addition to the most cursory view of society, to establish it" (Malthus 1985 [1798], 61, italics added).

The Poverty to Perversity Conversion Narrative

The final dimension of the perversity thesis's epistemological infrastructure is what we call a "conversion narrative." It is characteristic of all epistemically privileged ideas, especially religious ones, that they use narratives to "teach" people how to see the world differently (Barthes 1977; MacIntyre 1980; Ricoeur 1989; Somers 1999, 2008; White 1987). Narrative makes sense of our world by explaining cause and effect as we experience it, over time, in place, and through agency (Barthes 1977; Somers 1992, 1994b, 1997; Steinmetz 1992; White 1987). A conversion narrative differs from standard narrative in that it has only one goal—to convert a person, a culture, a people, a nation from one ideational regime to another by telling causal stories that change perceptions of reality. Its task is to *neutralize* and *delegitimate* the prevailing narrative by using its own alternative story to reveal the illusion and the reality of the true but hidden causal mechanisms of the social order. By identifying the now maligned ideational regime as something people have been fooled into believing by empirical trickery, it becomes easier to convert people to an alternative understanding of the causes and cures for poverty.

While it is well accepted that social movements must consciously frame their public discourse, the term "frame" evokes a static discursive image contained and enclosed inside a solid, immobile, airtight picture frame. But it takes the causal temporality of narrative to convert the intended audience from one ideational regime to another. A conversion narrative, therefore, begins with a present crisis, and then moves backward in time to a more harmonious past before the onset of the crisis, then forward again to the problematic present. Here again the conversion narrative differs from the standard form. Rather than automatically moving to a resolution, it uses the thought experiment to forecast two possible futures—one promising only more of the same strife, the second promising a future restored to an original state of harmony.

True to narrative form Malthus begins his story at the moment of crisis and paradox—a crisis of ever-worsening poverty despite ever-increasing levels of poor relief: "It is a subject often started in conversation, and mentioned always as a matter of great surprise that, notwithstanding the immense sum that is annually collected for the poor in England, there is still so much distress among them" (Malthus 1985[1798], 94).

After running through a standard catalog of all the other apparent causes of distress, Malthus argues that none is the culprit. Instead he insists in true theoretical realist intonations that a "man who looks a little *below the surface of things*" can readily perceive that it is not poverty that causes increasing poor relief but—now introducing the shock effect of the perversity thesis—it is *poor relief that causes poverty*. To make the case, Malthus uses causal narrativity (Somers 1998). He takes us backward to the story's "beginning," before political meddling with the laws of nature eroded the peasantry's "spirit of independence" (Malthus 1985 [1798], 98). In this pre-political Lockean state of nature (one readily recognizable as inspired by Townsend's island), scarcity creates a perfect equilibrium of food and population. As an historical claim, this lacks empirical foundations; Malthus could present no evidence that this harmonious past ever existed. His was a theory-driven logic, based on imputed theoretical entities. But it worked brilliantly as an axiomatic point of departure to develop, step-by-step, his poverty to perversion conversion narrative.

Malthus then returns us to the crisis-ridden present. Equilibrium has turned into chaos as population growth has far outpaced available resources. The reason is all too evident: By guaranteeing food and resources, the Poor Laws have dissolved the discipline that only scarcity can impose; they have distorted labor market signals and created perverse incentives to produce children doomed to live off parish relief.

The only solution is total abolition. In response to the skeptics, Malthus tells his audience that they have been captive to a worldview that for three centuries has been deceiving the English into believing that laws and institutions are stronger than the laws of nature—a case of deeply duplicitous reasoning used on unknowing but well-intentioned taxpayers. Unable to see deeper than the appearance of poverty, the empiricism of institutional pragmatism applies a pragmatic band-aid that only fiddles with the "hands of the clock." The Poor Laws will never work because they are trying to solve through political means what is in fact a natural phenomena: "What is this [the Poor Law requirement to provide work] but saying that the funds for the maintenance of labour in this country may be increased at will, and without limit by a fiat of government or an assessment of the overseers? Strictly speaking, this clause is as arrogant and as absurd as if it had enacted that two ears of wheat should in future grow where one only had grown before. *Canute, when he commanded the waves not to wet his princely foot, did not in reality assume a greater power over the laws of nature* . . . it is expected that a miraculous increase of these funds should immediately follow an edict of the government, used at the discretion of some ignorant parish officers" (Malthus 1992 [1803], 103–4, emphasis added). Pragmatic institutionalism cannot solve the crisis because it does not even understand that it is the result of natural laws. By showing how only social naturalism's laws of nature can explain why the Poor Laws not only have not but *cannot* solve the problem of poverty, Malthus is well on his way to making his own alternative ideational program the only viable definition of reality.

In a dazzling display of the powers of the thought experiment, Malthus uses a conversion narrative to project two possible futures. In the first, the Old Poor Laws remain untouched. As there has been neither the will nor the wisdom to adopt the practical implications of the perversity thesis, this future portends ever-darkening social ills. In this bleak outlook, misplaced compassion relentlessly induces more and more avoidance of market appropriate behavior. There will be only more poverty, higher taxes, more beggary and vagrancy, and ever-multiplying numbers of poor people demanding their "right" to assistance that the country can no longer provide. With generational continuity, the parasitic culture of dependence will only continue.

But Malthus presents an alternative future that people can choose. In this second one, the Poor Laws have been abolished and the state has converted to a new regime of free-market fundamentalism based on obedience to the laws of nature. New policy mandates would establish a definite time limit on the meager benefits that might still be bestowed under special circumstances: "[A] regulation [shall] be made, declaring that no child born from any marriage taking place after the expiration of a year from the date of the law, and no illegitimate child born two years from the same date, should ever be entitled to parish assistance"(Malthus 1992 [1803], 261).[15] And should any child be born in violation of these laws of state and nature, then the consequences be damned: "To the punishment, therefore, of nature he should be left, the punishment of severe want. He has erred in the face of a most clear and precise warning, and can have no just reason to complain of any person but himself when he feels the consequence of his error" (Malthus 1992 [1803], 262–63).

His Procrustean interpretation of scientific logic gives Malthus complete confidence to predict that when the poor are no longer protected from the consequences of their folly, their behavior will change. Absent the perverse incentives of the Poor Laws, in his utopian projection the poor will inevitably confront and anticipate the consequences of their own actions: "If this system were pursued, we need be under no apprehensions whatever that the number of persons in extreme want would be beyond the power and will of the benevolent [through private charity] to supply" (Malthus [1803] 1992, 263). While eliminating relief and letting children die of hunger might appear to be cruel, it is simply restoring the regulative laws of nature that have always kept population and food supply in balance.[16] This balance promises to be the foundation of Polanyi's "stark Utopia."

Ideational Re-Embedding

Malthus understood well the power of narrative to convert elite opinion to the truth of the perversity thesis, and in his invention of the poverty to perversity conversion narrative he displayed real genius. With a parsimonious elegance and logic, he uses both theoretical realism and social naturalism to move us from an initial focus on the "illusory" causes of poverty to an endpoint that reveals the "real" causes to be reckless and perverse violations of the laws of nature and population. Point by point, Malthus refutes the entire canon of institutional pragmatism. He fells the alleged benefits of a large and healthy population of working people. He demolishes the institutionalist belief in the social and political causes of unemployment. He ridicules the capacity of reason to alleviate suffering and improve humanity. And thanks to his adept use of theoretical realism, he has provided an explanation for how intelligent and well-meaning people could have been so misled by pragmatic institutionalism. The blame is placed squarely on the mystifying powers of wrongheaded *ideas,* not on those whom they deceived. It follows then that institutional pragmatism is an illegitimate regime whose policies are not solutions; they are actually themselves the problems.[17]

Inventing the "Undeserving" Poor

Of all Malthus's accomplishments, however, none was more portentous than his radically converting poverty from a structural status in society to a behavioral choice. Recall that "the poor" did not originally refer to a condition of want, indigence, or dependence on poor relief. Rather, the poor were a *class* of people whose lack of *property* compelled them to labor to survive—hence they were also called the "labouring" or the "working" poor. Extreme labor market volatility put them continually at risk of losing their livelihoods and being forced to seek temporary poor relief. But falling in and out of poverty was not due to changes in behavior; rather, it was the precariousness of the poor's propertyless status in the class structure.

Breaking centuries of tradition, Malthus tears apart this structural definition and transforms the poor from a class location to a moral condition based on personal behavior and lack of biological restraint. This allows him to bifurcate a once unified status into what later became codified as the "deserving" and the "undeserving" poor. The state of one's livelihood now became a matter of moral character, with independence and employment privileged as the highest moral achievements. Only those destitute through no "fault" of their own—the old, the crippled, the sick, the disabled—were deserving of charity, and even then not in the form of parish relief but of private (discretionary) alms. But *able-bodied* workers without work and in need exhibited failures of moral character—they were the *undeserving* poor. In this newly moralized taxonomy, the amalgam of being able-bodied, penniless, and seeking assistance (however temporary) made one a moral outlaw, newly condemned as a pauper. And if beseeched for aid by these morally undeserving, Malthus enjoined the authorities not to eliminate their poverty and provide relief, but to coerce them into suffering the consequences of their perverse and blameworthy behavior. Shame and disgrace were to be the means: "Hard as it may appear in individual instances, dependent poverty ought to be held disgraceful. Such a stimulus seems to be absolutely necessary to promote the happiness of the great mass of mankind; and every general attempt to weaken this stimulus, however benevolent its apparent intention, will always defeat its own purpose. If men be induced to marry from the mere prospect of parish provision, they are not only unjustly tempted to bring unhappiness and dependence upon themselves, but are tempted, without knowing it, to injure all in the same class with themselves" (Malthus 1992 [1803], 101).

Malthus thus ideationally re-embeds the labor market. For 500 years the poor had been a sociological classification of the propertyless that carried no moral judgment. Because the labor market was an institution over which people had no control, poverty and unemployment were also beyond control, and thus conditions with no shame attached. By grafting the moral categories of desert, merit, and self-sufficiency onto the structural condition of poverty and a volatile labor market, Malthus broke the pragmatic institutionalist social compact and replaced it with a market-based one. The ideational change from poverty to perversity was all but triumphant.

It was the 1834 Report of the Royal Commission that was the necessary last link before legislative change could be achieved. The commissioners—ardent converts all—made no attempt to interview the recipients of relief. Instead, they accumulated anecdotes from "reformed" parish authorities to prove that their Malthusian model of human behavior was correct (Royal Commission 1834, 227–61). In a skillful Malthusian maneuver, the commissioners claimed that they had scientifically tested their hypothesis of Poor Law reform and had real statistical evidence for their causal claims. Their report exemplifies the use of facts as ornaments in a model-driven thought experiment rather than as data in a genuine causal theory. And despite the implausibility of its findings, the report was hugely influential in both England and the United States for decades.

Delegitimating the old Poor Laws was quickened by the work of numerous Malthusian converts. It was often these zealous followers who took on the task of influencing opinion against the Poor Laws through rancorous public debate. Thomas Chalmers, a political economist who exerted great sway over public opinion, was one of the most significant of these. In 1811, Chalmers warns that a future with the Poor Laws still in place "would unhinge the constitution of society." It would be hard to find a more exacting representation of the poverty to perversity conversion narrative: "It is in the *power of charity to corrupt its object*; it may tempt him to indolence—it may lead him to *renounce all dependence on himself*—it may *nourish the meanness and depravity of his character*—it may lead him to *hate exertion*, and *resign without a sigh the dignity of independence* . . . Every man would *repose on the beneficence of another*; every *incitement to diligence would be destroyed*. The *evils of poverty would multiply* to such an extent as to be beyond the power of the most unbounded charity to redress them; and instead of an Elysium of love and plenty, the country would present the nauseating spectacle of sloth *and beggary and corruption*" (cited in Young 1969, 120, italics in original).

With the 1834 New Poor Law, the poverty to perversity ideational regime change triumphed.[18] The able-bodied but now undeserving poor would no longer be provided assistance unless they succumbed to the humiliation, degradation, and discipline of the work house (Driver 1993; Poynter 1969). The English labor market was restructured within a new ideational and institutional framework, one that overthrew the perversity of political meddling and reinstated the natural order in which degradation and scarcity would again teach the poor to respond appropriately to labor market signals. Labor market re-embedding, not its disembedding and setting free, was the perversity thesis's crowning achievement.

The Recycling of Malthus in the United States

As with the English Poor Law, Aid for Dependent Children from its inception was ideationally embedded in the institutional pragmatism of Roosevelt's New Deal. While the New Deal coalition was energized by the moral fervor of radical and socialist critics of capitalism, its architects did not set forth a full-fledged public narrative based on social democratic or other systematic principles (Brinkley 1996; Plotke 1996). Instead, not unlike mercantilism, most of the key policymakers responded on a piecemeal basis to particular problems believing that pragmatic government policies could overcome market failures. In the case of Aid to Dependent Children (the initial name for the program), the idea was to federalize the Widow's Pension laws, which had been funded at inadequate levels by the states (Katz 1986; Skocpol 1992).

And when government programs—including Aid to Families with Dependent Children—were further expanded in the Great Society, the justifications were also pragmatic. But just as England's pragmatic but inchoate approach to poverty suffered when confronted with the overarching narrative and utopian coherence of the perversity thesis, so too the New Deal / Great Society regime was equally vulnerable against the appeal of market fundamentalism's coherent, naturalistic, and visionary narrative.

As the U.S. welfare rolls expanded dramatically in the 1960s, there was talk of replacing AFDC with a more effective set of policies to reduce poverty. By the mid-1970s, however, the failure of reform efforts provided an opportunity for conservatives to launch an attack on welfare dependency. Although Martin Anderson (1978) was the first of the conservative intellectuals to revive the perversity thesis, the turning point was Charles Murray's *Losing Ground* (1984). Murray's role in shifting the welfare debate has been well recognized (Harpham and Scotch 1988; Katz 1989; O'Connor 2001; Schram 1995). That his arguments replicate those of Malthus has not.[19] Just as Malthus used the paradoxical conceit of ever-growing poverty in the midst of ever-increasing poor relief, so too Murray begins: "[Thirteen] percent of Americans were poor, using the official definition. Over the next twelve years, our expenditures on social welfare quadrupled. And, in 1980, the percentage of poor Americans was 13 percent." (Murray 1984, 8) By the next page, Murray shifts from the idea that the poverty rate had remained unchanged to the Malthusian reprise that: "We tried to provide more for the poor and produced more poor instead" (Murray 1984, 8–9).

Although he provides no textual or bibliographic reference, Murray's opening salvo against Great Society social policy recycles Malthus almost to the letter. Great Society programs failed because of their perverse behavioral inducements; instead of work discipline and sexual restraint, wrongheaded perverse incentives increased childbearing, female-headed households, and labor force withdrawal. Inevitably, the poor made themselves poorer in direct proportion to society's increasingly expenditures.[20] Once declaring the causal agent of poverty to be the perversity of welfare itself, Murray adopts the poverty to perversity conversion narrative in his efforts to change public opinion. As with Malthus before him, he invokes the social naturalism of a harmonious utopian existence before welfare created a culture of dependence, personal shame, and sexual irresponsibility (1984, 229). He proves his argument by directly replicating Malthus's thought experiment about two possible futures—one, a bleak culture of dependency and parasitism; the other a utopian restoration of character and moral redemption: "The proposed program, *our final and most ambitious thought experiment,* consists of scrapping the entire federal welfare and income-support structure for working-aged persons. . . . It would leave the person with no recourse whatsoever except the job market, family members, friends, and public or private locally funded services" (Murray 1984, 227–228, emphasis added).

The discipline of scarcity would induce parents to "become quite insistent about their children learning skills and getting jobs" and to exercise appropriate parenting by preventing "a daughter's bringing home a baby that must be entirely supported on an already inadequate income" (Murray 1984, 228). He invokes the natural harmony of a pre-welfare order when he predicts that the withdrawal of poor relief will lead to the moral redemption of the poor: "I am hypothesizing . . . that the lives of large numbers of poor people would be radically changed for the better" (Murray 1984, 229). He also reveals his affinity with Malthus in his derision of those who would be held back by lack of data: "Data are not essential to certain arguments about social policy and indeed can get in the way. The terms of debate can be grounded wholly in preferences about how the world ought to be, not how it is" (Murray 1984, 53). He continues to be unrepentant about his disdain for data: "[It is not] necessary to treat the hypotheses raised here as ones to be abruptly tested and accepted or discarded. They will not statistically test the validity of antipoverty programs. They deal with the complicated side of the welfare problem: human behavior. These hypotheses, rather, are more useful for the perspectives they provide. When ways to shrink the underclass are found, they will grow from a strategic understanding of how social policy shapes behavior . . . analysts of social policy badly need a place to stand" (Murray 1986b, 11).

Just as Malthus's success was reflected in his many converts who joined the battle for Poor Law repeal, so too Murray's arguments were reprised by other writers who were even more explicit in recycling the perversity framework of the early nineteenth century. In 1984 the conservative intellectual historian Gertrude Himmelfarb published *The Idea of Poverty,* in which she passionately revives the anti-Poor Law arguments of Malthus, Burke, de Tocqueville, and others. With much fanfare and acclaim, she also republished de Tocqueville's (1983 [1835]) attack on the English Poor Laws, itself a stunningly Malthusian artifact. Marvin Olasky (1992), mentor to Newt Gingrich and G. W. Bush, celebrated the thinking of Thomas Chalmers, the same enthusiastic Malthusian convert who was so influential in the passage of the New Poor Law almost two hundred years earlier (see above). And throughout the 1980s and 1990s, conservative think tanks mobilized the perversity thesis to criticize the welfare system with ever-greater intensity (George 1997; O'Connor 2001; Rich 2004; Schram 1995; Williams 1996).

Only shortly before the PRWORA passed into law, Murray himself returned to the Malthusian theme of runaway population growth with his influential essay, "The Coming White Underclass" (1993). Exploiting the widespread moral panic over the alleged epidemic of teenage pregnancy, Murray argued that the out-of-wedlock birthrate among whites was poised to replicate the spectacular increase that had already occurred among African American women—a direct consequence of welfare's perverse incentives for illegitimate childbearing. His solution: "To restore the rewards and penalties of marriage does not require social engineering. Rather, it requires that the state stop interfering with the natural forces that have done the job quite effectively for millennia. . . . Restoring economic penalties translates into the first and central policy prescription: to end all economic support for single mothers. The AFDC (Aid to Families with Dependent Children) payment goes to zero" (Murray 1993). And despite Luker's (1996) path-breaking discovery that the alleged epidemic of teenage pregnancy was illusory, Murray's naturalistic abstractions overwhelmed social science evidence and shaped the terms of the debate in public discourse and hastened the 1996 legislation (Weaver 2000, 150–151).

Ideational Re-Embedding Again

The U.S. transformation from a culture that supported AFDC to one that easily instituted the PRWORA was an ideational achievement. Weaver (2000, 104–105) writes, "Conservative ideas, including those on welfare, moved from the margins of public debate to the mainstream, while liberal ideas appeared increasingly bankrupt." There is little doubt that this can in large part be attributed to Murray (and others) recycling the discursive powers of the perversity thesis. Thanks especially to the highly favorable treatment of his work by influential publications, Murray's channeling of Malthus had a significant impact on both elite and public opinion. *Business Week* claimed that *Losing Ground* "lays out a stark truth that must be faced," while the *Wall Street Journal* wrote that Murray's "tone is steadfastly non-partisan; he marshals an immense amount of data in support of his views . . . and never ventures a conclusion for which he has not laid the most elaborate and convincing groundwork" (cited in Harpham and Scotch 1988, 199)—a stunningly Malthusian demonstration of how to use theoretical realism to convince readers that what are only voluminous illustrations are in fact genuine causal arguments.

It is hardly surprising that by 1994, 71% of respondents in a public opinion survey agreed with the following statement: "The welfare system does more harm than good, because it encourages the breakup of the family and discourages the work ethic" (Weaver, Shapiro, and Jacobs 1995, 611). Surveys in earlier years did not ask this same question, but respondents had been significantly less inclined to blame government programs for increasing poverty. Between 1978 and 1986, the number of respondents who said that government programs generally made things worse for the poor fluctuated between 14% and 20% (Shapiro, Patterson, Russell, and Young 1987).

By 1994, it was clear that ideational regime change had all but triumphed. The poverty to perversity conversion narrative had succeeded in delegitimating AFDC; both elites and the public were persuaded that it was doing more harm than good. The path was open to radical policy transformation.

Still, two additional developments were critical before the ideational change was converted into a new policy regime. The first derived from Murray's (1984) proposal that welfare benefits should be limited and recipients explicitly told that at a definite future time, all government assistance would end. This idea of an across-the-board time limit transformed into the idea of tailored time limits that would limit the assistance that any particular recipient could receive. David Ellwood, a Kennedy School analyst, was one of the first prominent liberals to embrace this type of time limit, but only as part of a broader program to raise both the Earned Income Tax Credit and the minimum wage while guaranteeing a minimum wage job (Ellwood 1988). As routinely happens, when Bill Clinton campaigned in 1992 in support of a two-year time limit, the time limit idea was quickly severed from this broader program. Offering no promise of guaranteed employment, Clinton never explained how a young mother with few skills could quickly become self-sufficient in a labor market marked by chronically high unemployment (O'Connor 2001; Schram 2002). No one seemed to notice. Once prominent Democrats had signed on to this dramatic change in perspective, it became increasingly difficult to protect the older notion of welfare assistance as a necessary compensation for the unfairness of circumstances. Malthusian logic triumphed again.

A second important development was the mobilization of illustrative "evidence" about the state welfare waiver experiments that had begun under Ronald Reagan in 1986 (Rogers-Dillon 2004; Teles 1996). In this program, states were allowed to experiment with different rules for welfare provision in specific localities. The research reports that emerged from these experiments played a role in the United States comparable to that of England's 1834 Royal Commission Report. The studies, principally written by the Manpower Development Research Corporation, found that programs designed to push welfare mothers into work could sharply cut the welfare rolls and government outlays without provoking protest. Hence, the studies appeared to confirm the perversity conversion story—that the poor would actually be better off without welfare (Gueron, Pauly, and Lougy 1991; Peck 2001; Weaver 2000).

Of course, the studies did not prove this at all. The data actually showed that most recipients who made the transition from welfare to work remained desperately poor, and a substantial percentage of the caseload was unable to find or sustain employment. In fact, the waiver studies were consistent with decades of careful empirical findings that the AFDC rolls were divided between a mobile group with short spells on the rolls and a second group that remained on the rolls for years (Blank 1997). Legislators, however, ignored all of this earlier research. Their now deeply held Malthusian expectations blinded them or allowed them to overwrite undesirable or inconvenient data—a stark example of how epistemic privilege equips the perversity thesis with its own internal standards of veracity. As with their predecessor in 1834, the Reports justified a bill with rigid work requirements and strict time limits by relying on dubious scientific data and thought experiments about how repealing welfare transformed the poor into productive citizens.

The 1996 legislation effectively re-embedded low-wage labor markets within a new ideational and institutional regime. The new legislation led to a transformation of the culture and organization of welfare offices as a new discipline of "work first" policies, and time limits were imposed on recipients. The hallmark of this new infrastructure was a dramatic increase in the use of sanctions to punish recipients for lack of compliance with the new and complex structure of rules (Hays 2003; Handler 2004; Pavetti and Bloom 2001; Shipler 2004). The new policies pushed millions of single mothers off the welfare rolls, further expanding the number for whatever low-wage work employers are willing to provide and exacerbating the trend toward growing wage inequality in the United States (Kuttner 2007).

Conclusion

Every nation has a story—a public narrative it tells to explain its place in the flow of history, to justify its normative principles, to delineate the boundaries of rational political decision-making, and to give legitimacy to its economic policies and practices. Under normal conditions, narratives that compete with the mainstream are marginalized beyond those boundaries; in crisis conditions, however, a contest over ideational hegemony is likely to erupt. Much is at stake in these battles of ideas, as the victor will dramatically transform how markets and society interact. Debates over market policies are thus fought out as battles of contending narratives. History, rival ideas, even crises may conspire to destabilize the ruling ideational regime, but as long as there is no more powerful alternative story, it will be unthreatened. Ideational regime change in a society's reigning narrative is a rare event.

Our goal is to understand and bring theoretical clarity to one such rare event—market fundamentalism's rise to hegemony in the late twentieth century. Its very uncommonness signals its importance, but it also poses a methodological challenge for theorizing beyond a case study. To gain leverage, we have focused our detailed analysis on its greatest successes in two very different historical eras. The 1996 PRWORA and the 1834 NPL were divided by enormous contextual differences of time and place. Yet the centuries between them only deepen the mystery of how such dissimilar environments could produce such similar outcomes. In both cases, long-prevailing policy regimes of institutional pragmatism were felled and replaced by market fundamentalism in just a few short decades. Market fundamentalist views once seen as extremist rapidly achieved mainstream status and moved the spectrum of political discourse to the right. In both cases, a public discourse that reassigned blame for the poor's condition from poverty to perversity played the key role. Ideational change was the engine of new welfare legislation that dramatically restricted the access of the poor to assistance.

That ideas matter is readily confirmed by our findings: market fundamentalist ideas served as the causal drive in both episodes of ideational re-embeddedness. In this we concur with O'Connor (2001, 17–18): "[Most] important in determining the political meaning and policy consequences of poverty knowledge . . . has been the power to establish the terms of debate—to contest, gain, and ultimately to exercise ideological hegemony over the boundaries of political discourse." Market fundamentalist political discourse and ideational practices thus matter not just as descriptors or extra variables but as causal mechanisms that embed and shape markets. This in turn highlights the significance of our concept of ideational embeddedness—it is a real force with real causal powers. It also corrects a common misunderstanding, namely that the victory of free market ideology is synonymous with market deregulation. Market fundamentalism, as our stories of the NPL and the PRWORA demonstrate, does not disembed markets. Rather, it simply imposes a different *kind* of embeddedness from that of institutional pragmatism, one that tells a different story about the urgency of liberating markets from the tyranny of policies that violate the autonomy of self-regulating natural entities. The struggle between institutional pragmatism and market fundamentalism was not over *whether* markets would be embedded, but *which* body of ideas would do the embedding.

That all ideas are not created equal has also been confirmed. Market fundamentalism is clearly a case of uncommon ideational powers, which we attribute to an epistemic privilege derived from its infrastructure of social naturalism, theoretical realism, and its use of the conversion narrative. Both Malthus and Murray used this epistemic clout not only to discredit structural explanations for poverty but also to create alternative definitions of reality and rationality. We also saw how market fundamentalism's epistemic privilege equips it with its own internal claims to veracity—Bourdieu's "means of making itself true" (1998, 95)—and, as the MDRC studies indicate, immunizes it against disconfirming evidence. Social scientists find themselves puzzled and frustrated that twenty years of high-quality research based on large empirical projects like the Panel Study of Income Dynamics changed public opinion so little on such basic facts as how long most people stay on welfare (Duncan 1984).

That the PRWORA and the NPL were so similar despite their great contextual differences reveals another advantage market fundamentalism has over theories that lack their own epistemological bootstraps: its ideas do not have to be rooted in specific historical circumstances to exert powerful influence. This poses a challenge for a sociology of knowledge that assumes winning ideas are those that fit local circumstances. In fact, the very strength of the perversity thesis is that it is *not* so rooted, but relies on abstract thought experiments and naturalistic models that have no empirical referents. Given the common assumption that, in the marketplace of ideas, successful theories are those that best confirm empirical data, these findings may be puzzling. But it seems inescapable that Malthus and Murray triumphed not despite but *because* they relied on arguments driven by the seemingly inevitable and timeless laws of nature and biology, rather than by empirical contextual referents.

This makes social naturalism perhaps the most potent weapon of market fundamentalism. Those who believe, even a little, in the sovereignty of nature cannot simultaneously accept the causal powers of human artifice, reason, and political institutions. If the laws of nature rule, then social and political laws cannot; there can only be one sovereign per ideational regime. Market fundamentalism achieves that status by taking control over what counts as reality. By defining the crises of the old regime as inevitable results of the failure to obey nature's laws, market fundamentalism establishes itself as the new gatekeeper of rational discourse and policy debate. While it is shocking, therefore, it is not surprising that when the House of Representatives was debating the PRWORA, a U.S. Congressperson biologized the poor as beasts who have been cheated of the natural order. The unconscious allusion to Townsend's island of the goats and the dogs that so influenced Malthus's vision of human nature is striking: "Mr. Chairman, I represent Florida where we have many lakes and natural reserves. If you visit these areas, you may see a sign that reads, 'do not feed the alligators.' We post these for several reasons. First, because if left in a natural state, alligators can fend for themselves. They work, gather food and care for their young. Second, we post these warnings because *unnatural feeding and artificial care creates dependency. When dependency sets in, these otherwise able-bodied alligators can no longer survive on their own.* Now, I know people are not alligators, but I submit to you that with our current handout, nonwork welfare system, *we have upset the natural order.* We have failed to understand the simple warning signs. We have created a system of dependency" (Mica 1995, emphasis added).

Still, as impressive and necessary as they are, market fundamentalism's internal causal powers are not sufficient to explain its triumph.[21] Outside opportunities were also necessary. One of these was the common cultural heritage of Lockean liberalism. In most non-Anglo-American developed societies, similar efforts to delegitimate welfare programs have been less successful, achieving only minor retrenchments without visible impact on rates of poverty and inequality. The United States, England, and perhaps Australia and New Zealand are the only exceptions (Handler 2004; Hicks 1999; Huber and Stephens 2001; Korpi and Palme 2003; Smeeding, Rainwater, and Burtless 2001; Solow 2000). These are all societies with a common Lockean ideational history in which social naturalism has deep roots. (That the Canadian welfare state has been growing suggests that the Lockean legacy is necessary but not sufficient for a society to be at risk for welfare retrenchment). Social naturalism allowed Locke to make civil society and markets natural and self-regulating entities free from coercive governmental authority. Distrust of the state, high confidence in the freedom of the market's natural laws, and the essential biologization of human nature are all part of this mix of social naturalism and the Lockean legacy.

Sequential patterns of external events also created openings and opportunities for market fundamentalism. In both cases, a cascade of problems became full-blown national political crises only when the old regimes could no longer absorb and neutralize them, making the government look unstable, weak, and floundering. The resulting policy vacuum created an opening for once-marginalized competing ideas to enter into public debates over what should be done, and in the ensuing battles of clashing ideational systems the persuasiveness of the perversity thesis accorded a new mainstream legitimacy to the once extreme challengers.

These patterns also reveal the vulnerability of institutional pragmatism. Its pragmatism pushes it toward technocratic fixes of immediate and urgent problems, rather than toward comprehensive moral visions. Mercantilism and the New Deal/Great Society were in many ways bricolages of problem-driven solutions that accumulated over time. When challenged by progressive social movements, pragmatic institutionalists often respond with reforms that morally strengthen the regime. But when challenged by market fundamentalism, the impulse to make concessions only serves to make these regimes appear incoherent relative to the moral purity of their opponents' proposals. *Pragmatic policy-making produces regime frailty.* When faced with problem overload, its very flexibility leaves it vulnerable to market fundamentalism's unbending visionary principles.

This points to another of market fundamentalism's advantages. Its leitmotif of a purely self-regulating market society cannot be achieved; it is a "stark Utopia" (GT, 3). As we documented and explored in Chapter 1, market fundamentalism has for two centuries been telling a free-market utopian story in which it is simply a midwife to a "natural" future that has yet to come into being. If markets fail to perform as promised, the fault cannot lie with the theory, since free-market utopianism is simply a reflection of nature's design. Instead, the blame is placed on political interferences that must have imposed perverse incentives and impaired its self-regulating laws by shielding some aspect of the social order from the market's logic. Hence, market fundamentalism engages in a double sleight of hand—using ideational and political powers to construct markets by means of draconian laws and policies, while simultaneously insisting that the process is entirely natural and apolitical.

Afterword

The Personal Responsibility and Work Opportunities Reconciliation Act of 1996 represented a significant turning point in U.S. politics. When Bill Clinton signed the bill, the Democratic Party had won only two out of the last six presidential elections. After he signed, the Democrats proceeded to win four out of the next five presidential elections, although George W. Bush was awarded the White House in 2000 by the Supreme Court without a recount of ballots in Florida. Victorious Republicans in the first period invariably tied their Democratic opponent to an unpopular program that much of the public perceived as providing benefits to an overwhelmingly minority population. From 1996 onward, Democrats could claim that their party had "ended welfare as we knew it" and thus render such Republican attacks impotent.[22]

To be sure, Republicans have gone on to deploy the rhetoric of perversity against virtually all remaining government benefit program, including food stamps, unemployment insurance, the earned income tax credit, social security, Medicare, and Medicaid. But these rhetorical attacks have, thus far, failed to discredit programs that are perceived by much of the public as providing necessary support to deserving people. In fact, Republican proposals to "privatize" or "voucherize" Social Security and Medicare have proven politically unpopular and have contributed to public perceptions of the party as being out of touch and indifferent to the needs of the middle class.

This problem for the Republcans was exemplified in the 2012 campaign by Mitt Romney's comments about the 47%. Speaking at a fundraiser at a private house with no press present, Romney was surreptitiously captured saying:

> There are 47 percent of the people who will vote for the president no matter what. All right, there are 47 percent who are with him, who are dependent upon government, who believe that they are victims, who believe that government has a responsibility to care for them, who believe that they are entitled to health care, to food, to housing, to you-name-it. That that's an entitlement. And the government should give it to them. And they will vote for this president no matter what. And I mean, the president starts off with 48, 49, 48—he starts off with a huge number. These are people who pay no income tax. Forty-seven percent of Americans pay no income tax. So our message of low taxes doesn't connect (http://www.motherjones.com/politics/2012/09/full-transcript-mitt-romney-secret-video#47percent).

The irony was that Romney ended up the election with just a little more than 47% of the vote, suggesting that he was unable to hold the votes of a significant number of those who he defined as productive and independent citizens.

While it is hard to dispute that the 1996 welfare legislation had a major impact on electoral politics, this "success" has effectively frozen the new policies in place and has largely immunized them from criticism. The Temporary Aid to Needy Families (TANF) program was reauthorized in 2005, and another reauthorization has been pending since 2010. However, the delays in reauthorization have little to do with progressive criticisms of TANF; they come almost entirely from continuing Republican efforts to reduce spending to the poor even further. In fact, no major voices have been raised in the Democratic Party for expanding benefits or for reconsidering the logic of the program.

Bill and Hillary Clinton have very visibly reconsidered certain policies enacted during the Clinton presidency; they have both rejected the "don't ask, don't tell" policy on gays in the military and they have repudiated the Defense of Marriage Act that had been signed just a month after the PRWORA. But they continue to defend "welfare reform" as a great success despite considerable evidence to the contrary. Moreover, because of its electoral potency, the establishment of the Democratic

Party—including, of course, President Obama—have enthusiastically embraced the Clintons' position. The result is an ongoing conspiracy of silence in which even some progressive academics have continued to defend the 1996 legislation (Jencks 2005).

But the shift from AFDC to TANF has cost poor families billions of dollars of assistance and the percentage of poor families receiving government assistance has fallen precipitously from 1996 to the present.[23] The United States has long been an outlier among developed nations in terms of the percentage of families living in poverty before taxes and transfers. But with the shift from AFDC to TANF, the United States now does far less than other nations to redress the very uneven distribution of market-based income. The consequence is that the percentage of children living in poverty in the United States is significantly higher than in other developed nations (Gornick and Jantti 2011). Even the U.K., which historically kept the United States company in the percentage of children growing up in poverty, has implemented policies that have substantially improved its performance on this indicator.

But the critical test for any social program is how it performs when disaster strikes. In 2008–2009, the U.S. economy experienced the most severe economic downturn since the Great Depression of the 1930s. In earlier post-World War II recessions, AFDC worked as a safety net. As unemployment rose, so also did the AFDC rolls—supporting many children driven into poverty by their parents' temporary economic distress. This was a vitally important part of the safety net because the system of unemployment insurance in the United States is deeply flawed. In 2010, only 32% of the unemployed were actually receiving unemployment benefits (National Employment Law Program 2010). First, states have allowed employers to exempt certain categories of employees from coverage. Second, coverage expires after fifty-two weeks or ninety-nine weeks, depending on Congressional action, even though joblessness in a severe recession can last much longer. The national unemployment rate remained above 8% four and a half years after the recession began.

TANF, however, was structured to give states strong incentives to make entry into the program difficult for new applicants. The consequence was that it was simply not available for many families that were either ineligible for unemployment insurance or who had exhausted their benefits. As Jason DeParle wrote in *The New York Times* in April 2012: " . . . much as overlooked critics of the restrictions once warned, a program that built its reputation when times were good offered little help when jobs disappeared. Despite the worst economy in decades, the cash welfare rolls have barely budged. Faced with flat federal financing and rising need, Arizona is one of 16 states that have cut their welfare caseloads further since the start of the recession—in its case, by half. Even as it turned away the needy, Arizona spent most of its federal welfare dollars on other programs, using permissive rules to plug state budget gaps" (DeParle 2012).

In short, in many states of the union, when children faced hunger and homelessness because their parents had lost employment in a global economic downturn, the TANF program refused to provide assistance. It is difficult to exaggerate the magnitude of this as a policy failure. Moreover, it is a policy failure that could only be justified by the most extreme version of the perversity thesis; one which insists that individuals, including children, are personally responsible for meeting their own needs even when unemployment had reached catastrophic levels. And yet, there has been virtually no debate about this policy failure.

TANF's massive inadequacies should not surprise, however; after all, they had already been revealed in an earlier disaster—Hurricane Katrina's catastrophic impact on New Orleans in 2005. Here again, the storm and its aftermath received enormous media coverage, but almost no one connected the dots and showed that the scale of the disaster was also linked to the 1996 PRWORA. It is thus worthwhile to revisit Somers' (2008) argument, which elaborates the Polanyian argument about the destructive consequences of market fundamentalist ideas.

Polanyi emphasizes that while the free-market utopia cannot be achieved, the ideologically driven effort to impose it on society will nevertheless have disastrous consequences for vulnerable sectors of society. In his view, the whole idea of protective measures such as the Old Poor Laws is that they buffer people from rapid shifts in the market. In rural counties of England, for example, in the seventeenth and eighteenth centuries, there was a sudden collapse of long-established rural crafts that had provided a significant amount of employment. But Poor Law assistance gave families time to adjust and find replacement sources of income. Without such buffering mechanisms, he stresses that the very survival of entire communities is put at risk (Somers 1993, 1995).

But market fundamentalists have argued that citizenship should be treated as a contractual quid pro quo market relationship in which once-basic rights and government assistance should be provided only in exchange for citizens meeting certain obligations, such as making themselves ready for poorly paid employment and cooperating with the authorities to reveal the paternity of any offspring who are to be supported with public funds. However reasonable such requests for responsibility might sound, this "contractualization of citizenship" is catastrophic for the significant numbers of people who have little of value to exchange. With few skills and a deficit of cultural capital, there is no demand for their services, and thus no right to full citizenship. They are, in effect, internally stateless.

This is exactly what happened in many inner city neighborhoods in the aftermath of the 1996 PRWORA. With a brief exception during the 1996–1999 economic expansion, unemployment rates in these communities have been at catastrophically high levels, particularly for young people of color. Without substantial job opportunities, young men in these communities drift towards the underground economy and have been incarcerated at astonishingly high rates (Alexander 2010; Wacquant 2009). Young women are left on their own to raise children, but time limits and other barriers make it extremely difficult for them to receive any forms of public assistance. Census data shows that the number of families living in extreme poverty—defined as incomes less than half of the federal poverty line—has been steadily increasing since the late 1990s.

This was the condition of the urban poor in New Orleans in 2005 when Hurricane Katrina devastated the city. New Orleans did not have an evacuation plan for those in isolated African American neighborhoods who lacked their own means of transportation. As the waters rose, several thousand died in their homes or the streets, and more than 25,000 suffered for days in the Louisiana Superdome and Convention Center without food, water, or other supplies. All the while, the world watched and wondered how this could occur in the world's only remaining superpower.

This tragic story was the logical result of the contractualization of citizenship. While the poor of New Orleans had nominally retained their formal rights as citizens, they had effectively lost the foundational capacity to make claims on their fellow citizens. Hannah Arendt analyzed what happened to Jews in Central Europe who were stripped of their citizenship rights by the Nazis and their allies in other countries; they were transformed into stateless people who had lost "the right to have rights." From that condition, mass extermination in the death camps followed. While not as extreme, the fate of the poor of New Orleans can be analyzed in similar terms; even within their own nation, they had lost the right to have the rights of social inclusion and citizenship.

Two separate disasters—Hurricane Katrina and the global financial crisis—have revealed the failure of the welfare legislation passed in 1996. And yet, there is still no hint that the political system is willing to revisit that legislation and devise a more humane and just response to millions of people living in poverty. By every indicator, the United States has the highest percentage of religiously observant Christians of any of the world's developed societies. And in the Gospel of Matthew, Jesus told his followers with great clarity: "Truly I tell you, whatever you did for one of the least of these brothers and sisters of mine, you did for me" (Matthew 25:40). At some level, the gap between this New Testament injunction and the cruelty of poverty policies in the United States is impossible to fathom. But we have tried to show that the rhetoric of perversity is an important element in making sense of this abiding paradox.

7

THE ENDURING STRENGTH OF
FREE MARKET CONSERVATISM
IN THE UNITED STATES

This chapter brings Polanyi's insights to bear on some contemporary political differences between the United States and Europe since the 1970s. Chapter 6 explained why the United States passed legislation that significantly reduced income transfers to poor families in 1996 despite ever-rising numbers of children growing up in poverty.[1] Those legislative changes, moreover, contributed to both the social disaster of Hurricane Katrina as well as the impoverishing impact of the 2008 economic crisis.

Behind both welfare retrenchment and the repeated loosening of financial regulations that accompanied it lies the extraordinary strength of an organized conservative movement. Polanyi's concepts can help us make sense of the intensity and success of this right-wing ascendance. Many observers took Barack Obama's initial election in 2008 as marking the end of this prolonged period of right-wing dominance in the United States, but hostility to Obama's legislative agenda fueled a revival of the right's political fortunes at both the grassroots level and in the electoral arena (Skocpol and Williamson 2012; Rosenthal and Trost, eds. 2012). And once again, in 2012 some believed that Obama's re-election and the defeat of Mitt Romney would signal a political turn-around; but time since the election has disappointed these expectations no less than in the previous term.

To be sure, in its first term the Obama Administration pushed through legislation to address the decades-old task of giving the United States a system of national health insurance that would include most citizens if and when it is fully implemented. But the price paid for this long awaited measure has been heightened and continuous resistance to what conservatives label "Big Government." In its fight against health care reform in 2009 and 2010, the right successfully mobilized both grassroots and "top-down" ("astro-turf") protest against what they called an "unprecedented" expansion in federal powers, and this widely publicized "Tea Party" activism contributed to major gains by the Republicans in the 2010 midterm elections.

The irony is that what many citizens have been convinced is huge government "overreach" is, in fact, small in comparison to most other developed market societies. U.S. taxes as a percent of GDP are dramatically lower than the average among European nations, even though the outlays for military and security purposes are many times greater than those in other developed nations.[2] The combination of lower taxes and much higher military and national security spending means that the United States allocates a far smaller share of GDP for domestic programs than most other developed nations, which are far more generous in assisting the elderly, the unemployed, and especially the poor (Huber and Stephens 2001; Pontusson 2005). In comparison, market inequalities in the United States have accelerated virtually unimpeded. More than 20% of children are living at any time in households below the poverty line; the comparable figures in most European nations are below 5%. In this respect, there is a marked continuity: despite brief periods of market regulations in the New Deal and the Great Society, the United States has been a laggard in public social provision since the last decades of the nineteenth century (Skocpol 1992), and the pattern persists today.

Even so, extreme hostility to government continues to be a far more potent political force in the United States than elsewhere.[3] The relatively modest Obama health care legislation produced an intense anti-government backlash virtually absent in other developed nations where universal health coverage has been routine for generations.

There is a puzzle here, since it seemed in the 1960s that the United States was converging with Western Europe (Shonfield 1969). That was a decade of major welfare state expansion in most developed countries, perhaps most dramatized by the Johnson Administration's Medicare and Medicaid Acts in 1965 that passed with bipartisan Congressional support. Even when the Republicans gained the presidency in 1968, the Nixon Administration proposed an ambitious welfare reform agenda that would have provided a floor under every citizen's income (see

Chapter 5). It seemed at that time that anti-government hostility had ceased to be a major force in U.S. political life.

This changed rapidly in the 1970s, as the right successfully mobilized a backlash against the social movements and political reforms of the 1960s. By mobilizing instead of taking advantage of distrust of government and hostility to taxation, the right wing of the Republican Party became increasingly powerful (Martin 2008). With Ronald Reagan's election in 1980 and the implementation of tax cuts and business-friendly regulatory reforms, the United States moved definitively away from the direction that had been set by Franklin Roosevelt's New Deal (Himmelstein 1990; Phillips-Fein 2009; Smith 2012).

Two distinct but interconnected processes are at the heart of this major shift that began in the 1970s. The first is the strengthening of a grassroots conservative movement that has had considerable autonomy from the Republican Party. The second is a dramatic shift in the political strategy of the nation's business community that began in the 1970s. Combined, these two dynamics have driven U.S. politics continually to the right for four decades.

But before examining these more closely, let us look in more detail at how the United States has developed over the last four decades in a quite different direction than most of Europe, particularly the U.K., France, and Germany.[4] While Europe is currently experiencing deep economic and social conflicts over some of the same social welfare issues,[5] the marked differences between the United States and its European partners still call out to be explained.

United States and European Divergences

Over the years, scholars have long anticipated that the processes of globalization would create greater convergence among developed nations. It is certainly true that luxury hotels and tangled downtown traffic are very similar whether one is in Paris, New York, Shanghai, Los Angeles, or Warsaw. And the transportation and communication revolutions have brought these global cities into closer daily contact. Nevertheless, the United States and Europe have been moving in different directions in three critical ways.[6]

As we have already stressed, the first dimension of difference is in social policy, particularly health and welfare policies that protect the population from uncertainty and risk. Years ago, Esping-Andersen

(1990) documented the huge gaps between the three different "worlds of welfare capitalism." He contrasted liberal welfare states like the United States and the U.K. with the more generous provision found in Continental and social democratic welfare states. More recently, Huber and Stephens (2001) showed that those gaps persisted through the 1990s. Data from the Luxemburg Income Survey show that the likelihood that a child will live in poverty is almost three times greater in the United States than in France or Germany (Block, Korteweg, and Woodward 2006). Moreover, government data show that rates of both poverty and extreme poverty have been rising in the United States since 2000 (U.S. Census Bureau 2012, table 22). European polities have been engaged in some welfare state retrenchment, but the European Communities commitment to reducing "social exclusion" has meant that programs targeted to protect children have generally been insulated from cuts. Even the U.K. made significant reductions in child poverty rates between 1998 and 2005 (Smeeding 2005; Brewer et al. 2010).[7]

As the only developed nation that lacks national health insurance, the United States has also long been an outlier in comparative health indicators. But the variance has grown even greater more recently as the role of prescription drugs in health care delivery has increased and the United States has given drug companies carte blanche to charge whatever the market will bear for their products (Angell 2004). The consequence is that, while many in Western Europe have confidence that they will be protected from health crises, the great majority of people in the United States live in fear that they will not be able to afford the health care necessary to keep a family member alive or healthy (Rifkin 2004; Hacker 2006).

The second area of difference is in measures of inequality of income and wealth. From the 1970s to the present, the United States has experienced a dramatic increase in the share of income that goes to the top 1% of households. Measures of income show the share of income going to that top 1% rising from 7.7% in 1973 to 17.4% in 2011 (Saez and Piketty 2013, with update at http://elsa.berkeley.edu/~saez/). While the pattern in the U.K. has been similar to that of the United States, albeit less extreme, both France and Germany have experienced declines in the share of income held by the top 1% in this same time period (Piketty and Saez 2012). These trends in income have produced a distribution of wealth that can only be described as oligarchic (Winters 2011). What follows from this oligarchic trend in the United States is that households in the bottom half of the income distribution have experienced a significant decline in their share of total income. Moreover, this shift has occurred at the same time that continuing fiscal crises at the local and state level have produced stagnation or actual declines in spending to support public education. One important consequence is that public colleges and universities across the nation are forcing students to pay an ever larger share of the costs of their community college or college experiences (Newfield 2008).

The combination of declining income, deteriorating schools, and significant economic barriers to higher education has dramatically diminished opportunities for upward social mobility for children born in the bottom half of the income distribution (U.S. Advisory Committee on Student Financial Assistance 2006). Recent studies that compare intergenerational mobility between the United States and Western Europe show that children who had their elementary educations in the United States in the 1980s—when these trends were only beginning—had lesser prospects of upward mobility than their counterparts in Europe (Smeeding, Erikson, and Jantti, eds. 2011). Since these barriers to upward mobility have been intensifying steadily, there is every reason to believe that children who entered school in the 2000s will trail comparable European children in upward mobility by an even larger margin. The irony of this as a reversal of the history of the United States as the land of opportunity cannot be overstated.

The third area of difference is in religious and cultural attitudes. While Europe has continued to secularize with falling rates of belief and church attendance since the 1970s, the United States has experienced a religious revival (Rifkin 2004). The greater salience of religion in the United States has contributed to intense polarization on issues such as abortion and gay rights that have not divided European societies to the same degree. Perhaps the most striking evidence of this divergence in attitudes is found in the World Values Survey, which uses a series of questions to measure where different nations stand on an axis called traditional versus secular-rational values. Traditional values include belief in God, an emphasis on the importance of religious observance, the idea that children should learn obedience and respect, and support for absolute standards of morality. On a scale that goes from -2.2 to +1.8, the United States is at -1.0, slightly below India, while Germany and Sweden are at the other end of the scale at +1.3 (Baker 2005).

These extremely important differences between the United States and Western Europe are unlikely to diminish any time soon. Even if the

United States were to take a left turn in its social policies and Europe were to move sharply to curtail welfare state spending, it would most certainly take decades before these patterns were likely to converge. It is important to bear these differences in mind as we look at the factors that have pushed the United States along its peculiar trajectory—the strength of its right-wing movement and the decision of its business community to build a political alliance with a grassroots conservative movement.

An Autonomous and Durable Right-Wing Social Movement

Far more so than other developed market societies, United States history has been fundamentally shaped by a series of social movements that emerged outside of the organized political party system. This was true in the nineteenth century with abolitionism, the women's rights movement, and agrarian populism, and in the twentieth century with progressivism, the industrial union movement, the civil rights movement, the environmental movement, and second-wave feminism (Piven, ed. 2006). But from the 1970s onward, the most powerful social movement in the United States has been movement conservatism—a set of organizationally diverse groups allied to the Republican Party that have combined support for traditional values, an embrace of market "freedom," and hostility to taxation and government.[8]

Some of the strands of this conservatism extend back to the 1930s or even earlier, but the movement achieved its modern form in the 1970s as a backlash against the movements of the 1960s and the expansion of the federal government's role in the society. Critical episodes in the movement's emergence in the 1970s were fights against the integration of public schools in both the South and the North, attacks on affirmative action, the emergence of a powerful anti-abortion movement in response to the Supreme Court's Roe v. Wade decision in 1973, the mobilization against feminist efforts to gain ratification of the Equal Rights Amendment to the U.S. Constitution, and campaigns against the extension of civil rights protections to gays and lesbians. As these efforts became integrated with the heightened political activism of pastors from thousands of evangelical Christian congregations, it became clear that millions of ordinary people could be incorporated into a durable movement that would strengthen the right wing's influence in the political arena.

Over forty years, there have been significant changes in the key mobilizing organizations of grass-roots conservatism. The Moral Majority lasted from 1979–1989, the Christian Coalition played a key role nationally from 1989 to the early 2000s, and Tea Party organizations of varying durations sprang to life suddenly in 2009. But while the specific organizations come and go, four durable features make it reasonable to categorize it as a relatively unified phenomenon.

1. *Organizational autonomy.* Since its inception, grassroots and populist conservatism has been a reliable element in the Republican Party's political coalition. But, for strategic reasons, the movement has been careful to maintain a significant degree of autonomy from the Party's organizational apparatus. So, for example, activists in the Moral Majority and the Christian Coalition routinely distributed campaign materials in support of Republican candidates, but they retained the ability to withhold support from candidates who they considered to be insufficiently conservative.[9] This allowed the movement to exert continual pressure on Republican politicians to avoid moving to the center or compromising with Democrats on those issues most important to the movement. The contrast to how the labor movement relates to the Democratic Party could not be greater. In the 1930s and 1940s, labor was strong enough to obtain concessions from the Democrats in exchange for their electoral support. By the 1950s and 1960s, however, labor had lost so much autonomy that it had little leverage in party debates (Plotke 1996).

2. *Ongoing funding support.* In August of 1971, Lewis Powell, at the time a corporate lawyer but soon to a Nixon appointee to the Supreme Court, wrote a manifesto in the form of a memo to a colleague at the Chamber of Commerce in which he outlined clear and present threats to the free enterprise system and the need for a concerted response by the business community (http://reclaimdemocracy.org/powell_memo_lewis/). In it he admonished the business community to take the offensive against their "anti-capitalist" critics or risk losing the battle of ideas. His argument is encapsulated in these two paragraphs: "While neither responsible business interests, nor the United States Chamber of Commerce, would engage in the irresponsible tactics of some pressure groups, it is essential that spokesmen for the enterprise system—at all levels and at every opportunity—be far more aggressive than in the past. There should be no hesitation to attack the [Ralph] Naders, the [Herbert] Marcuses and others who openly seek destruction of the system. There should not be the slightest hesitation to press vigorously in all political arenas for support of the enterprise system. Nor should there

be reluctance to penalize politically those who oppose it." The Powell memorandum catalyzed a new phase of institution building on the right that included the creation of new think tanks such as the Heritage Foundation and the Cato Institute, as well as a groundswell of financial giving on the part of business in the effort to construct a new network of organizations that proposed and lobbied for policies consistent with the "free enterprise" agenda (Medvetz 2012). And notwithstanding the elite sponsorship of this extensive organizational complex, the grassroots part of the movement benefited enough to continually enhance its mobilizing capacity. That in turn bolstered the movement's leverage over and autonomy from the Republican Party apparatus (Hacker and Pierson 2010; Phillips-Fein 2009).

3. *Ideological fusion.* While tactics and emphases have shifted over time, conservative organizations have sustained a core ideology that combines a defense of traditional values with market fundamentalism—a quasi-religious belief in the absence of any and all market regulations as the source of personal liberty. As we argue in Chapter 6, much of this ideology has been recycled from early nineteenth-century Christian political economy, especially that which blamed poverty on a perverse lack of personal responsibility and moral degradation, all caused by the very governmental institutions designed to prevent these very afflictions. Just as Malthus decried in the nineteenth century that governmental assistance threatens the individual's capacity to be self-sufficient and personally responsible, so too does today's conservative ideology relentlessly attack the "perversity" of government "compassion" (Frank 2004; Goldberg 2006; Hirschman 1991).

Decades ago, the political theorist Sheldon Wolin highlighted the contradictions in this ideological fusion between traditional moral dogma and laissez-faire political economy: "The destruction of traditional values is also the condition for the innovating economy to operate freely. The modernizing economy is voracious, not only of natural resources, but of the traditional human resources summed in traditions: resources of skill, craftsmanship, domesticity, personal ties, and common morality" (Wolin 1980, 10). The operation of the free market inevitably tends to subvert both traditional values and the communities that have sustained them. The big box retail stores such as WalMart force thousands of locally owned small businesses into bankruptcy. Nevertheless, these contradictions do not appear to have lessened the mobilizing power of this ideological fusion. On the contrary, repeated experiences of defeat appear to have made movement activists even more determined to defend traditional values and protect the sanctity of the free market.

4. *Regional concentrations.* While conservative ascendency has been national in its scope, it has always been far stronger as a political force in the Southern states—the same states that joined the Confederacy (Moreton 2009). There are several reasons for this. First, the expansion of the federal role in protecting the civil rights of racial minorities and women allowed activists to invoke the region's historic defenses of state's rights against an oppressive central government. Second, the region has historically had the highest concentration of the evangelical religious congregations, which have collectively become involved in right wing initiatives. At the same time, the movement has always been acutely aware of the vulnerabilities that come from its regional concentration and it has worked hard to expand its influence in other parts of the country. Young people have been recruited as college students, given ideological training, hired as Congressional aides, and then launched on their own political careers. By the 2000s, these efforts had paid off. Typical Republican legislators in many northern states were far closer to conservative positions on unions, abortion, voting rights, and public spending than to the kind of pragmatic "moderate" politics that had characterized the northeastern Republican Party in the North in earlier generations.[10]

A Polanyian Countermovement

It may seem ironic to use Polanyi's conceptual repertoire to understand a social movement that has been fervently committed to the very free market conservatism he so passionately criticized as a utopian impossibility. But it is precisely Polanyi's understanding of the effects of unfettered markets on both left and right that makes his ideas so pertinent for our analysis. Polanyi understood the power of nationalism to deflect the dislocations inflicted by the market. And indeed, populist conservatism has consistently deployed a strongly nationalist rhetoric and exhibited a deep distrust of other nations, international institutions, and foreign commitments as threats to the sovereignty of the United States. Thus the George W. Bush administration solidified its right-wing base with a militaristic and unilateralist response to the terrorist attacks of September 2001 (Block 2003).

More recently, Tea Party activists have agitated against "uncontrolled" immigration—both legal and illegal—from Latin America, the Middle East, and Asia (Skocpol and Williamson 2012). These hardened expressions of nationalism echo Polanyi's discussion in *The Great Transformation* of how the nineteenth-century gold standard engendered a nationalist response that "was everywhere producing the hard shell of the emerging unit of social life" (GT, 211). And it is therefore not surprising that the rise of extreme movement conservatism coincides with the same four-decade period over which globalization has so relentlessly undermined the socioeconomic lives of working and middle classes. The indicators are familiar—giant stores that are stocked almost entirely with imports from abroad, factories and other workplaces that have closed down or moved offshore, and a rising percentage of foreign born in the population.

These processes of economic globalization, it is true, have not only been disruptive; they have simultaneously generated new economic opportunities. Parts of the South, for example, have been particularly successful in attracting new manufacturing jobs provided by foreign-based multinationals. But even when its economic impact has been relatively benign, globalization is still perceived as deeply disruptive of established ways of living, and conservatism has been highly successful in channeling the anxieties it creates into greater loyalty to the movement (Wald, Owen, and Hill 1989; Hardisty 2004; Somers 2008, ch.3).

Evidence for the centrality of this anti-globalization current can be gleaned from Texas, where conservatism has had the greatest organizational strength. The movement has elected majorities to the State Board of Education and has successfully pushed the state's Republican Party far to the right. The Party's 2012 platform calls for the withdrawal of the United States from the United Nations, the International Monetary Fund, the World Trade Organization, and the World Bank, and it proposes an end to all foreign aid except in emergency circumstances (http://convention.texasgop.org/). Despite the fact that the state is deeply integrated into the global economy, the rejection of international organizations is indicative of a powerful xenophobia.

Furthermore, as we elaborate in Chapters 5 and 6, the peculiar blending of Christianity and free-market ideology at the core of the conservative belief system reincarnates the ideas of T. R. Malthus and the Christian political economy that flourished in the early decades of English industrialization, a similar era of severe economic dislocation on the working population. Polanyi argues that those ideas emerged precisely as trade, commercialization, and industrialization were accelerating in England and producing an expanding problem of poverty. In this as in so many other aspects of social life, Robert Owen—early nineteenth-century co-operative manufacturer, philanthropist, and alleged "utopian"—is Polanyi's hero in GT. Only Owen understood that in the face of these powerful forces, disdain for government and individual self-reliance was no longer sufficient to avoid poverty. He actively repudiated the then fashionable view that blamed poor relief for the very poverty it was supposed to alleviate. Instead he insisted that new forms of public provision were required to assure that the powers released by industrialization would not exacerbate poverty and other social evils. Against this Owenite view, Malthus and his followers attacked government assistance and claimed that individuals are entirely responsible for their own place in the social order—a theme consistent with contemporary conservative ideology dating back to the Reagan years.

The reality is exactly the opposite: globalization and new technologies have produced not a new ability for self-reliance but a dramatic intensification of social interdependence. Although there are "survivalists" who seek to live entirely "off the grid," the rest of us make do by depending on relationships and institutions amidst an increasingly complex global division of labor and instantaneous communication across vast distances. In this brave new world in which manufacturing plants can close, long-established businesses can liquidate, and occupations and livelihoods can disappear overnight, the idea that the individual can determine his or her own fate with enough discipline and hard work is ever more problematic (Block 2009).

Not surprisingly, these economic losses have generated calls for renewed forms of social insurance to protect people from forces that are beyond their immediate control. In response, conservative ideology has reasserted the perversity narrative of how social safety nets inexorably turn into dependency. Most importantly—from a Polanyian perspective—it is an ideology expressed and mobilized collectively in the form of a conservative countermovement, often organized through religious congregations that provide private charity in the form of both community and concrete material assistance to members who are going through hard times (Ehrenreich 2004). Tellingly then, while at the level of ideology the movement insists that individuals are on their own, conservative organizations its actual practices provide forms of protection from disruptions caused by market processes.

The anti-abortion movement has from the start exhibited a similar kind of displacement. As the social movement at the very epicenter of movement conservativism, it has explicitly adopted the language of "protection," declaring its mission is "to protect and save the unborn child from 'murder'." Perhaps inadevertently, these movement activists are displacing onto the fetus their own feelings of vulnerability in the face of powerful market forces they cannot control. Indeed, their rhetoric resembles the language of progressives who advocate government policies to protect children born in extreme poverty from a life with no prospects. The difference between conservatism and progressivism is that the "right to life" interventions called for by the anti-abortion movement are designed to protect only a fetus. When progressives and liberals claim similar protections for actual living human beings, the right rejects them as dangerous gateway drugs to government dependency.

Over the decades, populist grassroots conservatism has stumbled onto a remarkably durable organizing model. By championing the free market and opposing welfare-oriented policies aimed to assist the poor and the vulnerable among us, it assures that millions of people remain vulnerable to the economic and psychological pressures generated by globalization and heightened economic interdependence. At the same time, it reaches out to these same vulnerable individuals and organizes them into quixotic campaigns designed to restore traditional social values and uphold a hyper-individualist ideology in which we are each responsible for our own fate (Hacker 2006; Somers 2008).

Changing Business Alliances

In the 1960s, most of the business community in the United States had made its peace with Keynesianism by recognizing the benefits of a substantial role for government in the economy. In the Johnson and Nixon Administrations, business leaders supported initiatives to expand public provisions of health care and social provisioning, as well as acquiesced to new environmental and consumer protection legislation. But in the 1970s, spurred on by the Powell memo, things changed dramatically. The same business leaders who had earlier made peace with the Keynesian welfare state abruptly reversed course and entered a political alliance with the conservative right—a decision that has driven American politics ever since (Himmelstein 1990; Micklethwait and Woolridge 2004; Phillips-Fein 2009; Smith 2012).

There is a long history of America's exceptionally stingy public sphere. Before the New Deal, and contributing mightily to the tragic impact of the Great Depression, the United States had already been a welfare state laggard (Skocpol 1992). Public old-age pensions that were established in most European countries after World War I were not instated in the United States until 1935. Even then, many in the business community vehemently opposed Roosevelt and many of his reforms (Katznelson 2013). By World War II and through the following decades, however, American business made its peace with the expanded role of the federal government (Blyth 2002; Swenson 2002). It accommodated itself to the New Deal order because it benefited greatly from the government's putting an effective floor under aggregate demand and protecting firms from various forms of illegitimate competition. Furthermore, the passage of Taft-Hartley and the McCarthyite purges of left-wing unions weakened the corporation's most threatening opponents. Similarly, the shifts to "business Keynesianism" and "military Keynesianism" were reassuring bulwarks against the influence of European social democratic ideas, which had flourished among left Keynesians in the 1930s (Collins 1981).

Another important factor in business cooperation with government was the United States' global role during World War II and continuing during the Cold War. While the typical American firm was provincial in its business strategy and had little to gain from the billions spent on overseas military efforts, these companies were persuaded of the correctness of the government's foreign policy. They were eager participants in a powerful political coalition favoring the systematic projection of U.S. power globally that was led by the largest, internationally oriented corporations. From Pearl Harbor through the 1960s, U.S. foreign policy operated as the necessary lubricant to facilitate business cooperation with the expansion of the federal government's economic role. The existence of a coherent foreign policy establishment—with roots in the internationally oriented segment of the business community—operated as a bridge between the business community and successive administrations in Washington.[11] This foreign policy elite was particularly important in cementing relations between Democratic administrations and the business community. Under this elite sector, business abandoned its traditional anti-statist rhetoric, and "corporate liberals" who believed that government had an important role to play in solving social and economic problems assumed positions of great influence (Domhoff 1990).

But all of this changed in the 1970s. The broad anti-business sentiment fostered by the radical movements of the 1960s and early 1970s generated a full-scale conservative countermobilization. As outlined in Lewis Powell's 1971 memo, the strategy was to build counterinstitutions such as conservative think tanks and other policy organizations to challenge what they claimed was the liberal/left bias of the media and the intelligentsia. Most important, they reasserted traditional free-market economics, demeaned Keynesianism, and began a systematic effort to reverse the New Deal expansion in the government's economic role (Phillips-Fein 2009). Almost overnight, "corporate liberalism" went into decline and was replaced by the corporate embrace of market fundamentalism. This political alignment remained largely unchanged through 2008. Even the brief Clinton interregnum (1993–2000) had little enduring impact. Despite his administration's centrist policies, Clinton failed to bring any significant business constituencies back into a durable alliance with the Democratic Party. Corporate campaign contributions still flowed disproportionately to Republicans, who offered tax cuts, anti-labor policies, and reduced regulation as a quid pro quo (see Clawson, Neustadtl, and Weller 1998; more recent data are available at the Center for Responsive Politics, http://www.opensecrets.org).

What accounts for the swiftness of the transformation in the political allegiance of business between the late 1960s and the mid-1970s? No comparable shift occurred among European business leaders, who maintained their wary acceptance of the welfare state during this period. Indeed, as late as 1969, a business-dominated blue ribbon commission appointed by President Johnson endorsed the idea of a federal guaranteed income as a solution to problems of poverty and racial inequality (Katz 1989). By 1980, however, the most visible representatives of the business community were supporting Reagan's efforts to dismantle significant parts of the limited American welfare state. At the time of these shifts, some analysts offered an explanation of the transformation in sectoral or regional terms; new business interests rooted in the South and Southwest had dramatically come into their own and overwhelmed the traditional liberalism of East Coast business elites (Salt 1989). But the empirical foundations for this argument were always shaky, as was the idea that long-dominant business interests would lose power so suddenly.

A more persuasive explanation focuses on the severity of the crisis that U.S. society suffered in the decade between 1964 and 1974. There was not the mass unemployment and economic collapse of the 1930s, but it was nevertheless a period of acute strain on all social institutions, which resulted from the coincidence of three fundamental transformations. The first transformation in the United States was the exhaustion of the economic model based on mass-production manufacturing. The same transition would hit Europe, although not with the same intensity until the mid-1970s. With the support of military Keynesianism, suburbanization and the sale of consumer durables, especially autos, sustained economic growth in the United States for the first two postwar decades. But in the 1960s, it became clear that manufacturing employment would no longer be the great engine of employment growth (Block 1987, ch.7; see also Brick 2006). Economic and employment growth would have to be led by the expansion of service industries, and shifts in government policy would be needed to facilitate this transition. It was also clear that the resource profligacy that had accompanied the dramatic expansion of mass manufacturing would be more difficult to sustain.

The second transformation centered on the Vietnam War and the deep domestic conflicts that the war generated. While the Cold War had served to connect business interests to the Democratic coalition, the interplay between its global role, the rhetoric of anticommunism, and domestic partisanship made it increasingly difficult for the United States to devise a coherent foreign policy. The U.S. military became overextended and lost tens of thousands of lives waging an unnecessary war that served only to weaken the United States' international position (Hodgson 2005). Moreover, the war kept the United States from negotiating a trilateral understanding with Europe and Japan that would have allowed it to maintain its global influence at a much lower cost in resources and lives (Block 1977).

The final transformation was produced by the political mobilization of African Americans, other ethnic minorities, and women—all of whom had been marginalized or excluded from the New Deal settlement (Katznelson 2013). These groups campaigned for economic, political, and cultural inclusion, and their demands came into direct conflict with deeply established patterns of neighborhood and family life, as well as with the liberal and trade union establishment. The partial and gradual accommodation of these newly energized movements might have reinvigorated the Democratic coalition and allowed it to restore its electoral dominance. But the Johnson Administration was forced to choose between escalation of the Vietnam War and a project of domestic reform, and it opted for the former (Hodgson 2005). This, in turn, made it impossible to respond to underlying economic problems, or to make employment-related concessions to African Americans and other minorities. Instead of synergistic solutions, there were synergistic failures that escalated political polarization and radicalization (Piven and Cloward 1997).

While parts of Western Europe went through comparable periods of turmoil and transition in the late 1960s and early 1970s, they had the advantage of having only a marginal involvement in the Vietnam conflict (Marwick 1998). Without the added budgetary and cultural strains of a deeply unpopular war, their political systems were able to weather the transition in a way that sustained the continued support of employers for Keynesian welfare state measures. There was also no equivalent in Europe to the panicky response of the U.S. business community because European businesses had decades of experience contending with challenges from the left.

Significantly, the two presidents in this period were highly respected for their political prowess. Lyndon Johnson was both a direct heir of the New Deal legacy and one of the most skillful politicians of his generation. His crushing defeat of Goldwater's challenge in 1964 represented the high-water mark of business support for the Democratic Party. His failure to hold the political center and respond effectively to the crises of his time catalyzed business disillusionment with the New Deal tradition. The disillusionment only accelerated when Johnson was succeeded by Nixon, an equally effective politician. In comparison to later Republicans, Nixon was an unabashedly "big-government" conservative; he had no hesitation about enhancing the government's power and institutional reach in domestic policy. His administration created the Environmental Protection Agency and the Occupational Safety and Health Administration, used wage and price controls to contain inflation, dramatically increased the generosity of Social Security, and established the Supplemental Social Insurance program to federalize government assistance to the disabled. Nixon also declared, "We are all Keynesians now" (Hodgson 2005). Indeed, his rapprochement with China could have been a metaphor for the entire duration of the administration. In the manner of Disraeli in nineteenth-century England, Nixon could have reinvigorated American conservatism by using government to solve the threefold array of social problems he faced—all the while deploying a facade of conservative rhetoric that would have allowed the Republican coalition to incorporate millions of Democratic voters.

Yet Nixon also failed spectacularly. His economic policies were just a series of improvisations that lacked any long-term vision. He toyed with the idea of far-reaching reforms in relation to poverty with his tepid support for Moynihan's Family Assistance Plan, but he was unwilling to invest the political capital needed to push the initiative through Congress (see Chapter 5). In foreign policy, he and Kissinger had elements of a bold vision, but it was undermined by their inability to accept the reality of the U.S. defeat in Vietnam. And, of course, Nixon crowned these failures by the systematic abuse of executive power.

It is difficult to exaggerate the cumulative impact on business of the political missteps by Johnson and Nixon between 1964 and 1974. The fact that neither of these two highly skilled and centrist politicians was able to make headway against the multiple problems facing the United States led business leaders to an agonizing reassessment of their assumptions.[12] As a corporate body, business decided that the "vital center" could not hold and that it needed to abandon support for big-government politicians of both parties. This disillusionment coincided with the collapse of the bipartisan foreign policy establishment that had provided the intellectual leadership for U.S. foreign policy through the Cold War period (Hodgson 2005). To be sure, much of U.S. foreign policy in the 1970s and 1980s remained bipartisan, but it was no longer linked in the same way with a cohesive foreign policy establishment. With the erosion of these bridging institutions, business leaders were now free to form new political coalitions.

The urgent task facing the Democratic heirs of the New Deal coalition had been to respond to the difficult challenges of the 1970s by renewing and deepening the New Deal settlement. However, the Democratic coalition was not up to this difficult task. Instead, it fractured and left a void at the center of the nation's politics. In the early 1970s, a resurgent free-market conservatism began to fill this void by capitalizing on business disillusionment with the successive failures of big government initiatives. Their spokespeople explained the failures of both Johnson and Nixon as incarnations of a statist ideology that rejected the fundamental truth that the path to prosperity and freedom was through greater reliance on market forces. Whether the issue was energy policy, welfare policy, the crisis of Bretton Woods, or domestic inflation, conservatism mobilized a powerful "conversion narrative" that depicted the current crises as an inevitable consequence of failed liberal assumptions and insisted that salvation would come only from policies that restored the "natural order" of self-regulating markets (see Chapter 6).[13] The business community's fears further increased their attraction to conservative arguments. The radicalization of the 1960s had created broad distrust of business, and the consumerist and environmentalist critiques of standard business practices were becoming increasingly influential. The McGovern wing of the Democratic Party was perceived as anti-business and likely to unleash new rounds of regulatory reform if it ever achieved power in Washington.

Corporate liberalism experienced a spectacular decline, and most of the business community entered enthusiastically into an alliance with the Republican right that promised tax cuts, deregulation, and smaller government. But what is most striking about the rhetoric of business conservatism from the 1970s onward is the unrelenting refusal to take responsibility for any of society's problems. The rhetoric blamed all economic difficulties on rigid government regulators, rapacious unions, and a culture that failed to understand the heroic sacrifices of those who toiled to make profits.

The irony is that, as business leaders were almost unanimously adopting this rhetoric, it was apparent that many of the largest U.S. corporations had become rigidly bureaucratic, significantly overstaffed, and unable to respond swiftly to changes in the marketplace. The poster child of this weakness was the U.S. automobile industry, which was unable to respond effectively to the Japanese competitive challenge in the 1970s. But the auto industry was not atypical; many U.S. corporations had experienced the great post-World War II boom as a period in which polite oligopolistic competition among three or four dominant firms had allowed enormous growth with little competitive discipline. By the end of the 1970s, in fact, the need for these same corporations to become leaner and more entrepreneurial had become part of business common sense. The 1980s and 1990s were a period of dramatic corporate downsizing, as big firms belatedly sought to make themselves more flexible and more competitive to face a changing business environment (Harrison 1994).

But why were so many business leaders willing to embrace an ideology that blamed "big" government and "big" unions when it was apparent that big corporations had been in fact responsible for many of the economic problems? Shouldn't there have been enlightened business leaders in this period who advocated a reform program that was more balanced? Such a program would have emphasized the need for business to get its own house in order while also recognizing that the federal government still had a very significant regulatory role to play in helping move firms and the entire economy toward greater efficiency.

There were such voices, to be sure, and they won a few isolated policy victories. The Carter Administration's decision to organize a federal bailout of the Chrysler Corporation in 1979 can be seen as a last gasp of a domestic reform agenda that rejected the assumptions of market fundamentalism. But the larger story is that the handful of open-minded business leaders who were still around by 1976 was left without either credible potential allies or a plausible reform agenda. In the mid-1970s, labor and other progressive groups mobilized to pass "Humphrey-Hawkins"—a piece of legislation that would have obligated the federal government to become "employer of last resort," providing jobs to anyone who was unemployed. This was an initiative that was anathema even to relatively enlightened business interests, who feared improved employee bargaining power at a time of strong inflationary pressures and increasing international competition (Weir 1992).

Indeed, business disillusionment with the federal government was so deep by the time Carter came into office in 1977 that a revival of business cooperation with the Democratic Party was improbable. But the conflicting pressures on Carter from labor and other progressive constituencies and the absence of a persuasive economic reform agenda on the part of Democrats pushed business into the arms of the increasingly right-wing Republicans. By 1979, when Carter appointed Paul Volcker as chair of the Federal Reserve Board, the pattern of the next quarter century was set. From that point onward, all economic problems were to be solved through austerity policies that hurt wage earners while promising greater benefits to big corporations and the wealthy (Greider 1987; Kuttner 2013).

Changes in the Business-Movement Conservative Alliance

Political alliances, however, generate their own unique political dynamics. When the alliance between big business and movement conservatives began in the 1970s, business was the dominant partner in the coalition, and populist conservatism was definitely the junior partner. But as we argued earlier, the Reagan Administration's market oriented policies created economic dislocations that fueled the right wing and even created a new class of "Reagan Democrats." Corporate downsizing in the 1980s and 1990s eliminated millions of factory jobs and middle-management positions. Entire industries, such as meat packing, that had provided unionized jobs shifted to the employment of a low-wage labor force, including many undocumented immigrants. Big-box retailers, led by Walmart, expanded their domain, closing off many of the traditional niches for small retail businesses. Millions more people lost their access to health insurance as medical costs escalated dramatically. And, finally, continuing fiscal constraints on spending by state and local governments meant that there was no place to turn for help with medical emergencies or financing higher education for one's children (Harrison 1994; Blau 1999; Applebaum, Bernhardt, and Murmane, eds. 2003).

The modernizing economy that Reagan unleashed also continued to accelerate the racial and gender transformations of the 1960s that threatened much of "middle America" and fueled an explosive "culture war." As a consequence, grassroots conservatism transformed itself in the 1980s and 1990s into a powerful Polanyian countermovement driven by deep dissatisfaction with economic insecurities and the impact of continuing cultural modernization. At the same time, it maintained its organizational independence from the Republican Party and its business allies. This, combined with its increasing strength of numbers, allowed movement conservatism to become increasingly powerful relative to its business partners.

It was business Republicans who originally built the Reagan revolution in the 1970s and early 1980s and who opportunistically incorporated grassroots conservatives as their populist junior partners, but over the following thirty years power relations shifted and the position of business within the coalition became progressively weaker. When George H. W. Bush was defeated in 1992 by Bill Clinton, the result was intensified grassroots mobilization against the Democrats that culminated in the Republicans winning control of Congress in 1994. These newly empowered Congressional Republicans, moreover, showed little deference to business preferences for predictability; they forced a shutdown of the federal government in 1995 and 1996 and pursued impeachment of President Clinton over the Monica Lewinsky affair.

True, George W. Bush had campaigned as a compassionate conservative in 2000, but his administration pursued a more right-wing agenda under pressure from the conservative base.[14] Indeed, its new political clout helps to explain why the Bush administration turned away from multilateralism after 9/11 (Block 2003). A more logical response to the terrorist attacks would have been a concerted effort to strengthen the fabric of global cooperation, including a new Marshall Plan to jump-start economic growth in the developing world, and especially in Islamic regions. But, while such a policy would have been consistent with the history of U.S. business internationalism, it would also have strength-ened the international institutions that movement conservatives view with enormous suspicion.

Historically, conservative primary voters had shown considerable def-erence to the Party's leadership; as late as 2004 and 2006, for example, moderate Republican Senators Lincoln Chafee and Arlen Specter were able to defeat right-wing primary challengers. But after the election of Barack Obama in 2008, resentment towards the failures of the Bush Administration and intense hostility to the nation's first African Amer-ican president further expanded the conservative movement's influence over the Republican electorate. And in 2010 and 2012, Republican pri-mary voters began choosing far right candidates over more establish-ment figures, even when they were opposing incumbents. These more conservative candidates in Delaware, Kentucky, Pennsylvania, Nevada, Alaska, Utah, Colorado, Indiana, Missouri, Texas, and Florida were able to raise considerable funds from right wing PACs and conservative billionaires.[15] While a number of these far right candidates lost seats that Republicans had been favored to win, the success of the primary challenges sent a message to Republican incumbents that almost any cooperation with the Democratic Party could end their political careers.

Not surprisingly, its thirty-year alliance with movement conservatism has significantly transformed the business community—both in its per-ceptions and in its organizational capacities. The market fundamentalist doctrine that has served as the glue of this political coalition instructs business executives not to get tripped up on "social responsibility"; their only responsibility is to increase returns to the shareholders (Crouch 2009). Moreover, under the theory of "alignment," corporate executives are most effective if they act as "owners" of the firms that they are sup-posed to only be managing (Useem 1993). This, in turn, has encouraged an explosion in corporate compensation as executives have been show-ered with stock options, bonuses, and other incentives, all of which serve to reinforce executive fixation on short-term results, as these have an immediate influence on share prices. It also encourages a concentration on instrumental Washington deal making. After all, by far the quickest way to make next year's results look better is to win tax concessions that allow firms to hold on to a higher share of their profits. Those that rely heavily on their intellectual property rights, such as the Disney Corporation or the pharmaceutical industry, can promise shareholders higher returns simply by winning legislative and lobbying victories that extend their exclusive control over particular bits of intellectual property (Stiglitz 2003; Baker 2011).

Many firms are now dominated by myopic management strategies fixated almost exclusively on maximizing shareholder value in the short term (Bogle 2005; Davis 2009). These strategies assume that the market environment will remain unchanged and that there is little reason to prepare for a different future. General Motors and Ford, for example, were totally surprised by the post-Katrina increase in oil prices; despite all of the debates about global warming and "peak oil," they had been content to focus much of their domestic strategy on the production of energy-wasting trucks and sports utility vehicles. Similarly, the big energy companies have fought ferociously against new energy policies that might reduce the nation's dependence on fossil fuels.[16]

Such short-term orientation represents a significant shift in business policy since the Cold War years. At that time such towering figures as Dean Acheson, Douglas Dillon, and the Dulles brothers, all "organic intellectuals" of the business community, were deeply rooted in both the American business milieu as well as simultaneously preoccupied with the long-term outlook for the global economy. Many of these men moved back and forth between government offices and partnerships at elite law firms or top investment banking houses. Even when out of government office and working for the private sector, they concentrated their time not only on seeking corporate profits but also on pursuing their class-wide legislative and political policy agendas (Domhoff 2006).

But these arrangements had been a product of the comfortable and oligopolistic organization of U.S. big business after World War II. Those elite law firms and investment banking houses were supported by big firms that were willing and able to subsidize a small cadre of organic business intellectuals until disagreements over the Vietnam War irrevocably fractured their unity. Big corporations, moreover, faced increasing competitive pressures, and they were no longer willing to pay the padded bills of elite law firms and investment banks. At the same time, the law firms and investment banks also found themselves in a more competitive environment where even senior rainmakers were required to attend to their billable hours (Bradlow 1988). And as the norms of elite business compensation escalated dramatically in the 1980s and 1990s, fewer and fewer active business people were interested in taking valuable time away from such urgent tasks as managing their already considerable investment portfolios.

In addition to affecting its hierarchy of priorities, the long-term alliance with movement conservatism has also transformed the organizational capacities of the business community. This is the context in which the huge investment by right-wing foundations in think tanks and policy organizations has proven so important. In place of the earlier strata of organic intellectuals who had deep roots in actual businesses, these organizations have promoted and recruited new cohorts of "business intellectuals" whose primary ideological commitments are to market fundamentalism, more a political platform than an economic strategy. Not surprisingly, then, these hired guns are more loyal to the Republican coalition than to business itself.[17] At the same time, the Republican Party leadership has worked aggressively since 1994 on the "K Street Project"—a stratagem designed to ensure that the top positions at big business's trade associations and lobbying firms are dominated exclusively by litmus-tested ideological Republicans (Dubose and Reid 2004). The message is explicit: lobbyists on Capitol Hill will only be rewarded with access to legislators if they demonstrate themselves to be loyal Republicans who place partisan interests above specific business concerns.

Big business, in short, effectively outsourced its policy development and lobbying activities to conservative ideologues while focusing on the immediate bottom line. This locked business into its alliance with movement conservatism and to whatever foreign policy a Republican administration chose to pursue. Conservative think tanks are clearly not funded to consider or reconsider the successes and failures of market fundamentalism, nor to invent alternative policy paradigms. So even if some sectors of the business community develop serious reservations about their alliance with the right, their options are limited because the business policy apparatus has been effectively captured. To be sure, there have been signs of strain between business interests and the extreme right for years now. Especially on so-called cultural and social issues such as affirmative action, homosexual rights, embryonic stem cell research, immigration reform, and science education, there have recurring conflicts where business and conservative culture warriors end up on opposite sides. The 2006 and 2008 election cycles briefly reflected this and there was an uptick in business donations to Democrats, including considerable support for the successful campaign of Barack Obama.

Nevertheless, when the Republican Party responded to the election of Obama by refusing to cooperate with any part of his legislative program, big business did not protest. Instead, business rallied with generous financial support for Republicans in the midterm elections in 2010, giving them even more power to obstruct. The Obama Administration tried to counter this by assiduously courting business support and refusing to consider any criminal charges against the very Wall Street firms that nearly destroyed the world economy. But it was to no avail, and the bulk of business contributions in the 2012 election still went to Republican candidates.

Conclusion

This analysis of why the United States has moved along a different path for the last generation than most of its European allies is Polanyian in two distinct respects. First, Polanyi emphasizes the ironic and unexpected consequences of the project of implementing the unachievable utopia of a self-regulating market. He explains, for example, how the rush to empire by European powers in the last decades of the nineteenth century was, in fact, a direct consequence of the strains created by adherence to the rules of the international gold standard. Measures designed to create an open world economy had completely opposite effects. In the current case, the irony is that U.S. government efforts to create and maintain an open world economy and to impose "market-driven" domestic policies have created a powerful protective countermovement that has taken a distinctly right-wing form.

Second, Polanyi recognizes the disproportionate political influence wielded by big business, as well as its affinity for structural hypocrisy as it mobilizes market fundamentalist arguments to justify using state power to secure its advantaged position in competitive struggles. We have emphasized the centrality to U.S. politics of the recent alliance between big business and movement conservatives despite the considerable strains that should divide these very different constituencies.

Our story centers on how the U.S. business community forged an alliance with a newly insurgent populist conservatism, a social movement built more from burning resentment towards blacks, the poor, and Democratic welfare policies than any particular allegiance to a business elite. While big business initially dominated this alliance, its relative power began to diminish in the 1990s. As extreme right-wing conservatism gained control of the Republican Party apparatus, it was able to exert greater influence not only at the grassroots but also in Washington. By the time G. W. Bush was awarded a contested presidential victory in 2000, business had lost influence on both foreign policy and a range of domestic social policies. In return, business was rewarded with continuing tax cuts, supportive federal spending, and a lax regulatory environment. But the quid pro quo for these favors was a forced acquiescence to the conservative right's agenda for both foreign and domestic policy.

Much of the divergence between the United States and Europe can be traced to the 1970s, when these political dynamics began. Europe, in contrast to the United States, did not develop a comparable grassroots conservative countermovement. Until now, at least, national health insurance in combination with other forms of public provision has reduced the uncertainties of everyday life for most Europeans sufficiently to lock in solid electoral support for continuity in public spending. At the same time, Europe has not seen any similar resurgence of religious belief or affiliation. While right-wing countermovements have emerged in several European countries, they have been driven primarily by national chauvinism and focused on an anti-immigration ideology. With some exceptions, they have not exerted the kind of influence on socioeconomic provisioning policies that movement conservatism has achieved in the United States.

But it also must be emphasized that the future of the European Community remains highly uncertain. The crisis that unfolded in 2012, with the threat that Greece and possibly other nations might be forced to leave the Eurozone, exposed deep tensions in the project of European integration. In response to the European fiscal crisis, moreover, a broad retreat from the common currency remains a possibility. If such a retreat were to occur, it would be a grave threat to the future of European welfare states. Still, this scenario differs from the trajectory in the United States, where even more limited social insurance programs are under continuous threat by conservative political opposition. The future of U.S. politics may well depend on whether the business community is persuaded to reconsider its alliance with movement conservatism.

8

THE REALITY OF SOCIETY

It cannot be denied that however great a thinker Karl Polanyi was very much a failed prophet. In *The Great Transformation* (hereafter GT), he predicted that with the turmoil of the 1930s and 1940s, the idea of the self-regulating market had suffered a final and catastrophic defeat. While the early post-World War II decades seemed to confirm his prediction, this volume has told a different story. From the mid-1970s onward, free-market utopianism has been revived with disastrous consequences, including vastly increased inequality and greater economic instability.

The very mark of towering intellectuals, however, is that we can learn from them even when their predictions are proven wrong. For GT, along with its relatively optimistic anticipations of the post-World War II world, warns in no less pronounced a manner that without a deeper change in how we *understand* the social world, we might slide back into the views that were discredited by the global economic collapse of the 1930s. This call for a change in understanding Polanyi names *a new governance philosophy*. Its philosophy is that of *the reality of society,* which we explore in some depth in this concluding chapter.

Despite being much less well known than other major economic thinkers, Karl Polanyi provides us with the most incisive intellectual apparatus available to understand the actual workings and consequences of market economies (Stiglitz 2001). Chapters 2 through 4 presented this apparatus and its conceptual vocabulary, Chapter 5 explored in greater detail one of the historical transformations at the center of Polanyi's argument, while Chapters 6 and 7 employ a Polyani-inspired institutionalist approach to analyze several of the critical events and processes that have marked the recent rise of market fundamentalism in the United States.

In Chapter 1 we elaborated a three-part conceptual armature that forms the core of our interpretation of Karl Polanyi's thought. The first part is the idea that, while markets are necessary for organizing society, they also represent a fundamental threat to social order and human wellbeing. This is most dramatically demonstrated in the afterword to Chapter 6, where we briefly summarized Somers' argument that the transformation of citizenship from an equal right to a quid pro quo contract based on one's market value had the tragic consequence of socially excluding the poor of New Orleans, leaving them unprotected from the ravages of Hurricane Katrina and invisible, ultimately disposable, to those local, state, and federal agencies expected to provide emergency rescue services (Somers 2008).

The second dimension of our conceptual framework is that the self-regulating invoked by market fundamentalists exists only in ideology; in reality, markets are always and everywhere embedded in social structures of politics, law, and culture. So, for example, in Chapter 7 we argue that the business interests in the United States that began to mobilize in the 1970s for "free market" political solutions had no real intention of shrinking the government's role. They sought instead to dismantle those specific governmental regulations that were long in place to protect employees, consumers, and the environment and to substitute an alternative set of governmental rules and regulations to advance their own business interests (Galbraith 2008; Baker 2010). The resulting "reregulation" (*not* deregulation) of the financial sector empowered financial firms to engage in extremely risky speculation with the assurance that government would rescue them when disaster struck. In New Orleans, the poor had to fend for themselves in the face of disaster; the "Too Big to Fail" banks, by contrast, knew that when disaster struck, help would quickly be on the way.

The final dimension of our conceptual framework probes into the special appeal of the free-market doctrine; after all, despite all its notable and self-evident harms, it still endures beyond all expectations. Its exceptional powers, we believe, are rooted in its promise of a world without politics, a world of almost complete individual freedom where the role of government—so often feared as coercive and threatening to our rights—would be kept to an absolute minimum. Polanyi helps us to understand how this utopian promise allowed free-market doctrine to return to global power in the 1970s and 1980s despite having been decisively defeated and discredited four decades earlier.

This three-dimensional conceptual armature joins together the wide-ranging subjects we have covered in the preceding chapters. But it can also be seen as the foundation that underlies Polanyi's central metaphor of a long-term contestation between the two sides of his double movement. On the one side, the forces of laissez-faire justify an ever-expanding process of commodification by invoking the utopian promise of a fully self-regulating market society free of politics. On the other, multiple social movements mobilize in opposition to defend society against market domination by establishing institutional protections. While Polanyi demonstrates that protective countermovements can be reactionary and regressive as well as progressive, he leaves no doubt that he is above all committed to democratically-motivated procedures to manage markets.

It is a great theory that provides the conceptual tools to illuminate and understand its own flaws. Thus our three-pronged framework also helps explain Polanyi's overly optimistic prediction that the back and forth of the double movement would come to an end with the effective defeat of both free-market fundamentalism and fascism in the 1940s. While in GT Polanyi expresses confidence that, after World War II, the market would be subordinated to democratic politics, he appears substantially less sure about the paradigmatic shift towards a new understanding of freedom. The great passion and intensity that is evident in the final pages of the book betray his sense that his was still a voice in the wilderness, and that market liberalism's misleading concept of freedom remained hegemonic. Moreover, in an important article written just a few years after GT, he is more explicitly pessimistic that without a deeper paradigm shift away from "our obsolete market mentality," society would be on the precipice of disaster (Polanyi 1947).

In the short run, at least, his optimism was justified, as social democracy, greater equality, and expanding inclusiveness flourished over the course of the next three decades. But the paradigm shift towards a new governance philosophy never occurred, and social democracy was unable to draw sufficient support to sustain and renew itself when it ran into problems in the 1960s and 1970s. At that moment, free-market utopianism reasserted itself with undiminished force.

Polanyi's View of Socialism

Polanyi believed that it is possible to transcend the painful back and forth of the double movement by durably subordinating the economy to social life—this is what he means by the term *socialism*. His conception of socialism rests on his belief in democracy and his view of democratic institutions as extraordinary historical achievements. He believed that the only way to protect these achievements is by expanding democracy to include markets. He developed his vision of economic democracy during the interwar years, when democratically-elected governments failed to protect their populations from the devastation caused by deflationary policies—a failure that produced fascism as people turned to authoritarian solutions to protect themselves from exposure to markets. He recognized that the only way to preserve democratic institutions over the long term is to expand their capacity to protect citizens from market-driven instability.

Polanyi's vision depends on the possibility of a political-economic compromise by which businesses would continue to earn profits, but they would accept regulatory restraints, taxation, and the steady expansion of social welfare institutions. He had seen this in embryonic form in the social democratic experiments in the 1920s that were labeled "Red Vienna," where improvements in the living standards of the working class coexisted with viable business enterprises. That experience gave him confidence that an economy could simultaneously be productive and fair, as well as under democratic control.

While Polanyi does not discuss it, his intuition was vindicated in Sweden's social democratic breakthrough in the 1930s. Sheri Berman (2006) draws extensively on Polanyi's analysis to show the close affinity between Swedish Social Democracy and Polanyi's definition of socialism. Berman's argument is that the social democratic breakthrough depended on ideas that were distinct from both Marxism and conventional liberalism. The leaders of Swedish Social Democratic Party were committed to "the primacy of politics"—the idea that governmental power could be used to offset the destabilizing and unequal consequences of private property, and that reforms brought about by democratic means are both the means and the end of social transformation. Berman quotes Nils Karleby, an important theorist of Swedish Social Democracy: "All social reforms . . . resulting in an increase in societal and a decrease in private control over property [represent a stage in] social transformation. . . . [Furthermore], social policies are, in fact an overstepping of the boundaries of capitalism . . . an actual shift in the position of workers in society and the production process. This is the original [and uniquely] Social Democratic view." He suggested, in short, that "[r]eforms do not merely prepare the transformation of society, they are the transformation itself" (quoted in Berman 2006, 168).

These transformative reforms would be won through the combination of electoral victories and the continuing political mobilization of the trade union base of the Social Democratic Party. Building on this theoretical foundation, the Swedish Social Democrats were uniquely able in the 1930s to gain the political support they needed for a reform program that pulled Sweden out of depression, improved the living standards of workers and farmers, and ultimately institutionalized the Social Democrats as the party of government for the next forty years. Berman argues that this social democratic breakthrough provided the model for other governments in Europe after World War II. Working within the protective shield provided by the Bretton Woods regime of fixed exchange rates and limited capital mobility, governments in Western Europe were able to introduce reforms that tamed the market and significantly diminished class inequalities.

This aspect of Polanyi's vision was vindicated by the extraordinary achievements of European social democracy in the years after World War II. The late historian Tony Judt (2010) argues that social democratic policies produced steady economic growth and greater economic security for the population, which stabilized the political space and marginalized the radical forces that exerted such influence in the interwar years. Moreover, the advances in social equality have been truly extraordinary; most European nations very significantly narrowed the gap in life chances between the working class and the middle class. In fact, a series of recent studies show that the traditionally class bound European societies have surpassed the United States in intergenerational social mobility (Organization for Economic Cooperation and Development 2010; Smeeding, Erikson, and Janti, eds. 2011). Moreover, even after the last thirty years of the global dominance of market fundamentalism, the achievements of the Nordic Social Democracies—Sweden, Norway, Finland, and Denmark—continue to be remarkable (Pontusson 2011). These countries have the highest level of social welfare expenditures and they have successfully reduced the percentage of all children living in poverty to rates around 5% or lower (as compared to more than 20% in the United States). This means, as well, that households headed by a single female parent are effectively protected against poverty. The reduction of poverty and strong support for public education has produced rates of adult literacy and skill that are superior to those in most other European nations (Pontusson 2011; Block 2011b). The World Economic Forum (2011) ranked all four of the Nordic Social Democracies among the fifteen most competitive nations on the planet. This is a surprising result, since measures of competitiveness are business oriented and tend to mark countries down for having high tax rates. Nevertheless, the Nordic Social Democracies ranked very high because of the superior skill levels of their labor forces, the support for innovation as a result of large investments in science and technology, and the high degree of effectiveness of public programs.

Yet despite all of this, social democrats are in retreat. As Judt (2010, 6) noted: "Many European countries have long practiced something resembling social democracy: but they have forgotten how to preach it. Social democrats today are defensive and apologetic. Critics who claim that the European model is too expensive or economically inefficient have been allowed to pass unchallenged. And yet, the welfare state is as popular as ever with its beneficiaries: nowhere in Europe is there a constituency for abolishing public health services, ending free or subsidized education or reducing public provision of transport and other essential services."

Social democrats, in short, appear to have lost their social democratic convictions; they have not been able to reinvent their tradition to face the new circumstances of the twenty-first century and they have not been able to take the offensive against the resurgence of free-market doctrine. Instead, too often they have sought to emulate the market model, usually with only minimalist modifications (Crouch 2011). As we argued in Chapter 1 in pointing out the differences between Polanyi and Keynes, twentieth-century social democrats abandoned the moral critique of the inequalities and injustices of market society; for several generations, they instead made their political appeals solely on the pragmatic grounds that they would be better able than politicians in other parties to deliver the goods.

But this is simply the surface level of the deeper problem that Polanyi identified in the final pages of GT. While social democrats were successful in demonstrating that a more just economy that was subjected to democratic political constraints could be highly productive, they failed to advance the philosophic transformation that Polanyi called for. They did not articulate a new governance philosophy and a new conception of human freedom. And without that deeper transformation, they have had no compelling vision to counter free-market advocates who insist that a meddlesome government will inevitably destroy individual autonomy and freedom.

A New Public Philosophy: The Reality of Society

In the years after GT, Polanyi continued to be preoccupied by the idea of a necessary philosophic shift away from the obsolete market mentality of economic liberalism toward a necessary "acceptance of the reality of society" (GT, 268). Although never published, in the 1950s he drafted outlines for a book to be called *The Reality of Society* (Rotstein 1990). But while the phrase appears throughout Polanyi's writings, most prominently in GT, few commentators have tried to work out what he meant by this admittedly Delphic injunction that only "uncomplaining acceptance of the reality of society gives man indomitable courage and strength to remove all removable injustice and unfreedom" (GT, 268). Clearly, this was an aspirational plea—one that Polanyi put forth while the world war against fascism still raged. But it was also a warning to the victors that they should not return complacently to the kind of free-market economic philosophy that had contributed to the conflagration in the first place.

To begin to bring clarity to what Polanyi means by the reality of society, we must turn to the final chapter of GT (ch. 21), as that is where he most pointedly and frequently invokes the phrase. Entitled "Freedom in a Complex Society," the chapter reads as though it was a direct response to Friedrich Hayek's *The Road to Serfdom*, which was published just a few months before GT in early 1944. As an early entrant into the anti-communist literature soon to flood the Cold War marketplace, Hayek's book was from the start far more widely read than Polanyi's— ultimately being abridged and widely distributed in the popular magazine *The Reader's Digest*. But Hayek's treatise was not framed in terms of the Cold War opposition of East vs. West, or Communism vs. Capitalism. On the contrary, *The Road to Serfdom* claimed that the mild social democratic policies in the West (the New Deal in the United States and the U.K.'s emerging welfare state) were separated only by a difference in degree from the terrors of totalitarianism. He thus evoked the fear of "slavery" by insisting that it was just a matter of time before social democracies like Britain's would inevitably slide down the slippery slope from "planning" to "serfdom" (Hayek 2007 [1944]).

Hayek aimed his attack directly at the market socialism that Polanyi espoused. And Polanyi's multifaceted discourse on the reality of society in the final chapter of GT is, in effect, a direct refutation of Hayek's position in *The Road to Serfdom*. Interpreting the meaning behind the phrase helps us to understand the paradigm shift that Polanyi advocated.

It also remains fundamental to any project of progressive political transformation.

What Does Polanyi Mean by "Society"?

The public philosophy that Polanyi sought to displace was one informed by what he called our "obsolete market mentality" (Polanyi 1947), a term that is interchangeable with the "economistic fallacy," which we discussed at length in Chapter 2. The economistic fallacy comprises the unfounded assumption that human nature is that of a *homo economicus,* motivated above all by material self-interest or utility maximization. Moreover, it holds that our collective existence is that of homo economicus *writ large*; instead of simply having a market economy as *part* of collective life, we live in an entire market *society* shaped exclusively by the laws of the market. Finally, these market principles are, in effect perceived as part of the *natural* order of things; they are as immutable as the laws of nature and equally resistant to human intervention. When combined, these assumptions add up to the fallacy that society is not only in theory, but in actual fact, subordinate to the immutable natural laws of the market.

The implications for public philosophy and social policy are straightforward. With economic laws established as the foundation of social existence, practitioners of economic science are elevated to the reigning czars of public philosophy and policy influence. Because all aspects of human existence are subordinated to that of *homo economicus,* the kind of knowledge produced by sociologists, anthropologists, historians, and other social scientists is effectively marginalized. For Polanyi, such economic orthodoxy empties the social world of everything truly social. In this market mentality as public philosophy, policy solutions always involve applying the self-evident assumptions of economic knowledge, such as those we examine in detail in Chapter 6 on social welfare policy.

A new Polanyian public philosophy would first and foremost dethrone the privileged power of economic ideology and would instead establish the importance for public policy of social, cultural, and historical knowledge. Polanyi was certainly not suggesting that the materiality of life was outside the field of legitimate public policy. On the contrary, he believed that how to best provide for "the livelihood of man" (Polanyi 1977) was the central concern of all societies. And reckoning with social provisioning would always be a critical part of democratic governance. But instead of conceiving of livelihood as something driven by the natural laws of the market, he emphasizes the historical and cultural variations through which societies have established the appropriate institutional arrangements for social provisioning. This requires Polanyi to argue for a different understanding of what economics actually means. The orthodox meaning, which he calls the "formal" definition of economics, is built on abstract assumptions about human nature and social naturalism. In contrast, the "substantive" meaning focuses on social provisioning; it analyzes the varied means by which people cooperate to sustain the kinds of institutions, allocations, and social practices that support collective livelihood. From this perspective, understanding how to best meet the needs of livelihood requires anthropological and historical analysis of actual social practices rather than abstract assumptions and economic axioms.

Polanyi's approach involves seeing society as comprising multiple social institutions and dense networks of social relationships (Polanyi 1935, 371; Rotstein 1990, 100). Following both Marx and Durkheim, he challenges the self-evident quality of *homo economicus* by demonstrating through anthropological evidence the fundamentally social nature of human agency. He eviscerates the notion of a universal self-interested, utility-maximizing individual. As Marshall Sahlins (1976) and other anthropologists and historians have since demonstrated, the invention of the autonomous individual is itself a cultural totem and ultimately a conceit of modernity. Indeed, the very idea of modernity is a cultural artifact that tells a story about how modern individuals are "free to choose" as sovereign and independent actors.

Polanyi argues that the Christian Gospels played an important role in perpetuating this fanciful ontology by advancing a highly individualized understanding of freedom of conscience. He argues that because individuals are constituted by their societies and cultural practices, they can only develop a unique set of talents and understandings within that society—that is, in relation to other human beings. Individuals cannot exist outside of society not simply because they would starve and die (although they surely would), but because recognition as a moral and social equal by others is the very foundation of the self; membership in society is what it means to be human. Without that recognition, people will be pushed across the boundary that divides humans from animals (Arendt 1976 [1948] Somers 2008, chs. 2, 3).

Polanyi's view sharply departs from the social naturalist position that defines humans by their basic biological needs, and instincts, and then invokes markets as instruments that mobilize incentives to push those instinctual drives in the proper direction. Much of his life's work challenges the common assumptions that humans are divided between their material and ideal interests, and that it is the material or economic interests that take priority as the foundation for everything else. He believed that the concept of interest used by social scientists is an analytic abstraction, and that actual human beings make their decisions based on understandings in which material and ideal factors are deeply intertwined. Somers (1994b, 628) elaborates Polanyi's approach when she writes: " . . . social action can only be intelligible if we recognize that people are guided to act by the structural and cultural relationships in which they are embedded and by the stories through which they constitute their identities—and less because of the interests that we impute to them." This is a perspective in which individual action is deeply shaped by social ties and shared ideas. Where others emphasize material interests, Polanyi recognizes that people are motivated to preserve the non-contractual arrangements necessary for social life itself.

Polanyi also demonstrates how an elaborate division of labor gives rise to a complex interdependence of technologies, producers, and political bureaucracies. These require coordination through culture, through law, and ultimately through governing institutions. In his relational and institutional view of society, he targets the market fundamentalists, whose utopian vision rests on a minimalist state and a society free of political power. For Polanyi, just as the state is necessary and will never wither away, so too is our dependence on the institutions and cultural repertoires that support organized social life.

In the end, Polanyi is asking us to accept that we live in complex societies, the essence of which is the interdependence of persons and institutions. No person or action or institution is autonomous; every institutional movement or seemingly personal action will have consequences, often unknown, for people close and far. This changes the moral valence of individual choices; they have consequences well beyond one's own life and conscience, and make us ethically responsible to the whole of society. A new public philosophy must be built from this foundational commitment to the reality of a complex and interdependent society.

What Does Polanyi Mean by "Reality"?

Throughout GT, Polanyi invokes the word *reality* to serve as the positive counterpart to several of his most foundational criticisms of economic liberalism. First and foremost, the concept's critical task is to challenge the economists' practice of reducing society to their axiomatic economic assumptions. Just as he drew from anthropology and history to establish the priority of social relations in collective life, so too does he insist that the only way to construct realistic knowledge is to theorize based on observations of the world as it actually *is*—something again akin to the empirical work of anthropologists and historians. In the case of "society," Polanyi is making an ontological statement about the social nature of human agency and the interdependence of our collective existence. In the case of "reality," his critique is epistemological and methodological, and it is directed squarely against economic theory as a form of knowledge that is based on abstract logic and unobservable assumptions about human nature and social equilibrium. To see the world as it is in reality, not as we might like it to be in the logic of economic thought, is for Polanyi the only way to fashion public and social policies on moral and ethical foundations.

Polanyi traces the beginning of the denial of reality to the classical political economists of the late eighteenth and early nineteenth centuries, specifically to their appropriation of social naturalism, their utopian ideas about autonomous self-regulating markets, and their methods of deductive theory-driven abstract logic. Social naturalism, in the first instance, is an approach to understanding the social world that assumes that human society and the natural world both work according to the same laws of nature. Polanyi locates the origins of social naturalism in Joseph Townsend's allegorical fable of goats and dogs on a deserted island that, despite a natural predatory competition for survival, lived in a harmonious equilibrium (1971 [1786]). Townsend, whose fable became the inspiration for Malthus, Ricardo, and later Darwin, justified using goats and dogs as allegorical proxies for human beings because he saw no difference in the biological instincts that drove human and animal alike. This, in turn, justified social policies designed to trigger biological drives, rather than human morality or social responsibility.

Polanyi wants us to appreciate just how radical was this theory that reduced the meaning of what it is to be human to purely biological instincts, instincts that the political economists made to serve as proxies for economic motivations and activities. He argues, moreover, that reinventing the social world as a system that works according to the "laws of the jungle" was among the most significant—and egregious—of classical political economy's dictates, as it transformed our social world from a system of socially-constructed arrangements into one that achieved its own equilibrium by being left alone to self-regulate no differently from dogs and goats alone on an island. By defining human agency and the social world as as subject to the same laws as the natural world, Polanyi argues that classical political economy achieved three of its greatest accomplishments—1) to rule the economy as out of bounds for political intervention; 2) to make the sole criteria for public policies only those practices that played upon people's biological instincts for survival; and 3) to make the study of human livelihood an axiomatic science based on highly problematic assumptions.

The first accomplishment was deeply political, and the aim was to block any government efforts to regulate labor conditions or to bring relief to the poor. Polanyi identifies the target as Thomas Hobbes's celebration of the state (2008 [1651]). According to Townsend and the political economists, Hobbes was mistaken when he postulated that because people behave just like animals in their eternal battle for survival, a powerful government is necessary to prevent an endless war of all against all, and to ensure humanity the right to security and life itself. Townsend sought to delegitimize this idea that a strong government protected rights by preserving social order for the common good. In Polanyi's formulation, for Hobbes, people were *like* beasts, and thus needed a state to regulate them; for Townsend, people *are* beasts and because they are driven by the same laws of nature as say, tigers and gazelles, foxes and rabbits, no government was necessary. In using goats and dogs as proxies for humans, Townsend thus slipped from the metaphor of "likeness" to a condition of *being*. In the wilds of nature there exists no umpire.

The second accomplishment of social naturalism was to delegitimize public philosophy and those social policies that appeal to the common good, to social morality, to collective conscience or social compassion. Social naturalism dictated only those policies designed to mimic the brutalities of nature. By allowing the harshest of social conditions to prevail, people would act on their biological instincts to survive. Poverty policy, for example, would no longer provide relief to the hungry; instead, it would allow the natural condition of extreme hunger as an incentive to motivate the poor to work. Polanyi's achievement was to puncture the delusion that subordinating society to nature's laws would produce harmony. The perfect world envisioned by proponents of the self-regulating market could never be actualized by real human beings whose very existence is integrated with their social institutions. Hence he traces the cataclysms of World Wars I and II to the political economy of nineteenth-century England.

The final principle of social naturalism is that because people and beasts are one and the same, then the logic of natural science can generate the kind of knowledge needed to produce optimal social and political policies. Once again, Polanyi traces this methodological denial of a distinct human reality to the classical political economists. Townsend and his followers, after all, did not generate their theories through first observing and then theorizing real social practices. Rather they made up allegories and conducted thought experiments, which aimed to identify those social policies appropriate for a society in which humans are shaped by their biological drives. It was the logic of the thought experiment combined with deductive models that gave rise to their new theories of economics and society. Deductivist, theory-driven economics triumphed further with the marginalist revolution and the birth of neoclassicism in the last third of the nineteenth century. In the famous *Methodienstreit* (battle over methods) between the empirical and the neoclassical economists that followed, those scholars that Polanyi most admired from the German Historical School and the English tradition of historical economics were effectively marginalized because of their resistance to deductivism and formalism (Somers 1990).

As we discussed in Chapter 6, economic theory's self-styled scientific methodology is founded on a deductive model constructed through theoretical reasoning. The deductivist methodology in economics can be said to have reached its apex in 1953, when Milton Friedman famously pronounced the purpose of modern economic knowledge was to generate powerful and parsimonious economic predictions (Friedman 1953). This was a goal, he argued, which justifies, indeed necessitates, unrealistic "as if" assumptions about utility-maximizing rational actors and general equilibrium. This embrace of unrealistic foundations remains to this day central to much of mainstream economics and to the proselytizing of public economic pundits. Its rejection of reality-based empirical analysis can be understood as an expression of theoretical realism, a philosophy that builds on the classic Enlightenment distinction between the illusions of superficial empirical appearances and the profound level of reason, truth, and reality that remains hidden.

In response to accusations that they have built an entire theoretical edifice on postulates and assumptions about human nature that can never be either confirmed or disconfirmed by evidence, theoretical realists decry "empiricism"—what they define as the testing of theory with illusory superficial empirical evidence. Modern economic science reflects the philosophy of theoretical realism; it is not empirical observations but logical deduction that is the source of their foundational tenets. It is called theoretical realism because it is an approach to knowledge that uses rational logic to determine what is real, and rejects what seems self-evidentially real to the rest of us as superficial and surface illusion. They argue, for example, that human agency is biologically driven because logic dictates that it must be so. In this way, theoretical realism turns our common sense notion of reality upside down: that which is accessible to our senses, the empirical, is rejected as merely the stuff of misleading appearance and not real; if we want truth, then we must tear away the veil of the illusory exterior to find the hidden logic of reality.

Common sense, however, demands an answer to the question of how any generally accepted knowledge can be achieved if truth is hidden from all but the anointed knowers. Clearly, there is no impartial way to adjudicate which hidden truth gets to count as *the* truth. Reality becomes a matter of deductive reasoning, which builds from arbitrary assumptions that can never be democratically adjudicated. That is to say, whereas the level of the empirical can be observed by any and all, a hidden truth is only discernible to those who claim special abilities to access it. This type of economic reasoning relies on the special capacities of the few, those who are the priests of philosophical logic rather than of empirical observation (Somers 1998).

Polanyi was first and foremost an economic historian and rejected this theory-driven methodology. And while he never uses the concept of theoretical realism to describe economic theory, he spent a lifetime advocating for what he called the empirical economy. Against the abstractions of the economistic fallacy, Polanyi counterposed the necessity of empirical evidence and inductive reasoning drawn from the actual social practices of observable human beings. GT, while it is rich with social theory, is theory generated from actual human history, including the vast diversity of economic arrangements one finds through history. In this sense, his argument is clearly a rejection of theoretical realism.

Polanyi especially admired the late nineteenth and early twentieth century English and German historical economists whose research forms the backbone of GT (see pp. 269–303 on his sources). In addition to their holistic approach, the historical economists were distinguished by their belief in inductive reasoning and empirical data collection. This put them in intellectual and institutional conflict with the mathematically inclined marginalist economists. Polanyi embraced the institutionalism of the English historical economists and the German historical school to demonstrate the dangers that result from adhering to theories built not on what real men and women actually do, but on theoretical models based on a priori postulates about what human nature would dictate they do. Polanyi's allegiance to the reality of inductive reasoning challenged and served as a counterpoint to the dominant methods of political economy and economic liberalism, which adopted untestable and nonempirical assumptions about human nature and market equilibrium to justify their self-representations as true science (Somers 1990).

Paul Krugman has recently characterized the principles and practices of modern economics as "faith-based" (2009b, 37). By this he means economists place untestable economic logic—justified by a theology of faith in presuppositions and assumptions—over and above years and decades of historical and sociological evidence. Krugman, in fact, links the economists' failure to foresee the financial crisis of 2008 to exactly that kind of reasoning. "As a group," he writes, they "mistook beauty, clad in impressive-looking mathematics, for truth." He continues: "[T] he central cause of the profession's failure was the desire for an all-encompassing, intellectually elegant approach that also gave economists a chance to show off their mathematical prowess . . . this romanticized and sanitized vision of the economy led most economists to ignore all the things that can go wrong. They turned a blind eye to the limitations of human rationality that often leads to bubbles and busts; . . . to the imperfections of markets . . . that can cause the economy's operating system to undergo sudden, unpredictable crashes"(Krugman 2009b, 37).

Polanyi's pursuit of "reality" as the foundation of knowledge is the exact opposite of this hubristic approach. Indeed, it seems more than likely that he would embrace wholeheartedly Krugman's aspirational cure for his ailing discipline: "[w]hat's almost certain is that economists will have to learn to live with messiness . . . they will have to acknowledge the importance of irrational and often unpredictable behavior, face up to the often idiosyncratic imperfections of markets and accept that an elegant economic 'theory of everything' is a long way off" (Krugman 2009b, 37).

Re-Viewing the Reality of Society versus Economic Utopianism

We have conducted this tour through the complex thinking beneath Polanyi's commitment to the reality of society to give a fuller sense of what a new Polanyian public philosophy would look like. It would be informed by extensive empirical research and deep philosophical conviction alike. But there is one last angle on how prioritizing the reality of society motivates Polanyi's call for a new political philosophy. This is his juxtaposition of the reality of society against the stark utopianism of the self-regulating market. For Polanyi, one reason why economic liberalism and the self-regulating market are unrealistic and utopian is because of their abstract, theory-based approach to making sense of the social world. But even more important, he believes that the logic of economic liberalism is utopian because it denies two of the most foundational truths about actual social reality.

First, economic liberalism is blind to the harms associated with the fact that, for a market society to ever fully exist, land, labor, and capital all have to be converted into commodities. As Polanyi most memorably charges, the problem is that they are "fictitious commodities"—fictitious because commodities are things produced for the sole purpose of being bought and sold on the market. Since this is obviously not true of land, labor, or money, they are unreal (utopian) fictions that exist exclusively in the world of theories, models, and thought experiments. The tragedy is that this does not prevent the utopian architects of market societies from treating them *as if* they were real commodities. Because they are in reality nothing less than three of the vital substances of which social life is comprised, to rip them out of the fabric of society, as commodification requires, is to destroy the very stuff that makes society possible. A self-regulating market society is unrealizable because it would inevitably destroy its very being in the effort to come to fruition.

Secondly, Polanyi argues that economic utopianism denies that government, power, and politics are necessary for societal well-being. For both classical political economy and twentieth-century market fundamentalists, the presence of power and government is singularly portrayed as a threat to individual rights and freedoms. To be sure, Hayek and his allies were not anarchists; they embraced the "rule of law" for guaranteeing property rights and enforcing contracts, even going so far as to support the government's vigorous enforcement of anti-trust laws in the interest of ensuring a competitive market.[1] Beyond this minimum, however, Hayek's (2007 [1944]) most memorable declaration was that government involvement in the economy along the lines of Britain's infant welfare state would lead to nothing short of tyranny and "serfdom."

Polanyi's counterargument was that no human society can exist without the presence of power, especially governmental power to protect society and its people from the most destructive aspects of market society, as well as to ensure the rights and liberties of which Hayek speaks so eloquently. The economists' utopian dream of a perfect society without the exercise of power is the political expression of a story-book tale more appropriate for Kipling's *Just-So Stories* . Like other utopias, however, it provides an appealing escape from the obvious social problems and limitations of actual politics. Polanyi, by contrast, finds his solace in the reality of society as the foundation of a humane public philosophy.

Freedom, Democracy, and the Reality of Society

In its full-throated embrace of the reality of society, the last chapter of GT lays the foundation for Polanyi's new public philosophy—the core principles of which are *freedom* and *rights*. There he elaborates an enlarged conception and a new understanding of their meaning. At first glance it may seem surprising that Polanyi turns to concerns more commonly found in political theory. But Polanyi invokes a more expansive and social understanding of freedom and individual rights to defend against Hayek's claim that the pursuit of greater social justice through social and political provisioning inexorably takes us down the slippery "road to serfdom."

Polanyi's theory of freedom begins by challenging the narrowness, individualism, and anti-government stance of classical political and economic liberalism. In the final pages of GT, he explicitly calls for a paradigm shift that would redefine the way in which we conceptualize freedom for a complex society. He identifies three "constitutive facts in the consciousness of Western man [*sic*]: knowledge of death, knowledge of freedom, knowledge of society" (267). The knowledge of death he attributes to the Old Testament; the knowledge of freedom he attributes to the teachings of Jesus in the Gospels. While freedom is of course a great desideratum, Polanyi argues that by offering a vision of individual freedom premised on absolute freedom of conscience for isolated and autonomous individuals, the Gospels "ignored the reality of society." Polanyi's view is that once we recognize the complex interdependence of our collective existence, we can no longer justify an unlimited freedom to act solely according to one's own, too often self-serving conscience.

Polanyi identifies the great nineteenth-century social reformer Robert Owen as among the first to call into question the hyper-individualism of the Gospels. Owen looked squarely at the reality of life in the industrial revolution and rejected the free-market political economy that dominated at the time. In it he saw not the glory of autonomous and unfettered freedoms, but a society in which the fates of individuals are tragically interconnected. Specifically, a small group of factory owners inflicted great hardship on the working families who had no choice but to take work in the harsh Satanic mills of early industrialization. "Owen recognized that the freedom we gained through the teachings of Jesus was inapplicable to a complex [interdependent] society. His socialism was the upholding of man's claim to freedom in such a society" (GT, 268). Inspired by Owen, Polanyi argues that there are two kinds of freedom. The more familiar one is that of classical liberal political theory, which makes autonomous rights-bearing the natural condition of humanity and imagines that individual rights-bearers voluntarily enter into society through a social contract. Building on these foundations, economic liberals then tightly link the free market system to the very existence of human freedom, while simultaneously defining government actions as the negation of freedom. Polanyi explains that this understanding of freedom limits its benefits solely to "those whose income, leisure, and security need no enhancing," which in turns leaves "a mere pittance of liberty for the people, who may in vain attempt to make use of their democratic rights to gain shelter from the power of the owners of property" (GT, 265).

Polanyi's alternative conception of freedom begins with the recognition of the complex social interconnectedness of our society. Each individual act inevitably affects other people's lives, often without the original actor even knowing. Polanyi refuses to privilege the freedom of the well-heeled at the expense of unfreedom for anonymous others. While fully endorsing individual rights and liberties, he vigorously rejects the idea that they are "natural" and that their flourishing requires freedom *from* government. On the contrary, freedoms and rights are actually produced and sustained *through* politics and law. The only quality of human beings that can be considered natural is their relational sociality, and it is our work as social beings that will determine whether or not we shall have any rights at all.

Polanyi's new public philosophy is therefore founded on his alternative conception of freedom. He recognizes social interdependence as the foundation of humanity and knows that freedom and rights must be deliberately built on that foundation. The implications would most immediately impact social elites, who have long had the luxury of exercising their autonomous freedom, while being fully insulated from the suffering their actions inevitably inflict on everyone else. Instead, the privileges long associated with the control of wealth must ultimately be constrained, not redistributed but recognized and reconceptualized as having been collectively produced. To be sure, Polanyi understands that "the comfortable classes" will be "less anxious" to extend their own freedoms to "those whose lack of income must rest content with a minimum of [freedom]" (GT, 262). But Polanyi has faith that even the well-off can come to recognize that it is inside the interdependency of society that freedoms exist: "Such a shifting, reshaping and enlarging of freedoms should offer no ground whatsoever for the assertion that the new condition must necessarily be less free than was the old" (GT, 263). Placing limits on the exercise of individual autonomy will thus not rob people of their freedom. Rather, Polanyi is suggesting that by extending to others the vested freedoms so long enjoyed only by the wealthy few "the level of freedom throughout the land shall be raised." New and different kinds of freedoms will develop by accommodating ourselves to the constraints imposed on us by our complex interdependencies.

As for the celebrated "market view" of freedom, Polanyi argues that its exclusive focus on contractual market freedom "degenerates into a mere advocacy of free enterprise" (GT, 265). Ironically, he observes, even individual market freedom is an illusion in the face of the "hard reality of gigantic trusts and princely monopolies." This is a hard reality that has only multiplied in the twenty-first century. For Polanyi, every move toward "planning"—the term then in currency to denote social democratic economic policies—should "comprise the strengthening of the rights of the individual in society." He is as resolute in his commitment to individual freedom as he is toward the necessity of the social. But he insists that to be true freedom it had to expand into new "institutions . . . to make the rights effective." It is here that he breaks decisively with classical liberalism's conception of freedom, which limits the concept to civil rights protections against the state. Polanyi fully endorses such rights, but adds that "rights of the citizen hitherto unacknowledged must be added to the Bill of Rights," including the whole range of socio-economic rights from having a job to a decent education (GT, 264–265). Quite remarkably, and surely unbeknownst by the other, almost simultaneously FDR gave a too-little known speech advocating for a "Second Bill of Rights," also comprised of socioeconomic rights (Sunstein 2004).

For Polanyi, then, the maximum opportunity for real freedom can come only through expansive socioeconomic rights, which are firmly rooted in institutions. But for this to be accomplished in a durable fashion, people have to understand that the historical struggle to maximize only the freedom of the individual *from* government is a dead end, for it inevitably subverts the very social arrangements that are needed to provide us with real freedom. Polanyi's faith in government is not naïve optimism; after all, GT is an account of the *defeat* of democratic aspirations by fascist and totalitarian governments. But it also is an account of the survival of those aspirations over and against the formidable ideological and institutional obstacles that have continually frustrated and blocked them. That Polanyi still recognizes the necessity of government to secure rights and freedoms rests on his belief in the capacity of human populations to exercise influence and power over political institutions through democratic self-governance. Indeed, these capacities for self-governance are rooted in the same processes that make possible a complex division of labor and high levels of social interdependence. Just as his belief that people are social beings motivated not merely by economic interests but by the values of social relationships makes him optimistic that even the privileged can come to understand the desirability of his alternative view of freedom, Polanyi believes that we are able to create solidaristic bonds with each other for the purposes of achieving a wide variety of ends.

Despite his direct experience with the most brutal regimes, Polanyi chose to believe that democratic potentialities are deeply rooted in the noncontractual foundations of society. The ability to construct relationships based on deep reciprocity can be learned within family, intimate life, and neighborhood, and this form of reciprocity often continues even within modern political cultures that celebrate the sovereignty of the individual. As an increasingly complex division of labor requires that people acquire both more complex cognitive skills and a capacity to question received wisdom, these new abilities have been joined with the old to produce recurrent solidaristic initiatives to reshape society itself.

It is out of such initiatives that people have created a public sphere of debate and discussion and democratic institutions. While Polanyi sees the attainment of a perfect democratic society as yet another utopian illusion, he envisions democratization as a process that can advance over the decades as people learn how to construct political and economic institutions that are effective and allow for the preservation of individual freedoms. Echoing Polanyi, Somers (2008, 249) suggests that the conditions for such freedom are deeply relational and institutional: " . . . meaningful citizenship practices and durable relationships that are robust, relationally sturdy, reciprocally empowered, and characterized by high degrees of trust [that] depend on deep links to public spheres, the national state, and the rule of law."

While Polanyi does not speculate on what these processes of democratization would look like and what kinds of institutions they might involve, we read him as an advocate of radical democracy. Radical democracy includes parliamentary institutions elected on a territorial basis, but it also envisions an extension of democracy into the fabric of everyday life. This would include new institutions of "empowered participatory governance" (Fung and Wright 2001) through which citizens would directly influence the allocations made by local governments, have key input into decisions about how to build and maintain the complex physical infrastructure of contemporary societies, and have a direct voice in how schools and other key institutions function. It would also involve employee participation in the governance of the workplace as has been developed in systems of collective bargaining, works councils, and codetermination (Greider 2003; Alperovitz 2005). Finally, it would involve the creation of local economic institutions that would give citizens a direct voice in patterns of economic development. The best example we have of this has been the development of the solidarity economy in Quebec, which involves the proliferation of financial institutions that are directly accountable to citizen input. Citizens are able to use these mechanisms to shape job creation, the provision of key services, and to influence broader patterns of economic development (Mendell 2009; Mendell and Nogales 2011; Bouchard, ed. 2013).

This is not the place to outline here a vision of twenty-first-century social democracy that would be consistent with Polanyi's ideas. It would also take us too far afield to address the contemporary social movements, such as the World Social Forum or Occupy Wall Street, that have sought to galvanize opposition to the market fundamentalist policies that have been dominant for the last thirty years. Nevertheless in closing, we think there are several key insights from Polanyi that can illuminate our contemporary global condition.

First, social and economic thought about what needs to be done in the aftermath of the 2008 global financial crisis remains terribly impoverished. Conventional thinking has not yet even returned to the level of insight that Keynes, Polanyi, and others attained in the 1940s. This is exemplified in the single-minded and disastrous pursuit of public sector austerity as a way to muddle through the continuing weakness of economies (Kuttner 2013). The lesson learned in the United States under Herbert Hoover between 1929 and 1932 remains as relevant as ever; in response to a global economic downturn, nations cannot recover by slashing government spending and balancing budgets. The only solution to what is a lack of adequate demand is to add demand to the global economy, not to subtract it.

Not only are serious proposals for generating global demand glaringly absent; Polanyi's analysis of the crises of the 1930s also should alert us to the urgency of reforming the governing rules of the global economy. The policies and practices of organizations such as the International Monetary Fund, the World Bank, and the World Trade Organization need to be radically transformed to lay the foundation for a new period of sustainable global economic growth. Moreover, the dollar's central role as the key global currency must be phased out and replaced by a global mechanism that would provide the world economy with the expanding supply of money needed to sustain global demand (Block 2011a). Among the key reforms of the global institutions would be a new regulatory regime that would bring the world's largest financial institutions under far more rigorous control than has been so far accomplished. The threat of a new financial bubble that would again explode and endanger the global economy is still present; radical reforms are needed so that financial activity is once again supporting the real economy rather than undermining it in the pursuit of speculative profits. And yet global elites appear to believe that just a little tinkering around the edges might be sufficient to restore global prosperity.

The second charge we take from Polanyi is equally urgent: we must resolutely call attention to how "our obsolete market mentality" with respect to nature is a dangerous delusion that threatens the future of the human species. Throughout this book we have emphasized the economic side of this argument, but it is also important to recognize the ecological peril. As the world's population now exceeds seven billion people, it is obvious that our collective ability to survive requires a radical shift in our relation to nature. Only a perspective that ceases to treat nature and natural resources as commodities to be exploited will make it possible to meet the challenge of global climate change and overcome the current threats to the ocean and the supplies of clean water on which humanity relies.

All of our efforts to move beyond this crisis must be animated by our willingness, as Polanyi said, to embrace the reality of society. We must recognize that we will not be able to solve our collective problems without the instrumentalities of government, which inevitably involve the use of political power. But political power is not necessarily tyranny or even governmental paternalism. We can and must struggle continuously to expand and institutionalize rights, to subject our political leaders to the oversight of a democratically-mobilized citizenry, and to wage ongoing battles to deepen and enlarge democratic governance at the local, national, and global levels. For political power, in tandem with a democratically-empowered citizenry, is our best countervailing strength against the relentless expansionary drive of market forces.

Finally, we must vigorously strive to achieve the paradigm shift for which Polanyi argued with such passion. To live in a complex and interdependent global society with seven billion other people, it is no longer possible to define freedom as the maximal autonomy of the individual. The spiritual freedom enjoyed by the cloistered monk or the isolated hermit has ceased to be a meaningful marker of the free individual. We are social beings; we derive our meanings from our connections to other people, and we need to understand that genuine freedom comes from constructing human institutions that protect the rights of each and every one of us.

NOTES

1. Karl Polanyi and the Power of Ideas

1. Eurosclerosis is a diagnosis of Europe's difficulties as resulting from too much government spending, high tax rates, and excessive regulatory burdens on corporations.

2. In this, they were hardly alone. Other dissenters, who drew on Polanyi before the crisis, include Block (1996), Kuttner (1996), Harvey (2005), Klein (2007), Somers (2008).

3. Moreover, the problem did not end with the global financial crisis. Saez and Piketty (2013, Table 1) reports that from 2009 to 2011, 121% of income growth went to the top 1%.

4. Shortly afterwards, Concordia University in Montreal, Canada, established the Karl Polanyi Institute. Since then, there have been nine more Karl Polanyi International Conferences held throughout Europe and the Americas, all attended by scholars from as many as thirty countries, which have produced a series of edited volumes. Polanyi's work is increasingly discussed at important panels at professional meetings of social scientists and at conferences and symposia held around the world. We discuss his biography in more depth in Chapter 2.

5. One exception was Polanyi's centrality to a major two-decade-long debate among anthropologists over the "formal" versus the "substantive" meaning of the economy. His studies of Aristotle's economics and ancient Greek economies had an important impact on the discipline of classics, particularly through the work of the eminent classicist M. I. Finley, who had worked with Polanyi (Tompkins 2008). Polanyi was also an important influence on Immanuel Wallerstein's (1974–1980) development of world-system theory.

6. The distinguished economic historian Charles Kindelberger had written earlier (1974) of GT: "Some books refuse to go away. They get shot out of the water by critics but surface again and remain afloat."

7. Polanyi called this the "double movement" in which a protective counter-movement to that of the market is necessary for society to be able to survive market society.

8. FDR gave his now largely forgotten speech proposing a Second Bill of Rights the same year (1944) as GT was published. In that speech, FDR advocated expanding our conception of freedom beyond civil and political rights to embrace "freedom from want" and many other socioeconomic rights. Some of this had been foreshadowed in his 1941 "Four Freedoms" speech (Sunstein 2004).

9. More precisely, Polanyi emphasizes both discontinuities in social development and deep continuities in social and economic theories.

10. While our discussion of Polanyi focuses on his major work, *The Great Transformation*, his life's work encompassed many other writings—both published and unpublished. While some of these have not yet been translated into English, our interpretation draws on Polanyi's published writings, some of his unpublished work, and a number of important secondary analyses of Polanyi's work. Some of Polanyi's previously little-known works have been republished in European languages recently. See Cangiani, Polanyi-Levitt and Thomasberger, eds. (2002, 2003, 2005); Cangiani and Maucourant, eds. (2008); Laville and La Rose, eds. (2008); Maucourant, ed. (2011); Resta and Cantanzariti, eds. (2013).

11. Polanyi, however, stressed the important discontinuities between Smith on the one side, who was still oriented toward the nation-state, with Malthus and Ricardo, and the classical political economists on the other (GT, ch.10; see also Rothschild 2001).

12. The obvious problem with this idea that the government must remain a neutral arbiter is that the specifics of how governments protect property or enforce contracts cannot be derived from free market principles, and differing definitions of property rights or alternative ideas of what constitutes a valid contract or a legitimate competitive strategy will, in fact, shape the way that market processes evolve. One can see this in the ongoing struggles for legal advantage between large corporations and small businesses.

13. Polanyi was well aware that the gold standard never worked exactly as its adherents claimed. He discusses the way that central banks managed inflows and outflows of gold (GT, 206–207).

14. See Chapter 5 on Speenhamland for a more developed discussion of the implications of the gold standard.

15. One such paradigmatic instance was the Irish potato famine. The English authorities withheld assistance on the grounds that it violated the principles of laissez-faire and let hundreds of thousands starve. As Amartya Sen (1981) argues, however, this was a colonial situation. When people have democratic rights, governments almost always act to avert starvation. This has not, however,

stopped increasingly strident complaints in the United States by conservatives against the federal food stamp program—the nation's major bulwark against malnutrition.

16. It was the better-off developing countries that had to make use of international credit in the 1980s. Those countries that were not credit-worthy had been subject to the International Monetary Fund's discipline to pursue orthodox economic policies from the 1950s onward.

17. In our account, we emphasize the commonalities among von Mises, with whom Polanyi argued directly in Vienna, his student Hayek, and Friedman, whom Hayek effectively recruited into the free market crusade. But there are important differences among these thinkers. Von Mises consistently held an extreme position against virtually any state activity; he befriended Ayn Rand, who could not stand the somewhat more moderate Hayek (Burns 2011). Hayek wanted the Mont Pelerin group to develop a "neo-liberalism" that was not simply a rehash of nineteenth-century liberalism, but as Burgin (2012) makes clear, this never happened, and as Friedman became progressively more anti-state in the 1950s, he successfully took the Mont Pelerin group along with him. While Hayek was celebrated in his old age for reviving the free market idea, the truth is that he failed in the project of creating something new.

18. Burns (2011) reports that Greenspan was so close to the libertarian thinker and novelist Ayn Rand that he brought Rand and her husband to his swearing in as Gerald Ford's Chairperson of the Council of Economic Advisors in 1974.

19. As Keynes (1964 [1936], 383) famously put it, " . . . the ideas of economists and political philosophers, both when they are right and when they are wrong, are more powerful than is commonly understood. Indeed the world is ruled by little else. Practical men, who believe themselves to be quite exempt from any intellectual influence, are usually the slaves of some defunct economist."

20. Although, as Phillips-Fein (2009) demonstrates so effectively, despite surface political calm, conservative business opposition had been increasing for some time.

21. This process of transformation began very early. One of Keynes's key disciples, Joan Robinson, referred to this official version of Keynes's ideas as "Bastard Keynesianism" (Marcuzzo, Pasinetti, and Roncaglia, eds. 1996).

22. In the U.S., the practices of Keynesianism were also compromised by an alliance with military and commercial interests (Block 1977; Collins 1981).

23. We are grateful to John Judis for bringing this quote to our attention.

24. Dale (2010, 29) shows that in Polanyi's 1925 response to von Mises in the *Archiv fur Sozialwissenschaft und Soczialpolitik,* one of his key points is that property includes both rights of disposition and rights of appropriation that need "not be invested in the same hands."

25. Daniel Bell (1981) writes that building theory "as if" certain things were true is the foundation of modern economic thought.

26. It is possible to identify cycles in governmental management of the fictitious commodities in which existing policy repertoire becomes progressively less effective until replaced by new policies.

27. In this respect, the American Bill of Rights is an ideal encomium to popular fears of government power.

2. Beyond the Economistic Fallacy

1. A biography of Polanyi is being written by Berkeley Fleming at Mount Allison College in Canada, and Gareth Dale currently has one in the works.

2. The biographical data are pieced together from Levitt (1964); Zeisel (1968); Congdon (1976); Duczynska (1977); and personal communications from G. Markus, Hans and Eva Zeisel, and G. Litvan. See also Cangiani (2009), Dale (2009), and Polanyi-Levitt 2013. Note that the chapter on the Polanyis in Drucker (1979), while vastly entertaining, is completely unreliable. For a critique of Drucker, see McRobbie 2006.

3. The process of publishing or republishing Polanyi's remaining writings is further advanced in other languages than in English. See particularly Cangiani, Polanyi-Levitt, and Thomasberger 2002, 2003, and 2005.

4. His wife wrote: "It is given to the best among men somewhere to let down the roots of a sacred hate in the course of their lives. This happened to Polanyi in England. At later stages, in the United States, it merely grew in intensity. His hatred was directed against market society and its effects, which divested man of his human shape" (Duczynska 1977, xiv).

5. In emphasizing the ways in which medieval towns were part and parcel of feudalism and not an oppositional force, Polanyi anticipated later discussions of the transition from feudalism to capitalism. In particular, see Anderson (1974), Wallerstein (1974), and Merrington (1975). But Polanyi's main focus lay elsewhere since he was emphasizing the importance of changes at the beginning of the 19th century in England.

6. In this section, we explicate Polanyi's analysis of the Speenhamland episode as he wrote it, but in Chapter 5 we subject it to an extended historical critique.

7. On this point, we think Polanyi was wrong, as we explain in Chapter 5.

8. For a revisionist interpretation of the New Poor Law as legislation constructed to maintain the traditional power of the landed classes, see Brundage (1974, 1978). For a parallel reinterpretation of the 1832 Reform Bill, see Moore (1976).

9. On holism as an explanatory strategy in the social sciences, see Diesing (1971).

10. Polanyi's views on this issue are stated most forcefully in *The Livelihood of Man* (1977, 5–56).

11. For more on Polanyi's use of the concept of utopia, see Chapter 4.

12. Both Thompson and Polanyi were influenced by John and Barbara Hammond (1970 [1911]).

13. Northrop Frye, in commenting on Spengler and Toynbee, remarks that "every historical overview of this kind . . . is and has to be metaphorical" (1973, 11). See also Stinchcombe (1978).

14. Wallerstein's coworker in the 1970s, 1980s, and 1990s, Terence Hopkins, worked directly with Polanyi at Columbia.

3. Karl Polanyi and the Writing of *The Great Transformation*

1. In personal correspondence, Kari Polanyi-Levitt has suggested that this was Polanyi's third encounter with Marxism, since his second occurred in Vienna when he confronted the arguments of the Austro-Marxists.

2. This is cited in GT as K. Marx, *Nationalokonomie und Philosophie* at the beginning of ch.13.

3. Although this piece is not signed, the archivists have confirmed through an interview with Irene Grant (a member of the group) that Polanyi was the author.

4. Burawoy (2003) takes the further step of identifying Gramsci and Polanyi as the fathers of a fundamentally new variant of Western Marxism. As Burawoy indicates in his essay, there are some tensions between his reading of GT and the one that is elaborated here.

5. For more on the intellectual convergence between Gramsci and Polanyi, see Burawoy (2003).

6. On Polanyi's theory and practice of workers education, see Mendell (1994).

7. Some of these complex issues are addressed in Litvan (1991, 265). In a letter to his old friend, Oskár Jászi in October 1950, Polanyi asserts that "I have not been interested in Marxism since the age of 22" (p. 265). While this claim is very much at odds with the argument being made here, the statement has to be understood in its historical context. It was written at the very peak of McCarthyism in the U.S. and to an old Hungarian friend with whom relations had become quite strained because of their differing views toward the Cold War.

8. The concept of fictitious commodities appears in Polanyi's notes for a lecture course called "Conflicting Philosophies in Modern Society," that he taught at the University of London in 1937–1938 (Karl Polanyi Archive, Concordia University, Montreal, Canada), but it does not appear to carry the same meaning as in GT. Immerwahr (2009) has recently shown that Peter Drucker used a quite similar idea in a book published in 1942. He sees this as an outcome of the intense conversations that Polanyi and Drucker were having when they were both in Bennington in the early 1940s.

9. See, for example, O'Connor (1998).

10. See, for example, Vajda (1981, ch.4). On the direct links between Polanyi and the Budapest school of which Vajda was a part, see Brown (1988).

11. The issue is complicated because Marxist formulations suggest that the separation between the political and the economic in capitalism is simultaneously both real and illusory.

12. The best source on this period in Polanyi's life is Fleming (2001).

13. Letter to MacIver, October 12, 1946, Karl Polanyi Archive, Concordia University, Montreal, Canada.

14. A letter to Polanyi's publisher provides further testimony of the rushed nature of the book's completion. Polanyi proposes to "submit to you the Ms. in a fortnight or sooner, with some of the last chapters not quite finished" and the final chapter would be mailed from abroad. Letter to Gordon, May 7, 1943, Karl Polanyi Archive, Concordia University, Montreal, Canada.

15. This is in marked contrast to preindustrial England, during which working people saw the state—and its labor statutes in particular—as their ally. See Somers (1993, 1994a, 1995).

16. In this respect, Polanyi remained orthodox in GT; he continued to see the working class as central to the project of social transformation.

17. Such a reading is offered by Barber (1995) in his valuable review of the embeddedness concept.

18. This more vigorous concept of embeddedness avoids the dualism between markets and society that is effectively critiqued by Krippner (2001).

19. It was only after his retirement that he returned to issues of world politics by founding the journal *Co-existence*.

20. Or as Peck (2005) suggests "the always and everywhere embedded economy."

4. Turning the Tables

1. It would be ironic, indeed, if Hayek had been inspired to embrace utopianism after reading Karl Polanyi's indictment of free-market utopianism. But it is certainly possible, since Hayek studied the writings of his opponents on the left and Michael Polanyi, Karl's brother, who had read GT in draft form, was in contact with Hayek and had attended the first Mont Pelerin meeting in 1947.

2. This definition is from Dictionary.com, which is based on the Random House Dictionary, 2013. http://dictionary.reference.com/browse/dystopia?s=t Accessed on Sept. 12, 2013.

3. As we note in Chapter 5, during Malthus's lifetime and after, there was a major focus in England on emigration as the solution to the growth of population.

5. In the Shadow of Speenhamland

1. Among the most important reports were Parliamentary Papers, *Report from the Select Committee on the Poor Laws* (1817), *Report from the Committee on*

the Poor Laws (1819), and *Report from the Select Committee on Labourers Wages* (1824). The Royal Commission Report was published as *Report from His Majesty's Commissioners for Inquiring into the Administration and Practical Operation of the Poor Laws* (London: B. Fellowes, 1834).

2. Also relevant is the work of the important English institutional historian who emphasized the negative consequences of Speenhamland (Cunningham 1922, 718–723).

3. Polanyi did try to respond to some of Cole's criticisms in the additional note on "Poor Law and the Organization of Labor" that he appended to the 1945 English edition of the book. But while Polanyi added some qualifications to his argument, he did not change its main thrust.

4. To be sure, in those years in which wheat prices were unusually high, Poor Law outlays would rise across the whole country since parishes had to adjust the income of dependent populations. On declining rural industry, see Kriedte, Medick, and Schlumbohm (1991).

5. On London, see Sharpe (1997); Steinberg (1999). On the role of trade unions and secret societies in providing assistance, see Leeson (1980).

6. Webb and Webb (1927, 221–240), provide the classic account of the failure of numerous efforts to make profits from the labor of those who were in need of relief.

7. On the other hand, high rates of unemployment certainly played a role in radicalizing employed farm workers, such as those who participated in the Captain Swing rebellion in 1830. One of the main targets of the rebels was the threshing machines that increased seasonal unemployment (see Hobsbawm and Rude 1968; Charlesworth, ed. 1983; Reay 1990; Wells 2000).

8. Our definition of Speenhamland also excludes child allowances. The justification is simply practical—to make the story more manageable. Child allowances represented only a small proportion of Poor Law outlays and played little role in arguments about work disincentives.

9. Napoleon abdicated for the first time in early April 1814 and then returned from Elba for three more months of war in 1815. Hence, in annual series, 1813 generally marks the peak of the wartime boom since it was the last full year of war.

10. On the threshing machine, see Fox (1978). On Swing, see Hobsbawm and Rude (1968). On the rise in unemployment, see Gash (1935); Snell (1985); Boyer (1990).

11. With this change in meaning, there was also a change in generosity. The post-1813 scales, even holding the price of wheat constant, were considerably less generous than those used in famine years. But the famine payments established a floor for full-time *employed* workers, while the post-1813 payments were going to households of *unemployed* workers. For a somewhat misleading comparison of the scales, see Hammond and Hammond (1970[1911], 181–182).

12. Eric Jones (1974) estimated that yields per acre rose 16% between 1815–1819 and 1832–1836; see Jones (1974).

13. Drawing on settlement hearings, Snell (1985), argues that there was a significant decline in women's employment opportunities in the wheat-growing regions from the 1790s onward. However, Horrell and Humphries (1995) use family budget data to show women and children providing an increasing share of family income in the later period.

14. Malthus's distrust of appearances is indicated by the following passage: "If I saw a glass of wine repeatedly presented to a man, and he took no notice of it, I should be apt to think that he was blind or uncivil. A juster philosophy might teach me rather to think that my eyes deceived me and that the offer was not really what I conceived it to be" (Malthus 1985 [1798], 70).

15. Marx was bitterly critical of Malthus, but he generally treated Ricardo with respect as an intellectually honest defender of the interests of the bourgeoisie. For Marx's writings on Malthus, see Meek (1954). Keynes (1951 [1933]) reversed this ordering and praised Malthus's underconsumptionist views while criticizing Ricardo's confidence that markets would reach equilibrium.

16. In an essay first published in 1923, "Alternative Aims in Monetary Policy," Keynes was explicit about the parallel when speaking of his contemporaries who favored an immediate return to the prewar parity: "This view is in accordance with that expressed by Ricardo in analogous circumstances a hundred years ago." Keynes (1963 [1923], 194). Polanyi also recognized the parallels between the two postwar periods in a short unpublished piece titled "1820 vs. 1920" that is in the Karl Polanyi Archive (Concordia University, Montreal, Canada), but he chose not to emphasize this parallel in GT.

17. The actual impact of the New Poor Law is still intensely debated. For discussions, see Driver (1993); King (2000).

18. For the precariousness of Ricardian orthodoxy in this period, see Checkland (1949). On the intensity of the anti-Ricardo backlash after the 1825 crash, see Gordon (1976, ch. 4).

6. From Poverty to Perversity

1. With the exception of Foucault (1970), social scientists have generally paid insufficient attention to ideational causal mechanisms. Other works that have closely engaged the causal influence of ideas include Bourdieu (1998); Dean (1991); Fraser and Gordon (1994, 1998); Glasman (1996); Hall (1989); Hirschman (1991); O'Connor (2001); Schram (1995, 2000); Steinmetz (1993, 2000).

2. Pimpare (2004) argues persuasively that the attacks on local welfare provision in the United States in the 1880s and 1890s paralleled the impact and justification of the 1996 legislation. His case differs, however, from the ones we address because the anti-welfare initiative was decentralized.

3. Cases that differ along every parameter except the dependent variable are particularly suited for comparative sociology's method of agreement (Skocpol and Somers 1980)—a method that makes a robust causal argument for the one hypothesized independent variable common to both cases. To avoid the charge of selecting on the dependent variable, we will also be asking why significant changes in welfare legislation did not occur at earlier points in these periods.

4. The classic formulation of this idea was Weber's (1969 [1922]) use of the notion of "elective affinity" to explain how certain religious ideas were embraced by certain social groups because those ideas made sense of their lived experience.

5. While there are overlaps, the logic of the perversity thesis is distinct form arguments about the "unintended consequences" of social action (Merton 1936). While the latter emphasize the impossibility of predicting the outcome of social policies, the perversity thesis is unambiguous in predicting that outcomes will be the reverse of what was intended.

6. Outlays increased from .99 % of GDP in 1749 to 2.15% in 1801–1803 (Lindert 1998), with the highest per capita relief outlays largely in the rural wheat growing and rural industrial textile regions of the southeast (Blaug 1963; Snell 1985). See also Chapter 5.

7. It was referred to as an "Act," but it was never made a Parliamentary statute, as we explain in Chapter 5.

8. Congress passed a major expansion of the Earned Income Tax Credit (EITC) in 1993 that substantially increased transfers to low income households. This partially offset the economic impact of the shift from AFDC to TANF.

9. See Polanyi's essay, "Aristotle Discovers the Economy," reprinted in Polanyi (1968) for a brilliant discussion of the invention of the "scarcity postulate" by classical and neoclassical economics.

10. It was not until the second edition that he adds "moral restraint" as a sop to his theological critics.

11. The gendered character of Malthus's argument is addressed by Gallagher (1987) and Valenze (1995).

12. So significant was the role of Townsend's fable and its influence on Malthus and free-market utopianism that we reprise some of our discussion from earlier chapters.

13. Malthus's appropriation of Smith still does not make Smith himself a market fundamentalist or free-market utopian.

14. The English term "thought experiment" dates to the end of the nineteenth century. Philosophers of science have identified the use of thought experiments at least as far back as Galileo (Kuhn 1977).

15. Malthus is using "illegitimate" to cover any child born to parents who would turn to the parish for assistance.

16. In light of this, it is remarkable that Malthus's story professes to be sympathetic to the poor. To be sure, he does not attribute the behavioral shortcomings

of relief recipients to any unique biological traits or deficiency. Rather, Malthus insists that all human beings are driven by the same overriding biological drive for sexual pleasure; it is just that the middle and upper classes have been able to control those drives.

17. In this we should hear echoes to some of President Ronald Reagan's famous paradigm-changing discourse of the 1980s: "Government is not the solution; government is the problem."

18. The literature on the legislative machinations involved in the bill's passage is enormous and would have to be explored in depth for a full-scale account of how the law made it through Parliament. See especially Brundage (1978); Poynter (1969); Winch (1996).

19. The major exception, of course, is Hirschman (1991). And although Malthus is not specifically identified, Harpham and Scotch (1988) attribute much of *Losing Ground's* popularity and influence "to the fact that it has put old wine into a new bottle . . . In many ways, the policy proposal presented by Murray at the end of *Losing Ground* can be seen as an updating of the proposal for English Poor Law Reform in 1834" (201).

20. For other critiques of Murray, see Katz (2001) Danziger and Gottschalk (1985); Danziger and Haveman (2001);; O'Connor (2001).

21. In explaining these two pieces of legislation, our intention is to supplement rather than replace the scholarship that examines the role of partisanship, economic resources, and political institutions in shaping outcomes.

22. Early in the 2012 election cycle, the Republicans charged that Obama was undermining the welfare rules by granting waivers to the states. Bill Clinton refuted this charge in his speech at the Democratic National Convention—once again affirming that Obama was on board with the goals of the 1996 legislation.

23. For recent studies that document negative long-term consequences of the 1996 legislation, see Collins and Mayer (2010); Morgen, Acker, and Weigt (2010); Self (2012).

7. The Enduring Strength of Free Market Conservatism in the United States

1. This chapter is in part a response to Hicks (2006), who suggested a need to focus more explicitly on the religious dimension of the turn to market fundamentalism in the United States.

2. In 2010, taxes in the United States were 24.8% of GDP while the U.K. was at 34.9%, Germany was 36.1%, and France was 42.9%. (Data are from the OECD, Tax Ration Changes, available at *http://www.oecd.org/ctp/taxpolicyanalysis/revenuestatisticstaxratioschangesbetween1965and20102012edition.htm.*) At the same time, military spending was 4.8% of GDP in the United States, 2.6% in the U.K., 1.3% in Germany, and 2.2% in France. (Data are from the

World Bank, available at *http://data.worldbank.org/indicator/MS.MIL.XPND. GD.ZS.*) Moreover, this data source probably does not capture the spending of U.S. civilian intelligence agencies.

3. Europe has its own right-wing political movements, but hostility to the national government has not been one of the central themes. See, for example, Berezin (2009).

4. There were, of course, close parallels between social policies under Reagan and Thatcher. The difference, however, is that U.S. domestic politics continued to move rightward after Reagan, while Labour Party governments between 1997 and 2010 moved back towards the center.

5. For example, Streeck (2009) emphasizes how deeply the Germany economy has been transformed in recent decades.

6. For a rich historical account of this divergence, see Nolan (2012).

7. Since the global financial crisis in 2008, official child poverty rates in the U.K. have continued to fall, but since the poverty line is defined as 60% of median income, this might be an artifact of a downward trend in median income.

8. There has been considerable disagreement about the best label to use for this social movement, especially because it has continually evolved and changed. For example, when the Tea Party emerged in 2009, it represented itself as completely new rather than a continuation of earlier forms of activism. We use the term "movement conservatism" to convey that there has been a high degree of ideological continuity over forty years and that the movement has retained considerable independence from the apparatus of the Republican Party.

9. For insights on how this autonomy was managed when George W. Bush was in office, see Medvetz (2006).

10. In the 2010 midterm elections, Republicans gained control of state legislatures in Pennsylvania, Wisconsin, Ohio, and Virginia, leading to a torrent of aggressive new legislation targeted at the right's opponents.

11. See Mizruchi (2013) for a somewhat different analysis of the transformation of the U.S. corporate elite over the last four decades.

12. For a contemporaneous account of business anxieties, see Silk and Vogel (1976).

13. For analysis of change in one of the more liberal business groups, see Domhoff (2006). See also Peschek (1987), Himmelstein (1990), and Phillips-Fein (2009).

14. According to one study, Christian conservatives exerted strong influence over eighteen, and moderate control, over twenty-six of fifty state Republican parties in 2000 (Conger and Green 2002). See also Guth et al. (2003).

15. In 2010, the more moderate Republicans withdrew from the Republican primary. Crist in Florida ran as an independent and Specter as a Democrat, but both lost. In Alaska, Murkowski lost in the primary but won re-election as a write-in candidate in the general election.

16. The focus on shareholder value is part of the larger process of financialization that has driven both banks and corporations towards increasingly short-term strategies (Lazonick 2009; Krippner 2011).

17. On the think-tank infrastructure of the Right, see Micklethwait and Wooldridge (2004), Rich (2004), and Medvetz (2012).

8. The Reality of Society

1. A practice readily discarded in the late twentieth century in favor of the "general welfare" to be gained from corporate monopolies (Crouch 2011).

BIBLIOGRAPHY

Adaman, Fikret, Pat Devine, and Begum Ozkaynak. 2003. "Reinstituting the Economic Process: (Re)embedding the Economy in Society and Nature." *International Review of Sociology* 13(2): 357–374.

Adams, Vincenne. 2013. *Markets of Sorrow, Labors of Faith: New Orleans in the Wake of Katrina.* Durham, NC: Duke University Press.

Alexander, Jeffrey. 2006. *The Civil Sphere.* Oxford: Oxford University Press.

Alexander, Michelle. 2010. *The New Jim Crow: Mass Incarceration in the Age of Colorblindness.* New York: The New Press.

Allen, Robert C. 1992. *Enclosure and the Yeoman.* Oxford: Clarendon.

Alperovitz, Gar. 2005. *America beyond Capitalism.* Hoboken, NJ: Wiley.

Anderson, Martin. 1978. *Welfare: The Political Economy of Welfare Reform in the United States.* Stanford, CA: Hoover Institution Press.

Anderson, Perry. 1974. *Lineages of the Absolutist State.* London: New Left Books.

——— 1976. *Considerations on Western Marxism.* London: New Left Books.

Andrews, Edmund L. 2008. "Greenspan Concedes Error on Regulation." *New York Times* October 24: B1.

Angell, Marcia. 2004. *The Truth about the Drug Companies.* New York: Random House.

Applebaum, Eileen, Annette Bernhardt, and Richard Murnane, eds. 2003. *Low-Wage America: How Employers are Reshaping Opportunity in the Workplace.* New York: Russell Sage.

Appleby, Joyce. 1978. *Economic Thought and Ideology in Seventeenth-Century England.* Princeton, NJ: Princeton University Press.

Arendt, Hannah. 1976 [1948]. *The Origins of Totalitarianism.* New York: Harcourt Brace.

Arrighi, Giovanni and Beverly Silver. 2003. "Polanyi's 'Double Movement': The Belle Époques of British and U.S. Hegemony Compared." *Politics & Society* 31(2): 325–355.

Arsneault, Shelly. 2000. "Welfare Policy Innovation and Diffusion: Section 1115 Waivers and the Federal System." *State and Local Government Review* 32: 49–60.

Baker, Dean. 2008. *Plunder and Blunder.* Sausalito, CA: PoliPoint Press.

——— 2010. *Taking Economics Seriously.* Cambridge, MA: MIT Press.

——— 2011. *The End of Loser Liberalism.* Washington, DC: Center for Economic and Policy Research.

Baker, Wayne. 2005. *America's Crisis of Values.* Princeton, NJ: Princeton University Press.

Balibar, Etienne. 2004. *We, The People of Europe?: Reflections on Transnational Citizenship.* Princeton, NJ: Princeton University Press.

Banks, Sarah. 1988. "Nineteenth-Century Scandal or Twentieth Century Model? A New Look at 'Open' and 'Close' Parishes." *Economic History Review* 41(1): 51–73.

Barber, Bernard. 1995. "All Economies Are 'Embedded': The Career of a Concept and Beyond."*Social Research* 62 (2): 387-413.

Barnett, D. C. 1967. "Allotments and the Problem of Rural Poverty, 1740–1840." In *Land, Labour, and Population in the Industrial Revolution,* ed. E. L. and G. E. Mingay Jones, 162–183. London: Edward Arnold.

Barrett, L. 2004. "Yankee Go Home." *Marketing Week,* Nov. 11: 24–27.

Barthes, Roland. 1977. *Image-Music-Text.* Tr. by Stephen Heath. London: Fontana.

Baugh, D. A. 1975. "The Cost of Poor Relief in South-East England, 1790–1834." *Economic History Review* 28: 50–68.

Baum, Gregory. 1996. *Karl Polanyi on Ethics and Economics.* Montreal: McGill-Queen's Press.

Bell, Daniel. 1976. *The Cultural Contradictions of Capitalism.* New York: Basic Books.

——— 1981. "Models and Reality in Economic Discourse." In *The Crisis in Economic Theory,* ed. Daniel Bell and Irving Kristol, 46–80. New York: Basic Books.

Berezin, Mabel. 2009. *Illiberal Politics in Neoliberal Times: Culture, Security, and Populism in the New Europe.* Cambridge: Cambridge University Press.

Berg, Maxine. 1994. *The Age of Manufacturers, 1700–1820.* London: Routledge.

Berman, Sheri. 1998. *The Social Democratic Moment: Ideas and Politics in the Making of Interwar Europe.* Cambridge, MA: Harvard University Press.

——— 2006. *The Primacy of Politics.* Cambridge: Cambridge University Press.

Bernstein, Jared. 2007. "Is Education the Cure for Poverty?" *American Prospect* 18 (May): 17.

Blank, Rebecca. 1997. *It Takes a Nation: A New Agenda for Fighting Poverty.* New York: Russell Sage Foundation.

Blau, Joel. 1999. *Illusions of Prosperity: America's Working Families in an Age of Insecurity.* New York: Oxford.

Blau, Judith, and Alberto Moncada. 2005. *Human Rights: Beyond the Liberal Vision.* Lanham, MD: Rowman & Littlefield.

Blaug, Mark. 1963. "The Myth of the Old Poor Law and the Making of the New." *Journal of Economic History* 23: 151–184.

——— 1964. "The Poor Law Reexamined." *Journal of Economic History* 24: 229–245.

Bloch, Marc. 1961. *Feudal Society.* Chicago: University of Chicago Press.

Block, Fred 1977. *The Origins of International Economic Disorder.* Berkeley: University of California Press.

——— 1987. *Revising State Theory.* Philadelphia: Temple University Press.

——— 1990. *Postindustrial Possibilities.* Berkeley: University of California Press.

——— 1996. *The Vampire State.* New York: The New Press.

——— 2000. "Deconstructing Capitalism as a System." *Rethinking Marxism* 12(3): 83–98.

——— 2001. "Introduction." In Karl Polanyi, *The Great Transformation,* xviii–xxxviii. Boston: Beacon.

——— 2003. "The Global Economy in the Bush Era." *Socio-Economic Review* 1(3): 439–456.

——— 2005. "Towards a New Understanding of Economic Modernity." In *The Economy as Polity: The Political Constitution of Contemporary Capitalism,* ed. Bo Strath, Christian Joerges, and Peter Wagner, 3–16. London: UCL Press.

——— 2009. "Read Their Lips: Taxation and the Right Wing." In *The New Fiscal Sociology,* ed. Isaac Martin, Ajay Mehrotra, and Monica Prasad, 68–85. New York: Cambridge University Press.

——— 2011a. "Breaking with Market Fundamentalism: Toward Domestic and Global Reform." In *Globalization and Beyond,* ed. Jon Shefner and Patricia Fernandez-Kelly, 210–227. University Park: Penn State University Press.

——— 2011b. "Reinventing Social Democracy for the 21st Century." *Journal of Australian Political Economy* 67: 5–21.

Block, Fred, Anna Korteweg, and Kerry Woodward. 2006. "The Compassion Gap in American Poverty Policy." *Contexts* 5(2):14–20.

Block, Fred, and Matthew R. Keller, eds. 2011. *State of Innovation: The U.S. Government's Role in Technology Development.* Boulder, Colorado: Paradigm Publishers.

Block, Fred and Peter Evans. 2005. "The State and the Economy." In *The Handbook of Economic Sociology,* 2nd ed., ed. Neil Smelser and Richard Swedberg, 505–526. Princeton, NJ: Russell Sage.

Bluestone, Barry, and Teresa Ghilarducci. 1996. "Rewarding Work." *The American Prospect* 7(26): 40–46.

Blyth, Mark. 2002. *Great Transformations: Economic Ideas and Institutional Change in the Twentieth Century.* Cambridge: Cambridge University Press.

Bogle, John C. 2005. *The Battle for the Soul of Capitalism.* New Haven, CT: Yale University Press.

Bosniak, Linda. 2006. *The Citizen and the Alien: Dilemmas of Contemporary Membership.* Princeton, NJ: Princeton University Press.

Bouchard, Marie, ed. 2013. *Innovation and the Social Economy: The Quebec Experience.* Toronto: University of Toronto Press.

Bourdieu, Pierre. 1998. *Acts of Resistance: Against the Tyranny of the Market.* New York: New Press.

Boyer, George R. 1990. *An Economic History of the Poor Law, 1750–1850.* Cambridge: Cambridge University Press.

Boyer, Robert, and Daniel Drache, eds. 1996. *States against Markets.* London: Routledge.

Bradlow, David. 1988. "The Changing Legal Environment: The 1980s and Beyond." *ABA Journal,* Dec. 1: 72.

Brenner, Robert. 1977. "Origins of Capitalist Development: A Critique of Neo-Smithian Marxism." *New Left Review* 104: 25–93.

Brewer, John. 1989. *The Sinews of Power: War, Money and the English State, 1688–1783.* New York: Knopf.

Brewer, John, and John Styles, eds. 1980. *An Ungovernable People.* New Brunswick, NJ: Rutgers University Press.

Brewer, Mike, James Browne, Robert Joyce, and Luke Sibieta. 2010. "Child Poverty in the UK since 1998–99: Lessons from the Past Decade." *Institute for Financial Studies Working Papers* 10/23. http://www.ifs.org.uk/wps/wp1023.pdf. Accessed July 12, 2013.

Brick, Howard 2006. *Transcending Capitalism: Visions of a New Society in Modern American Thought.* Ithaca, NY: Cornell University Press.

Brinkley, Alan. 1996. *The End of Reform: New Deal Liberalism in Recession and War.* New York: Vintage.

Brooks, Clem, and Jeff Manza. 2004. "A Great Divide? Religion and Political Change in U.S. National Elections, 1972–2000." *Sociological Quarterly* 45(3): 421–450.

Brown, Douglas M. 1988. *Towards a Radical Democracy: The Political Economy of the Budapest School.* London: Unwin Hyman.

Brown, William Adams, Jr. 1940. *The International Gold Standard Reinterpreted.* 2 vols. Washington, DC: Brookings.

Brundage, Anthony. 1974. "The English Poor Law of 1836 and the Cohesion of Agricultural Society." *Agricultural History* 48: 405–417.

———— 1978. *The Making of the New Poor Law: The Politics of Inquiry, Enactment, and Implementation, 1832–1839.* New Brunswick, NJ: Rutgers University Press.

———— 2002. *The English Poor Laws, 1700–1930.* New York: Palgrave.

Buğra, Ayşe, and Kaan Agartan, eds. 2007. *Reading Karl Polanyi for the Twenty-First Century.* New York: Palgrave Macmillan.

Burawoy, Michael. 1985. *The Politics of Production: Factory Regimes under Capitalism and Socialism.* London: Verso.

———— 2003. "For a Sociological Marxism: The Complementary Convergence of Antonio Gramsci and Karl Polanyi." *Politics & Society* 31(2): 193–261.

Burgin, Angus. 2012. *The Great Persuasion: Reinventing Free Markets since the Depression.* Cambridge, MA: Harvard University Press.

Burns, Jennifer. 2011. *Goddess of the Market: Ayn Rand and the American Right.* New York: Oxford.

Callaghan, John. 2000. *The Retreat of Social Democracy.* Manchester: Manchester University Press.

Callinicos, Alex. 2001. *Against the Third Way.* Cambridge: Polity.

Callon, Michel. 1998. *The Laws of the Market.* Oxford: Blackwell.

Camic, Charles, and Neil Gross. 2001. "The New Sociology of Ideas." In *The Blackwell Companion to Sociology,* ed. Judith R. Blau, 236–250. Malden, MA: Blackwell.

Campbell, John. 1998. "Institutional Analysis and the Role of Ideas in Political Economy." *Theory and Society* 27: 377–409.

Campbell, John, J. Rogers Hollingsworth, and Leon Lindberg. 1991. *Governance of the American Economy.* Cambridge: Cambridge University Press.

Campbell, John, and Ove K. Pedersen, eds. 2001. *The Rise of Neoliberalism and Institutional Analysis.* Princeton, NJ: Princeton University Press.

Cangiani, Michele. 2009. "The Unknown Karl Polanyi." *International Review of Sociology* 19(2): 367–375.

Cangiani, Michele, and Jerome Maucourant, eds. 2008. *Essais de Karl Polanyi.* Paris: Seuil.

Cangiani, Michele, Kari Polanyi-Levitt, and Claus Thomasberger, eds. 2002, 2003, 2005. *Chronik der grossen Transformation,* 3 vols. Marburg: Metropolis.

Cass, Ronald. 2003. *The Rule of Law in America.* Baltimore, MD: Johns Hopkins University Press.

Cassidy, John. 2009. *How Markets Fail.* New York: Farrar, Straus, and Giroux.

Chang, Ha-Joon. 2002. *Kicking Away the Ladder.* London: Anthem Books.

Charlesworth, Andrew, ed. 1983. *An Atlas of Rural Protest in Britain, 1548–1900.* Philadelphia: University of Pennsylvania Press.

Checkland, S. G. 1949. "The Propagation of Ricardian Economics in England." *Economica* 16(61): 40–52.

Christopherson, Susan, and Michael Storper. 1989. "The Effects of Flexible Specialization on Industrial Politics and the Labor Market: The Motion Picture Industry." *Industrial and Labor Relations Review* 42: 331–347.

Chwialkowska, Luiza. 2000. "Subsidies Paid in Loaves of Bread in England in 1700s." *National Post* (Canada), Dec. 12: A6.

Clark, Greg. 1991. "Labour Productivity in English Agriculture, 1300–1860." In *Labour and Livestock: Historical Studies in European Agricultural Productivity,* ed. Bruce M. S. Campbell and Mark Overton, 211–235. Manchester: Manchester University Press.

——— 1999. "Too Much Revolution: Agriculture and the Industrial Revolution, 1700–1860." In *The British Industrial Revolution: An Economic Assessment,* 2d ed., ed. Joel Mokyr, 206–240. Boulder, CO: Westview.

——— 2001. "Farm Wages and Living Standards in the Industrial Revolution: England, 1670–1869." *Economic History Review* 54(3): 477–505.

Clarke, Peter. 2009. *Keynes.* New York: Bloomsbury Press.

Clawson, Dan, Alan Neustadtl, and Mark Weller. 1998. *Dollars and Votes.* Philadelphia: Temple University Press.

Clement, Alain. 1997. "Revenue Minimum: Les Lecons de Speenhamland." *Lien Social et Politique* 42: 49–60.

Cohen, Joshua, and Joel Rogers, eds. 2001. *What's Wrong with a Free Lunch?* Boston: Beacon.

Cole, G. D. H. 1920. *Self-Government in Industry.* London: G. Bell & Sons.

——— 1943. "Notes on *The Great Transformation.*" The Karl Polanyi Archive, Concordia University, Montreal, Canada.

Coleman, Donald C., ed. 1969. *Revisions in Mercantilism.* London: Methuen.

——— 1980. "Mercantilism Revisited." *The Historical Journal* 23: 773–791.

Collins, Jane, and Victoria Mayer. 2010. *Both Hands Tied: Welfare Reform and the Race to the Bottom of the Low-Wage Labor Market.* Chicago: University of Chicago Press.

Collins, Robert M. 1981. *The Business Response to Keynes, 1929–1964.* New York: Columbia University Press.

Congdon, Lee. 1976. "Karl Polanyi in Hungary, 1900–1919." *Journal of Contemporary History* 11: 167–183.

——— 1990. "The Sovereignty of Society: Polanyi in Vienna." In *The Life and Work of Karl Polanyi,* ed. Kari Polanyi-Levitt, 78–84. Montreal: Black Rose.

Conger, Kimberly, and John Green. 2002. "Spreading Out and Digging In: Christian Conservatives and State Republican Parties." *Campaigns and Elections* 23(1): 58–60, 64–65.

Continetti, Matthew 2006. *The K Street Gang.* New York: Doubleday.

Cowan, Deborah. 2008. *Military Workfare: The Soldier and Social Citizenship in Canada.* Toronto: University of Toronto Press.

Cowherd, Raymond G. 1977. *Political Economists and the English Poor Laws.* Athens: Ohio University Press.

Crouch, Colin. 2009. *Post-Democracy.* Cambridge: Polity.

―――― 2011. *The Strange Non-Death of Neoliberalism.* Cambridge: Polity.

Crouch, Colin, and Wolfgang Streeck, eds. 1997. *The Political Economy of Modern Capitalism.* Thousand Oaks, CA: Sage.

Cunningham, William. 1922 [1892] *The Industrial Revolution.* Cambridge: Cambridge University Press.

Dale, Gareth. 2008. "Karl Polanyi's *The Great Transformation:* Perverse Effects, Protectionism, and Gemeinschaft." *Economy and Society* 37(4): 495–524.

―――― 2009. "Karl Polanyi in Budapest: On his Political and Intellectual Formation." *European Journal of Sociology.* 50 (1): 97–130.

―――― 2010. *Karl Polanyi: The Limits of the Market.* Cambridge: Polity.

Danziger, Sheldon H., and Peter Gottschalk. 1985. "The Poverty of Losing Ground." *Challenge* 28: 32–38.

Danziger, Sheldon H., and Robert H. Haveman. 2001. *Understanding Poverty.* Cambridge, MA: Harvard University Press.

Davis, Gerald F. 2009. *Managed by the Market.* New York: Oxford University Press.

Davis, Martha. 1993. *Brutal Need: Lawyers and the Welfare Rights Movement, 1960–1973.* New Haven, CT: Yale University Press.

de Tocqueville, Alexis. 1983 [1835]. "Memoir on Pauperism." *Public Interest* 70: 102–120.

Dean, Mitchell. 1991. *The Constitution of Poverty: Toward a Genealogy of Liberal Governance.* London: Routledge.

Denning, Michael. 1997. *The Cultural Front.* London: Verso.

DeParle, Jason. 2012. "Welfare Limits Left Poor Adrift as Recession Hit." *New York Times,* April 8: A1.

Dershowitz, Alan M. 2004. *America on Trial: Inside the Legal Battles that Transformed Our Nation.* New York: Warner Books.

Diesing, Paul. 1971. *Patterns of Discovery in the Social Sciences.* Chicago: Aldine.

Digby, Anne. 1978. *Pauper Palaces.* London: Routledge and Kegan Paul.

Dobson, C. R. 1980. *Masters and Journeymen: A Pre-history of Industrial Relations, 1717–1800.* London: Croon Helm.

Domestic Policy Council Low Income Opportunity Working Group. 1986. *Up From Dependency: A New National Public Assistance Strategy.* Washington, DC: U.S. Government Printing Office.

Domhoff, G. William. 1990. *The Power Elite and the State.* New York: Aldine.

———— 2006. *Who Rules America? Power, Politics, and Social Change*, 5th ed. New York: McGraw Hill.

Drew, Elizabeth. 2000. *The Corruption of American Politics*. New York: Overlook Press.

Driver, Cecil. 1956. *Tory Radical: The Life of Richard Oastler*. Oxford: Oxford University Press.

Driver, Felix. 1993. *Power and Pauperism: The Workhouse System, 1834–1884*. Cambridge: Cambridge University Press.

Drucker, Peter. 1979. *Adventures of a Bystander*. New York: Harper & Row.

Dubose, Lou, and Jan Reid. 2004. *The Hammer: God, Money, and the Rise of the Republican Congress*. New York: Public Affairs.

Duczynska, Ilona. 1977. "Karl Polanyi: Notes on His Life." In Karl Polanyi, *The Livelihood of Man*, ed. Harry W. Pearson, xi-xx. New York: Academic Press.

Duczynska, Ilona and Karl Polanyi, eds. 1963. *The Plough and the Pen: Writings from Hungary 1930-1956*. London: P. Owen.

Duncan, Greg J. 1984. *Years of Poverty, Years of Plenty*. Ann Arbor, MI: Institute for Social Research.

Dunkley, Peter. 1982. *The Crisis of the Old Poor Law in England: An Interpretative Essay*. New York: Garland.

Durkheim, Emile. 1964 [1893]. *The Division of Labor*, trans. George Simpson. New York: Free Press.

Eccleston, Bernard. 1986. "Malthus, Wages, and the Labour Market in England, 1790–1830." In *Malthus and His Times*, ed. Michael Turner, 143–156. New York: St. Martin's.

Edsall, Nicholas. 1970. *The Anti-Poor Law Movement, 1834–1844*. Manchester: Manchester University Press.

Ehrenreich, Barbara. 2004. "The Faith Factor." *The Nation*, Nov. 29.

Eichengreen, Barry. 1996. *Globalizing Capital: A History of the International Monetary System*. Princeton, NJ: Princeton University Press.

Ellwood, David T. 1988. *Poor Support: Poverty in the American Family*. New York: Basic.

———— 2001. "Welfare Reform as I Knew It." *The American Prospect* 26: 22–29.

Emmison, F. G. 1933. "The Relief of the Poor at Eaton Socon, 1706–1834." *Publications of the Bedfordshire Historical Record Society* 15: 3–98.

Engels, Friedrich. 1958 [1845]. *The Condition of the Working Class in England*. Stanford, CA: Stanford University Press.

Epstein, Richard. 2005. *Takings: Private Property and the Power of Eminent Domain*. Cambridge, MA: Harvard University Press.

Esping-Andersen, Gosta. 1990. *The Three Worlds of Welfare Capitalism*. Princeton, NJ: Princeton University Press.

Evans, Peter. 2008. "Is an Alternative Globalization Possible?" *Politics & Society* 36(2): 271–305.

Febvre, Lucien. 1973. *A New Kind of History,* ed. Peter Burke. New York: Harper and Row.

Feinstein, Charles. 1998. "Pessimism Perpetuated: Real Wages and the Standard of Living in Britain during the Industrial Reovlution." *Journal of Economic History* 58(3): 625–658.

Fetter, Frank W. 1965. *Development of British Monetary Orthodoxy, 1791–1875.* Cambridge, MA: Harvard University Press.

Finer, S. E. 1972. "The Transmission of Benthamite Ideas, 1820–1850." In *Studies in the Growth of Nineteenth-Century Government,* ed. by Gillian Sutherland, 11–32. London: Routledge and Kegan Paul.

Fischer, Wolfram, and Peter Lundgreen. 1975. "The Recruitment and Training of Administrative and Technical Personnel." In *The Formation of National States in Western Europe,* ed. Charles Tilly, 456–561. Princeton, NJ: Princeton University Press.

Fitzpatrick, Peter. 1992. *The Mythology of Modern Law.* New York: Routledge.

Fleming, Berkeley. 2001. "Three Years in Vermont: The Writing of Karl Polanyi's *The Great Transformation.*" Paper presented at the Eighth International Karl Polanyi Conference, Mexico City. November 14.

Foucault, M. 1970. *The Order of Things: An Archaeology of the Human Sciences.* New York: Vintage.

Fourcade-Gourinchas, Marion, and Sarah Babb. 2002. "The Rebirth of the Liberal Creed: Paths to Neoliberalism in Four Countries." *American Journal of Sociology* 108: 533–579.

Fox, N.E. 1978. "The Spread of the Threshing Machine in Central Southern England." *Agricultural History Review* 26(1): 26–28.

Frank, Robert. 2007a. *The Economic Naturalist: In Search of Explanations for Everyday Enigmas.* New York: Basic Books.

——— 2007a. *Falling Behind: How Rising Inequality Harms the Middle Class.* Berkeley: University of California Press.

——— 2011. *The Darwinian Economy: Liberty, Competition, and the Common Good.* Princeton, NJ: Princeton University Press.

Frank, Thomas. 1997. *The Conquest of Cool.* Chicago: University of Chicago Press.

——— 2004. *What's the Matter with Kansas?* New York: Metropolitan.

——— 2006. "What is K Street's Project?" *New York Times,* Aug. 19: A15.

Fraser, Derek, ed. 1976. *The New Poor Law in the Nineteenth Century.* New York: St. Martin's Press.

Fraser, Nancy, and Linda Gordon. 1994. "A Genealogy of Dependency: Tracing a Keyword of the U.S. Welfare State." *Signs* 19: 309–336.

——— 1998. "Contract vs. Charity: Why Is There No Social Citizenship in America?" In *The Citizenship Debates*, ed. Gershon Shafir, 113–130. Minneapolis: University of Minnesota Press.

Friedman, Milton. 1953. *Essays in Positive Economics*. Chicago: University of Chicago Press.

——— 1962. *Capitalism and Freedom*, Chicago: University of Chicago Press.

Friedman, Thomas. 1999. *The Lexus and the Olive Tree*. New York: Farrar, Straus, and Giroux.

Frye, Northrop. 1973. "Spengler Revisited." *Daedalus* 103(1): 1–13.

Fukuyama, Francis. 1992. *The End of History and the Last Man*. New York: Free Press.

Fung, Archon, and Erik Olin Wright. 2001. "Deepening Democracy: Innovations in Empowered Participatory Governance." *Politics & Society* 29 (March): 5–41.

Furniss, Edgar. 1920. *The Position of the Laborer in a System of Nationalism: A Study in the Labor Theories of Later English Mercantilists*. Boston: Houghton Mifflin.

Fussell, G. E., and M. Compton. 1939. "Agricultural Adjustments after the Napoleonic Wars." *Economic History* 3(14): 184–204.

Galbraith, James. 2000. "How the Economists Got It Wrong." *The American Prospect* 11:18–20.

——— 2008. *The Predator State*. New York: Free Press.

Gallagher, Catherine. 1987. "The Body versus the Social Body in the Works of Thomas Malthus and Henry Mayhew." In *The Making of the Modern Body: Sexuality and Society in the Nineteenth Century*, ed. Catherine Gallagher and Thomas Laquer, 83–106. Berkeley: University of California Press.

Gao, Bai. 1997. *Economic Ideology and Japanese Industrial Policy*. Cambridge: Cambridge University Press.

Gash, Norman. 1935. "Rural Unemployment, 1815–1834." *Economic History Review* 6(1): 90–93.

Gemici, Kurtulus. 2008. "Karl Polanyi and the Anitmonies of Embeddedness." *Socio-Economic Review* 6(3): 5–33.

George, Susan. 1997. "How to Win the War of Ideas: Lessons from the Gramscian Right." *Dissent* 44: 47–53.

Gerschenkron, Alexander. 1962. *Economic Backwardness in Historical Perspective*. Cambridge, MA: Harvard University Press.

——— 1966. *Bread and Democracy in Germany*. New York: Howard Fertig.

Gerth, Hans, and C. Wright Mills, eds. 1946. *From Max Weber: Essays in Sociology*. New York: Oxford.

Gibbs, David. 2004. "Pretexts and U.S. Foreign Policy: The War on Terrorism in Historical Perspective." *New Political Science* 26(3): 293–321.

Gilens, Martin. 1999. *Why Americans Hate Welfare*. Chicago: University of Chicago Press.

Glasman, Maurice. 1996. *Unnecessary Suffering: Managing Market Utopia*. London: Verso.

Goldberg, Michelle. 2006. *Kingdom Coming: The Rise of Christian Nationalism*. New York: Norton.

Gordon, Barry. 1976. *Political Economy in Parliament, 1819–1823*. London: Macmillan.

Gornick, Janet and Markus Jantti. 2011. "Child Poverty in Comparative Perspective: Assessing the Role of Family Structure and Parental Education and Employment." LIS Working Paper No. 570. http://www.lisdatacenter. org/wps/liswps/570.pdf. Accessed Oct. 1, 2013.

Gottschalk, Marie. 2000. *The Shadow Welfare State: Labor, Business, and the Politics of Health Care in the United States*. Ithaca, NY: Cornell University Press.

Goulden, Joseph C. 1972. *The Superlawyers: The Small and Powerful World of the Great Washington Law Firms*. New York: Weybright and Talley.

Gouldner, Alvin. 1980. *The Two Marxisms: Contradictions and Anomalies in the Development of Theory*. New York: Seabury Press.

Gourevitch, Peter. 1978. "The International System and Regime Formation: A Critical Review of Anderson and Wallerstein." *Comparative Politics* 10(4): 419–438.

Gourevitch, Peter, and James Shinn. 2005. *Political Power and Corporate Control: The New Global Politics of Corporate Governance*. Princeton, NJ: Princeton University Press.

Graham, Otis L., Jr. 1992. *Losing Time: The Industrial Policy Debate*. Cambridge, MA: Harvard University Press.

Gray, John. 2000. *False Dawn: The Delusions of Global Capitalism*. New York: New Press.

Greider, William 1987. *Secrets of the Temple: How the Federal Reserve Runs the Country*. New York: Simon and Schuster.

——— 1997. *One World Ready or Not: The Manic Logic of Global Capitalism*. New York: Simon and Schuster.

——— 2003. *The Soul of Capitalism*. New York: Simon and Schuster.

Gross, Daniel. 2007. "Income Inequality, Writ Larger." *New York Times*, June 10: III, 7.

Gueron, Judith, Edward Pauly, and Cameran M. Lougy. 1991. *From Welfare to Work*. New York: Russell Sage.

Guth, James L., Linda Beail, Greg Crow, Beverly Gaddy, Steve Montreal, Brent Nelsen, James Penning, Jeff Walz. 2003. "The Political Activity of Evangelical Clergy in the Election of 2000: A Case Study of Five Denominations." *Journal for the Scientific Study of Religion* 42(4): 501–514.

Hacker, Jacob. 2006. *The Great Risk Shift*. New York: Oxford University Press.

Hacker, Jacob, and Paul Pierson. 2010. *Winner-Take-All Politics*. New York: Simon and Schuster.

Hall, Peter A., ed. 1989. *The Political Power of Economic Ideas*. Princeton, NJ: Princeton University Press.

Hall, Peter, and David Soskice, eds. 2001. *Varieties of Capitalism: The Institutional Foundations of Comparative Advantage*. Oxford: Oxford University Press.

Halperin, Rhoda. 1994. *Cultural Economics: Past and Present*. Austin: University of Texas Press.

Hammond, John, and Barbara Hammond. 1970 [1911]. *The Village Labourer, 1760–1832*. New York: Harper & Row.

Handler, Joel. 2004. *Social Citizenship and Workfare in the United States and Western Europe*. New York: Cambridge.

——— 2006. "On Welfare Reform's Hollow Victory." *Daedalus* 135: 114–117.

Hardisty, Jean. 2004. *Mobilizing Resentment*. Boston: Beacon.

Harpham, Edward J., and Richard K. Scotch. 1988. "Rethinking the War on Poverty: The Ideology of Social Welfare Reform." *Western Political Quarterly* 41: 193–207.

Harrison, Bennett. 1994. *Lean and Mean*. New York: Basic Books.

Harriss-White, Barbara. 1996. "Free Market Romanticism in an Era of Deregulation." *Oxford Development Studies* 24(1): 27–46.

Harvey, David. 2005. *A Brief History of Neoliberalism*. New York: Oxford University Press.

Harvey, Philip. 1999. "Joblessness and the Law before the New Deal." *Georgetown Journal on Poverty Law and Policy* 6: 2–41.

Hasbach, Wilhelm. 1920 [1908]. *A History of the English Agricultural Labourer*, trans. Ruth Kenyon. London: King & Son.

Hayek, Friedrich A. 1949. "The Intellectuals and Socialism." *University of Chicago Law Review*. 16 (3): 417–433.

——— 2007 [1944]. *The Road to Serfdom*. Chicago: University of Chicago Press.

Hays, Sharon. 2003. *Flat Broke with Children: Women in the Age of Welfare Reform*. New York: Oxford University Press.

Heckscher, Eli. 1955 [1935]. *Mercantilism*, trans. Mendel Shapiro. New York: Macmillan.

Henriques, Ursula R. Q. 1979. *Before the Welfare State: Social Administration in Early Industrial Britain*. London: Longman.

Herbert, Bob. 2010. "This Raging Fire." *New York Times*, Nov. 16: A31.

Hicks, Alexander. 1999. *Social Democracy and Welfare Capitalism*. Ithaca, NY: Cornell University Press.

———— 2006. "Comment on Somers and Block." *American Sociological Review* 71(3): 503–510.

Hill, R. L. 1929. *Toryism and the People, 1832–1846*. London: Constable.

Hilton, Boyd. 1977. *Corn, Cash, Commerce: The Economic Policies of the Tory Governments, 1815–1830*. Oxford: Oxford University Press.

Himmelfarb, Gertrude. 1984. *The Idea of Poverty: England in the Early Industrial Age*. New York: Knopf.

———— 1994. "A De-moralized Society." *The Public Interest* 117: 57–80.

———— 1995. *The De-moralization of Society: From Victorian Virtues to Modern Values*. New York: Knopf.

Himmelstein, Jerome. 1990. *To the Right: The Transformation of American Conservatism*. Berkeley: University of California Press.

Hirschman, Albert O. 1977. *The Passions and the Interests*. Princeton, NJ: Princeton University Press.

———— 1991. *The Rhetoric of Reaction: Perversity, Futility, Jeopardy*. Cambridge, MA: Harvard University Press.

Hitchcock, Tim, Peter King and Pamela Sharpe. 1997. *Chronicling Poverty: The Voices and Strategies of the English Poor, 1640–1840*. Houndsmill, Hampshire: Macmillan.

Hobbes, Thomas. 2008 [1651]. *Leviathan*. Ed. Marshall Missner. New York: Pearson Longmen.

————1998 [1642]. *Hobbes: On the Citizen,* ed. Richard Tuck and Michael Silverthorne. Cambridge: Cambridge University Press.

Hobsbawm, E. J., and George Rude. 1968. *Captain Swing*. New York: Pantheon.

Hodgson, Godfrey. 2005. *America in Our Time*. Princeton, NJ: Princeton University Press.

Holderness, B. A. 1972. "'Open' and 'Close' Parishes in England in the Eighteenth and Nineteenth Centuries." *Agricultural History Review* 20: 125–139.

Hollander, Samuel. 1997. *The Economics of Thomas Robert Malthus*. Toronto: University of Toronto Press.

Hollingsworth, Rogers J., and Robert Boyer, eds. 1997. *Contemporary Capitalism: The Embeddedness of Institutions*. Cambridge: Cambridge University Press.

Horrell, Sara, and Jane Humphries. 1995. "Women's Labour Force Participation and the Transition to the Male-Breadwinner Family, 1790–1865." *Economic History Review* 48(1): 89–117.

Howard, Dick and Karl Klare, eds. 1972. *The Unknown Dimension: European Marxism since Lenin*. New York: Basic Books.

Howell, David. 1997. "Block and Manza on the Negative Income Tax." *Politics & Society* 24(4): 533–539.

Huber, Evelyne, and John D. Stephens. 2001. *Development and Crisis of the Welfare State: Parties and Policies in Global Markets.* Chicago: University of Chicago Press.

Hudson, Pat. 1986. *The Genesis of Industrial Capital: A Study of the West Riding Wool Textile Industry, c. 1750–1850.* Cambridge: Cambridge University Press.

——— 1989. *Regions and Industries: A Perspective on the Industrial Revolution in Britain.* Cambridge: Cambridge University Press.

——— 1992. *The Industrial Revolution.* London: E. Arnold.

Huzel, James. 1989. "The Labourer and the Poor Law." In *The Agrarian History of England and Wales,* vol. 6, ed. G. E. Mingay, 755–810. Cambridge: Cambridge University Press.

Ignatieff, Michael. 2005. "The Broken Contract." *New York Times Magazine,* Sept. 25: 15–17.

Immerwahr, Daniel. 2009. "Polanyi in the United States: Peter Drucker, Karl Polanyi, and the Midcentury Critique of Economic Society." *Journal of the History of Ideas* 70(3): 445–466.

Jacobs, Michael 1991. *Short-Term America: The Causes and Cures of Our Business Myopia.* Cambridge, MA: Harvard Business School Press.

Jencks, Christopher. 2005. "What Happened to Welfare?" *New York Review of Books* Dec. 15: 76.

John, A. H. 1989. "Statistical Appendix." *The Agrarian History of England and Wales,* ed. G. E. Mingay, 972–1155. Cambridge: Cambridge University Press.

Johnson, Simon, and James Kwak. 2010. *13 Bankers.* New York: Pantheon.

Jones, Eric L. 1974. "The Agricultural Labor Market in England, 1793–1872." In *Agriculture and the Industrial Revolution,* ed. E. L. Jones. 211–233. Oxford: Basil Blackwell.

Jones, Daniel Stedman. 2012. *Masters of the Universe: Hayek, Friedman, and the Birth of Neoliberal Politics.* Princeton, NJ: Princeton University Press.

Jones, Gareth Stedman, and New Left Review, eds. 1977. *Western Marxism: A Critical Reader.* London: New Left Books.

Judt, Tony. 2010. *Ill Fares the Land.* New York: Penguin Press.

Kahneman, Daniel, Paul Slovic, and Amos Tversky. 1985. *Judgment under Uncertainty: Heuristics and Biases.* Cambridge: Cambridge University Press.

Kanter, Rosabeth 1977. *Men and Women of the Corporation.* New York: Basic Books.

Karst, Kenneth. 1989. *Belonging to America: Equal Citizenship and the Constitution.* New Haven, CT: Yale University Press.

Katz, Michael. 1986. *In the Shadow of the Poorhouse: A Social History of Welfare in America.* New York: Basic.

——— 1989. *The Undeserving Poor.* New York: Pantheon.

—— 2001. *The Price of Citizenship*. New York: Henry Holt.

Katznelson, Ira. 1979. "Community, Capitalist Development, and the Emergence of Class." *Politics & Society* 9(2): 203–237.

—— 2005. *When Affirmative Action Was White*. New York: W.W. Norton.

—— 2013. *Fear Itself: The New Deal and the Origins of Our Time*. New York: Liveright.

Kennedy, Duncan. 1991. "The Stakes of Law, or Hale and Foucault!" *Legal Studies Forum* 15(4): 327–366.

Keynes, John Maynard. 1925. *Economic Consequences of Sterling Parity*. New York: Harcourt.

—— 1951 [1933]. "Robert Malthus: The First of the Cambridge Economists." In *Essays in Biography*, 81–124. London: Rupert Hart-Davis.

—— 1963. [1923]. "Alternative Aims in Monetary Policy." Reprinted in J.M. Keynes, *Essays in Persuasion*. 186–212. New York: Norton.

—— 1963 [1925]. "The Economic Consequences of Mr. Churchill." In *Essays in Persuasion*, 244–270. New York: Norton.

—— 1963 [1930]. "Economic Possibilities for our Grandchildren." Reprinted in J.M. Keynes, *Essays in Persuasion*, 358–374. New York: Norton.

—— 1964 [1936]. *The General Theory of Employment, Interest, and Money*. New York: Harcourt, Brace, and World.

—— 1982 [1939]. "Democracy and Efficiency." In *The Collected Writings of John Maynard Keynes*, ed. Donald Moggridge, vol. 21, 491–500. London: The Royal Economic Society.

Kindleberger, Charles P. 1974. "The Great Transformation by Karl Polanyi." *Daedalus* 103(1): 45–52.

—— 1975. "The Rise of Free Trade in Western Europe, 1820–1875." *Journal of Economic History* 35(1): 20–55.

King, Steven. 2000. *Poverty and Welfare in England, 1700–1850*. Manchester: Manchester University Press.

Klein, Naomi. 2007. *The Shock Doctrine*. New York: Metropolitan Books.

Knott, John. 1986. *Popular Opposition to the 1834 Poor Law*. London: Croon Helm.

Korpi, Walter and Joakim Palme. 2003. "New Politics and Class Politics in the Context of Austerity and Globalization: Welfare State Regress in 18 Countries." *American Political Science Review* 19: 425–446.

Kriedte, Peter, Hans Medick, and Jügen Schlumbohm. 1991. *Industrialization before Industrialization*. Cambridge: Cambridge University Press.

Krippner, Greta R. 2001. "The Elusive Market: Embeddedness and the Paradigm of Economic Sociology." *Theory and Society* 30: 775–810.

—— 2011. *Capitalizing on Crisis: The Political Origins of the Rise of Finance*. Cambridge, MA: Harvard University Press.

Krippner, Greta, and Anthony S. Alvarez. 2007. "Embeddedness and the Intellectual Projects of Economic Sociology." *Annual Review of Sociology* 33: 219–240.

Krugman, Paul. 1989. *Exchange Rate Instability*. Cambridge, MA: MIT Press.

——— 2009a. "The Crisis and How to Deal with It." Symposium with George Soros, Niall Ferguson, Paul Krugman, Robin Wells, Bill Bradley, et.al. *New York Review of Books,* June 11. http://www.nybooks.com/articles/archives/2009/jun/11/the-crisis-and-how-to-deal-with-it/?pagination=false. Accessed July 12, 2013.

——— 2009b. "How Did Economists Get It So Wrong?" *New York Times Magazine,* Sept. 2: 36.

——— 2012. *End This Depression Now*. New York: Norton.

Kuhn, Thomas. 1977. "A Function for Thought Experiments." In *The Essential Tension,* 240–265. Chicago: University of Chicago Press.

Kumar, Krishan. 1988. "Employment and Unemployment: The English Experience." In *On Work: Historical, Comparative, and Theoretical Approaches,* ed. R. E. Pahl, 138–164. London: Blackwell.

Kussmaul, A. S. 1981. *Servants in Husbandry in Early Modern England*. Cambridge: Cambridge University Press.

Kuttner, Robert. 1996. *Everything for Sale: The Virtues and Limits of Markets*. New York: Knopf.

——— 2007. *The Squandering of America: How the Failure of Our Politics Undermines Our Prosperity*. New York: Vintage Books.

——— 2013. *Debtor's Prison: The Politics of Austerity Versus Possibility*. New York: Knopf.

Kwon, Hyeong-Ki. 2003. "Divergent Constitution of Liberal Regimes: Comparison of the U.S. and German Automotive Supplier Markets." *Politics & Society* 31(1): 93–130.

Lakatos, Imre. 1970. "Falsification and the Methodology of Scientific Research Programames." In *Criticism and the Growth of Knowlege,* ed. Imre Lakatos and A. Musgrave, 91–196. Cambridge: Cambridge University Press.

Lakoff, George. 1996. *Moral Politics: What Conservatives Know that Liberals Don't*. Chicago: University of Chicago Press.

Laville, Jean-Luis, and Michele La Rose, eds. 2008. *Per una critica all'economicismo?* Milan: FrancoAngeli.

Lazonick, William. 2009. *Sustainable Prosperity in the New Economy?* Kalamazoo, MI: Upjohn.

Lees, Lynn. 1998. *The Solidarities of Strangers: The English Poor Laws and the People, 1700–1948*. Cambridge: Cambridge University Press.

Leeson, R. A. 1980. *Travelling Brothers: The Six Centuries' Road from Craft Fellowship to Trade Unionism*. London: Granada.

Leonhardt, David. 2007. "Larry Summer's Evolution." *New York Times Magazine,* June 10: 22.

Levitt, Kari. 1964. "Karl Polanyi and Co-Existence." *Co-Existence* 2: 113–121.

Leys, Colin. 2003. *Market-Driven Politics: Neoliberal Democracy and the Public Interest.* London: Verso.

Lieberman, Robert C. 1998. *Shifting the Color Line: Race and the American Welfare State.* Cambridge, MA: Harvard University Press.

—— 2002. "Ideas, Institutions, and Political Order: Explaining Political Change." *American Political Science Review* 96: 697–712.

Lindblom, Charles E. 2001. *The Market System: What It Is, How It Works, and What to Make of It.* New Haven, CT: Yale University Press.

Lindert, Peter. 1998. "Poor Relief before the Welfare State: Britain versus the Continent, 1780–1880." *European Review of Economic History* 2:101–140.

Link, Robert G. 1959. *English Economic Fluctuations, 1815–1848.* New York: Columbia University Press.

Lipson, Ephraim E. 1943. *The Economic History of England.* London: A. and C. Black.

Litvan, Gyorgi. 1991. "Democratic and Socialist Values in Karl Polanyi's Thought." In *The Legacy of Karl Polanyi,* ed. Marguerite Mendell and Daniel Salee, 251–271. New York: St. Martin's.

Lowenstein, Roger. 2000. *When Genius Failed.* New York: Random House.

—— 2007. "The Inequality Conundrum." *New York Times Magazine,* June 10: 11–14.

Lukacs, Georg. 1971 [1923]. *History and Class Consciousness,* trans. Rodney Livingstone. Cambridge, MA: MIT Press.

Luker, Kristin. 1996. *Dubious Conceptions: The Politics of Teenage Pregnancy.* Cambridge, MA: Harvard University Press.

Lukes, Steven. 2004. "Invasions of the Market." In *Worlds of Capitalism: Institutions, Governance and Economic Change in the Era of Globalization,* ed. Max Miller, 298–321. London: Routledge.

MacIntyre, Alasdair. 1980. "Epistemological Crisis, Dramatic Narrative, and the Philosophy of Science." In *Paradigms and Revolutions,* ed. Gary Gutting, 54–74. Notre Dame, IN: University of Notre Dame Press.

MacKenzie, Donald. 2006. *An Engine, Not a Camera.* Cambridge, MA: MIT Press.

MacKenzie, Donald, Fabian Muniesa, and Lucia Su, eds. 2007. *Do Economists Make Markets?* Princeton, NJ: Princeton University Press.

Maier, Charles. 1975. *Recasting Bourgeois Europe.* Princeton, NJ: Princeton University Press.

Malthus, T. R. 1985 [1798]. *An Essay on the Principle of Population,* ed. Anthony Flew. London: Penguin Books.

———1992 [1803]. *An Essay on the Principle of Population,* 2nd ed., ed. Donald Winch. Cambridge: Cambridge University Press.

Mandler, Peter. 1987. "The Making of the New Poor Law Redivivus." *Past and Present* 117: 131–57.

——— 1990. "Tories and Paupers: Christian Political Economy and the Making of the New Poor Law." *The Historical Journal* 33(1): 81–103.

Mannheim, Karl. 1968 [1936]. *Ideology and Utopia,* trans. Louis Wirth and Edward Shils. New York: Harcourt, Brace & World.

Mantoux, Paul. 1962 [1928]. *The Industrial Revolution in the Eighteenth Century,* trans. Marjorie Vernon. New York: Harper and Row.

Marcuzzo, Maria Cristina, Luigi L. Pasinetti, and Alessandro Roncaglia, eds. 1996. *The Economics of Joan Robinson.* London: Routledge.

Marglin, Stephen and Juliet Schor, eds. 1990. *The Golden Age of Capitalism.* Oxford: Clarendon Press.

Marshall, Dorothy. 1926. *The English Poor in the Eighteenth Century.* London: Routledge.

Marshall, J. D. 1985. *The Old Poor Law, 1795–1834.* London: Macmillan.

Marshall, T. H. 1964 [1950]. "Citizenship and Social Class." In *Class, Citizenship, and Social Development,* ed. S. M. Lipset, 65–123. Garden City, NY: Doubleday.

Marshall, T. H., and Tom Bottomore. 1992. *Citizenship and Social Class.* Concord, MA: Pluto.

Martin, Isaac William. 2008. *The Permanent Tax Revolt.* Stanford, CA: Stanford University Press.

Marwick, Arthur. 1998. *The Sixties: Cultural Revolution in Britain, France, Italy and the United States, c. 1958–c.1974.* New York: Oxford University Press.

Marx, Karl. 1930 [1890]. *Capital,* vol. 1, trans. Eden and Cedar Paul. New York: E.P. Dutton.

——— 1966 [1932]. *The Economic and Philosophic Manuscripts of 1844.* Tr. by Martin Milligan, ed. by Dirk J. Struik. New York: International Publishers.

——— 1978 [1859]. "Preface to the Contribution to the Critique of Political Economy." In *The Marx-Engels Reader,* 2nd ed., ed. Robert C. Tucker, 3–6. New York: W.W. Norton.

Maucourant, Jerome, ed. 2011. *Avez-vous Lu Polanyi?* Paris: Collection Champs.

McCulloch, J. R. 1938 [1845]. *The Literature of Political Economy.* London: London School of Economics.

McNamara, Kathleen R. 1998. *The Currency of Ideas: Monetary Politics in the European Union.* Ithaca, NY: Cornell University Press.

McRobbie, Kenneth. 2006. "'Old, Badly Peeled, Half-Raw Potatoes' and Peter F. Drucker's Other Myths about Karl Polanyi." In *Karl Polanyi in Vienna,* ed. Kenneth McRobbie and Kari Polanyi Levitt, 359–377. Montreal: Black Rose.

McRobbie, Kenneth and Kari Polanyi Levitt, eds. 2006. *Karl Polanyi in Vienna.* 2nd ed. Montreal: Black Rose.

Medvetz, Tom. 2006. "The Strength of Weekly Ties: Relations of Material and Symbolic Exchange in the Conservative Movement." *Politics & Society* 34(3): 343–368.

———— 2012. *Think Tanks in America.* Chicago: University of Chicago Press.

Meek, Ronald. 1954. Ed. *Marx and Engels on Malthus.* New York: International Publishers.

Mendell, Marguerite. 1994. "Karl Polanyi and Socialist Education." In *Humanity, Society, and Commitment: On Karl Polanyi,* ed. Kenneth McRobbie, 25–42. Montreal: Black Rose.

———— 2009. "The Three Pillars of the Social Economy: The Quebec Experience (1996–2007)." In *The Social Economy.* ed. Ash Amin, 176–207. London: Zed Books.

Mendell, Marguerite, and Rocio Nogales. 2011. "Working Paper on Solidarity Finance." Forum International de L'Economies Sociale et Solidaire (FIESS), October. http://base.socioeco.org/docs/fiess_wp_solidarity-finance_oct.-20115.pdf Accessed September 24, 2013.

Merrington, John. 1975. "Town and Country in the Transition to Capitalism." *New Left Review* 93: 71–92.

Merton, Robert K. 1936. "The Unanticipated Consequences of Purposive Social Action." *American Sociological Review* 1: 894–904.

Mica, Daniel. 1995. "Personal Responsibility Act of 1995." *House of Representatives: Congressional Record,* March 24.

Micklethwait, John, and Adrian Wooldridge. 2004. *The Right Nation: Conservative Power in America.* New York: Penguin.

Mills, C. Wright. 1959. *The Sociological Imagination.* New York: Oxford University Press.

Mills, D. R. 1980. *Lord and Peasant in Nineteenth-Century Britain.* London: Croon Helm.

Minchinton, Walter F. 1972. *Wage Regulation in Pre-Industrial England.* New York: Barnes and Noble.

Minsky, Hyman. 1986. *Stabilizing an Unstable Economy.* New Haven, CT: Yale University Press.

Mirowski, Philip 1989. *More Heat than Light: Economics as Social Physics, Physics as Nature's Economics.* Cambridge: Cambridge University Press.

Mirowski, Philip, and Dieter Plehwe, eds. 2009. *The Road to Mont Pelerin.* Cambridge, MA: Harvard University Press.

Mishel, Lawrence, Jared Bernstein, and Heather Boushey. 2003. *The State of Working America 2002 / 2003.* Ithaca, NY: Cornell University Press.

Mishel, Lawrence, Jared Bernstein, and Sylvia Allegretto. 2006. *The State of Working America, 2006 / 2007.* Ithaca, NY: ILR Press.

Mitchell, B. R., and Phyllis Deane. 1962. *Abstract of British Historical Statistics.* Cambridge: Cambridge University Press.

Mitchell, Timothy. 2002. *Rule of Experts.* Berkeley: University of California Press.

Mizruchi, Mark. 2013. *The Fracturing of the American Corporate Elite.* Cambridge, MA: Harvard University Press.

Molotch, Harvey. 2012. *Against Security: How We Go Wrong at Airports, Subways, and Other Sites of Ambiguous Danger.* Princeton, NJ: Princeton University Press.

Moore, Barrington. 1966. *Social Origins of Dictatorships and Democracy.* Boston: Beacon Press.

Moore, D. C. 1976. *The Politics of Deference.* London: Harvester Press.

Moreton, Bethany. 2009. *To Serve God and Wal-Mart.* Cambridge, MA: Harvard University Press.

Morgen, Sandra, Joan Acker, and Jill Weigt. 2010. *Stretched Thin: Poor Families, Welfare Work, and Welfare Reform.* Ithaca, NY: Cornell University Press.

Moynihan, Patrick Daniel. 1973. *The Politics of a Guaranteed Income: The Nixon Administration and the Family Assistance Plan.* New York: Vintage.

Murray, Charles. 1984. *Losing Ground: American Social Policy, 1950–1980.* New York: Basic Books.

——— 1986a. "White Welfare, White Families, White Trash." *National Review* 38(5): 30–34.

——— 1986b. "No, Welfare Isn't Really the Problem." *Public Interest* 84: 3–11.

——— 1993. "The Coming White Underclass." *Wall Street Journal,* Oct. 29: A14.

National Employment Law Project. 2010. *Unemployment Insurance Modernization: Questions and Answers,* originally posted Jan. 30, 2009, updated Dec. 14, 2009. http://nelp.3cdn.net/d2e0a0eb686ddc0826_v4m6bx17s.pdf. Accessed July 12, 2013.

Neuman, Mark. 1982. *The Speenhamland County: Poverty and the Poor Laws in Berkshire, 1782–1834.* New York: Garland.

Newfield, Christopher. 2008. *Unmaking the Public University.* Cambridge, MA: Harvard University Press

Newman, Nathan. 2002. *Net Loss: Internet Prophets, Private Profits, and the Costs to Community.* University Park: Penn State University Press.

Nolan, Mary. 2005. "Anti-Americanism and Americanization in Germany." *Politics & Society* 33(1): 88–122.

——— 2012. *The Transatlantic Century: Europe and America, 1890–2010.* Cambridge: Cambridge University Press.

Nozick, Robert. 1974. *Anarchy, State, and Utopia.* New York: Basic Books.

O'Connor, Alice 2001. *Poverty Knowledge: Social Science, Social Policy, and the Poor in Twentieth-Century U.S. History.* Princeton, NJ: Princeton University Press.

O'Connor, James. 1998. *Natural Causes: Essays in Ecological Marxism.* New York: Guilford.

Organization for Economic Cooperation and Development. 2010. *Economic Policy Reforms: Going for Growth.* Paris: OECD Publishing.

O'Riain, Sean 2006. "Time Space Intensification: Karl Polanyi, the Double Movement and Global Informational Capitalism." *Theory and Society.* 35 (5–6): 507–528.

Offe, Claus 1984. "The Crisis of Crisis Management: Elements of a Political Crisis Theory." In *Contradictions of the Welfare State,* 35–61. London: Hutchinson.

Olasky, Marvin. 1992. *The Tragedy of American Compassion.* Wheaton, IL: Crossway.

Osborne, David, and Ted Gaebler. 1993. *Reinventing Government: How the Entrepreneurial Spirit Is Transforming the Public Sector.* New York: Penguin.

Overton, Mark. 1989. "Agricultural Revolution? England 1540–1850." In *New Directions in Economic and Social History,* ed. Anne Digby and Charles Feinstein, 9–21. Houndsmill, Hampshire: Macmillan.

——— 1996. "Re-establishing the English Agricultural Revolution." *Agricultural History Review* 44(1): 1–20.

Palmer, Robert. 1993. *English Law in the Age of Black Death, 1348–1381: A Transformation of Governance and Law.* Chapel Hill: University of North Carolina Press.

Parsons, Talcott. 1966. *Societies.* Englewood Cliffs, New Jersey: Prentice Hall.

Pavetti, LaDonna, and Dan Bloom 2001. "State Sanctions and Time Limits." In *The New World of Welfare,* ed. Rebecca Blank and Ron Haskins, 245–269. Washington, DC: Brookings.

Peck, Jamie. 2001. *Workfare States.* New York: Guilford.

——— 2005. "Economic Sociologies in Space." *Geography* 81(2): 129–176.

——— 2010. *Constructions of Neoliberal Reason.* Oxford: Oxford University Press.

Peck, Jamie, and A. Ticknell. 2002. "Neoliberalizing Space." *Antipode* 34(3): 380–404.

Perren, Richard. 1989. "Markets and Marketing." In *The Agrarian History of England and Wales, 1750–1850,* vol. 6. ed. G. E. Mingay, 190–274. Cambridge: Cambridge University Press.

Perrow, Charles. 1984. *Normal Accidents.* New York: Basic Books.

Persky, Joseph. 1997. "Classical Family Values: Ending the Poor Law as They Knew Them." *Journal of Economic Perspectives* 11(1): 178–189.

Peschek, J. G. 1987. *Policy-Planning Organizations: Elite Agendas and America's Rightward Turn*. Philadelphia: Temple University Press.

Phillips-Fein, Kim. 2009. *Invisible Hands: The Making of the Conservative Movement from the New Deal to Reagan*. New York: Norton.

Pierson, Paul. 1994. *Dismantling the Welfare State? Reagan, Thatcher, and the Politics of Retrenchment*. Cambridge: Cambridge University Press.

Piketty, Thomas, and Emmanuel Saez. 2012. "Top Incomes and the Great Recession: Recent Evolutions and Policy Implications." Paper presented at the 13th Jacques Polak Annual Research Conference, Washington D.C., November 8–9http://www.imf.org/external/np/res/seminars/2012/arc/pdf/PS.pdf. Accessed July 12, 2013.

Pimpare, Stephen. 2004. *The New Victorians: Poverty, Politics, and Propaganda in Two Gilded Ages*. New York: New Press.

Piore, Michael, and Charles Sabel. 1984. *The Second Industrial Divide*. New York: Basic Books.

Piven, Francis Fox, ed. 1977. *Poor People's Movements: Why They Succeed, How They Fail*. New York: Vintage Books.

———— 1991. *Labor Parties in Postindustrial Societies*. New York: Oxford University Press.

———— 1997. *The Breaking of the American Social Compact*. New York: New Press.

———— 2006. *Challenging Authority*. Lanham, MD: Rowman and Littlefield.

Piven, Frances Fox, and Richard Cloward. 1993 [1971] Regulating the Poor: The Functions of Public Welfare. New York: Pantheon.

Plotke, David. 1996. *Building a Democratic Political Order: Reshaping American Liberalism in the 1930s and 1940s*. New York: Cambridge University Press.

Polanyi, Karl. 1934. "Marxism Restated." *New Britain,* July 4: 187–188.

———— 1935. "The Essence of Fascism." In *Christianity and the Social Revolution,* ed. John Lewis, Karl Polanyi, and Donald Kitchin, 359–394. London: Gollancz.

———— 1937–38. English Economic, Social and Industrial History from the 16th Century. Lecture notes for a course at Heathfield W.E.A. Karl Polanyi Archive, Concordia University, Montreal, Canada, 94.

———— 1938. "Notes of a Week's Study on the Early Writings of Karl Marx and summary of a discussion on British Working Class Consciousness." Bulletin 2, Christian Left Group. Karl Polanyi Archive, Concordia University, Montreal, Canada, 5.

———— 1941. History of the Labour-market in England (cont). Bennington College Seminar Outline, May 9, 1941. Karl Polanyi Archive, Concordia University, Montreal, Canada.

———— 1947. "Our Obsolete Market Mentality." *Commentary* 3:109–117.

———— 1966. *Dahomey and the Slave Trade.* Seattle: University of Washington Press.

———— 1968 [1957]. "Aristotle Discovers the Economy." In K. Polanyi, *Primitive, Archaic, and Modern Economies,* ed. George Dalton, 78–115. New York: Doubleday Anchor.

———— 1968. *Primitive, Archaic, and Modern Economies,* ed. George Dalton. New York: Doubleday Anchor.

———— 1977. *The Livelihood of Man,* ed. Harry W. Pearson. Waltham, MA: Academic Press.

———— 2001 [1944]. *The Great Transformation: The Political and Economic Origins of Our Time.* Boston: Beacon.

Polanyi, Karl, Conrad M. Arensberg, and Harry W. Pearson, eds. 1957. *Trade and Market in the Early Empires.* Glencoe, Illinois: The Free Press.

Polanyi, Michael. 2009 [1966]. *The Tacit Dimension.* Chicago: University of Chicago Press.

Polanyi-Levitt, Kari. 1990. "Origins and Significance of the Great Transformation." In *The Life and Work of Karl Polanyi,* ed. Kari Polanyi-Levitt, 111–126. Montreal: Black Rose.

———— 1994. "Karl Polanyi as Socialist." In *Humanity, Society, and Commitment: On Karl Polanyi,* ed. Kenneth McRobbie, 115–134. Montreal: Black Rose.

———— 2013. *From the Great Transformation to the Great Financialization.* Halifax, Nova Scotia: Fernwood.

Polanyi-Levitt, Kari, and Marguerite Mendell. 1987. "Karl Polanyi: His Life and Times." *Studies in Political Economy* 22: 7–39.

Pontusson, Jonas. 1992. *The Limits of Social Democracy: Investment Politics in Sweden.* Ithaca, NY: Cornell University Press.

———— 2005. *Inequality and Prosperity: Social Europe vs. Liberal America.* New York: Century Foundation.

———— 2011. "Once Again a Model: Nordic Social Democracy in a Globalized World." In *What's Left of the Left: Democrats and Social Democrats in Changing Times,* ed. James Cronin, George Ross, and James Shoch, 89–115. Durham, NC: Duke University Press.

Powell, Lewis. 1971. "The Powell Memo." August 23, 1971. Reprinted at ReclaimDemocracy.org. Accessed July 12, 2013. Poynter, J. R. 1969. *Society and Pauperism: English Ideas on Poor Relief, 1795–1834.* London: Routledge & Kegan Paul.

Procacci, Giovanna. 1991. "Social Economy and the Government of Poverty." In *The Foucault Effect: Studies in Governmentality,* ed. Graham Burchell, Colin Gordon, and Peter Miller, 151–168. London: Harvest Wheatsheaf.

Prothero, Rowland. 1912. *English Farming Past and Present.* London: Longmans, Green.

Quadagno, Jill. 1994. *The Color of Welfare: How Racism Undermined the War on Poverty.* New York: Oxford University Press.

Quiggin, John. 2010. *Zombie Economics: How Dead Ideas Still Walk among Us.* Princeton, NJ: Princeton University Press.

Rahman, Sabeel. 2011. "Conceptualizing the Economic Role of the State: Laissez-Faire, Technocracy, and the Democratic Alternative." *Polity* 43(2): 264–286.

Rawls, John. 1971. *A Theory of Justice.* Cambridge, MA: Belknap Press of Harvard University Press.

Reay, Barry. 1990. *The Last Rising of the Agricultural Labourers.* Oxford: The Clarendon Press.

——— 1996. *Microhistories: Demography, Society and Culture in Rural England, 1800–1930.* Cambridge: Cambridge University Press.

Redman, Deborah A. 1997. *The Rise of Political Economy as a Science: Methodology and the Classical Economists.* Cambridge, MA: MIT Press.

Reekie, Gail. 1998. *Measuring Immorality: Social Inquiry and the Problem of Legitimacy.* Cambridge: Cambridge University Press.

Reese, Ellen. 2005. *Backlash against Welfare Mothers.* Berkeley: University of California Press.

Resta, Giorio, and Mariavittoria Catanzariti, eds. 2013. *Karl Polanyi: Per un nuovo Occidente.* Milan: Il Saggiatore.

Rich, Andrew. 2004. *Think Tanks, Public Policy, and the Politics of Expertise.* Cambridge: Cambridge University Press.

Richardson, T. L. 1991. "'Agricultural Labourers' Wages and the Cost of Living in Essex, 1790–1840: A Contribution to the Standard of Living Debate." In *Land, Labour, and Agriculture: Essays for Gordon Mingay,* ed. B. A. Holderness and Michael Turner, 70–90. London: Hambleton.

Ricoeur, Paul. 1989. *The Narrative Path: The Later Works of Paul Ricoeur,* ed. T. Peter Kemp and David Rasmussen. Cambridge, MA: MIT Press.

Rifkin, Jeremy. 2004. *The European Dream.* New York: Penguin.

Ringmar, Erik 2005. *Surviving Capitalism.* London: Anthem Press.

Rogers-Dillon, Robin. 2004. *The Welfare Experiments: Politics and Policy Evaluation.* Stanford, CA: Stanford University Press.

Roland, Alex, with Philip Shiman. 2002. *Strategic Computing: DARPA and the Quest for Machine Intelligence 1983–1993.* Cambridge, MA: MIT Press.

Rose, Michael. 1970. "The Anti-Poor Law Agitation." In *Popular Movements c. 1830–1850,* ed. J. T. Ward. London: Macmillan.

Rosen, Jeffrey. 2005. "The Unregulated Offensive." *New York Times Magazine,* April 17: 42.

Rosenthal, Lawrence, and Christine Trost. eds. 2012. *Steep: The Precipitous Rise of the Tea Party*. Berkeley: University of California Press

Rothschild, Emma. 2001. *Economic Sentiments*. Cambridge, MA: Harvard University Press.

Rotstein, Abraham. 1990. "The Reality of Society: Karl Polanyi's Philosophical Perspective." In *The Life and Work of Karl Polanyi*, ed. Kari Polanyi-Levitt, 98–110. Montreal: Black Rose.

Royal Commission. 1834. *Report from His Majesty's Commissioners for Inquiring into the Administration and Practical Operation of the Poor Laws*. London: B. Fellowes.

Rueschemeyer, Dietrich, and Theda Skocpol, eds. 1996. *States, Social Knowledge, and the Origins of Modern Social Policies*. Princeton, NJ: Princeton University Press.

Rule, John. 1979. *The Experience of Labour*. London: Croon Helm.

Rule, John, and Roger Wells. 1988. *Crime, Protest, and Popular Politics in Southern England, 1750–1850: The Formative Years*. London: Longman.

Saez, Emmanuel, and Thomas Piketty. 2013. "Income Inequality in the United States, 1913–1988." Tables and Figures updated to 2012, September 2013, http://elsa.berkeley.edu/~saez/. Accessed October 8, 2013.

Sahlins, Marshall. 1976. *Culture and Practical Reason*. Chicago: University of Chicago Press.

Salt, James. 1989. "Sunbelt Capital and Conservative Political Realignment in the 1970s and 1980s." *Critical Sociology* 16: 145–163.

Santos, Boaventura de Sousa. 2008. "The World Social Forum and the Global Left." *Politics & Society* 36(2): 247–270.

Schmoller, G. 1989 [1897]. *The Mercantile System and Its Historical Significance*. New York: A. M. Kelley.

Schram, Sanford. 1995. *Words of Welfare: The Poverty of Social Science and the Social Science of Poverty*. Minneapolis: University of Minnesota Press.

——— 2000. *After Welfare: The Culture of Postindustrial Social Policy*. New York: NYU Press.

——— 2002. *Praxis for the Poor: Piven and Cloward and the Future of Social Science in Social Welfare*. New York: New York University Press.

Scott, James C. 1985. *Weapons of the Weak: Everyday Forms of Peasant Resistance*. New Haven, CT: Yale University Press.

Self, Robert O. 2012. *All in the Family: The Realignment of American Democracy Since the 1960s*. New York: Hill and Wang.

Semmel, Bernard. 1970. *The Rise of Free Trade Imperialism*. Cambridge: Cambridge University Press.

Sen, Amartya. 1981. *Poverty and Famines: An Essay on Entitlement and Deprivation*. Oxford: Oxford University Press.

—— 1982. "The Right not to be Hungry." In *Contemporary Philosophy: A New Survey*, vol. 2, ed. G. Floitstad, 343–360. The Hague: Martinus Nijhoff.

—— 1999. *Development as Freedom*. New York: Knopf.

—— 2009. *The Idea of Justice*. London: Allen Lane.

Shafer, Byron 2003. *The Two Majorities and the Puzzle of Modern American Politics*. Lawrence: University of Kansas Press.

Shapiro, Ian. 1995. "Resources, Capacities, and Ownership: The Workmanship Ideal and Distributive Justice." In *Early Modern Conceptions of Property*, ed. John Brewer and Susan Staves, 21–42. London: Routledge.

Shapiro, Robert Y., Kelly D. Patterson, Judith Russell, and John T. Young. 1987. "The Polls: Employment and Welfare." *Public Opinion Quarterly* 51: 268–281.

Sharlet, Jeff 2005. "Soldiers of Christ: Inside America's Most Powerful Megachurch." *Harper's*, May: 41–54.

Sharpe, Pamela. 1997. "'The Bowels of Compassion': A Labouring Family and the Law, c. 1790–1834." In *Chronicling Poverty: The Voices and Strategies of the English Poor, 1640–1840*, ed. Tim Hitchcock, Peter King, and Pamela Sharpe, 87–108. Houndsmill, Hampshire: Macmillan.

Shipler, David K. 2004. *The Working Poor: Invisible in America*. New York: Knopf.

Shklar, Judith. 1991. *American Citizenship: The Quest for Inclusion*. Cambridge, MA: Harvard University Press.

Shonfield, Andrew. 1969. *Modern Capitalism: The Changing Balance of Public and Private Power*. Oxford: Oxford University Press.

Sievers, A. M. 1949. *Has Market Society Collapsed? A Critique of Karl Polanyi's New Economics*. New York: Columbia University Press.

Silk, Leonard, and David Vogel. 1976. *Ethics and Profits: The Crisis of Confidence in American Business*. New York: Simon and Schuster.

Silver, Beverly. 2003. *Forces of Labor*. Cambridge: Cambridge University Press.

Skidelsky, Robert. 1994. *John Maynard Keynes: The Economist as Savior*. New York: Penguin Press.

—— 2009. *Keynes: The Return of the Master*. New York: Public Affairs.

Skocpol, Theda. 1977. "Wallerstein's World System." *American Journal of Sociology* 82: 1075–1090.

—— 1992. *Protecting Soldiers and Mothers*. Cambridge, MA: Harvard University Press.

Skocpol, Theda, and Margaret Somers. 1980. "The Uses of Comparative History in Macrosocial Inquiry." *Comparative Studies in Society and History* 22: 174–197.

Skocpol, Theda, and Vanessa Williamson. 2012. *The Tea Party and the Remaking of Republican Conservatism*. New York: Oxford University Press.

Smeeding, Timothy. 2005. "Public Policy, Economic Inequality, and Poverty: The United States in Comparative Perspective." *Social Science Quarterly* 86: 955–983.

Smeeding, Timothy, Lee Rainwater, and Gary Burtless. 2001. "U.S. Poverty in a Cross-national Context." In *Understanding Poverty,* ed. Sheldon H. Danziger and Robert H. Haveman, 162–189. Cambridge, MA: Harvard University Press.

Smeeding, Timothy, Robert Erikson, and Markus Janti, eds. 2011. *Persistence, Privilege, and Parenting.* New York: Russell Sage.

Smith, Adam. 1976 [1776]. *The Wealth of Nations.* Chicago: University of Chicago Press.

Smith, Hedrick. 2012. *Who Stole the American Dream?* New York: Random House.

Smith, Rogers M. 1993. "Beyond Tocqueville, Myrdal, and Hartz: The Multiple Traditions in America." *American Political Science Review* 87(3): 549–566.

―――― 1999. *Civic Ideals: Conflicting Visions of Citizenship in US History.* New Haven, CT: Yale University Press.

Snell, K. D. M. 1985. *Annals of the Labouring Poor: Social Change and Agrarian England.* Cambridge: Cambridge University Press.

Sokoll, Thomas. 1993. *Household and Family among the Poor.* Bochum: Universitatsverlag Dr. N. Brockmeyer.

Solar, Peter M. 1995. "Poor Relief and English Economic Development before the Industrial Revolution." *Economic History Review* 38:1–22.

Solow, Robert M. 2000. "Welfare: The Cheapest Country." *New York Review of Books,* March 23: 20.

Somers, Margaret R. 1990. "Karl Polanyi's Intellectual Legacy." In *The Life and Work of Karl Polanyi,* ed. Kari Polanyi-Levitt, 152–160. Montreal: Black Rose.

―――― 1992. "Narrativity, Narrative Identity, and Social Action: Rethinking English Working-Class Formation." *Social Science History* 16(4): 591–630.

―――― 1993. "Citizenship and the Place of the Public Sphere: Law, Community, and Political Culture in the Transition to Democracy." *American Sociological Review* 58: 587–620.

―――― 1994a. "Rights, Relationality, and Membership: Rethinking the Making and Meaning of Citizenship." *Law and Social Inquiry* 19: 63–114.

―――― 1994b. "The Narrative Constitution of Identity: A Relational and Network Approach." Theory and Society 23 (5): 605–649.

―――― 1995. "The 'Misteries' of Property: Relationality, Families, and Community in Chartist Narratives of Political Rights." In *Early Modern Conceptions of Property*, ed. John Brewer and Susan Staves, 62–92. London: Routledge.

———— 1996. "Class Formation and Capitalism." *European Journal of Sociology* 37: 180–202.

———— 1997. "Deconstructing and Reconstructing Class Formation Theory: Narrativity, Relational Analysis, and Social Theory." *In Reworking Class,* ed. John R. Hall, 73–106. Ithaca, NY: Cornell University Press.

———— 1998. "We're No Angels: Realism, Relational Choice, and Relationality in Social Science." *American Journal of Sociology* 104: 722–784.

———— 1999. "The Privatization of Citizenship: How to Unthink a Knowledge Culture." In *Beyond the Cultural Turn,* ed. Victoria E. Bonnell and Lynn Hunt, 121–161. Berkeley: University of California Press.

———— 2008. *Genealogies of Citizenship: Markets, Statelessness, and the Right to Have Rights.* New York: Cambridge University Press.

Somers, Margaret, and Fred Block. 2006. "Poverty and Piety: Reply to Hicks." *American Sociological Review* 71 (June): 511–513.

Somers, Margaret, and Christopher N. J. Roberts. 2008. "Toward a New Sociology of Rights: A Genealogy of 'Buried Bodies' of Citizenship and Human Rights." *Annual Review of Law and Social Science* 4: 385–425.

Song, Byung Khun. 1998. "Landed Interest, Local Government, and the Labour Market in England, 1750–1850." *Economic History Review* 51(3): 465–488.

Soros, George. 1998. *The Crisis of Global Capitalism.* New York: Public Affairs.

———— 2000. *Open Society: Reforming Global Capitalism.* New York: Public Affairs.

———— 2002. *On Globalization.* New York: Public Affairs.

Spencer, Herbert. 1940 [1881]. *The Man versus the State.* Caldwell, IA: Caxton Printers.

Standing, Guy. 1999. *Global Labour Flexibility: Seeking Distributive Justice.* New York: Macmillan.

Steinberg, Marc. 1999. *Fighting Words: Working-class Formation, Collective Action, and Discourse in Early Nineteenth-Century England.* Ithaca, NY: Cornell University Press.

———— 2003. "Capitalist Development, the Labor Process, and the Law." *American Journal of Sociology* 109: 445–495.

Steinmetz, George. 1992. "Reflections on the Role of Social Narratives in Working-Class Formation: Narrative Theory in the Social Sciences." *Social Science History* 16(3): 489–516.

———— 1993. *Regulating the Social: The Welfare State and Local Politics in Imperial Germany.* Princeton, NJ: Princeton University Press.

———— ed. 1998. *State / Culture: State-Formation after the Cultural Turn.* Ithaca, NY: Cornell University Press.

Stiglitz, Joseph. 1989. "Markets, Market Failures and Development." *American Economic Review* 79(2):197–202.

——— 2000. "What I Learned at the World Economic Crisis." *The New Republic.* April 17: 56–60.

——— 2001. "Foreword." In *The Great Transformation.* K. Polanyi. vii–xvii. Boston: Beacon Press.

——— 2002. *Globalization and Its Discontents.* New York: Norton.

——— 2003. *The Roaring Nineties.* New York: Norton

——— 2010. *Freefall.* New York: Norton.

Stiglitz, Joseph, Amartya Sen, and Jean-Paul Fitoussi. 2010. *Mismeasuring Our Lives: Why GDP Doesn't Add Up.* New York: New Press.

Stiglitz, Joseph, and Andrew Charlton. 2005. *Fair Trade for All.* New York: Oxford University Press.

Stinchcombe, Arthur. 1978. *Theoretical Methods in Social History.* New York: Academic Press.

Streeck, Wolfgang. 2009. *Re-forming Capitalism: Institutional Change in the German Political Economy.* New York: Oxford University Press.

——— 2011. "The Crises of Democratic Capitalism." *New Left Review* 71 (Sept.-Oct.): 5–29.

Stroshane, Tim. 1997. "The Second Contradiction of Capitalism and Karl Polanyi's The Great Transformation." *Capitalism, Nature, and Society* 8: 93–116.

Sunstein, Cass. 2004. *The Second Bill of Rights.* New York: Basic Books.

Swenson, Peter. 2002. *Capitalists against Markets.* New York: Oxford University Press.

Tabb, William. 2012. *The Restructuring of Capitalism in Our Time.* New York: Columbia University Press.

Tamanaha, Brian. 2004. *On the Rule of Law: History Politics, Theory.* Cambridge: Cambridge University Press.

Tawney, R. H. 1972 [1938]. "The Assessment of Wages in England by the Justices of the Peace." In *Wage in Regulation in Pre-Industrial England,* ed. Walter Minchinton, 37–92. New York: Barnes and Nobles.

Tawney, R. H., and Eileen Power, eds. 1924. *Tudor Economic Documents.* London: Longmans.

Taylor, Arthur J. ed. 1975. *The Standard of Living in Britain in the Industrial Revolution.* London: Methuen.

Teles, Steven M. 1996. *Whose Welfare? AFDC and Elite Politics.* Lawrence: University Press of Kansas.

Thomasberger, Claus. 2013. "The Belief in Economic Determinism, Neoliberalism, and the Significance of Polanyi's Contribution in the Twenty-first Century." *International Journal of Political Economy* 41(4): 16–33.

Thompson, E. P. 1963. *The Making of the English Working Class.* New York: Pantheon.

———— 1971. "The Moral Economy of the English Crowd." *Past and Present* 50: 76–136.

Thomson, David. 1991. "The Welfare of the Elderly in the Past: A Family or Community Responsibility." In *Life, Death and the Elderly: Historical Perspectives,* ed. Margaret and Richard M. Smith Pelling, 194–221. London: Routledge.

Tilly, Charles. 1995. *Popular Contention in Great Britain 1758–1834.* Cambridge, MA: Harvard University Press.

Tilman, Robert H., and Michael L. Indergaard. 2005. *Pump and Dump: The Rancid Rules of the New Economy.* New Brunswick, NJ: Rutgers University Press.

Tompkins, Daniel. 2008. "Webster, Polanyi, and Finley." *History and Theory* 47: 123–136.

Townsend, Joseph. 1971 [1786]. *A Dissertation on the Poor Laws.* Berkeley: University of California Press.

Uchitelle, Louis. 2006. *The Disposable American.* New York: Knopf.

———— 2007. "Age of Riches: The Richest of the Rich, Proud of a New Gilded Age." *New York Times,* July 15: A1.

ul Haq, Mahbub, Inge Kaul, and Isabelle Grunberg, eds. 1996. *The Tobin Tax.* Oxford: Oxford University Press.

United States Advisory Committee on Student Financial Assistance. 2006. *Mortgaging Our Future: How Financial Barriers to College Undermine America's Global Competititveness.* Washington, DC. http://www2.ed.gov/about/bdscomm/list/acsfa/mof.pdf. Accessed July 12, 2013.

United States Bureau of the Census. 2005. *Income, Poverty, and Health Insurance Coverage in the United States.* Current Population Reports, P60–229. Washington, DC: U.S. Government Printing Office.

———— 2012. *Statistical Abstract of the United States.* http://www.census.gov/compendia/statab/. Accessed July 12, 2013.

United States Domestic Policy Council Low Income Opportunity Working Group. 1986. *Up From Dependency: A New National Public Assistance Strategy.* Washington: U.S. Government Printing Office.

United States House of Representatives, Ways and Means Committee. 2012. *Green Book.* http://greenbook.waysandmeans.house.gov/. Accessed July 12, 2013.

Useem, Michael 1993. *Executive Defense: Shareholder Power and Corporate Reorganization.* Cambridge: Harvard University Press.

Vajda, Mihaly 1976. *Fascism as a Mass Movement.* London: Allison & Busby.

———— 1981. *The State and Socialism.* London: Allison & Busby.

Valenze, Deborah. 1995. *The First Industrial Woman.* Oxford: Oxford University Press.

Van Parijs, Philippe. 1992. *Arguing for Basic Income: Ethical Foundations for a Radical Reform.* London: Verso.

Viner, Jacob. 1965 [1937]. *Studies in the Theory of International Trade.* New York: Augustus Kelley.

Vogel, Ezra. 1979. *Japan as Number 1: Lessons for America.* New York: Harper & Row.

Wacquant, Loic. 2009. *Punishing the Poor: The Neoliberal Government of Social Insecurity.* Durham, NC: Duke University Press.

Wade, Robert. 1990. *Governing the Market: Economic Theory and the Role of Government in East Asian Industrialization.* Princeton, NJ: Princeton University Press.

Wald, Kenneth D. 1997. *Religion and Politics in the United States,* 3rd ed. Washington, DC: Congressional Quarterly.

Wald, Kenneth D., Dennis E. Owen, and Samuel S. Hill, Jr. 1989. "Evangelical Politics and Status Issues." *Journal for the Scientific Study of Religion* 28(1): 1–16.

Wallerstein, Immanuel. 1974. *The Modern World-System: Capitalist Agriculture and the Origins of the European World-Economy in the Sixteenth Century.* New York: Academic Press.

Walter, John, and Keith Wrightson. 1976. "Dearth and the Social Order in Early Modern England." *Past and Present* 71: 22–42.

Ward, J. T. 1962. *The Factory Movement 1830–1855.* New York: St. Martin's

Waterman, A. M. C. 1991. *Revolution, Economics, and Religion; Christian Political Economy, 1798–1833.* Cambridge: Cambridge University Press.

Weaver, Kent. 2000. *Ending Welfare as We Know It.* Washington, DC: Brookings.

Weaver, Kent. Robert Y. Shapiro, and Lawrence R. Jacobs. 1995. "The Polls-Trends: Welfare." *Public Opinion Quarterly* 59: 606–627.

Webb, Sidney, and Beatrice Webb. 1927. *English Local Government: English Poor Law History: Part I: The Old Poor Law.* London, England: Longmans, Green.

Weber, Max. 1946 [1919]. "Politics as a Vocation." In *From Max Weber,* ed. Hans Gerth and C. Wright Mills, 77–128. New York: Oxford University Press.

——— 1969 [1922]. *The Sociology of Religion,* trans. Ephraim Fischoff. Boston, MA: Beacon.

Weir, Margaret. 1992. *Politics and Jobs: The Boundaries of Employment Policy in the United States.* Princeton, NJ: Princeton University Press.

Wells, Roger A.E. 1988. *Wretched Faces: Famine in Wartime England, 1793-1801.* Gloucester: Sutton.

——— 2000. "The Moral Economy of the English Countryside." In *Moral Economy and Popular Protest: Crowds, Conflict and Authority,* ed. Adrian

Randall and Andrew Charlesworth, 209–271. Houndsmill, Hampshire: Macmillan.

Wessel, David. 2009. *In Fed We Trust*. New York: Crown Business.

White, Hayden. 1987. *The Content of the Form: Narrative Discourse and Historical Representation*. Baltimore, MD: Johns Hopkins University Press.

Wilkinson, Richard, and Kate Pickett. 2009. *The Spirit Level: Why Greater Equality Makes Societies Stronger*. New York: Bloomsbury Press.

Williams, Karel. 1981. *From Pauperism to Poverty*. London: Routledge & Kegan Paul.

Williams, Lucy A. 1996. "The Right's Attack on Aid to Families with Dependent Children." *The Public Eye* Fall–Winter: 1–18.

Wilson, Charles. 1969. "The Other Face of Mercantilism." In *Economic History and the Historian: Collected Essays*, 73–93. London: Weidenfeld and Nicolson.

Winch, Donald. 1992. "Introduction." In *T. R. Malthus's Essay on Principle of Population*, ed. Donald Winch, vii–xxiii. Cambridge: Cambridge University Press.

——— 1996. *Riches and Poverty: An Intellectual History of Political Economy in Britain, 1750–1834*. Cambridge: Cambridge University Press.

Winters, Jeffrey A. 2011. *Oligarchy*. Cambridge: Cambridge University Press.

Wolfe, Alan. 1989. *Whose Keeper? Social Science and Moral Obligation*. Berkeley: University of California Press.

Wolin, Sheldon. 1960. *Politics and Vision*. Boston: Little Brown.

——— 1980. "Reagan Country." *New York Review of Books*, Dec. 18: 9.

Womack, James P., Daniel T. Jones, and Daniel Ross. 1990. *The Machine that Changed the World*. New York: HarperCollins.

World Economic Forum. 2011. *The Global Competitiveness Report 2010–2011*. Geneva: World Economic Forum.

Wright, Erik Olin. 2010. *Envisioning Real Utopias*. London: Verso.

Wrightson, Keith. 1980. "Two Concepts of Order: Justices, Constables, and Jurymen in Seventeenth-Century England." In *An Ungovernable People*, ed. John Brewer and John J. Styles, 21–46. New Brunswick, NJ: Rutgers University Press.

——— 2000. *Earthly Necessities: Economic Lives in Early Modern Britain*. New Haven, CT: Yale University Press.

Wrigley, E. A. 1983. "The Growth of Population in Eighteenth Century England: A Conundrum Resolved." *Past and Present* 98: 121–150.

——— 1986. *Men on the Land and Men in the Countryside: Employment in Agriculture in Early-Nineteenth Century England*. London: Basil Blackwell.

Yamamura, Kozo, and Wolfgang Streeck, eds. 2003. *The End of Diversity? Prospects for German and Japanese Capitalism*. Ithaca, NY: Cornell University Press.

Yonay, Yuval. 1998. *The Struggle over the Soul of Economics*. Princeton, NJ: Princeton University Press.

Young, Robert M. 1969. "Malthus and the Evolutionists: The Common Context of Biological and Social Theory." *Past and Present* 43:109–145.

Zeisel, Hans. 1968. "Karl Polanyi." *International Encyclopedia of the Social Sciences* Vol. 12: 172. Ed. David L. Sills. New York: Macmillan.

Zukin, Sharon, and Paul DiMaggio. 1990. "Introduction." In *Structures of Capital: The Social Organization of the Economy,* ed. Sharon Zukin and Paul DiMaggio, 1–36. Cambridge: Cambridge University Press.

Zysman, John. 1983. *Governments, Markets, and Growth*. Ithaca, NY: Cornell University Press.

INDEX

Acheson, Dean, 214
agricultural crisis, 112, 144, 147
Aid to Families with Dependent Children (AFDC), 115–116, 160–161, 178–182, 189
aid-in-wages, 51–52, 77, 117, 122–123, 128
Alger, Horatio, 203
"allowance system," 90, 120–122, 128, 134, 147, 159
Althusser, Louis, 74–75
"always and everywhere embedded economy," 9–10, 31–34, 219
"always embedded economy:" ambiguities of, 94–97; autonomous economy and, 31–34; cultural understanding of, 9–10; human economy and, 9, 26, 59–60; idea of, 9–10, 73–74, 79–81; ideational embeddedness, 155; interventions and, 105–107. *See also* economy
Anderson, Martin, 87, 114, 116, 178
Arendt, Hannah, 191
Aristotle, 30, 49, 58
Arnold, Thurman, 93
autonomous economy: appeal of, 34–35; concept of, 31–33; embedded economy and, 31–34; organizational autonomy, 199. *See also* economy

Benjamin, Walter, 75
Berman, Sheri, 221, 222
"big business," 40–41, 211–217

"big government," 19, 194, 208–210
Bill of Rights, 7, 237
Bismarck, Otto von, 14, 27
Blaug, Mark, 123, 135
Bloch, Marc, 58
Blyth, Mark, 2
boom-bust cycles, 33, 112–113
Bourdieu, Pierre, 155, 156, 184
bread scale, 87–90, 133–142
Bretton Woods, 15–17, 85, 97, 209, 222
Brown, William Adams, Jr., 16
Burke, Kenneth, 75, 116, 179
Burns, Arthur, 114
Bush, George H. W., 212
Bush, George W., 1, 116, 180, 187, 201, 212–213, 217
Bush Administration, 1, 201, 213
Business Week, 181
business-movement conservative alliance, 211–213, 216

Callon, Michel, 107
Capital, 74–75, 120
capitalism: analysis of, 74–81, 92; contradictions of, 79, 92; critics of, 121, 124, 177; feudalism and, 80–81, 88, 92, 244n5; forms of, 1–2, 57, 76–79, 84, 87–88, 151; industrial capitalism, 76–77, 87–88; liberal capitalism, 57; market capitalism, 52; market society and, 78; modern capitalism, 27, 47; rise of, 47; welfare capitalism, 196

capitalist societies, 27, 59–61, 79–81
Captain Swing riots, 136, 144, 146
Carlyle, Thomas, 101
Carter, Jimmy, 20, 160, 211
Carter Administration, 211
causal mechanisms: of change, 155; influences of, 151, 184; perversity thesis and, 158, 170–171; social processes and, 39, 68; theoretical realism and, 169–170, 181
central banks: creation of, 33; growth of, 41, 55–56, 94; purpose of, 33, 112–113
Chafee, Lincoln, 213
Chalmers, Thomas, 176–177, 180
Chretien, Jean, 115
Christianity and the Social Revolution, 47
Churchill, Winston, 85
citizenship, contractualization of, 111, 191
civil rights, 34, 198, 201, 237
classical economics, 6, 31, 54, 90–91, 100
Clinton, Bill, 1, 161, 181, 187–189, 206, 212
Clinton, Hillary, 188–189
Clinton Administration, 20
Co-Existence, 48, 246
Cole, G. D. H., 26, 124
Combination Acts, 90
"Coming White Underclass, The," 180
"commodification of labor," 83, 87
"compassionate conservatism," 116
complex society, freedom in, 72, 224
conservatism: compassionate conservatism, 116; market conservatism, 193–217; movement conservatism, 198–202, 211–217, 251n8; populist conservatism, 199, 201, 211–212, 216–217; strength of, 3, 193–217
"contractualization of citizenship," 111, 191
conversion narrative, 158, 166, 171–178, 181, 184, 210
"corporate liberalism," 205–206, 210–211

countermovements: double movement and, 10, 13–15, 242n7; explanation of, 53–54; Polanyian countermovement, 201–204, 212; for protection, 14–15, 53–54, 60–68, 92–95, 216–220, 242n7
credit cycles, 33
credit default, 20–21
credit system, 33, 55, 112–113, 144–146

Dahomey and the Slave Trade, 47, 71
Dalton, George, 47
"dark Satanic mills," 37, 77, 108, 235
Darwin, Charles, 228
DeParle, Jason, 189
de Tocqueville, Alexis, 116, 179
deflationary pressures, 14–19, 94, 143–145, 149, 221
democratic politics: economy and, 11, 25–28, 41–45, 220–223; "reality of society" and, 234–240
Denning, Michael, 75
deregulation, 1, 9–10, 19–20, 40, 184, 210, 219
determinism, 44, 59, 82–86
Dillon, Douglas, 214
disembeddedness, 91–92, 155
Dissertation on the Poor Law, 118
division of labor, 12, 203, 227, 237–238
"double movement," 10, 13–15, 94, 220–221, 242n7
Duczynska, Ilona, 5, 45, 46, 47
Dulles brothers, 214
Durkheim, Emile, 30, 61, 93, 108, 226
dystopia, 101, 108
dystopian consequences, 9, 101, 108–112

Economic and Philosophical Manuscripts, 74
economic cycles, 13–14, 33, 112–113
economic definition, 59–60
economic democracy, 220–221
economic determinism, 44, 59, 82–86
economic growth, 12, 17, 23, 162, 207, 213, 222, 239

economic imperialism, 56
economic liberalism: criticisms of, 228; diffusion of, 147; embeddedness and, 80; ideology of, 52–53; market liberalism and, 99; market self-regulation and, 84, 233; political economy and, 232; reality of society and, 224; tradition of, 7; utopianism and, 150, 233–234
economic orthodoxy, 22–23, 96, 225
economic sociology, 155–156
economic utopianism, 233–234
"economistic fallacy:" critique of, 38, 44–72; cultural disaster and, 62–63; obsolete market mentality and, 225; views on, 7, 30–31, 231
economy: "always embedded economy," 9–10, 31–34, 74, 79–81, 94–97, 105–107, 155, 219; autonomous economy, 31–35; democratic politics and, 11, 25–28, 41–45, 220–223; growth of, 12, 17, 23, 162, 207, 213, 222, 239; human economy, 9, 26, 59–60; as instituted process, 29–31; substantive economy, 29–30, 59–60, 226, 241n5; of today, 18–19, 238–240
Ellwood, David, 181
embedded economy: ambiguities of, 91–97; autonomous economy and, 31–34; cultural understanding of, 9–10; idea of, 79–81; ideational embeddedness, 96–97. See also economy
Engels, Friedrich, 80–81, 98, 120–121
English crisis, 158–163
Equal Rights Amendment, 198
Esping-Andersen, Gosta, 195–196
Essay on the Principle of Population, 38, 98, 119, 145, 148, 163–171
"Essence of Fascism, The," 47
Europe: financial crisis in, 195–198, 216–217; free market conservatism and, 194–198, 205–208; United States and, 193, 195–198, 217

Factory Acts, 14, 93
fascism: deflationary policies and, 220–221; global economy collapse and, 84, 108; market society and, 57; origins of, 47–49; rise of, 2, 5, 42, 67, 75–76, 84, 94; world market collapse and, 67
Federal Reserve, 21, 41–42, 112, 211
feudalism, 80–81, 88, 92, 244n5
fictitious commodities: constructing markets for, 96; dystopian consequences of, 108; embedded economy and, 81–82; governing markets for, 36, 113; labor and, 82–83, 93, 112–113, 233; land and, 112–113, 233; market societies and, 61, 86–87; nature and, 112–113; theory of, 31–33, 78–83, 79–80
free enterprise, 41, 199–200, 236
free market conservatism: divergences in, 195–198; movement conservatism, 198–202, 211–217; populist conservatism, 199, 201, 211–212, 216–217; strength of, 193–217; in United States, 193–217; welfare reform and, 194–195; welfare state and, 194–198, 204–208, 217
free market ideas, 2–7, 19–20, 99–100
free market ideology, 2–3, 10, 41, 184, 202
free market utopia, 34–35, 190, 218
free market utopianism: economic liberalism and, 150, 233–234; elements of, 100–101; free market ideas, 34–35, 99–100; ideals of, 101–113; individual freedom and, 218–220; market self-regulation and, 187
freedom: in complex society, 72, 224; of conscience, 226, 235; individual freedom, 71–72, 219, 234–238, 240; preserving, 238, 240
"Freedom in a Complex Society," 224
"freedom of conscience," 226, 235
Freud, Sigmund, 8
Friedman, Milton: on economic predictions, 230; global financial system and, 19; ideas of, 4, 23–25, 28, 41; market society and, 103–104; on tax cutting, 110
funding support, 199–200

General Theory, The, 23, 156
George, Lloyd, 93
Gerschenkron, Alexander, 67
Gingrich, Newt, 180
global economy collapse, 67, 82–84, 207, 218
global economy today, 18–19, 238–240
global financial crisis: aftermath of, 84–86, 108, 238–240; agricultural crisis and, 112, 144, 147; key reforms for, 238–240; reasons for, 3, 11–21; unemployment and, 138; welfare policies and, 192
global financial markets, 2, 16–18
global financial system, 16–18
Godwin, William, 98
gold standard mechanism, 15–18, 69–70, 85–86
gold standard system: international gold standards, 11–12, 16, 85–86, 216; market forces and, 11–14, 55–61; market self-regulation and, 14–16, 55; mechanisms of, 15–18, 69–70, 85–86; Speenhamland and, 143–147
Goldwater, Barry, 208
Gospels, 226, 234–235
governance philosophy, 218–220, 223. *See also* "reality of society"
government assistance, 14, 181, 189, 200–203, 208
Gramsci, Antonio, 75–76
Gray, John, 2
Great Depression: economic downturns and, 54, 83, 93, 189; impact of, 1–2, 205
Great Society, 2–3, 160, 178, 186, 194
Great Transformation, The: ambiguities in, 81–91; analysis of, 44–72; inspiration from, 2–4; on Marxism, 46, 59, 74–79; nationalism and, 202; One Hundred Year's Peace and, 11–15; publication of, 2, 82, 99; reality of society and, 218–237; Speenhamland and, 114–124; writing of, 48–58, 73–97
Greenspan, Alan, 21–22, 112

Hammond, Barbara, 121
Hammond, J. L., 121
Hasbach, Wilhelm, 121
Hayek, Friedrich: fascism and, 42; free market ideas of, 99–102; global financial system and, 19; ideas of, 4, 28; market society and, 103–104; reality of society and, 233–234; on serfdom, 98–102, 224, 234; Speenhamland and, 123
health policies, 195–196
Hegel, G. W. F., 49
high finance, 56
Himmelfarb, Gertrude, 116, 179
Hirschman, Albert, 38, 98–99, 116, 157–158
History and Class Consciousness, 73
Hitler, Adolf, 16, 57, 69
Hobbes, Thomas, 103, 119, 167, 229
Hobsbawm, E. J., 121
holism, 58–59, 61–66, 129, 232
Hook, Sidney, 75
Hoover, Herbert, 85, 239
household income, 133, 141–142
householding, 30, 92
human beings: as commodities, 47–53, 83, 87, 111–112; fate of, 79; labor and, 32, 60–61, 108–109; society and, 79, 96–98, 108–109, 226–231, 235–236; understanding of, 38–39
human economy, 9, 26, 59–60
Hurricane Katrina, 111–112, 190–193, 214, 219

Idea of Poverty, The, 116, 179
"ideal interests," 58, 227
ideational embeddedness: of market, 39–40, 96–97, 107; perversity thesis and, 174–177, 180–183; re-embedding, 174–177, 180–183; theoretical realism and, 174–175; welfare debate and, 150–161, 178–198
"ideational institutionalism," 156
ideological fusion, 200–201
imperialism, 56
income inequality, 2–3, 20, 196–197
"industrial capitalism," 76–77, 87–88

Industrial Revolution: autonomous economy and, 31; capitalism and, 76–77, 87–88; as cultural catastrophe, 107–109; defenders of, 62; impact of, 88–89, 107–109, 133, 235; market economy and, 50; as "social revolution," 88–89

"institutional pragmatism," 161–169, 173–177, 183–186, 232

institutionalism: decline of, 5; economy and, 29–31; ideational institutionalism, 156; pragmatic institutionalism, 161–169, 173–176, 186, 232

International Gold Standard Reinterpreted, 1914–1934, 16

International Monetary Fund, 18, 202, 239

interventionism, 36, 40, 84, 94, 123

interwar years, 15–16, 23, 58, 221–222

"invisible hand," 12

James, C. L. R., 75

Jaszi, Oscar, 46

Jesus, 192, 234–235

Johnson, Lyndon, 2, 206, 208–209

Johnson Administration, 160, 194, 204, 208

Judt, Tony, 222, 223

Just-So Stories, 234

Karleby, Nils, 221

Kennedy, John F., 23

Kennedy-Johnson Administration, 160

Keynes, John Maynard: on classical economics, 54; contributions of, 142–143; on economic orthodoxy, 22–23, 156, 225; global financial crisis and, 239; global financial system and, 16, 19; ideas of, 4, 8, 22–28; on market society, 223

Keynesian ideas, 3, 19–25, 204–209

Kipling, Rudyard, 234

Kissinger, Henry, 209

Korsch, Karl, 75

Krugman, Paul, 232

Kun, Béla, 46, 47

labor: commodification of, 47–50, 83, 87, 111–112; division of, 12, 203, 227, 237–238; human beings and, 32, 60–61, 108–109

"law of population," 122, 163–166

Lenin, Vladimir, 85

Lewinsky, Monica, 212

"liberal capitalism," 57

"liberal socialism," 24–26. *See also* socialism

liberal state, 11–16

Lippman, Walter, 83, 85, 93

Livelihood of Man, The, 47

Losing Ground, 178, 181

Lukacs, Georg, 5, 73, 75, 79

MacKenzie, Donald, 107

Malthus, Thomas Robert: contributions of, 142–143; on government assistance, 200–203; on human population, 38–39, 98, 163–166; ideas of, 4, 12, 24, 91; influence of, 31; inspiration for, 228; New Poor Law and, 145–148; perversity thesis and, 101–104, 129, 142, 163–166, 171–172, 184–185; recycling of, 177–180; social naturalism and, 117, 166–169; Speenhamland and, 116–122; theoretical realism and, 39, 169–171; thesis of, 38–39, 98, 101–104, 163–180; on undeserving poor, 175–177; utopianism and, 101

Mannheim, Karl, 4–5

Marcuse, Herbert, 199

market economy: development of, 105–107; embedded economy, 10–12, 73–74, 94–97; fall of, 68–69; Industrial Revolution and, 50; political embedding of, 36–37; reform of, 52–57; self-correcting market, 41; self-regulating market, 83, 108–109, 220

market fundamentalism: big government and, 210–211; countermovements and, 206; dystopian consequences and, 108–112; global dominance of, 222; ideological fusion and, 200; movement conservatism and, 215–217; opposition to, 238–239; revival of, 3–4, 19–20; rise of, 218–222; state and, 64–65, 102–103; terms for, 3; utopianism and, 227, 233–234; welfare debate, 150–161, 178–198

market liberalism, 79–80, 87, 90–96, 99–100

market self-regulation: advocates of, 3; autonomous economy and, 34–35; crisis of, 55–60, 71–72, 83–86; economic liberalism and, 84, 233; free market utopianism, 187; goal for, 13–15, 32, 91–95; gold standard and, 14–16, 55; liberal state and, 13–14; market society and, 102–108, 150, 167–168, 187, 233–234; social naturalism and, 103–104; society and, 102–108, 150, 167–168; stark utopia and, 41–42, 80, 92, 101, 187, 233

market society: analysis of, 66–72, 78–94, 97, 103, 223–225, 233–234; collapse of, 49, 66–67, 84; contradictions of, 57–58; creation of, 53; crisis of, 58–63; end of, 7; history of, 47–53; market self-regulation and, 102–108, 150, 167–168, 187, 233–234; principles of, 53–54; terms for, 78; war and, 57–58; weakness of, 53

market utopianism: critique of, 98–113; elements of, 100–101; free market ideas, 99–100; ideals of, 101–113

Marshall Plan, 213

Marx, Karl: on capitalism, 81, 84, 92; contributions of, 142–143; ideas of, 8, 27; influences of, 74–81, 84; reality of society and, 226; social naturalism and, 166; Speenhamland and, 120–121

Marxism, 46, 59, 73–81, 99, 221

Marxist thoughts, 7, 10, 24–26, 46–49, 73–90

"material and ideal interests," 227

"material interests," 46, 76

McCulloch, J. R., 122

Medicaid, 187, 194

Medicare, 187, 194

mercantilism, 49, 61, 161–164, 169–170, 177, 186

metaphors, 65–68, 148, 169–170, 208–209, 220, 229

Methodienstreit, 230

"modern capitalist society," 27

Modern World-System, The, 68

Moore, Barrington, 67

More, Thomas, 100

movement conservatism, 198–202, 211–217, 251n8. *See also* conservatism

Moynihan, Daniel Patrick, 114–115, 209

Murray, Charles, 178–181

Mussolini, Benito, 15, 85

Nader, Ralph, 199

National Post, 115

neoclassical economy, 6, 31, 100, 230

New Deal: legacy of, 208–209; market regulations in, 194–195; reform measures of, 2–4, 57, 70–71, 205–209; regime of, 177–178; views of, 57, 186–187

New Poor Law: fictitious commodities and, 82–83; household income and, 133, 141–142; labor and, 82–83, 93; policies of, 9, 37, 51–52; poverty and, 151, 161, 177, 180, 183–185; Speenhamland and, 86–89, 118, 121–122, 143–149. *See also* Old Poor Law

New Statesman and Nation, The, 24

New Testament, 192

New York Times, 189

Newton, Isaac, 39, 142, 168, 170

Nixon, Richard, 114–115, 160, 208–209

Nixon Administration, 114, 116, 194, 204

Obama, Barack, 110, 189, 193–194, 213, 216

Obama Administration, 1, 193, 216

"obsolete market mentality," 71, 95, 224–225, 239–240

Oesterreschische Volkswirt, 46
Olasky, Marvin, 116, 180
Old Poor Law: analysis of, 77; labor and, 83; policies of, 36–38; poverty and, 151, 159–163; social policy and, 114–149; Speenhamland and, 87–88; views of, 173, 176, 190. *See also* New Poor Law
Old Testament, 234–235
One Hundred Year's Peace, 11–15
opportunity structures, 69–70
organizational autonomy, 199
"Our Obsolete Market Mentality," 71, 95
Owen, Robert, 49, 100, 203, 235

Pearson, Harry, 47
Personal Responsibility and Work Opportunities Reconciliation Act (PRWORA), 116, 148, 151, 155, 161, 180–187
perversity thesis: causal mechanisms of, 158, 170–171; ideational embeddedness and, 174–177, 180–183; logic of, 142–143; policies of, 103–104, 116; population and, 163–166; poverty and, 157–161, 171–174, 177–186; power of, 37–39, 180–185; PRWORA and, 148, 151, 155, 161, 180–187; social naturalism and, 158, 166–169, 178, 184–186; strength of, 37–39, 180–185; TANF and, 190; theoretical realism and, 158, 166, 169–171; welfare system and, 178–180
Plough and the Pen, The, 48
Polanyi, Karl: alternatives of, 25–28; birth of, 45; concepts of, 8–11, 58–65; contributions of, 65–72; countermovements and, 201–204, 212; death of, 5, 47–48; early years of, 4–5, 44–46; family of, 28–29, 45–46; on free market utopianism, 98–113; on *Great Transformation*, 73–97; ideas of, 1–43; inspiration from, 2–4; as institutionalist, 29–31; introduction to, 1–8
Polanyi, Michael, 28–29, 45

Polanyian countermovement, 201–204, 212. *See also* countermovements
political democracy, 11, 25–28
Poor Law Amendment Act, 9, 37, 151, 159. *See also* New Poor Law
Poor Law History, 122
Poor Law Reform Act, 51, 146, 151
population, law of, 122, 163–166
population growth, 38–39, 120, 162–165, 172, 180, 239–240
populist conservatism, 199, 201, 211–212, 216–217. *See also* conservatism
poverty: market fundamentalism and, 150–192; New Poor Law and, 151, 161, 177, 180, 183–185; Old Poor Law and, 151, 159–163; perversity thesis and, 157–161, 171–174, 177–186; "undeserving" poor, 175–177
Powell, Lewis, 199–200, 206
"pragmatic institutionalism," 161–169, 173–177, 183–186, 232. *See also* institutionalism
Primitive, Archaic, and Modern Economies, 47
Principles, 143
protection: agricultural protection, 55–56; constitutional protection, 34; copyright protection, 40–41; countermovements for, 14–15, 53–54, 60–68, 92–95, 216–220, 242n7; of individual rights, 234–240; rights to, 50–51, 110–113, 198, 204–205, 234–240; social protection, 7–10, 53–54, 63–64, 71; of trade secrets, 40–42
public policy, 103, 116, 143, 225

radical democracy, 238
Rahman, Sabeel, 25
Reader's Digest, 224
Reagan, Ronald, 3, 6, 19–20, 160, 182, 195, 203, 206
Reagan Administration, 19, 212
reality, meaning of, 228–233
"reality of society:" acceptance of, 11, 240; democracy and, 234–240; embracing, 240; freedom and, 234–240; governance philosophy and,

218–220, 223; *Great Transformation* and, 218–237; meaning of, 225–233; philosophy of, 224–225; re-viewing, 233–234; socialism and, 220–223; for societal repair, 113, 218–240; utopianism and, 233–234
Reality of Society, The, 224
reciprocity, 30, 66–67, 92, 237
"Red Vienna," 25, 221
redistribution, 30, 66–67, 92, 135, 136, 236
Reform Bill of 1832, 159
regulation, 13–17, 40, 49, 61, 113, 206. *See also* market self-regulation
regulatory reforms, 195, 211–211, 239
re-regulation, 9, 20–21, 219
Rhetoric of Reaction, The, 98
Ricardo, David: contributions of, 142–143; debates with, 170; ideas of, 4, 12, 24, 27, 91; influence of, 31; inspiration for, 228; social naturalism and, 117; theoretical realism and, 39; utopianism and, 101
"right to live," 50–51
rights: civil rights, 34, 198, 201, 237; individual rights, 234–237; protecting, 50–51, 110–113, 198, 204–205, 234–240; socioeconomic rights, 237–238
Road to Serfdom, The, 98, 224
Roe v. Wade, 198
Romney, Mitt, 188, 193
Roosevelt, Franklin D., 2, 7, 34, 57, 70, 95, 177, 195, 205, 237
Roosevelt, Theodore, 93
Royal Commission Report, 118–122, 130, 134–136, 145, 159, 182
Rude, George, 121
rural distress, 143–146

Sahlins, Marshall, 226
Satanic mills, 37, 77, 108, 235
"Second Bill of Rights," 7, 237, 242n8
self-regulation, 3, 13–15. *See also* market self-regulation
self-sufficiency, 165, 176, 181, 200–201
Sen, Amartya, 135, 143, 163

Silver, Beverly, 15
Skidelsky, Robert, 23–24
Smith, Adam, 8, 12, 59
Snell, K. D. M., 140
social arrangements, 30, 39, 47–48, 57–59, 98, 237
social classes, 44, 58, 62–64
social democracy, 6, 220–223, 238
social exclusion, 35, 196, 219
social naturalism: accomplishments of, 229–230; explanation of, 6–7, 38–39, 102–103; government policies and, 103–104; origins of, 102–103, 228; perversity thesis and, 158, 166–169, 178, 184–186; pragmatic institutionalism and, 173–174; self-regulating market and, 103–104; Speenhamland and, 117; understanding, 226–230; utopianism and, 105–106
social policy: debates on, 114, 117, 178–179; differences in, 195–198; impact on, 120–121, 142–143; mercantilist social policies, 162–164; modern social policy, 162; Old Poor Law and, 114–149; philosophy of, 99, 225–229; Speenhamland and, 114–115
social protection, 7–10, 53–54, 63–64, 71. *See also* protection
social safety net, 52, 110, 189
social security, 8, 160, 187, 208
social welfare, 26–28, 126, 178, 195, 221–222, 225
socialism: crisis of, 6; definition of, 26–27; failures of, 81; ideals of, 34, 71–72; impracticality of, 99–100, 123; liberal socialism, 24–26; transitions to, 57–58, 70–71; view of, 220–225; working class and, 76–80, 89; world market collapse and, 67–72
society, meaning of, 225–227
society, reality of, 11, 113, 218–240. *See also* "reality of society"
socioeconomic rights, 237–238. *See also* rights
Sokoll, Thomas, 136, 138

Soros, George, 2, 150
Specter, Arlen, 213
Speenhamland: analysis of, 51–54; bread scale and, 133–138, 140–142; causal gaps of, 124, 129–133; complexities of, 124–129; contribution to, 123–124; critique of, 114–149, 159–163; gold standard and, 143–147; household income and, 133, 141–142; impact of, 87–91, 114–124, 138–149; New Poor Law and, 86–89, 118, 121–122, 143–149; Old Poor Law and, 87–88; productivity and, 118, 131, 134, 138–142, 148; reality of, 133–138; revisionist narrative of, 142–148; stories of, 36–37, 86–91, 117–149; system of, 51–54, 114–116, 133–134, 145, 159–163; wages and, 115–123, 131–133, 137–142, 149
Speenhamland Act, 36, 49–50, 114, 159
Spencer, Herbert, 104
stark utopia: explanation of, 13; free-market utopianism, 150; of self-regulating market, 41–42, 80, 92, 101, 187, 233; view of, 13, 26, 174, 187
Stiglitz, Joseph, 2, 4
substantive economy, 29–30, 59–60, 226, 241n5

Tawney, R. H., 122
tax cuts, 1, 21, 39, 42, 110–111, 195, 206
Temporary Aid to Needy Families (TANF), 161, 188–190
Thatcher, Margaret, 2, 6
theoretical realism: causal mechanisms, 169–170, 181; definition of, 39–40; explanation of, 175; ideational embeddedness and, 174–175; perversity thesis and, 158, 166, 169–171; philosophy of, 230–231
Thompson, E. P., 62
Townsend, Joseph, 102–103, 118–120, 145, 167–168, 172, 185, 228–230
Toynbee, Arnold, 166

Trade and Markets in the Early Empires, 47
trade unions, 28, 54, 63, 93, 100, 131, 205
Tragedy of American Compassion, The, 116

"undeserving" poor, 175–177
United States: business alliances in, 204–217; countermovements and, 201–204; crisis of Great Society in, 160–161; cultural attitudes in, 197; different directions of, 195–198, 216–217; Europe and, 193, 195–198, 217; free market conservatism in, 193–217; funding support in, 199–200; health policies in, 195–196; ideological fusion and, 200–201; income inequality in, 2–3, 20, 196–197; organizational autonomy in, 199; regional concentrations in, 201; religious beliefs in, 197; social movements in, 198–201; traditional values in, 197–198
utopia: dystopian consequences of, 9, 108–111; elements of, 100–101; ideal scheme, 100–105; as planned project, 105–107; stark utopia, 13, 26, 41–42, 80, 92, 101, 150, 174, 187, 233; tragedy of, 108–113
utopianism: critique of, 98–113; economic liberalism and, 150, 233–234; economic utopianism, 233–234; elements of, 100–101; free-market utopianism, 34–35, 98–113, 150, 187, 218–220; ideals of, 101–113; market fundamentalism and, 227, 233–234; as planned project, 105–107; "reality of society" and, 233–234; social naturalism and, 105–106; stark utopianism, 26, 41–42, 233; as tragedy, 108–113

von Mises, Ludwig, 42, 83, 85, 101, 104, 123

Wall Street Journal, 181
Wallerstein, Immanuel, 68–69

Waxman, Harry, 21
wealth inequality, 2–3, 20, 196–197
Wealth of Nations, 168
Webb, Beatrice, 121–122
Webb, Sidney, 121–122
Weber, Max, 8, 27, 81
Welfare, 87, 116
welfare capitalism, 196
welfare debate, 150–161, 178–198
welfare dependency, 157, 178, 184
welfare legislation, 116, 184, 188, 192
welfare policies, 14, 116, 155–157, 195–196, 217, 225

welfare reform, 160–161, 188–189, 194–195
welfare revolutions, 158–163
welfare state, 25, 32, 186, 194–198, 204–208, 223–224
welfare system, 178–180
Weyrich, Paul, 41
White, Harry Dexter, 16, 27
Winters, Jeffrey, 3
Wolin, Sheldon, 99, 200
World Bank, 18, 202, 239
world market collapse, 67, 82–84
World Trade Organization, 202, 239